Automobile Manufacturers
of Cleveland and Ohio,
1864–1942

ALSO BY FRANK E. WRENICK
*WITH THE EDITORIAL ASSISTANCE
OF* ELAINE V. WRENICK

*The Streamline Era Greyhound Terminals: The Architecture
of W.S. Arrasmith* (McFarland 2007; paperback 2011)

Automobile Manufacturers of Cleveland and Ohio, 1864–1942

FRANK E. WRENICK *with*
ELAINE V. WRENICK
Foreword by JOHN J. GRABOWSKI

McFarland & Company, Inc., Publishers
Jefferson, North Carolina

Unless otherwise identified, all images are courtesy the Antique Automobile Club of America Library and Research Center, Hershey, Pennsylvania.

Names: Wrenick, Frank E., 1939– author. | Wrenick, Elaine V., author.
Title: Automobile manufacturers of Cleveland and Ohio, 1864–1942 / Frank E. Wrenick with Elaine V. Wrenick ; foreword by John J. Grabowski.
Description: Jefferson, N.C. : McFarland & Company, Inc., Publishers, 2016. | Includes bibliographical references and index.
Identifiers: LCCN 2016021253 | ISBN 9780786475353 (softcover : acid free paper) ∞
Subjects: LCSH: Automobile industry and trade—Ohio—Cleveland—History. | Automobile industry and trade—Ohio—History. | Automobiles—Marketing. | Industries—Ohio—History.
Classification: LCC HD9710.3.O3 W74 2016 | DDC 338.4/76292220977109041—dc23
LC record available at https://lccn.loc.gov/2016021253

ISBN (print) 978-0-7864-7535-3
ISBN (ebook) 978-1-4766-2356-6

BRITISH LIBRARY CATALOGUING DATA ARE AVAILABLE

© 2016 Frank E. Wrenick with Elaine V. Wrenick. All rights reserved

No part of this book may be reproduced or transmitted in any form or by any means, electronic or mechanical, including photocopying or recording, or by any information storage and retrieval system, without permission in writing from the publisher.

On the cover: 1908 Peerless advertisement.

Printed in the United States of America

McFarland & Company, Inc., Publishers
Box 611, Jefferson, North Carolina 28640
www.mcfarlandpub.com

Table of Contents

Foreword by John J. Grabowski — 1
Preface — 3
Introduction — 5

Part I. The Automobiles of Cleveland — 7
    An Overview — 7
    The Manufacturers — 30

Part II. The Automobiles of Ohio — 143
    An Overview — 143
    The Manufacturers — 145

Appendix 1: Cleveland Automobile Manufacturers by Year — 237
Appendix 2: Leading Cleveland Automobile Marques by Name and Address — 240
Appendix 3: Ohio Automobile Manufacturers by City — 243
Appendix 4: Unusual Vehicle Names — 250
Bibliography — 251
Index — 253

Foreword
John J. Grabowski

In 1920, Cleveland, Ohio, with a population of 796,841, was the fifth largest city in the United States. Its population consisted of a wide mixture of recent immigrants and migrants as well as descendants of families who had arrived in the area decades earlier. The city's growth had been rapid. Only fifty years earlier the population was 92,829, and Cleveland's rank in the nation was fifteenth.

It was industrial expansion that catalyzed the rise of Cleveland as a great American city—indeed, by 1920, the value of products made in Cleveland was also fifth in the nation. While the city's location—close to abundant natural resources and central to an expanding Midwest—was key to its industrial power, it was inventiveness and risk-taking that truly powered Cleveland's growth. Perhaps nowhere was this spirit of inventiveness better exemplified than in the rise of the automotive industry. By 1907, Cleveland and northeastern Ohio generally were considered the center of American automotive manufacturing. The existing steel and machine tool industries provided a platform for this relatively new product, and the experience in producing earlier consumer goods, ranging from sewing machines to roller skates and bicycles, nurtured the skills necessary to produce automobiles.

While Detroit would eclipse Cleveland as the national center for automotive production in the following decade, the city and region remained (and remain to this day) major producers of components ranging from frames to pistons, valves, and even window seals. And, until the Great Depression intervened, the city and the region still produced particular marques, including the Jordan and Peerless.

The Automobile Manufacturers of Cleveland and Ohio, 1864–1942, provides an encyclopedic overview of the companies and entrepreneurs that formed the basis of the automotive industry there. Importantly, the book looks beyond the period usually considered as the heyday of automotive production in Cleveland and Ohio. By doing so it provides a sense of just how compelling the concept of a self-propelled vehicle was in the years before the invention of the internal combustion engine, and it also shows that the door on automotive production in the state did not fully close with the advent of the Depression.

However, what is most significant about this volume is its attention to small endeavors. The tendency in many histories is to celebrate success and longevity. But that narrative neglects the story of failure, and it obscures the enormous risk that entrepreneurs in any field take. Not all succeed, and that fact is amply demonstrated within this book. In some instances production ended with a concept and not a car, and in many instances one, two, or three years represented a corporate lifespan.

Equally important is the geographic scope of this volume. While Cleveland and northeastern Ohio remain central to the story, Frank E. and Elaine V. Wrenick's detailed research shows just how widespread the industry was in the Buckeye State. That the automotive industry spread so far, and so fast, is a measure of how important the concept of personal mobility was and is in the United States and, today, around the globe. The pages that follow ably detail the seminal role Cleveland and Ohio played in setting the world—and each one of us—in motion.

John J. Grabowski holds a joint appointment as the Krieger-Mueller associate professor of applied history at Case Western Reserve University and senior vice president for research and publications at Western Reserve Historical Society, both in Cleveland. Much of his academic career has focused on the preservation and interpretation of the history of Cleveland and northeastern Ohio.

Preface

Ohioans were actively and energetically engaged in pursuing the dream of inventing and manufacturing a self-propelled vehicle from the earliest days of the automobile. Among Ohio cities, Cleveland was the leading automobile center, which is not surprising as it was one of the country's foremost industrial centers. Between 1895 and 1932 there were 158 automobile ventures and experimenters in Cleveland that stepped up to the challenge of producing an automobile. The rest of the state brought forth another 408 up to the onset of World War II.

Most of those outside of Cleveland were situated in large metropolitan centers while others could be found in a scattering of the smallest villages and farm communities. The most successful were usually located in larger metropolitan centers such as Cincinnati, Toledo, Dayton, Youngstown, Springfield, and Sandusky. The industrial base in these cities was commensurate with their size and played a role in facilitating the ultimate number of automobile ventures that existed in each particular location. And it was the state's strong manufacturing base that helps tell the story of the part Ohio, its cities, and its people played in the creation and evolution of the automobile.

Ohio's contribution to the automobile industry is a significant one, and among all of Ohio's cities, it is Cleveland that made the greatest contribution to what would become the newly evolving automobile industry. Surprisingly, Cleveland's automobile manufacturing history has gone largely unremarked over the years since the last Cleveland built automobile, a 1932 Ford, left a Euclid Avenue plant on the city's East Side. This is unfortunate because the city has a fascinating story to tell about the part it played during the formative years of America's automobile industry.

This oversight is especially remarkable inasmuch as it was in Cleveland in 1898 that our nation's automobile industry actually began, thanks to the genius of one of its own citizens. Between then and 1900, there were more than twenty automobile marques that called Cleveland home. In addition, Cleveland became the world's leading automobile center in 1902 and remained America's leading automobile city until 1908.

Preeminent among the names of Cleveland's pioneering automobile companies were Winton, Stearns, Peerless, Baker, and White. These companies designed and manufactured automobiles that set the standard for advanced design, engineering excellence, and quality construction.

The people who guided these companies exemplified the best of what America's leading inventors, entrepreneurs, and engineers could accomplish. They ranged from experienced businessmen leading successful manufacturing companies to a young college drop-out with just a dream and absolutely no business or manufacturing experience. Their stories demonstrate the power of ability and enthusiasm at the turn of the century in America.

These inspiring stories, as well as those of many other Ohioans in cities large and small, are best told through their material achievements, the companies they created, the automobiles they designed and manufactured, and the perseverance and ultimate success of their efforts. They were intent on presenting their own unique interpretations of what type of automobile would best meet the challenge of self-propelled transportation. Many of these company names and efforts are lost to history, others survived briefly to produce and demonstrate a one-off example of their ideas, while a select number succeeded in presenting vehicles that were innovative enough to attract public acceptance and continued support.

Each of these people contributed to the advancement of the automobile, some with ideas that took hold, others by showing that a particular idea or approach was not viable. Little attention is often paid to those who, most would say, failed. In fact their efforts contributed essential knowledge to the ongoing effort to produce a successful automobile. Many more names would find their way to the list of the forgotten than to a list of those who realized success.

Pioneer automotive inventors had to imagine what was necessary, conceive a solution, then realize the solution in the form of individual physical pieces. Those newly created pieces then had to work in harmony with all the others that had been made, or were yet to be created. All this had to occur before an automobile could be brought into existence, and before there could be an industry that would ultimately arise to support and serve automobile manufacturers and motorists alike. The invention of the automobile generated more innovation and resulting economic and societal impact in America than anything that had come before, and arguably since.

We will first take a look at the leading part Cleveland played in Ohio's story. As of this date only two of Cleveland's most important automobile entrepreneurs have received biographical treatment, Alexander Winton and Ned Jordan. While this book is not intended to be biographical, the pages that follow introduce all of those Cleveland entrepreneurs and adventurers who rose to the challenge of inventing and manufacturing an automobile. It focuses on the tangible result of their efforts which laid the foundation for what is the automobile and the automobile industry we know today. We will then take a look at the other Ohio entrepreneurs living outside of Cleveland who pursued the dream of making an automobile.

As with all research, there is always more to be done and it is hoped that this book serves to encourage others to explore the significant contribution made by so many Ohio inventors, entrepreneurs, and experimenters to automotive history.

* * *

Note: In the interest of providing images of as many marques as possible, the author and publisher have chosen to include various images of poor quality when none better could be found, in recognition of their historical value and rarity.

Introduction

The earliest example of a self-propelled road vehicle in America appeared in 1805 and was the creation of Oliver Evans of Philadelphia, Pennsylvania. It came about as a matter of necessity. Evans had built a steam dredge for the city of Philadelphia to use at the city docks. In order to get the dredge from his shop down to the water, Evans fitted it with four road wheels, which were driven by the steam engine that powered the dredge's paddle wheel. With this modification, Evans drove his dredge down to the waterfront, where it was launched and began its dredging operations. The dredge was a success, but when Evans sought financing for the production of a road vehicle based on his unique adaptation, he was unable to interest any investors. It was an idea too far ahead of its time.

This idea seems to have lain dormant for almost sixty years. Then in 1864, Cleveland experimenter John Grant mounted a steam engine in a small carriage and drove what was the first purpose-built self-propelled vehicle to appear on the city's streets, and may well have been the first of its kind anywhere in the country.

During the remainder of the 19th century, more experimentation, with a greater range of motive power and vehicle configuration, led to increasingly practical versions of the horseless carriage. Cleveland, especially, nourished this nascent industry, and soon became the leading automobile center among Ohio's cities, as well as the nation. This was due in part to the city's exceptional manufacturing infrastructure, as the city was one of the country's foremost industrial centers. And thus it was in Cleveland that the young automobile industry thrived.

The inventors, engineers, and entrepreneurs who guided early Cleveland automotive ventures had incredibly varied backgrounds, ranging from an experienced businessman running a highly successful manufacturing company, Alexander Winton, to a teenager without even a college degree, Frank B. Stearns.

The Cleveland Era of automotive manufacturing and creativity was truly impressive. It began slowly in 1864 and then gradually gained momentum for some forty-four years, but began to wane due to Ford's introduction of the Model T in 1908. It was not until 1932 that the last Cleveland-built automobile, a Ford, finally rolled off the assembly line on the city's East Side.

Companies such as Winton, Stearns, Peerless, Baker, and White designed and manufactured vehicles that set the standard for advanced automotive design, engineering, and quality construction. Between 1898 and 1900, more than twenty-four automobile marques called Cleveland home and, by 1932, there had been no fewer than 158 automobile ventures in Cleveland.

Much of this success can be attributed to Alexander Winton and the various manufacturing and marketing innovations which he instituted in Cleveland in 1898. It is arguably from this date that our nation's automobile industry as such actually began in earnest, and it is generally acknowledged that Winton is the father of America's automobile industry.

Meanwhile, the rest of Ohio was making automotive history as well, bringing forth another 408 marques by 1942.

Notwithstanding the natural advantages possessed by larger cities in attracting and nurturing automotive ventures, the degree of success of any automotive endeavor did not always relate to the size of its home community, and many could be found in a scattering of the smallest villages and farm communities. One entrepreneur whom no one would have expected to triumph was Fred Patterson. Not only was he a resident of Greenfield, one of the state's smallest population centers, but he was also the son of a freed slave. Another such success was one of the most renowned automobile pioneers, Harry C. Stutz, who hailed from rural southern Ohio. Stutz got his start by combining a stationary engine with a farm implement binder-chain to propel his home-made vehicle.

At the turn of the 20th century, people in America who possessed ability, enthusiasm, and unfettered imagination could achieve whatever they set their minds to.

It was at this time that Ohio, and especially Cleveland, shone. During the early days of the automobile and its industry, Ohio and Cleveland provided a most hospitable environment for development of the automobile.

Ohio's major contribution to the birth of the nation's automobile industry is undeniable, and the part played by Cleveland is even more significant. Although the automobile manufacturing history of Cleveland and Ohio has gone relatively unheralded, there is no question that, when the automobile age began, Ohio—and especially Cleveland—was the place to be.

Part I.
The Automobiles of Cleveland

An Overview

In 1864, the first self-propelled automobile to make an appearance on Cleveland city streets was a steam powered vehicle created by John J. Grant. Oddly enough, Grant's steam vehicle also holds the distinction of being involved in the city's, if not the country's, first traffic accident involving a self-propelled conveyance. (See Grant, John J.)

The second of Cleveland's earliest automobiles was the 1886 creation of Charles Francis Brush. It was an experimental electric powered three-wheeled vehicle which was intended to prove that electricity was capable of powering a wheeled conveyance. The vehicle was successful and met all expectations although there were no plans to put it into production. (See Brush, Charles Francis.)

These two inventors presented Cleveland with the first glimmerings of what was to become one of the city's, and the country's, major industries. A host of others would follow their lead and make Cleveland the center of the automobile industry as America was on the eve of the twentieth century.

In 1898, thirty-four years after the introduction of Grant's steam vehicle, the stage was set for the birth of the country's automobile industry. Into the limelight stepped Alexander Winton, who became the first person to build automobiles on a production basis and make them available to the general public for immediate sale. That first sale of a vehicle from inventory, rather than bespoke, was made to Robert Allison of Port Carbon, Pennsylvania. The very same year, Winton also made the new industry's first export sale, to a purchaser in Canada.

Alexander Winton was not the only Cleveland automobile manufacturer on the scene during the automobile's nascent years. By 1900 the city could boast other pioneers, including Walter Baker, Elmer Sperry, Paul Gaeth, Frank B. Stearns, George A. Washburn, Walter L. Marr, Frank Rogers, George Hanford, Rollin White, Raymond and Ralph Owen, as well as the Peerless Manufacturing Company. Of these Baker, Stearns, Peerless, and White became the most successful, going on to produce thousands of automobiles over the ensuing years.

Until the end of 1908 Cleveland held pride of place as the country's leading manufacturer of automobiles. During this span of years, 57 new names were added to the original list of Cleveland automobile manufacturers. However, by about 1908, when Henry Ford began production of the Model T, the epicenter of the automobile industry shifted to Detroit.

Better than Horse or Bicycle

Price $1,000. No Agents.

One of the most delightful of modern possessions is a motor carriage. No danger of overworking a horse or of its bolting.

The Winton Motor Carriage

is in every respect a well-built conveyance. It is of pleasing design, finished in Brewster green, with leather cushions and nickel trimmings. Driving mechanism concealed. Single hydro-carbon motor. Speed from 3 to 20 miles an hour, at driver's option. Suspension Wire Wheels, Pneumatic Tires, Ball Bearings. *Price list sent free on application.*

THE WINTON MOTOR CARRIAGE CO., Cleveland, Ohio.

The advertisement that launched America's automobile industry.

Nevertheless, Cleveland continued to nurture new and prominent automobile marques including Chandler in 1913, Owen Magnetic in 1915, Jordan and H.A.L. Twelve in 1916, Templar in 1917, Cleveland in 1919, Leon Rubay in 1922, and Hupmobile in 1929. And, Ford built a plant in Cleveland in 1915, where it produced automobiles until 1932.

By 1932 Cleveland had been home to over 158 automobile enterprises and, as might be expected, this resulted in many Cleveland automobile firsts, including:

- 1864: first self-propelled automobile (John Grant)
- 1886: first electric automobile in the country (Charles F. Brush)
- 1896: first design for a hybrid gasoline/electric vehicle (George Washburn)
- 1897: first automobile long-distance reliability run (Alexander Winton)
- 1898: first sale of a standard production internal combustion powered automobile (Alexander Winton)
- 1899: first automobile mail truck (Alexander Winton); first use of the word "automobile" by *Cleveland Plain Dealer* journalist Mr. Shanks, in reporting on Alexander Winton's Cleveland to New York City reliability run
- 1900: first steering wheel (Alexander Winton); first American automobile to compete in a European event (Alexander Winton)
- 1901: first all-steel automobile body (Eastman Metallic Body Company)

1902: first fully streamlined automobile body (Walter Baker)
1903: first cross-continental automobile run (Alexander Winton)
1906: first complete line of specialized motorized road vehicles including automobiles, trucks, and buses (White Company)
1909: first remote self-starter (Alexander Winton); first shock absorber (Gabriel Company)
1910: first placement of all operating levers and controls, including brake lever and gearshift, inside the automobile body (White Company)
1912: first gasoline/electric hybrid vehicle (Walter Baker)
1913: first American-designed diesel engine (Alexander Winton)
1914: first electric traffic signal (Garrett Morgan)
1923: Ned Jordan's famous "Somewhere West of Laramie" magazine advertisement
1940: first sealed-beam automobile headlamp (Cleveland-based General Electric Company)

Even though Cleveland experienced a decline in the number of automobile manufacturing establishments during the early part of the twentieth century, the city continued to play an important role in the automotive industry. It possessed an extensive and thriving manufacturing infrastructure as well as being home to a large number of skilled workers. In addition, the city was a major hub on a rail distribution system served by such important lines as the New York Central and the Pennsylvania Railroad. American automobile manufacturers increasingly turned to Cleveland for a variety of essential components for their vehicles, ranging from humble nuts and bolts to engines, bodies, and electrical systems. Even much of the gasoline which fueled the burgeoning automobile market came from the refineries of Cleveland-based John D. Rockefeller's Standard Oil Company.

The Early Twentieth Century

In the early years of the twentieth century Cleveland's automobile industry flourished along with that of the nation in general. Total nationwide annual automobile production increased over six-fold, from slightly more than 20,000 in 1903 to nearly 130,000 by 1909. In 1912 there were almost 600 manufacturers of pleasure automobiles. Michigan led with 54, Indiana had 38, and Ohio counted 34.[1]

The trade journal *Automobile* reported that the total national output of automobiles had reached 300,000 in 1912, and by 1913 there were almost one million automobiles registered in the United States. The following year's output of pleasure automobiles was projected to be no less than 564,650.[2]

At this time Cleveland and Chicago boasted similar levels of automobile ownership, with about 12,000 individually registered vehicles in each city. What is especially impressive about this is the fact that Cleveland's population stood at 560,663, approximately one-fourth of Chicago's 2,185,283 people.[3] This reflects the high per capita wealth in Cleveland at the time, and the community's fascination with the automobile.

Cleveland's prosperity was due in large part to its industrial base, of which the automobile was a major contributing factor. The city was not only an automobile manufacturing center, but it was also home to a variety of nationally prominent industrial firms, including American Ball Bearing Company, Otis Steel Company, Corrigan McKinney Steel Company, American Steel and Wire Company, National Carbon Company, Sherwin-Williams Paint Company, and

Standard Oil Company, which was the nation's leading supplier of petroleum and gasoline products.

By 1913 paved roads had become relatively common in urban centers like Cleveland. Beyond the cities, roadside amenities catered to motorists, and it was no longer difficult to find fuel, or even overnight accommodations when out on a motoring excursion.

It was Cleveland that excelled immediately prior to World War I, despite Detroit's surge to prominence at the end of the century's first decade. In 1916 the city added a large number of new automobile and support facilities to its roster.[4] This included automobile factories for H. A. Lozier Company (1915), Denneen Motor Company (1915), Baker R&L Company (1915) which began production of the Owen Magnetic at that time, Disbrow Motor Corporation (1916), Jordan Motor Car Company (1916), Grant Motor Car Company (1916), and Abbott Corporation (1917) which opened its plant less than a week before the United States entered World War I. Also at this time, one of the city's greatest construction projects was under way, as the Willard Storage Battery Company was quadrupling factory space to meet the soaring demand for its automobile batteries.[5]

The Impact of World War I

Barely had the automobile industry passed its fifteenth year when it was thrown into considerable confusion regarding the part it was to play in the country's war effort.

Conflicting statements were made by government officials, and numerous rumors were circulating. Would automobile production be permitted to continue as before? Would automobile manufacturers be required to retool in order to produce materiel for the war effort? There was even the fear that some factories might be nationalized to support the war effort.

In light of all of this, it was impossible for any automobile manufacturer to make clear plans. Decisions regarding production, employment, inventory maintenance, and possible plant expansion all had to be deferred.

In addition to this were three other important questions: Would steel be available for automobile manufacturers? Would the possible curtailment of gasoline supplies discourage automobile sales? Would rail transport, essential to the automotive industry, prove capable of handling domestic as well as war needs?

What this meant for Cleveland's automobile community was that the strong survived and the weak succumbed. The situation was especially difficult for new companies that had been formed immediately before the country's involvement in World War I.

Those companies that were well financed and were managed by people with extensive experience in the automobile industry, such as Jordan and Chandler, did reasonably well. Others like Abbott and Grant, which lacked adequate financial reserves, were unable to survive. On the other hand, for companies like Templar, the war effort meant large government contracts. In the end, most automobile companies in Cleveland and around the country were able to continue automobile production to at least some degree during the war.[6]

Immediately after the war, economic recovery was unpredictable. This created financial uncertainties which severely hampered automobile companies' planning and decision making process. Cleveland banks were attuned to the needs of the city's automobile industry and in 1921 stepped forward to provide additional capital for half a dozen Cleveland companies that were making automobile parts and accessories. At the same time a syndicate of bankers and financiers offered to provide needed working capital through stock purchases and bond exchanges.[7]

An Overview

Notwithstanding these efforts, there were other factors in play, and it turned out to be a classic case of too little, too late. So much financial cushion had been lost by the smaller manufacturers that the weak continued to fail and, during the ensuing years, things drew to a close for automobile manufacturing in Cleveland.

In 1931 there were 149 plants worldwide producing American automobiles. Of these, 82 were in America and 67 were in other countries. While Ford had a total of 67 plants worldwide, and General Motors had 37, Cleveland now hosted only five plants including Ford, Hupmobile (two), Jordan, and Peerless.

Although the attrition in Cleveland automobile manufacturers was significant, Cleveland still remained second only to Detroit, and Ohio second to Michigan, in the number of automobile plants located within their boundaries.[8]

Manufacturers and the Stock Exchanges

Although Cleveland was a major automobile production center for decades, only relatively few of its enterprises were publicly traded. The Chandler Motor Car Company was Cleveland's only automobile company that was traded on the New York Stock Exchange. Six other Cleveland companies were traded on the Cleveland Stock Exchange: Grant Motor Company, Jordan Motor Car Company, Peerless Motor Car Company, F.B. Stearns Company, White Company, and Winton Motor Carriage Company.[9]

The Cleveland Stock Exchange opened in 1900 and was active well beyond 1932 when the last Cleveland automobile was produced. In 1949 it was absorbed by the Midwest Stock Exchange, which became the Chicago Stock Exchange in 1993.

Automotive trading activity on the Cleveland Exchange varied widely from company to company. Peerless seemed to be far and away the most actively traded of the six companies, followed by Stearns. Trading activity for the other companies was relatively light, indicating that they were, for all intents and purposes, closely held companies. Jordan and Winton common voting stock seldom changed hands, although their preferred stock saw activity.

Stock of the Fisher Body Company, which had a huge plant in Cleveland, was also listed on the Cleveland Exchange. Other Cleveland automobile-related entities traded on the exchange included Allyne Industries, Eaton Manufacturing Company, Elwell-Parker Electric Company, Fostoria Pressed Steel, Grant-Lees Company, Midland Steel Products, Murray Ohio Manufacturing Company, Sparks Worthington, and Thompson Products.[10]

This concentration of stock trading activity in the Cleveland Stock Exchange seems to indicate that Cleveland automobile interests preferred to keep stock ownership in the hands of local investors.

And, Cleveland investment influence extended well beyond the city and its own stock exchange: Gordon S. Macklin, whose father had been president of the Cleveland Stock Exchange from 1935 to 1937, became the founder and first president of NASDAQ in 1971.[11]

Ned Jordan and the Selling of Automobiles

It wasn't long after the advent of the automobile as a commercial entity that advertising came to play an important part in the industry. Previously, there had been no need for, nor consideration given to, advertising. Vehicles were custom-made for purchasers who approached the manufacturer in person.

However, once automobiles began to be manufactured in advance of commissioned sales, it was necessary to acquaint the general public with a manufacturer's offerings, and national publications provided the perfect venue for this.

Typical of the earliest advertisements was this one in the July 30, 1898, issue of *Scientific American*, for the 1898 Winton:

> Dispense with a horse and save the expense, care and anxiety of keeping it. To run a motor carriage costs about ½ cent a mile. It is handsomely, strongly and yet tightly constructed and elegantly finished. Easily managed. Speeds from 3 to 20 miles an hour. The hydrocarbon motor is simple and powerful. No odor, no vibration. Suspension Wire Wheels. Pneumatic Tires. Ball Bearings. Send for Catalog.

Soon, other companies began to utilize mass media to inform the buying public of features and technical improvements which they had introduced on their vehicles. In the October 3, 1912, edition of *Life*, Baker Electric proudly proclaimed the following: "Baker silence is tangible evidence of the correctness of Baker engineering. Into this superb car are concentrated the mechanical and electrical principles that fourteen years of experience have proved to be RIGHT."

By the end of World War I, the automobile had demonstrated practicality as transportation for a multitude of applications. As the automobile's popularity grew, a wide range of components became available for the repair, and even assembly, of vehicles. It was no longer necessary for a potential automobile manufacturer to make his vehicle from scratch: virtually everything necessary to build an automobile was available on the general market.

Enter Ned Jordan.

Jordan never claimed to be an engineer. Rather, his expertise was in marketing. He prided himself on being able to identify a market and then offer the appropriate commodity to satisfy the needs of that market. To achieve this, he employed talented engineers and craftsmen, and provided them access to components with which to create vehicles of the highest quality. (See Jordan Motor Car Company.)

Jordan always presented his vehicles to the public in a unique and innovative manner. Rather than touting the Jordan's technical characteristics, he spoke of the experience of driving a Jordan, of being on the open road and encountering adventure.

The best insight into Ned Jordan's philosophy comes from his book *The Inside Story of Adam and Eve* (New York: Howard Coggeshall, 1945). Jordan's imaginative approach to automobile marketing dates from a casual social encounter. In January 1918 Ned Jordan was at Cleveland's elite Mayfield Country Club. He was dancing with the young debutante Eleanor Borton, whom he described as being a "real outdoor girl." While they were dancing she said to him "Why don't you build a swanky roadster for the girl who loves to swim and paddle and shoot ... and for the boy who loves the roar of the cut-out?" Ned responded, "Girl, you've given me an idea worth a million dollars! Thanks for the best dance I've ever had."

The next day Jordan took the train to New York to meet with his friend, custom automobile body designer Harry Huntington, and was given a private peek at a roadster being designed by Huntington for Billie Burke, as a present from her husband, Florenz Ziegfeld. On his way back to Cleveland, Ned sketched his idea for a similar automobile based on what he had seen. It was dashing and debonair. It had a slanted windshield, crowned fenders, a boot, saddle bag, vanity case, and a Waltham clock. Such a combination would be a first in a production automobile. The name of this new automobile was to be the Playboy, a name Jordan adopted from the 1907 play by John Millington Synge, *Playboy of the Western World*.

The advertising copy introducing the Playboy in a 1919 *Saturday Evening Post* remains impressive and original even to this day:

> We might as well tell it. The secret will soon be out. It's a wonderful companion for a wonderful girl and a wonderful boy. How did we happen to think of it? A girl who loves to swim and paddle and shoot described it to a boy who loves the roar of the cut-out. So we built one just for the fun of doing it ... stepped on it ... and the dogs barked and the chickens ran...

In the first year of production, Jordan sold 2,000 Playboys and the net profit per car was $500. The result was Ned Jordan's first million dollars.

The most famous of all Jordan ads was the fabled "Somewhere West of Laramie," which introduced the 1923 Jordan Playboy. Accounts vary as to the exact circumstances that triggered the ad's creation, but Ned's recollections are set forth in his book.

Jordan's daughter Jane was an accomplished western-style rider. Several days after watching her ride at a Fourth of July event in Point Judith, Rhode Island, Ned was westwardbound on the Overland Limited headed for San Francisco and was chatting in the lounge car with a Mr. Austin, a New York lawyer. They passed a station in Wyoming, too fast to catch the town's name on the sign. As Ned Jordan put it:

> Just then a husky somebody whirled up on a rarin' cayoose which was acting as if he'd never seen a Union Pacific train. She reminded me of Jane. "Where are we now?" I inquired, to make conversation. "Oh, somewhere west of Laramie," yawned my companion.
> I took an envelope from my pocket ... wrote down the phrase ... and added, as I looked from the window ... "there's a bronco-busting steer-roping girl who knows what I'm talking about," and so on.

This casual pencil notation evolved into the iconic magazine advertisement which is inextricably identified with Jordan, and was published in June 1923 in *The Saturday Evening Post*.

Jordan's marketing techniques present a clear contrast with such other contemporary automotive luminaries as Alexander Winton. Whereas Alexander Winton would hold contests among chauffeurs to demonstrate their driving prowess, Jordan sponsored slogan contests open to the general public, with the first-place winner receiving a new Jordan automobile. One contest, to promote the Little Custom Tomboy, generated a flurry of entries, some of which included "A Tomboy with Six Appeal," "The Little Custom Jordan—A Young Man's Fancy and an Old Man's Delight," and "Roll, Jordan Roll" which was the most often submitted slogan. The winner of the new Jordan was R.L. McGean for his slogan "A Glorious Challenge to an Eager Generation—The Little Custom Jordan."[12]

Jordan did not limit himself to media promotion of his vehicles. He travelled widely and was often on the road promoting the Jordan automobile, meeting with his distributors and dealers, and making those associated with his company feel a part of the Jordan family. His extensive traveling was so demanding that he had his own private railroad car for this purpose. He regularly hosted plant visitations for distributors and conducted dealer drive-aways. One time, he even hired an entire Santa Fe railroad train to haul new Jordan Playboys to Los Angeles for delivery to the company's largest West Coast dealership.

To follow Ned Jordan's career is to follow the evolution of modern American advertising. He had the ability to not only present a product in a way which would appeal to potential purchasers, but also to create an interest and therefore a market for the product itself.

Ned Jordan's talents did not go unremarked by his peers. *Advertising Age*, in its January 28, 1952, issue, referred to him as "one of the 'advertising greats' of all time."

Somewhere West of Laramie

SOMEWHERE west of Laramie there's a broncho-busting, steer-roping girl who knows what I'm talking about.

She can tell what a sassy pony, that's a cross between greased lightning and the place where it hits, can do with eleven hundred pounds of steel and action when he's going high, wide and handsome.

The truth is—the Playboy was built for her.

Built for the lass whose face is brown with the sun when the day is done of revel and romp and race.

She loves the cross of the wild and the tame.

There's a savor of links about that car—of laughter and lilt and light—a hint of old loves—and saddle and quirt. It's a brawny thing—yet a graceful thing for the sweep o' the Avenue.

Step into the Playboy when the hour grows dull with things gone dead and stale.

Then start for the land of real living with the spirit of the lass who rides, lean and rangy, into the red horizon of a Wyoming twilight.

JORDAN
JORDAN MOTOR CAR COMPANY, Inc., Cleveland, Ohio

Ned Jordan's "Somewhere West of Laramie" advertisement for the Jordan Playboy pointed the way to a new approach for selling the automobile.

An Overview

The Second Automobile Industry

Cleveland's participation in the manufacture of automobile parts and supplies was a natural adjunct to its burgeoning automobile industry, and included many well-known firms. From the very beginning of Cleveland's "second automobile industry," a multitude of companies provided a broad range of parts and services, including assembling automobiles for brand name manufacturers, building engines, turning out complete automobile bodies, designing and making electrical systems, and producing a wide variety of essential parts and accessories.

It all began with the earliest automobile inventors themselves who, of necessity, manufactured all of the components which they could not obtain commercially. Soon a cadre of parts suppliers, small manufacturers, and machine tool companies came on the scene, providing the ever-growing market of automobile manufacturers with everything needed for producing a finished automobile. It wasn't long before a variety of specialized automobile parts such as pistons, rings, rods, bearings, carburetors, radiators, water pumps, valves, boilers, and transmissions became readily available to meet the increasing demand of local automotive entrepreneurs.

It is important to recognize how much of the basic starting point for most of this technology came from the horse-drawn buggy, and also, how much modification was required. Clearly, the technology and the skills required for producing the automobile's unique components would have to be far superior to that which had theretofore been adequate for the manufacture of wagons and carriages.

The Cleveland-built Standard Steel Rims were relied on to take a Stanley Steamer to a record speed of over 120 miles per hour (author's collection).

The emergence of this technology began with the development of new machine tools and machine tooling techniques. This was necessary for producing the highly specialized fine tolerance components needed for constructing automobiles.

Fortunately, this capability existed in turn-of-the-century Cleveland. There were many precision machine tool manufacturing firms which, thanks to over a century of the city's industrial growth and the resulting manufacturing infrastructure, had on hand the technology which was needed. And these companies quickly adapted to meet the new challenge.

Thus, the transition from horse power to horseless power proceeded quite smoothly and quickly in Cleveland. Many small companies adjusted their production to service the growing automobile manufacturing market. In addition, ancillary services, offered specifically for the motorist, cropped up from very early on. After-market modifications and accessories quickly became a common offering of the supporting industry.[13] So many, in fact, that it is impossible to note all of them here.

Two of the earliest support industries were already in existence before the automobile appeared. Although not initially intended for use in self-propelled vehicles, batteries and electric motors were perhaps the first automobile-related parts that were adaptable for use by early automobile manufacturers. Similarly, carriage and wagon makers were already producing bodies which were suitable for the earliest automobiles. Although modifications were required, it has been said that, "with a little tweaking here and there, the carriage became the horseless carriage."

Among the pioneering companies which became primary suppliers to the automotive trade, one was the Cleveland Cap Screw Company, which was organized in 1900. Known today as TRW Automotive, it continues to act as a supplier of parts to the world's major automobile manufacturers. Another early arrival was Torbensen Axle Co., which moved to Cleveland from New Jersey in 1915. One of its officers, Joseph Eaton, left the company in 1919 to form what is now known as the Eaton Corporation, which is today a leading worldwide supplier of automobile parts. In 1921 General Motors' Fisher Body Division built the world's largest automobile body plant in Cleveland, furnishing bodies to Chandler, Cleveland, Oakland, Chevrolet, and others.

Cleveland's tradition as a major supplier to the automobile industry continued unabated long after the city ceased to be the country's automobile manufacturing center. Ford Motor Company's Cleveland Engine Plant #1 produced its first engine in 1951 and has since made over 35 million engines. In addition, Ford's Cleveland stamping plant, which began operations in 1954, continued to make doors, decks, fenders, floor pans and side panels in its 2.1 million square foot plant through the first decade of the twenty-first century.

There were many other early Cleveland companies which grew along with the manufacturers to whom they provided support. The Cleveland Machine Screw Company was the assembly site for the early Baker electric automobile, and was a major supplier of a variety of parts for the White Automobile Company. The Gabriel Company, which began in 1907 as the producer of a musical horn, driven off of a motor's exhaust, evolved into shock absorbers.

Automobile frames were manufactured by Hydraulic Pressed Steel Company, and W.W. Taylor Machine Company offered to make any transmission gear required. The Lamson & Sessions Company manufactured a complete line of bolts, nuts, rivets and even wrenches for automobiles. Perfection Spring Company boasted that its "thin leaf" springs were the easiest riding and most durable made in the world. The company also made the Perfection Tire Holder for mounting a spare tire on the running board which the company called "an ornament to your car."

Ferro Machine & Foundry Company of Cleveland built more than fourteen different types of automobile engines. Park Drop Forge Company cast engine blocks, many of which were purchased by its neighbor, the White Company, for installation in its automobiles. Allyne Foundries participated in the motive power arena as well, and cast engine blocks for the trade.

In an unusual, but very practical arrangement, Cleveland's Chandler Motor Car Company had two on-site suppliers: H. J. Walker Company and Briggs Company. Walker built engine and mechanical components exclusively for Chandler, and employed over five hundred men, while Briggs operated an adjacent auto body assembly facility. All final assembly work and testing was done by Chandler itself.[14]

Willard Storage Battery Company constructed a new plant adjacent to Chandler in 1917, where it was capable of producing 12,000 batteries per day. All components were made at the Willard plant, including wooden battery boxes and grids. The Willard plant was not one of Chandler's on-site suppliers, but had selected the location because of its superior rail connections and service. By 1918 Willard was supplying batteries to eighty-five percent of the nation's automobile factories.[15]

The Body Builders

In the early days of Cleveland's automobile industry, those automobile manufacturers which did not produce their own bodies had them made by nearby Cleveland carriage, wagon, and cabinet makers. Among these were the Broc Carriage and Wagon Company, which eventually offered its own vehicles in 1909, the Hanson Car Company, builder of wooden bodies, and the Kuntz Company, which made sewing machine cabinets and supplied automobile bodies to the White Company.

There were also a number of small body building companies which catered directly to the early automobile manufacturing trade. Wilson & Hayes Manufacturing Company was a manufacturer of metal bodies,[16] and the Bender Body Company of Cleveland built bodies for the Kurtz Automatic automobile from 1921 to 1924.

Some Cleveland automobile manufacturers, such as Leon Rubay, produced their own automobile bodies and also supplied bodies to the trade. Others, like Eastman Automobile Company, re-directed their efforts from the building of complete vehicles to concentrate on the manufacture of automobile bodies. In 1901, Eastman made this shift, changed its name to Eastman Metallic Body Company, and began offering all-steel bodies.

Also serving the industry was the Lang Body Company, an offshoot of the 1915 reorganization of electric automobile builder Rauch & Lang Carriage Company, when it became the Baker R&L Company. Formed in 1915 by E. J. Lang, son of the Carriage company's founder Charles E. J. Lang, the Lang Body Company constructed a new facility on West 106th Street and Lorain Avenue, where it began manufacturing bodies for Peerless, Lincoln, Ford, and others,[17] as well as truck, and aeroplane bodies.[18]

Four years later, in 1919, when the Baker R&L Company discontinued the manufacture of electric automobiles, it was reorganized into two divisions: The Baker-Rauchlang Company, which built automobile bodies for the trade, including such automobile manufacturers as Packard, Chandler, Peerless, and Duesenberg; and the recast Baker R&L Company which now made only commercial electric trucks for industrial use.[19]

By 1924 Baker R&L had expanded its operations, taking over the West Side body plant of the Rubay Company, which had been making a limited number of bodies for Stearns-Knight, Peerless, and Franklin. All of these Rubay clients were added to Baker's existing list of customers, which included Reo and Wills Sainte Claire.[20] Baker R&L's continuing success in body building resulted in further expansion. It took over the Lang company's Ford business in 1928, and went on to build steel bodies for the Cleveland Ford plant from 1928 to 1932, at which time the last Cleveland-built automobile rolled off the Ford assembly line.

The Briggs Manufacturing Company was another important supplier of automobile bodies. Briggs built a facility adjacent to the Chandler Automobile Company plant in 1916 for the sole purpose of furnishing finished bodies to Chandler. Briggs bodies were manufactured in Detroit and shipped to the company's Cleveland facility, where they were finished, painted and upholstered before being moved to the Chandler plant for mounting on chassis. This arrangement lasted for five years.

In 1921 Cleveland's automobile body building industry took a giant leap forward. That year General Motors completed its East Side Fisher Body plant, designed by the famous industrial architect Albert Kahn. General Motors had acquired the Fisher Body company from its founders, the Fisher brothers of Norwalk, Ohio, in 1916. Its new Cleveland factory enclosed over one million square feet of floor space, which made it the largest single-unit automobile body plant in existence, even at a time when Detroit was the automobile capital of the world.

Initially the plant supplied bodies for Chandler and Cleveland automobiles, which together made more vehicles than all the other Cleveland manufacturers combined. Beginning in 1921, Fisher also supplied bodies for Chevrolet. By 1924 the plant was turning out 600 bodies per day, having added Chrysler and Oakland to its list of customers.

The Fisher plant could claim several innovations. In 1923 it introduced the use of lacquer paints and the knock-down system for shipping bodies. In 1925 it became the first auto body manufacturer to use a moving conveyer line in its assembly process.[21]

Unfortunately, in the late 1920s Fisher lost two of its major customers. With the consolidation of the Chandler and Cleveland manufacturing operations in 1926, the new Chandler-Cleveland Motors Corporation began to construct its own automobile bodies, utilizing the facilities at the Cleveland Automobile Company's Euclid Avenue plant. When Hupp Motor Car Corporation bought Chandler-Cleveland in 1929 it continued to utilize the Euclid Avenue plant to build bodies until 1931 when it moved all operations to Detroit.

Early Automobile Assemblers

Automobile assemblers such as Cleveland Machine Screw Company, Federal Manufacturing Company, and the Garford Company played a significant but unheralded role in Cleveland's early automobile history. Although not manufacturers of automobiles in their own name or for their own marque, they were essential partners in the manufacture of numerous Cleveland automobiles.

More often than not, Federal was responsible for most of the component parts, while Cleveland Machine did the assembly and performed incidental manufacturing functions. Federal also supplied parts directly to a variety of Cleveland automobile companies, including providing chassis for Royal Tourist. Federal made virtually everything for automobiles except bodies, and its Cleveland ball bearing plant was the largest in the world.[22]

Federal and Cleveland Machine Screw built complete automobiles on contract for a number of manufacturers including Baker, Sperry, Berg, Meteor, and Cleveland.

Walter Baker and Elmer Sperry had their prototypes built by Federal and Cleveland Machine Screw. Federal and Cleveland Machine Screw collaborated to build Berg and Meteor vehicles for out-of-town interests which did not have manufacturing facilities of their own. The Cleveland automobile (not to be confused with Chandler's Cleveland automobile of 1919) was completely built and assembled by Federal and Cleveland Machine, until facilities for completing the assembly and finish work were obtained by the Cleveland company.[23]

Another important participant in this scheme was the Garford Company of Elyria, Ohio. Owned by Arthur L. Garford of Cleveland, who was the president of Federal and an officer in Cleveland Machine, this company built the chassis which were used in many of the vehicles produced by Federal and Cleveland Machine Screw.

On May 1, 1905, A.L. Garford formed the Garford Company to take over the operations and business of Federal Manufacturing Company. Garford's Elyria operation was combined with Federal. The Elyria plant concentrated on the manufacture of general automobile parts, while the Cleveland-based Federal facility specialized in assembly and heavier production work, as explained in *Motor Age*, May 18, 1905.

The Garford company produced a withering array of all imaginable types of automobile parts an extensive list of which can be found in *Cycle and Automobile Trade Journal*, December 1904.

Cleveland-Made Accessories, After-Market Components and Services

From the very beginning, motorists had the urge to improve and customize their automobiles with accessories and accoutrements to suit their personal tastes. Cleveland publications of the era contain many examples of advertisements which catered to this market.

Globe Machine & Stamping Company advertised twenty-seven styles of storage boxes and exterior trunks for mounting on an automobile. The Liberty Bell Company made five-inch bells, which it touted as being more reliable and attention-getting than horns.

McCauley Storage Battery Company offered Kremlo lighting and ignition batteries, which they guaranteed to replace free of charge if your McCauley battery failed. The Nungesser Carbon & Battery Company manufactured Acme Rapid Fire dry ignition system batteries, which the company stated would "Get Under Way & Get There."

Adams-Bagnall Electric Company specialized in the manufacture of AbAutoLites, "the most efficient automobile lamps in existence," and Guide Motor Lamp Manufacturing Company pointed out that it made and repaired all varieties of electric automobile lamps. The Auto Plating & Mfg. Company advertised a complete line of electric automobile lamps, and also carburetor floats. One of their products was a combination dash lamp and ventilator which, when opened for ventilation, illuminated both the inside and outside of the automobile.

Soon there was no shortage of companies that offered to revitalize your automobile in various ways. For example, the Gabriel Auto Company stated that it could remodel the body on your automobile by installing fore-doors and new up-to-date fenders. The company pointed out that the shape of a fender, and the fact that you had only rear-door access to the front seats in the automobile, were telltale signs of a vehicle's age.

You could, of course, have an entirely new body built for your automobile. If so, the Arter Auto Carriage Company was at your disposal. If mere modifications were all that you required, then the Standard Top & Equipment Company could be of assistance, as they manufactured automobile tops, seat covers, wind guards, curtains, storm aprons, storm fronts, roller curtains, and jiffy curtains.

An interesting upgrade was available from the Cleveland Speed Indicator Company, which noted that "An Unreliable Indicator Is a Mechanical Prevaricator, a Breeder of Distrust and Profanity" in an effort to convince manufacturers and motorists to use their "eternally dependable" speed and time indicators.

The need for vehicle maintenance and repair services was also important, and numerous Cleveland establishments were available to satisfy this need.

Lakewood Chemical Company manufactured an Autopower Carbon Remover to keep your engine in the best of health. Boden Brothers provided retreaded tires that were guaranteed to last for 2,000 miles, and were said to be priced at a fraction of what a new tire would cost. The Kurtzner Radiator Company built and repaired radiators. Kurtzner is still in business, doing that very same work, after over 100 years. The Auto Lamp & Radiator Company manufactured fenders, hoods, mufflers, sod pans, and any type of automobile sheet metal items, as did the Bunn, Hutchinson & Company.

If you wanted to protect your vehicle from the weather, The Geo. A. Rutherford Company or F. C. Pinyoun & Son would build a garage for you. Once your garage was built, Scientific Heater Company would furnish garage heaters to "protect your automobile from cracked engine blocks due to unreliable anti-freeze mixtures." Or you could choose to rely on Horstman Auto Top Company which made a combination auto hood and radiator cover that "keeps the motor warm for several hours and will do away with a lot of unnecessary cranking."

Other types of protection also became available, and the insurance industry was there to serve. Schlaudecker & Company would ensure you and your automobile, as would Mr. F. I. Burke, or the Cleveland agent of the Aetna Company. For assistance in the event of actual theft of your machine, the well-named W. W. Sly Mfg. Company was the firm to consider. The slogan for its line of automobile locks was "We Fool the Thief."

Finally, to look your best in proper motoring apparel, you had only to consult Browning, King & Company for "everything to wear in the machine for men," such as fur coats with fur inside or outside, detachable leather-lined overcoats, suits, leggings, puttees, caps, gloves, sweaters, lap robes, and more. The MacAdams Company offered "English shower-proof coats and lightweight Throw-Ons" for motoring weather protection. This was a time when motoring was truly an outdoor sport.

Enhancing the Motoring Experience

While the automobile was becoming more reliable and practical, other transportation-related developments were taking place, which both nurtured and benefited from the automobile culture.

Perhaps one of the most fortuitous of these symbiotic relationships was the near-simultaneous development of the petroleum industry. Once again at the forefront, Cleveland was home to John D. Rockefeller's Standard Oil Company, the pre-eminent producer of petroleum products.

At the very same time as the automobile was evolving from a vehicle for the wealthy into a reliable means of transportation with commercial applications, the petroleum industry was coming into its own, and the two industries contributed to each other's development.

Even seemingly small technological improvements contributed to this mutual success. For example, the introduction of the self-starter for internal combustion engines had a significant impact on the demand for gasoline. Once the self-starter was commonly available, women's preference for electric vehicles was eclipsed, resulting in an enlarged market and increased demand for gasoline-powered automobiles and, of course, for gasoline. Clearly, the gasoline-powered automobile, with its greater flexibility, convenience, and performance than either steam or electric vehicles, had won the day, and the petroleum industry flourished.

With a reliable and growing market, gasoline production and distribution grew steadily. No longer did a motorist have to seek out a hardware store or friendly farmer to obtain fuel for his vehicle. Gas stations and service garages grew almost like weeds along the roadside.

Paved roads were another benefit which was encouraged by increased road traffic. Although the League of American Wheelmen had been agitating for road paving ever since the 1880s, it was not until the automobile became common that the demand for good roads was finally met.

Roads paved by municipalities and governmental bodies, including Cleveland, were critical to the popularity of the automobile. As early as 1913, Ohio was addressing construction of a network of 440 roads which together would connect all "main market" centers of every county in the state. It was a known fact that paved all-weather roads significantly increased land value and economic growth.

For those motorists who ventured beyond their home town, finding fuel, food and accommodation could be something of a challenge. As a result, roadside eateries, campgrounds, and then motels sprang up along the highways to serve the long distance motorist.

An example of one of the more elegant alternatives is the Portage Hotel in Akron, which advertised 250 rooms, 175 baths, and a lavatory and toilet in every room. Its European Plan rooms began at $1.50, and the hotel's brochure boasted that it was located on a "continuous paved route" of thirty-five miles from Cleveland to Akron.

One of the major concerns for early motorists was, simply, not getting lost when trying to travel from Point A to Point B. Early route directions were obtained by word-of-mouth, from friends who had travelled that direction previously, or by stopping and asking for directions from a local resident.

The need for more reliable route advice quickly became apparent. Automobile clubs were the first to fill this need. They supplied detailed route directions for their members, and installed road signs on popularly travelled routes. It wasn't long before local clubs, such as the Cleveland Automobile Club, began to offer compact folding road maps to their members. This was a vast improvement over consulting a compass and looking for landmarks.

The Cleveland Automobile Club

In addition to being the automobile industry's capital from 1898 to 1908, Cleveland was home to the country's second automobile club. Founded January 8, 1900, the Cleveland Automobile Club (CAC) came into existence only six months after the Automobile Club of America was established in New York City in June of 1899.[24]

By 1916 the CAC had become the largest automobile club in the nation and, since 1978, is the oldest automobile club in existence. Initially formed as a gentlemen's social club, the CAC's founding members included both wealthy automobile enthusiasts and members of the automobile manufacturing community. Among these were Alexander Winton, Walter C. Baker, Frank B. Stearns, Fred White, and Windsor White.[25]

Fairly early on in its existence the CAC began to sponsor races, in which members could test their skills and manufacturers had the opportunity to demonstrate the abilities of their automobiles. In 1902 the club sponsored its first race.[26]

By 1903 the CAC had begun issuing brochures containing information about traffic laws, and it provided a listing of local automobile owners, whether or not they were members of the club. The first *Journal of the Cleveland Automobile Club*, a very substantial and attractive publication, appeared in 1911.

In 1912 CAC took over the Dover Bay Club, situated west of Cleveland on the shores of Lake Erie, and turned it into a retreat for club members. This magnificent establishment had a bathing beach, imposing club house with parlors, dining rooms, and sleeping accommodations, a dance pavilion, and a pier for boating and fishing. The dining room was overseen by a renowned chef and fresh Lake Erie catch was kept in an aquarium until selected and served. There were tennis courts, a baseball diamond, and golf links. Appropriately, the club was renamed the Automobile Country Club. Membership in the country club was a modest $15 for any CAC member.[27]

Travel assistance today is so commonplace and easily accessible that it is difficult to appreciate how many of the services offered by CAC, which we now take for granted, were considered innovative at the turn of the 20th century.

The CAC enthusiastically supported member touring, providing detailed information for a variety of point-to-point travel routes. By 1924, its *Automobile Route Book* contained 396 different itineraries.[28]

The club maintained an extensive library of touring information from around the country, and made available road maps for the asking. In addition, its monthly publication regularly featured suggested drives.

The May 1913 issue of CAC's publication *The Cleveland Motorist*, contains an excellent example of the type of information provided for its members.

Odometer readings and landmark sightings were essential for navigating. Over half of the entries describing the 171.5 mile route from Cleveland to Columbus mentioned trolley lines, which were often paralleled. Following utility poles was another reliable means of keeping to the route, as over one half-dozen entries mentioned these poles. Almost half of the route entries used railroad tracks and crossings as important reference points. References to "good macadam," "dirt track," and "brick pavement" were equally helpful to the early motorist.

In describing the route from Cleveland to Columbus, it is noted that the route goes "via Bellevue, Bucyrus and Marion" and is "Over level country on gravel or macadam practically all the way."

The trip begins in downtown Cleveland:

0.0 Cleveland, Public Square at monument. Go west with trolley on Superior street keeping left 0.4 onto long viaduct.
0.8 25th St. Jog left and immediately right with trolley onto Detroit Ave., following same direct under R.R.
7.5 Turn right with trolley and brick pavement over Rocky River Viaduct.

Once out into rural areas, a different type of landmark was of greater importance:

 69.4 Curve right with road at pond; cross 4 RRs
 72.0 BELLEVUE, 4-corners, stone foundation on left
 82.2 Fork, blacksmith shop on left; bear right
127.1 Ford; bear left with trolley following same direct through Norton

As can be seen from these period route plans, one close eye had to be kept on the odometer, and another on the passing scenery. Clearly, a navigator in the passenger seat would have been a definite asset.[29]

To further aid motorists, the club initiated a campaign in 1912 to erect road signs throughout Cuyahoga County and called upon its membership to actively participate by being a petitioner and prod their respective townships to comply with the State law requiring postings of road signs at all significant points. By 1924 CAC had installed signs on over 4,000 miles of roadways in the county, which clearly aided not only its members, but all motorists using those routes.

It would come as no surprise that roads and their condition remained a constant concern of the club. Paved roads first appeared thanks to the efforts of bicycle enthusiast and wheelmen organizations during the late 1800s. In 1893 the first paved stretch of rural road in Ohio, the Wooster Pike, was constructed south of Cleveland and surfaced in brick.

Not surprisingly, as motor vehicles began using these paved roadways, they deteriorated at a rapid pace. Although Cuyahoga County had what was said to be the best paved road system in the country, Cleveland lagged far behind in its street maintenance program and was often taken to task for this by the club. The CAC received immediate action on its complaints, which had been made directly to Mayor Newton D. Baker, and the city promptly undertook repaving and repair work on the worst of the offending streets.[30] Other municipalities were also often slow to attend to road maintenance, and the club waged a constant battle to correct this negligence.

Upon occasion, when an activity of interest to CAC members was too far distant to be practical for a motoring excursion, the club made alternative travel arrangements for its members, even if this necessitated travel by train. Members interested in attending the 1913 "500 mile Speedway Race at Indianapolis" could take advantage of CAC's arrangement with the Pennsylvania Railroad for overnight Pullman tickets to Indianapolis, starting at $6.10 each way, with a drawing room accommodation for an additional $7. Tickets for seats at the Speedway were not included.[31]

CAC was the only club in the country to maintain its own map and road route-aide department 365 days a year. Members could, on request, receive an itinerary for a trip anywhere in the country, and as a result, the Club's Touring Bureau was quite busy, fielding some 297,000 calls in one year in the 1920s alone. The club also conducted periodic inspections of gasoline filling stations, to ensure fair measure on every purchase, and even provided roadside breakdown services for members.[32]

In many instances, the club provided services which benefited non-members as well. For example, the club distributed motor car licenses, saving the State of Ohio some $250,000 annually.

The club's Anti-Theft Department was effective in reducing automobile thefts, and its Legal Department was always available to aid members. In one year alone, 30,000 people utilized this service. CAC also kept an eye on legislation and regulations affecting motorists, as well as possible threats of taxation focused on automobiles and their owners. On more than one occasion, CAC took affirmative action to thwart burdensome rules and taxes.

Civic events were sponsored on a regular basis, most notable and popular of which was an annual orphans outing. So well regarded was the service provided to members by CAC that its membership grew to cover one-third of all automobile owners in Cuyahoga County.

The Waning of Manufacturing

The decline of the Cleveland automobile manufacturing community occurred slowly, over a number of years. Many factors were involved. In fact, each automobile manufacturer failed in its own way.

Financing, although important, was not always a major issue. During the early years of their existence, most of Cleveland's successful automobile manufacturers were able to maintain complete control of their companies.[33] Alexander Winton and Frank B. Stearns were wealthy and able to manage all aspects of their ventures independently. Companies such as White and Peerless, already successful manufacturing establishments before they entered the automobile business, had ample resources within their own organizations to carry out their automobile ventures. Other companies such as Chandler and Jordan relied largely on satisfying their monetary needs through the sale of stock.

Financial support for Cleveland's automobile industry was available from other sources as well.

In 1910 a private Cleveland investment group was formed for the purpose of supporting the city's automobile industry. Capitalized at $4 million, the Consolidated Motor Car Company was organized to purchase select Cleveland automobile manufacturers with the objective of forming a conglomerate of automobile companies along the lines of General Motors. Unfortunately, it did not realize its goal.

In 1914 the Cleveland Chamber of Commerce supported the formation of an organization which was intended to encourage "outside" automobile companies to move their operations to Cleveland, promising them financial assistance for their relocation. This promotional venture proved to be quite successful and manufacturers including Grant, Abbott, Jordan, Chandler and Templar came to Cleveland as a result.

But, in the end, even this was not enough.

By the mid-teens many of Cleveland's existing factories were reaching obsolescence. Over the years, innovations had made mass production increasingly efficient. But, it became apparent that such adaptation would come at a hefty price. Rather than a question of re-tooling, this was something that would require entire plant re-configuration, and major investment.

The city's automobile manufacturers were clearly caught at a crossroads.

Cleveland automobile factories such as those of Winton, White, Stearns and Peerless had been designed for assembly on either a batch-type basis or a progressive station-by-station basis.

The batch construction process involved bringing the parts to a fixed location where they were assembled into a finished automobile as it sat in place on the factory floor. In the station-by-station system, chassis were moved manually along an assembly route and stopped at a number of locations along the way, where specific parts were mounted on the chassis before they progressed to the next station for the addition of other components.

To convert production from either of these systems to the more modern continuously moving assembly line would have been prohibitively expensive and impractical, even necessitating the construction of entirely new plants to accommodate a moving assembly line.

Even such a forward-looking company as Hupp fell victim to this. Hupp had acquired its Cleveland plant from the Chandler Company in 1929 and totally rebuilt the facility in 1930. Despite the fact that the Hupp plant itself was one of the most advanced of all Cleveland automobile manufacturing facilities at the time, the company was unable to justify the expense of any further modernization. Hupp closed its Cleveland plant only one year later, in 1931, and moved its operations to Detroit.

Other Cleveland automobile manufacturers also left the scene without fanfare.

Winton simply closed its doors. Chandler and Stearns were sold outright to third parties. Templar went bankrupt. Peerless, Baker and White successfully switched to non-automotive pursuits. Only Jordan struggled on until it simply expired.

Subsequent Endeavors

By 1932 Cleveland was no longer a major automobile manufacturing center.

However, many pioneering automobile individuals and concerns which had spearheaded Cleveland's success in the motoring field were quick to adapt to new opportunities and became involved in a variety of other manufacturing endeavors.

Looking back to the first decade of the 20th century, Elmer Sperry was perhaps the earliest among Cleveland's automotive pioneers to quit the automobile business and successfully re-direct his efforts.

Sperry originally formed the Sperry Electric Co. in 1880. Although his company had begun to produce electric automobiles by 1898, Sperry decided to leave the automobile business in 1901 in order to concentrate his efforts on the products of an electro-chemical laboratory which he had established in 1900. In this research facility Sperry developed a process for making caustic soda, and another for recovering tin from scrap metal. He also experimented with diesel engines. Most noteworthy was his work with gyroscopic compasses and stabilizers for ships and aircraft, which resulted in the invention of the Sperry Gyroscope in 1910.

Many other Cleveland automobile manufacturers were equally successful in adapting to the change in Cleveland's motor vehicle environment.

Winton

Change was nothing new to Alexander Winton; he had always focused on the future. In 1895 Winton left his highly successful bicycle company in order to concentrate on building an automobile. Then, in 1924 he liquidated his Winton Motor Car Company in order to devote full time to the Winton Engine Company, which he had established in 1912. From 1924 on, Winton focused his energies on the design and manufacture of diesel engines, which found use in a wide variety of applications, including the powering of Navy vessels and railroad locomotives.

The quality and success of Winton's diesel engines was widely recognized, and by 1930 his engine company had become a division of General Motors. In 1934 General Motors provided a Winton-designed diesel engine to power the Chicago Burlington & Quincy Railroad's Zephyr streamline train on its record-breaking run from Denver, Colorado to Chicago, Illinois. In 1935, GM's Winton division was split in two. Part of it was folded into GM's Electromotive Division, which became the country's largest producer of diesel locomotives. The other part became the Cleveland Diesel Engine Division in 1937, where diesel engines were made for the Navy and stationary applications.

Two GM-built Winton marine engine installations are worthy of particular note.

The United States Presidential yacht, powered by a GM-Winton diesel engine, was originally built in 1931 for Montgomery Ward & Company Chairman Sewell Avery. It subsequently served five U.S. Presidents during the years from 1945 through 1998, and was variously named Williamsburg (Truman), Barbara Anne (Eisenhower), Patricia (Nixon), and Honey Fitz (Kennedy and Johnson). The yacht is now privately owned and has been restored.

The USS *Cod*, a World War II submarine on exhibit at Cleveland's lakefront, is the last completely intact World War II submarine in existence, and is powered by five GM-Winton diesel engines built at Cleveland's Berea Road plant. Three of the engines are still operational.

Alexander Winton's elegant home in the north-Cleveland suburb of Lakewood no longer exists. However, the location itself remains highly visible, as Winton Place, a residential high-rise constructed on the original Alexander Winton estate.

Baker

Walter Baker resigned from the Baker Motor Vehicle Company in 1906 to concentrate on his American Ball Bearing Company interests. In 1918 he collaborated with others to form the Standard Parts Company, and in 1919 he became a member of the Peerless Motor Car Company board of directors.

The Baker company itself continued quite successfully up until the point in the mid-teens when electric vehicles were of fading interest to the motoring public. In 1915 it joined forces with two other Cleveland automobile manufacturers, Rauch & Lang, and the R.M. Owen Company. The merged companies went on to produce the Baker, Rauch-Lang, and Owen Magnetic automobiles, which were variously manufactured through 1920. After that time, the company redirected its focus to the making of industrial equipment such as forklifts, and the electric vehicle business was sold to interests outside of Ohio.

Stearns

Frank B. Stearns retired from the Stearns company in 1916. The company continued to manufacture Stearns-Knight automobiles and was purchased in 1925 by John North Willys, who manufactured Stearns-Knight automobiles until 1929, at which time the F.B. Stearns Company was dissolved. Like Winton, Stearns went from the manufacture of high quality automobiles to the design of diesel engines. One of Stearns' greatest successes was his design for a two-stroke overhead cam engine, which he sold to the U.S. Navy in 1935.

Peerless

In 1921 the Peerless Motor Car Company was sold to Richard H. Collins, the former president and general manager of Cadillac. Subsequent management conflicts plagued the company for a number of years until the last Peerless automobile was finally produced in

1931. Despite company optimism, which had led to the production of a magnificent 1932 Peerless prototype vehicle, it became apparent that the company needed to re-direct its efforts.

Historically, Peerless had always been adaptable. The company originally produced bicycles and washing machine wringers before entering into the automobile market in 1902. Thus, it was quite in character when Peerless once again re-directed its efforts and entered the brewing business in 1932.

In an agreement with the Carling Brewing Company of Canada, Peerless re-configured its plant and began producing Carling Black Label Beer. The timing was perfect, as the end of Prohibition was only one year away. This endeavor was very successful and endured until 1971, at which time Carling sold the Peerless plant and Cleveland brewing operation to C. Schmidt & Sons, which continued to produce Strohs beer at the old Peerless plant until 1986.

WHITE

When Thomas H. White died in 1914, the White story took two separate paths, each following the endeavors of Thomas's two sons, Rollin and Windsor.

Rollin left the White Company in 1914 and organized what became the Cleveland Tractor Company, in order to manufacture his Cletrac farm tractors.

In 1922 Rollin joined with E.E. Allyne and Fred M. Zeder to build an automobile of advanced design. However, Zeder opted instead to join the Chrysler corporation in Detroit, and his departure ended the endeavor. Undaunted, Rollin moved on to incorporate the Rollin Motors Company in 1923, and undertook the production of the Rollin automobile, the first to have four-wheel brakes. The relatively high price and small size of the four-cylinder Rollin were a detrimental combination and, by 1925, it was decided to cease production of the Rollin and to concentrate once again on the manufacture of farm equipment.

The original White Motor Company, now under the direction of Rollin's brother Windsor, continued the manufacture of automobiles until 1918. At that time the company switched to the exclusive manufacture of trucks, buses and military vehicles, and produced a variety of outstanding commercial vehicles over the subsequent sixty-plus years of its existence. Perhaps most noteworthy are the Yellowstone National Park yellow buses of the 1930s, which are still with us today, and the Army half-tracks of World War II.

Over the years White expanded, acquiring such respected names in trucks as Autocar, Diamond T, and REO. Although the White name was finally dropped from trucks in 1981 by its then acquirer, Volvo, it still survived briefly on a limited offering of farm equipment.

All of this brings us back to Rollin White and Cletrac. In 1944, Cletrac was sold to Oliver, a manufacturer of farm equipment. Then, in 1954, Oliver was purchased by the White Motor Company, bringing the family of White back together once again.

A Chronological Overview

1864 to 1895: Glimmerings. The prelude to the automobile industry in Cleveland came in 1864 when John Grant's steam-powered automobile made its inaugural run. (See Grant, John J.) The next noteworthy event occurred over twenty years later with the appearance of the Brush Electric three-wheeler in 1886. (See Brush, Charles Francis.) These two vehicles were harbingers of Cleveland's automobile industry.

1896 to 1900: The Beginning. During the years from 1896 to 1900 all of America was experiencing and participating in the invention of the automobile. In Cleveland, this brought about a rush of intensive activity that would establish the city as the home of America's automobile industry.

From 1896 to 1900 Cleveland hosted twenty-three automobile enterprises, fourteen of which became well-established. The most famous of these were Baker, Peerless, Stearns, White, and Winton, all of which remained at the forefront of the automobile industry well into the first quarter of the twentieth-century, and beyond.

1901 to 1905: Burgeoning of Creative Individual Inventors. By 1901 the basic concept of the automobile had been realized. What followed over the ensuing years was the refinement, improvement, and sorting-out of an almost infinite variety of technological aspects surrounding the engineering and manufacture of a self-propelled vehicle. By now it had been established that there were three viable sources of motive power: internal combustion, steam, and electricity. During these five years, the contest to establish which of the three offered the best overall alternative would determine the direction automobile power plants would take in the future.

It was also at this time that a flood of new names was brought to the Cleveland auto arena, as many budding entrepreneurs and inventors were attracted to the prospects for this new personal conveyance. In this short span of time, forty-three new automobile manufacturing names appeared in Cleveland.

1906 to 1910: Honing Techniques. Twenty-seven new automobile manufacturing names made their debut in Cleveland during these years. However, things were beginning to change.

Although Cleveland was home to White, the country's premier steam vehicle manufacturer, there was no other company in the city which was producing steam-powered vehicles. There were seven Cleveland firms which still offered electric vehicles, but it was becoming apparent that the internal combustion engine would be the ultimate choice for automotive power.

Likewise, there were changes brewing in the factories themselves. Manufacturing techniques had remained virtually unchanged since the first automobiles were constructed, and most of these methods had been in use since the earliest days of the horse-drawn wagons and buggies. But now mass production was beginning to take hold, especially by economy automobile manufacturers.

Fortunately, Cleveland was able to sidestep many of the issues arising from the need to adapt to mass production methods which confronted competitors in the lower-price field. This was primarily due to the fact that the city was home to many luxury automobile producers, which required a labor-intensive approach to achieve a high quality product.

Additionally, Cleveland was gaining increasing repute at this time as a major supplier of automobile components, which were being supplied to a variety of automobile manufacturers nationwide.

1911 to 1915: Refining the Automobile. In all, thirty-two new automobile manufacturing ventures were launched in Cleveland during these years. The waning demand for electric and steam-powered vehicles was clearly felt in Cleveland. The city's two remaining electric vehicle producers, Rauch-Lang and Baker, consolidated forces in an effort to remain viable, while White, Cleveland's sole manufacturer of steam vehicles had simply left the field, and refocused its efforts on internal combustion-powered automobiles exclusively. By now it was clear that the internal combustion engine would be the automotive powerplant of choice.

However, just offering a vehicle with an internal combustion engine was not enough to ensure success. One example of this fact is the cyclecar. Eight cyclecar companies appeared in Cleveland during the years before World War I, which was the heyday of the cyclecar craze. The cyclecar was a bare-bones, small, light, inexpensive vehicle which catered to those who were in the market for cheap four-wheel transportation. Once mass-produced vehicles like the Model T became available, offering better features at an equal or lesser price, the cyclecar was quickly eclipsed.

1916 to 1920: Marketing Takes Precedence. By now the automobile was no longer a novelty. It had become a functional vehicle possessing performance characteristics which the buying public now expected. Thus, successful entry into the automotive field at this point required innovation and the introduction of significant new features.

Fortunately at this time Cleveland's financial and industrial interests took an active role in bringing new automobile enterprises to the city. As a result, a number of outstanding new automobile companies relocated or established new manufacturing plants in Cleveland.

Twenty-three new automobile ventures started up in Cleveland during this time. They included Cleveland's Rubay Company, a well-established and successful automobile body manufacturer, and Jordan, a company which would go on to achieve fame as much for its innovative advertising as for its distinctive vehicles.

These successes were especially noteworthy because they occurred at a time when the industry was consolidating, and new independent brands were at a decided disadvantage. This was also a challenging time for another reason: World War I.

American manufacturers experienced many restrictions during the years of the war effort, as the production of war materiel took precedence over all domestic production. This of course included automobiles, and not all Cleveland manufacturers were able to maintain steady production during these years.

1921 to 1932: Leveling Off. The automobile industry was now mature. Entirely new ventures were virtually a thing of the past. Also, by this time many of Cleveland's most important names, including those that had come into existence during the very first years, had left the field. Those which had not already closed their doors before the onset of the depression now fell victim to its ravages.

By 1932, only three of the city's automobile manufacturers, Peerless, Ford, and Jordan, had managed to survive. And yet, nine new automobile endeavors were launched during these years. Most surprising of these was the Baker Motors Company, which was intent on building a steam-powered automobile.

The Cleveland automobile community never ceased to adapt. Having been at the forefront during the advent of America's automobile industry, Cleveland continued to be a leading automobile center for a period that spanned thirty-five years. It was home to one hundred fifty-eight automobile ventures during that time, and to this day remains a major supplier of a wide variety of automobile components to the industry.

Notes

1. *The Cleveland Motorist*, January 1913.
2. Ibid.
3. United States Census Bureau, 1910.
4. *The Automobile*, September 28, 1916, and March 22, 1917.
5. *The Automobile and Automobile Industries*, August 1917.
6. *Automotive Industries*, November 22 1917.

7. *Automobile Industries*, March 26, 1921.
8. *Automotive Industries*, April 18, 1931.
9. This information was obtained by an examination of the Cleveland Exchange records and a random sampling of daily stock reports listed in the *Cleveland Plain Dealer* from 1900 through 1929. See also Cleveland Stock Exchange–Statement of Sales, 1925–1928 and 1929–1933.
10. Manual of Cleveland and Northern Ohio securities, 1936.
11. William Ganson Rose, *Cleveland: The Making of a City* (Kent, OH: Kent State University Press, 1950); *Wall Street Journal*, February 3, 2010.
12. James H. Lackey, *The Jordan Automobile: A History* (Jefferson, NC: McFarland, 2005).
13. *The Automobile*, September 28, 1916.
14. Ibid.
15. David D. Van Tassel and John J. Grabowski, *The Encyclopedia of Cleveland History* (Bloomington: Indiana University Press, 1987).
16. *The Automobile*, October 3, 1903.
17. *Automotive Industries*, June 17, 1926.
18. *The Automobile*, February 8 and September 3, 1917.
19. *Automotive Industries*, March 20, 1919.
20. *Automotive Industries*, January 17, 1924.
21. Historic American Engineering Record, HAER OH-11H.
22. *The Automobile*, October 3, 1903.
23. Cleveland Machine Screw Company became Cleveland Automatic Machine Company in 1902. Federal Manufacturing Company was formerly the Automobile & Cycle Parts Company. Although it was mentioned in *The Horseless Age* of January 1899 and *Electrical World and Engineer* on July 21, 1900, that Cleveland Machine Screw was entering into the manufacture of motor vehicles of all styles, it never marketed an automobile under its own name. The vehicles referred to were in fact built for Sperry and known as the Cleveland Electric.
24. Van Tassel and Grabowski, *Encyclopedia of Cleveland History*.
25. Rose, *Cleveland*.
26. Van Tassel and Grabowski, *Encyclopedia of Cleveland History*.
27. *The Cleveland Motorist*, May 1913.
28. *Automobile Route Book* (Cleveland Automobile Club, 1924).
29. *Automobile Route Book* (Cleveland Automobile Club, 1924); *The Cleveland Motorist*.
30. *The Cleveland Motorist*.
31. Ibid.
32. *Road Map of North Eastern Ohio* (Cleveland Automobile Club, 1924); *Emergency Service of the Cleveland Automobile Club*, 1924.
33. Naomi R. Lamoreaux, et al., *Financing Invention During the Second Industrial Revolution: Cleveland, Ohio, 1870–1920*, (Cambridge, MA: National Bureau of Economic Research, 2004); Margaret Levenstein, University of Michigan and NBER; Kenneth L. Sokoloff, University of California, Los Angeles and NBER, June 7, 2004.

The Manufacturers

Abbott Corporation (1917 to 1918)

Timing is everything, and in the case of Abbott, the timing of a move from Detroit to Cleveland was most unfortunate. Bucking the trend of fledgling auto manufacturing companies to relocate in Detroit, Abbott took the opposite route.

As the manufacturer of the reliable and highly successful Abbott automobile from 1909 to 1916, the Abbott Motor Car Company of Detroit had recently been reorganized as the Consolidated Car Corporation. By 1916, production had reached an impressive level of between fifteen and twenty automobiles per day, and the company clearly needed to expand its manufacturing facilities to accommodate its growing sales success.

Encouraged by two major Cleveland investors[1] who knew that the Cleveland manufacturing infrastructure offered the perfect location for an expanded Abbott plant, the company arranged to lease a purpose-built factory in Cleveland. Initially, the decision appeared to be an excellent one. Cleveland had many auto parts manufacturing suppliers, a superb rail transportation network, a handsome tax abatement offer from the city, and a large number of skilled but unemployed auto workers. The company name was once again changed—to the Abbott Corporation—and by July 1917 production had begun in Cleveland.[2]

That September, Abbott optimistically announced its 1918 models,[3] but the economics of the situation were no longer favorable. During the year while Abbott was out of production, there was little sales income to support the major capital outlay demanded by the move. Then, with the entry of the United States into World War I, all auto-related manufacturing was stalled, and the automobile market itself shrank appreciably. Abbott was left with hefty financial obligations.

Thought was given in November 1917 to cutting overhead by way of a merger with Cleveland's Hal Motor Car Company (see Hal Motor Car Company), but the large cash outlay required for Abbott to purchase Hal's assets was not a realistic possibility,[4] and the Abbott Corporation ceased operation. Its name and good will, along with its service facilities and all machinery, were purchased by Standard Motor Parts of Cleveland.[5] General Electric Company acquired the factory, together with its adjacent railroad tracks, and converted the building for use as a machine shop in March 1918.[6]

1. *The Automobile*, August 24 and November 16, 1916.
2. *The Automobile*, August 2, 1917.
3. *The Automobile*, September 20, 1917.
4. *The Automobile*, November 15, 1917.
5. Wager, *Golden Wheels*.
6. *The Automobile*, March 7, 1918.

Aerocar Company (1906)

Aerocar was incorporated in the spring of 1906 with a $10,000 capitalization. The company's stated purpose was the manufacture of automobiles and parts. The organizers of this venture were F.C. Howe, James C. Brooks, W.J. Rudolph, and A. Welch. Apparently nothing came of this undertaking. The Cleveland Aerocar company should not be confused with the Detroit-based Aerocar Company of 1906 to 1908.[1]

1. *Automobile Topics*, March 16, 1907; Kimes and Clark, *Standard Catalog of American Cars, 1805–1942*, 3d ed.

Altman, Henry J. (1901)

Mr. Altman and his wife, after two years of effort, built a rear-entrance tonneau-bodied vehicle capable of going twenty miles per hour. The Altmans used their tonneau for personal excursions and later rebodied it as a roadster. Ultimately, it was sold to a paper hanger for $200, at which point the Altmans ended their automotive experimentations.[1]

1. Kimes and Clark, *Standard Catalog of American Cars, 1805–1942*, 3d ed.

Aluminum Manufacturers, Inc. (1919 to 1922)

English engineer Lawrence H. Pomeroy, who was famous for his work on both Vauxhall and Daimler automobiles, came to the United States in 1919 intending to build Vauxhalls here. Upon his arrival he visited the Cleveland plant of the Aluminum Company of America, later ALCOA, to observe their operation. When he saw them forging alloy automobile engine rods, he told President A.V. Davis that if the company could do that it could make a totally aluminum automobile. Davis responded by asking Pomeroy to do exactly that for his company.[1]

Davis' intention was to demonstrate the multiple uses which could be made of aluminum in automobile construction, and a separate organization, Aluminum Manufacturers, Inc., was formed for this purpose in 1919. Among those involved in the new company were Clevelanders Rollin White (see Rollin Motors Company), E.E. Allyne, and East Coast transplant Forrest Cameron (see Cameron, Forrest F.), all of whom were experienced in automobile manufacturing. The company hired Lawrence H. Pomeroy to design and build a demonstration vehicle, which was to bear his name and which was to be the first real effort anywhere to build an all-aluminum automobile.[2]

Activities surrounding this effort were held under the tightest security and word about the endeavor did not surface until May 3, 1922. After having spent several hundred thousand dollars on the Pomeroy, the company introduced its automobile, which was said to be eighty-five percent aluminum. The engine received special attention as it was designed to achieve a high degree of economy, power, and simplicity. Specific information about its four-cylinder engine and other aspects of the Pomeroy remained

One of six experimental Pomeroy automobiles constructed in Cleveland by the Aluminum Company of America in 1922. The four cylinder Pomeroy demonstrated the widest possible variety of automobile applications suitable for aluminum.

under wraps, with company engineers and officers repeatedly declining to comment.[3]

Six Pomeroys were built and were given extensive testing. Two of the four-cylinder models were driven a combined distance of 376,000 miles between 1920 and 1928. One was then stored indoors out of the weather, while the other was left unprotected outside until 1930. Both automobiles were then completely dismantled and inspected. Examination showed that wear was negligible and corrosion relatively slight on both automobiles.[4]

At all times, inquiries about when the Pomeroy would be available for sale fell on deaf ears and, in fact, the vehicle was never offered to the public. Most likely the company had no interest in marketing the Pomeroy from the very beginning, and the six experimental 126-inch wheelbase four-cylinder Pomeroy automobiles were the only ones constructed in Cleveland.

In 1923 operations of the Aluminum Manufacturers, Inc. moved to the Pierce-Arrow Motor Car Company factory in Buffalo, New York. A six-cylinder aluminum engine similar to the Pierce-Arrow 80 was developed there and mounted in a larger 133-inch wheelbase automobile. Three of these vehicles were built between 1923 and 1924. None were marketed and apparently that ended all Pomeroy production.[5]

Notwithstanding some of the obvious advantages which aluminum afforded, automobile manufacturers were reluctant to consider building an all-aluminum automobile for several reasons. Most important was the fact that the Aluminum Company of America had a virtual monopoly on the alloys and technology for producing the necessary components. Lawrence Pomeroy returned to England in 1926 taking with him one of the Pomeroy automobiles which he drove regularly until at least 1939. A 1925 Pomeroy is in the Dearborn, Michigan, Ford Museum collection.

---

1. *The Veteran and Vintage Magazine*, October 1963, p. 3: Lawrence E. Pomeroy account of his father's visit to Aluminum Company of America, Antique Automobile Club of America Library.

2. *The Veteran and Vintage Magazine*, October 1963;

Kimes and Clark, *Standard Catalog of American Cars, 1805–1942*, 3d ed.
  3. *Automotive Industries*, May 4, 1922.
  4. *The Veteran and Vintage Magazine*, October 1963.
  5. Kimes and Clark, *Standard Catalog of American Cars, 1805–1942*, 3d ed.; Wager, *Golden Wheels*.

American Automobile Company (1904)

Organized with a capitalization of $50,000 to manufacture automobiles and parts, it is believed that the American company achieved neither objective.[1]

  1. Kimes and Clark, *Standard Catalog of American Cars, 1805–1942*, 3d ed.

American Motor Carriage Company (1901 to 1904)

Walter L. Marr went to Cleveland from Detroit in 1901, after leaving the employ of David Dunbar Buick, for whom he had built the first Buick automobile. When Marr departed, he promised his wife that he was going to Cleveland to build his own automobile, and that he would not return until he had done so.[1]

When he arrived in Cleveland, Marr began looking for someone who wanted to get into the business of building automobiles. It is not known exactly how he happened to make contact with Frank D. Dorman, but Dorman was a manufacturer of furnaces who was in search of someone to help him build an automobile. The two men formed the American Motor Carriage Company to achieve their joint aim. It was agreed that Marr would design the prototype automobile, to be called the American Gas, and Dorman would supervise the corporate framework for the endeavor.

Marr made a trip back to Detroit, persuaded David Buick to sell him the automobile which he had built there, and returned with it to Cleveland, where it was to serve as the template for the American Gas prototype.

To save money, it was decided to purchase a ready-made single-cylinder five horsepower engine similar to the one which Marr had designed for Buick. Marr made improvements to the engine and designed the balance of the American Gas to his liking.

When the time came to prepare for production, Marr and Dorman could not agree on modifications to the prototype. As a result, Marr returned to Detroit in 1902 and went to work once again for David Buick.[2]

However, Marr had finally built an automobile of his own.

The American Gas was a handsome runabout with many impressive features, including a steering wheel rather than a tiller. The engine had an automatic spark advance, a compression relief valve to facilitate cranking, and a float-feed carburetor. The car had a two-speed transmission, and rode on four artillery wheels with pneumatic tires.[3] The proposed price for the production automobile was set at $1,000, which was higher than that of many similar vehicles at that time.

In addition to this gasoline-powered automobile, American Motor Carriage Company intended to simultaneously manufacture an electric vehicle. The plan was to use a battery of the company's own design, which was said to be thirty percent more efficient than other available batteries.[4] The electric version, however, never materialized.

Undaunted, the company announced its intention to enlarge its manufacturing facilities and upgrade its offices, rather than to focus on the manufacture of marketable vehicles. Even before production began, an impressive amount of money was spent. This lack of practical business judgement ultimately was its undoing.

The company offices were located in a handsome and imposing historic home which had most recently served as the headquarters of an interior decorating firm.[5] At the rear of the property was a workshop building, which was to be converted for the production of automobiles. The first thing that the company did was to completely remodel the house, installing a first floor showroom, offices and a restaurant for employees on the second floor, and drafting rooms on the third floor. After that, the plans called for building a two-story structure over and around the existing workshop, in order to increase factory space without interfering with proposed production.[6]

They never got that far.

Although orders for the American Gas were

in hand, by 1903 capital had run out and the company was having trouble obtaining parts from suppliers.[7] Despite claims of being capable of building 200 automobiles annually, it is doubtful that anything near this goal was ever achieved. Total production is unknown. American Motor Carriage Company went into receivership in early 1904, having survived only two years after Marr's departure.

1. Kimes and Cox. *Walter L. Marr*.
2. *Motor Age*, October 1902. The *Standard Catalog of American Cars, 1805–1942*, 3d ed., lists the date as August 1901.
3. *Cycle and Automobile Trade Journal*, December 1902.
4. *The Automobile and Motor Review*, September 1, 1902.
5. *Motor Age*, May 1902.
6. *The Automobile and Motor Review*, June 14, 1902.
7. Wager, *Golden Wheels*.

Amstutz-Osborn Company (1902)

Although it had built experimental vehicles and other devices for a variety of inventors, Amstutz-Osborn did not attempt to produce its own automobile until 1902.[1] Its prototype Durabile, a gasoline-powered runabout with a French-style hood, was successful enough that the company announced intentions to place the Durabile in production. How far things progressed along these lines is not known.

In November 1902, the company's successor, the Osborn-Morgan Company, assumed control with the stated intention of establishing a subsidiary to oversee production of the Durabile, while Osborn-Morgan itself pursued experimental work and the production of arc lamps. However, it appears that the Durabile project was abandoned and the automobile never entered into production.[2]

1. *The Automobile and Motor Review*, September 1902.
2. *The Automobile and Motor Review*, November 22, 1902.

Arter Auto Carriage Company (1912)

The company was formed in 1912 to manufacture, sell, and repair automobiles. Those who participated in its formation included James G. Arter, C.A. Chapman, James B. Ruhl, and C.M. Lemmon. The initial purpose was short lived, as the following year the company was re-formed to manufacture automobile bodies instead. Even if a prototype was constructed, it appears that no Arter vehicle went into actual production. The outcome of its body business is unknown.[1]

1. Kimes and Clark, *Standard Catalog of American Cars, 1805–1942*, 3d ed.

Automobile Carriage Supply Company (1900)

Listed as a manufacturer of automobiles in a 1900 trade compilation, the company was not listed in the city directory for that year. Actual manufacture of an automobile is doubtful.[1]

1. Kimes and Clark, *Standard Catalog of American Cars, 1805–1942*, 3d ed.

Baker, Walter C. (1897); Baker Motor Vehicle Company (1898 to 1916)

Walter Baker, one of Cleveland's foremost industrialists, joined with his father-in-law Rollin C. White and two others to found the American Ball Bearing Company in 1895, with the intention of making bearings and axles for a variety of applications. Baker soon became fascinated by the automobile and by 1897, while still actively overseeing the operations of the ball bearing company, began to design his first electric vehicle.

At this early stage in the development of the automobile, electric power had definite advantages. The motor was quiet, easy to control, smooth in operation, and relatively clean. Electric vehicles had an additional advantage: they appealed to the emerging market of female motorists, who preferred this form of quiet and decorous transport.

To complete the development of his prototype electric vehicle, Baker joined with his father-in-law Rollin C. White, his brother-in-law Fred R. White, and others to form the Baker Motor Vehicle Company in 1898.

Construction and assembly of Baker's prototype was accomplished in 1899 by the Cleveland Machine Screw Company, an affiliate of White Sewing Machine Company of Cleveland, one of whose founders was Baker's father-in-law.

From a drawing.
FACTORY OF BAKER MOTOR VEHICLE CO.

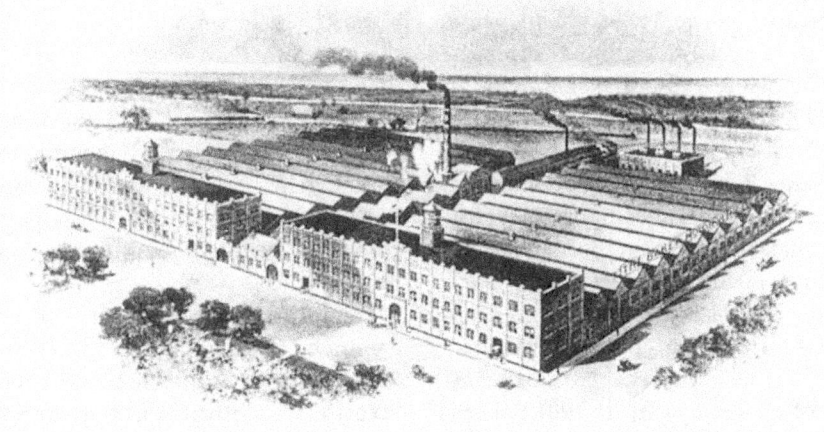

The Factory of The Baker Motor Vehicle Company
80th Street, N. W.
Cleveland, Ohio, U. S. A.

Top: Cleveland's first purpose-built automobile factory, constructed in 1900 by Walter Baker for the production of his electric vehicle. **Above:** Walter Baker's manufacturing complex, built in 1906, housed his ball bearing business in the left half of the complex and his electric automobile plant in the right half.

In 1900, after successfully testing its prototype, the Baker company moved ahead with the construction of Cleveland's first purpose-built automobile factory. It was located on the city's East Side, just a few steps away from Baker's ball bearing plant. The new five-story manufacturing plant, although relatively small by modern standards, was sufficient to contain all necessary operations for the vehicle's manufacture and assembly.[1] Materials were delivered by horse-drawn wagon and the manufacturing process flowed from the upper floors down to ground level where the completed vehicle emerged. This was essentially the same system which was being used to build wagons and carriages at that time.

Walter Baker's first customer was none other than Thomas Edison, who became a life-long friend. Like Edison, Baker was an innovator. Both men were familiar with the use of ball bearings to reduce friction, and this fact, along with carefully engineered weight reduction, enabled Baker to manufacture an electric vehicle that could go 100 miles between charges. This was due in large part to the fact that the rolling resistance of a Baker Electric was half that of its competitors.[2]

Baker was also a pioneer in the introduction of a shaft drive in place of the chain drive, and in the adoption of left-hand drive.[3]

Due in part to its relative simplicity, a Baker Electric was not as expensive as a contemporary Winton or Stearns vehicle. These other two fine automobiles were priced starting at approximately $2,500, while a 1903 Baker Runabout could be had for $850, and the most expensive Baker model was $1,600.

One of Walter Baker's hobbies produced an idea for a major aerodynamic improvement for his race cars. Baker was an avid sportsman who enjoyed sailboat racing. His two famously successful racing automobiles were based on a body profile which was the epitome of streamlined design, having bodies shaped like the inverted hull of a racing yacht. In 1901 Baker's Torpedo race car set an electric vehicle speed record of over 78 miles per hour, and in 1902 it reached 104 miles per hour, using just half of its battery power. The Torpedo Kid, a smaller version of the Torpedo, using a ¾ horsepower motor with a twelve-cell battery, averaged forty-five miles per hour for five miles the following year.[4]

Walter Baker also demonstrated the long-range capabilities of his Electrics, by driving one from Cleveland to Buffalo, New York.

Sales of the Baker Electric increased rapidly and the plant, with a capacity of 200 vehicles per year, was becoming inadequate. The ability to produce at least twice as many vehicles per year was now a necessity.[5] In 1906 Baker moved to a much larger newly constructed manufacturing complex on Cleveland's West Side, which featured two separate plants: one to serve Walter Baker's ball bearing company, and the other for his automobile operations.

The design of this new automobile factory was completely different from that of the first Baker plant. It was a single-story structure with a sky-lighted sawtooth roof.[6] A rail spur served the facility, and electricity came from an on-site steam-powered generation plant. This facility was said to be the largest factory in America devoted to the exclusive manufacture of electric vehicles.[7] The benefits in material handling and efficiency were significant, as all operations now took place on one floor. The fact that natural light flooded the building was a great improvement over the first factory where light was admitted only through casement windows, and was rapidly diffused the father away a worker was from a window. As a result of these and other innovations, 800 vehicles could now be produced annually.

That same year, however, Walter Baker seemed to lose interest in building automobiles. Although he retained a financial interest in the Baker company, he resigned his operating positions in order to focus full time on his ball bearing enterprise.

Following his departure, the Baker company continued to expand on its successes. By 1908 Baker Electrics had become more refined and luxurious, with prices as high as $4,000, although most Baker automobiles were priced in the $2,000 range. As always, the Baker Electric was the epitome of elegance, with interior appointments that rivaled those of any other motorized vehicle.

It was reported in 1910 that Baker was selling three times more electric vehicles than any other similar manufacturer, while offering ten different models to choose from. In addition, a purchaser could select either chain or shaft drive on any model. In 1913, the company guaranteed that some Baker Electric models would achieve a minimum of 65 miles per charge, and perhaps go as far as 100 miles on a single charge.

As always, research on the ultimate capabilities of an electric vehicle was on-going. It was

This 1912 advertisement for a Baker Electric Victoria is proof that electric vehicles did not have to look like telephone booths. The Baker was touted as being "the most noiseless of all electrics," one of several features that contributed to the preference of many women for an electric vehicle rather than a gasoline powered automobile (author's collection).

reported that a Baker Electric fitted with an Edison nickel-alkaline battery went over 224 miles on a single charge.[8] If this level of endurance could have been wedded to the impressive speed capabilities that Baker had already amply proven with his racing models, the path ultimately followed by America's automobile industry might have been quite different. But, top speed for the publicly offered vehicle was still only twenty-two miles per hour.

Baker Motor Vehicle Company expanded into production of electric trucks in 1915, but it became apparent that joining with another electric vehicle manufacturer would be necessary if Baker were to survive. Consequently, that same year the Baker company merged with Rauch & Lang, another Cleveland manufacturer of electric automobiles, to form the Baker R&L Company.[9] (See Baker R&L Company.)

A modern development which would have put a smile on Walter Baker's face occurred when the original Baker Electric showroom and service facility on Cleveland's East Side became the region's first public recharging station for electric vehicles in 2010.

---

1. *The Automobile*, October 3, 1903.
2. *Cycle and Automobile Trade Journal*, April 1906.
3. Wager, *Golden Wheels*.
4. *Cycle and Automobile Trade Journal*, October 1903.
5. Ibid.; *Motor Age*, April 1903.
6. *The Automobile*, November 12 and December 28, 1905, and January 15, 1906.
7. Baker sales brochure, 1908.
8. Wager, *Golden Wheels*.
9. *The Automobile*, December 16, 1915; Wager, *Golden Wheels*.

Baker Motors, Inc. (1923 to 1928)

This company is not to be confused with Baker Motor Vehicle Company (1898 to 1916), which was the manufacturer of the Baker Electric automobile.

Baker Motors was incorporated in 1923, with William E. Baker (no relation to Walter C. Baker, of Baker Electric fame) as Vice President. A contemporary advertisement stated that the company was engaged in the business of manufacturing high- and low-pressure rotary steam engines, high-pressure steam generators, and industrial fuel-oil burners. There is no mention of motor vehicles.[1]

There is an interesting sidelight to this company, however, as one source mentions a third Baker.[2]

Hartley O. Baker, no relation to either of the two Cleveland Bakers above, was a medical doctor in Colorado, who used a Stanley steamer on his rounds, and was inspired to make a better vehicle of his own. Hartley's Baker Steam Car and Manufacturing Company was incorporated in 1918 with the stated purpose of manufacturing steam railroad cars, steam automobiles, tractors, engines, generators, and fuel-oil burners. The company did manufacture a small number of passenger and commercial steam vehicles before 1925.

It was at about this time that one source suggests that Hartley came to Cleveland, possibly to connect up with Baker Motors, Inc., to manufacture steam automobiles.[3] There are no facts to support this Cleveland Baker connection, and even Hartley's family biographer states that the inventor most likely went west to California, rather than east to Cleveland, with his business ventures.[4]

---

1. *Cleveland City Directory*, 1925.
2. Kimes and Clark, *Standard Catalog of American Cars, 1805–1942*, 3d ed.
3. Ibid.
4. Baker, *Steamy Dreamer*.

Baker R&L Company (1915 to 1920)

With the waning interest in electric automobiles becoming apparent to both Baker Motor Vehicle Company (see Baker Motor Vehicle Company) and Rauch & Lang Carriage Company (see Rauch & Lang Carriage Company), a merger between the two makers of electric vehicles was effected in June 1915, and the new organization was named Baker R&L Company, popularly called "Baker-Raulang." In November of that year one hundred four acres of land were purchased to be used for the construction of a new factory for this joint venture. Baker and American Ball Bearing Company occupied adjoining facilities. One of the two was to move to the new factory and the other would take over the then-vacated adjoining plant.[1] Before the year was out, Owen Magnetic Company (see Owen Magnetic Company), owned by R. M. Owen of Cleveland, was added to the corporate fold.[2]

Baker R&L continued to manufacture the Baker Electric into 1916 and the Rauch & Lang Electric until 1920, but the company's main focus was on the production of the Owen Magnetic. Notwithstanding the expectation of a decline in public interest in electric automobiles, demand for the company's 1916 offerings saw a surprising increase, so much so that the company had to erect circus tents to accommodate additional assembly and storage needs.[3] This surge continued into early 1919, at which time a decision, based on earlier projections, was made to dispose of the electric automobile business and concentrate on industrial and commercial vehicles instead.

The Baker R&L electric automobile division was sold in 1920 to Raymond S. Deering, who moved it to Chicopee Falls, Massachusetts, and renamed it Rauch & Lang, Inc.[4] This new company manufactured electric passenger automobiles and taxis, although in ever-diminishing numbers, until 1928 when the last Rauch & Lang was built.[5] With the exception of the taxicabs, all of these Rauch & Lang electric automobiles retained the tall and upright appearance which had been a company tradition since at least 1910.

In 1919, shortly before divesting itself of its electric automobile division, Baker R&L added a line of industrial and commercial trucks. Over the years, a variety of products were introduced, and the truck division continued to thrive well into the middle of the twentieth century as part of the Baker-Raulang Company.

Amongst its many accolades, Baker R&L was recognized by the United States War Department for its efforts during World War I.

Electric passenger car manufacturing was nearing its end in 1919. The Raulang Electric, manufactured by the Baker R&L Company, was virtually identical to the 1915 Baker electric.

1. *The Automobile*, December 2, 1915.
2. *The Automobile*, December 16, 1915.
3. *The Automobile*, August 31, 1916.
4. *Automotive Industries*, April 8, 1920.
5. Kimes and Clark, *Standard Catalog of American Cars, 1805–1942*, 3d ed.

Benson Automobile Company (1901)

In 1901 Henry Eastman decided to focus on building steel bodies instead of manufactureing automobiles. (See Eastman Automobile Company.) A former Eastman employee, L.P. McLouth, joined with two others to form the Benson company which then took over Eastman's automobile enterprise. Small changes were made to the original Eastman which now bore the name

Benson. The new Benson featured an Eastman steel body, a flash steam boiler and a price of $750. It does not appear that this venture survived more than a few months, although perhaps a dozen examples were produced.[1]

---

1. Kimes and Clark, *Standard Catalog of American Cars, 1805–1942*, 3d ed.; Wager, *Golden Wheels*.

Berg Automobile Company (1902 to 1904)

Hart O. Berg was not a Cleveland resident and really had no connection with the city, which was unusual among those involved with automobiles made in Cleveland. Berg had organized the Berg company in New Jersey in 1902. The company's offices were located in New York City, which is where all design and management facilities were located. However, the company did not have its own factory.

Berg looked to Cleveland for the actual production of his automobile.[1] Parts for the Berg were manufactured by the Federal Manufacturing Company of Cleveland, and the finished automobile was assembled by Cleveland Machine Screw Company.[2]

The Berg was a large European-style automobile, and company advertising proudly proclaimed that it came with an 8 or 15 horsepower engine, cost $4,000, and boasted "hundreds of original body designs" from which purchasers could choose.[3]

Beginning in 1903, the Berg Company also offered the Cleveland-built Euclid, a smaller automobile of more conventional design. The Euclid, which was priced at $2,750, lasted no more than one year.

By mid–1904, Hart Berg had sold out to the Worthington Automobile Company of New York.[4] When the Worthington company was acquired by the Cleveland Motor Car Company, production of the Berg continued only briefly, until January 1905[5] (see Cleveland Motor Car Company).

---

1. *The Automobile*, October 3, 1903.
2. *The Automobile and Motor Review*, November 22, 1902.
3. *The Horseless Age*, vol. 10, no. 13 (1902).
4. Kimes and Clark, *Standard Catalog of American Cars, 1805–1942*, 3d ed.
5. *The Horseless Age*, vol. 18, no. 10 (1906).

In 1904 Berg offered customers the opportunity to browse through its pattern book and choose from hundreds of original body designs.

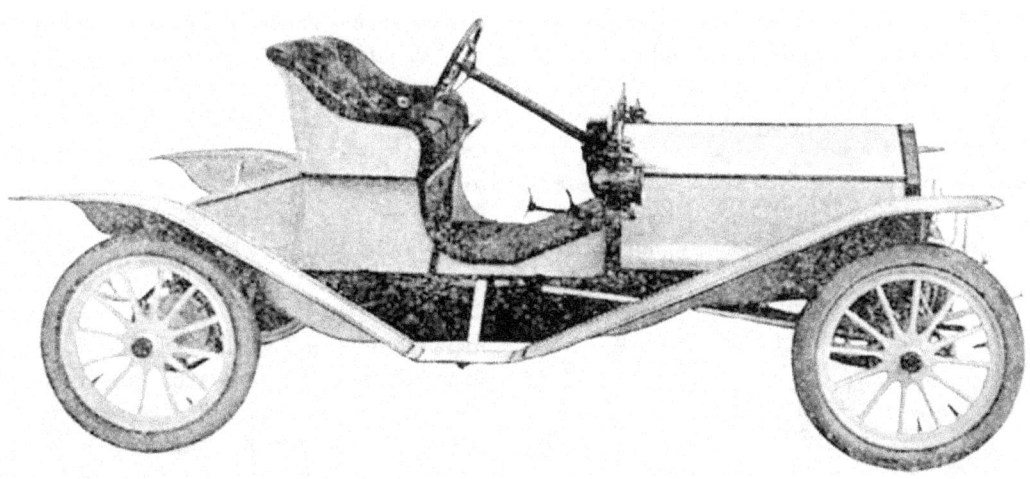

This 1903 Euclid was powered by a three cylinder air cooled 20 horsepower engine. It had chain drive and weighed 1,300 pounds. The Euclid's clean, uncluttered appearance exemplified the simplicity of its overall design and function.

Bingham Manufacturing Company (1911 to 1912); Bingham Motor Car Company (1912 to 1914)

Organized by Herbert Bingham, William H. Gillie, C.B. Dickey, C.F. Schied, and W.C. Rhoades, the company intended to manufacture automobiles and other vehicles. Changing its corporate mind in 1912 the company became the Bingham Motor Car Company, now with the intention of producing automobiles and trucks. Finally, in 1914, at least one truck was built, but it appears that no automobile ever materialized.[1]

 1. Kimes and Clark, *Standard Catalog of American Cars, 1805–1942*, 3d ed.

Blakeslee Electric Vehicle Company (1906)

(See Demars Electric Vehicle Company.)

Brew & Hatcher (1903); Brew-Hatcher Company (1904 to 1905)

A partnership operating under the name Brew & Hatcher was formed in early 1903 by William A. Hatcher and Francis O. Brew for the purpose of making automobile parts and performing contract work for automobile manufacturers.[1]

This pair of entrepreneurs was quite talented, as they offered a variety of items, all of which were to be produced under their own patents: carburetors, oil pumps, engines, transmission gears, and "change-speed devices," which were among the earliest examples of 3-speed slide-gear transmissions.[2] William Hatcher had a very distinguished background, having worked previously as an engineer and designer for both Alexander Winton and James Ward Packard during their companies' formative years. (See Winton, Alexander; also see Packard & Weiss in Part II.)

Brew & Hatcher exhibited a vehicle of its own design and construction at the 1904 Cleveland and Chicago automobile shows. It was powered by an opposed two-cylinder engine mounted in a five-passenger tonneau body. The rather novel chassis side members consisted of square wood bars reinforced by L-shaped arched steel strips along the interior side.[3] The vehicle was assembled primarily to demonstrate the numerous parts that were available from the firm, and to test the waters for the possible development of a line of vehicles for sale.

Shortly after the shows, Brew & Hatcher was reorganized as the Brew-Hatcher Company, with the stated purpose of manufacturing both parts and automobiles. Later that same year the company began manufacturing automobiles for other makers, and went on to produce at least seventeen of its own automobiles under the Brew-Hatcher and B & H names.[4]

A new B & H model was presented for 1905, but the parts business proved to be the more profitable venture. In November Francis Brew left the company, and William Hatcher carried on the parts business under the name Hatcher Auto Parts Company.[5]

---

1. *The Automobile*, April 4, 1903.
2. *Cycle and Automobile Trade Journal*, January 1904.
3. *The Horseless Age*, vol. 13, no. 6 (1904).
4. Wager, *Golden Wheels*.
5. *The Automobile*, November 2, 1905; *Motor*, November 1905.

Broc Carriage and Wagon Company (1909 to 1910); Broc Electric Vehicle Company (1910 to 1914)

For a company that ultimately produced a well-known and highly regarded luxury electric vehicle over a span of five years, relatively little is known about Broc. Broc Carriage company, formed in 1901, had been in the business of making automobile bodies and trim before introducing a motor vehicle of its own design. In 1904 the company enlarged its factory to accommodate an increase in production, and added a general automobile repair department as well.[1] But there was no indication that it was making any plans to go into the full-scale production of an automobile. In 1906 Broc did rent out a portion of its factory to the Monarch Motor Car Company (see Monarch Motor Car Company) which intended to begin the manufacture of a large gasoline powered automobile, but Broc was not involved with that endeavor.[2]

Broc's first electric vehicle appeared at the Cleveland Automobile Show in February 1909, and met with enough success that 1910 saw the continuation of the brand.[3] The new models were priced from $2,000 to $2,500 and weighed from 1,950 to 2,350 pounds. The company claimed that the Broc was the perfect car, offering such features as theft-proof safety devices, a simple control mechanism, interchangeable bodies, interchangeable parts, and the use of high quality materials throughout.[4]

The company changed its name in 1910 to the Broc Electric Vehicle Company.

The Broc Electric continued to sell well and by 1914 Broc had expanded its line of vehicles to eight models ranging in price from $2,900 to $3,200, all of which featured interior appointments that were as elegant as the most expensive automobiles, whether they be gasoline or electric.

This was the last year that Broc would be manufactured in Cleveland. By the end of 1914 Broc had been taken over by the American Electric Car Company and all equipment and operations were moved to Saginaw, Michigan.[5] The Broc continued in production there, as the American Broc, until late 1916.

---

1. *The Automobile*, September 10, 1904.
2. *The Automobile*, December 20, 1906.
3. Wager, *Golden Wheels*.
4. *Cycle and Automobile Trade Journal*, May 1909.
5. *The Automobile*, August 27, 1914.

Brush, Charles Francis (1886)

The second of Cleveland's earliest automobiles was the creation of Charles Francis Brush. During his lifetime he was the holder of over fifty patents. Brush invented what was considered to be the modern electric generator in 1876 and followed that in 1878 with the arc light. In 1880 he formed the Brush Electric Company to develop these inventions. Under his leadership the Brush company constructed an experimental electric three wheeled vehicle in 1886 which was intended to prove that electricity could power a wheeled conveyance. The vehicle was successful and met all expectations. However, there was no plan to put it into production. The Brush electric was the first electric vehicle to have been built in America and was reported upon in *Electrical World* magazine and cited in *The Encyclopedia of Cleveland History*, by Van Tassel and Grabowski.

Byrider Electric Automobile Company (1907 to 1910)

(See DeMars Electric Vehicle Company.)

Cameron, Forrest F. (1922)

Forrest F. Cameron, an engineer by training,

came to Cleveland in 1921 from the East Coast where he and his brother Everett had been in the automobile business off and on from 1900 to 1920.

The Cameron brothers' first vehicle was built in 1900, and by 1904 their light air-cooled Cameron automobile was achieving great success in competitions, setting a world speed record on a half-mile dirt track in Cincinnati as well as being the first air-cooled automobile to climb Mt. Washington without a stop. Another claim to fame was the Cameron's rear-mounted transmission, which became the only immutable aspect of the whole undertaking. After numerous factory relocations, engine design and type changes, investor and company name changes, the East Coast Cameron venture came to an end in 1920.[1]

Forrest Cameron now appeared in Cleveland and was initially involved with the design of the Marsh (see Marsh Motors Company) and Pomeroy automobiles (see Aluminum Manufacturers, Inc.), after which he began to work on the design for his own automobile. The Cleveland Cameron had an air-cooled four-cylinder engine, an electric starter, constant mesh herringbone transmission gears for silent running, and a 104-inch wheelbase chassis with disc type wheels. The Cameron weighed 1,000 pounds and could give thirty miles per gallon. It was said that the prototype had been built with a view toward achieving the lowest production cost possible, which helps explain the amazingly low selling price of $400. The prototype was built by the F. H. Bultman Company, a Cleveland machine shop. At the time the intention was to go forward with full-scale production in Cleveland as well as in England.[2] The idea for a Cameron plant in England may have arisen as a result of the acquaintanceship that Cameron developed with Englishman Lawrence Pomeroy while he was working on the Pomeroy automobile at Aluminum Manufactures, Inc.

It is not known to what extent Cameron utilized aluminum in the construction of his new automobile, but it may have played a significant role in view of the relatively light weight of the vehicle and its excellent gasoline mileage.

Financing for the venture was to have come from East Coast interests, but never developed and the Cleveland Cameron did not proceed beyond the single prototype model.

---

1. Kimes and Clark, *Standard Catalog of American Cars, 1805–1942*, 3d ed.
2. *Automotive Industries*, June 29, 1922: The machine shop was F.H. Bultman Company, at 2801 Superior Avenue N.E.

Canzol (1931)

This one-off propeller-driven midget vehicle was the official messenger car for the 1931 Cleveland National Air Races. The Canzol seated one person and was powered by an air-cooled engine that spun the rear mounted propeller which was caged in protective screening. It was claimed that the midget could attain speeds up to ninety miles per hour but, judging from the appearance of the vehicle, such a speed would have been foolhardy.[1]

---

1. Kimes and Clark, *Standard Catalog of American Cars, 1805–1942*, 3d ed.

Central Automobile Company (1903)

All that is known about this attempt to produce a self-propelled vehicle is that one example of the Central was built and displayed at the Chicago Automobile Show in 1903 under the auspices of the Ralph Temple & Austin Company. Powered by an opposed two-cylinder engine, it was chain-driven, had a tilting steering wheel, and the gasoline and water tanks were housed under a front hood. Whether the vehicle actually entered into production is not known.[1]

---

1. Kimes and Clark, *Standard Catalog of American Cars, 1805–1942*, 3d ed.

Champion Motor Car Company (1920)

Although capitalized at $525,000, which was in excess of most ventures of this type, Champion failed almost immediately, but not before it was able to construct a prototype automobile which was displayed at a local Cleveland industrial event in April 1920. The Champion touring car rode on a 108 inch wheelbase, had a four-cylinder engine, and was to be priced at $950. Nothing more was heard from Champion.[1]

1. Kimes and Clark, *Standard Catalog of American Cars, 1805–1942*, 3d ed.

Chandler Motor Car Company (1913 to 1926); Chandler-Cleveland Motors Corporation (1926 to 1929)

"Local boy makes good" could well be the headline for a story about Cleveland-born Frederick C. Chandler. Chandler got his start with H.A. Lozier & Company in 1890 selling the Lozier company's Cleveland brand bicycles. In 1899 as the bicycle fad began to fade, Henry Lozier sold his bicycle business to Albert Pope's American Bicycle Company and began manufacturing marine gasoline engines. Chandler, having risen to a position of considerable responsibility with Lozier, stayed on. When the Lozier organization turned its attention to building automobiles in 1904, Chandler became manager of sales for what was now the Lozier Motor Company. He was subsequently promoted to Vice President of sales in 1910 and General Manager in 1911.[1] By now the Lozier automobile was well known as a high quality luxury vehicle that ranked among the best in America.

However, Frederick Chandler had gone as far as he could with Lozier, and he had even bigger plans in mind. In January 1913, he and three other members of the Lozier company's upper management resigned and together announced the formation of the Chandler Motor Car Company.[2] It is evident that things had been quietly brewing for some time because the new company had a prototype of its Chandler

Recognizing that it was now a buyer's market, Chandler for 1923 introduced its New Chummy Sedan, which combined low cost with rich appointments and a metal body that offered permanency (author's collection).

automobile completed and on display at the 1913 Chicago Automobile Show in February 1913.[3] By early August of that same year the company had completed construction of a new factory in Cleveland and had begun full production of Chandler automobiles.[4]

Frederick Chandler deserves to be considered the "Henry Ford of the mid-price automobile." At a time when the least expensive six-cylinder automobiles were commonly priced around $2,500, the new Chandler Six was introduced at $1,785, and the next year the price was dropped to $1,595. In addition, this 3,000 pound automobile with its 120-inch wheelbase had a distinctly Lozier look that lent an air of luxury and set it apart from the competition. Needless to say, Frederick Chandler and his team of executives used their Lozier-based experience to the utmost in an effort to bring forth an automobile that offered the highest possible value at a very reasonable price.

The new Chandler met with instant acceptance. In 1915 7,000 automobiles were manufactured and the plant was expanded to double its capacity.[5] The year 1915 was also the first year for closed body styles in the form of a four-door sedan and a seven-passenger limousine, both of which were priced at a reasonable $2,750, while the standard open touring Chandler remained at $1,595. Sales for 1916 shot up to 16,000 vehicles, making the Chandler company Cleveland's biggest automobile manufacturer, and the plant was undergoing almost continual expansion to keep up with demand.[6] In addition, Briggs Manufacturing Company erected a body plant at the Chandler site, and was joined there by Detroit-based engine manufacturer W. J. Walker engine company.[7] By now Chandler automobiles were being shipped to a growing number of dealers around the world.[8]

Frederick C. Chandler, and the huge success of the Chandler company, had become the talk of the automobile industry. In an attempt to imitate the Chandler success story, many other leading manufacturers began to build lightweight sixes.[9]

Hopes for production of 20,000 in 1917 were hampered by restrictions on material put in place as a result of the country's entrance into World War I. Nevertheless, 15,000 automobiles were made that year.[10] In 1918 Chandler produced 1,000 tractors for the army and still managed to turn out just short of 9,200 automobiles. The difficulties encountered during the war did not divert management's attention from expanding its automobile offerings and in 1919 the Cleveland Automobile Company was formed to produce a smaller, less expensive six-cylinder automobile to be named the Cleveland.[11] This new automobile, like its larger brother, met with immediate success. (See Cleveland Automobile Company.)

The Chandler company hit its highest level of production in 1920 when 23,832 Chandler automobiles were manufactured. Chandler was now getting its bodies from the newly completed General Motors Fisher Body plant which had been constructed on Cleveland's East Side to serve Chandler and Cleveland, as well as other automobile manufacturers.

During all its years of production, Chandler strove to offer attractive features. From the beginning it had a six-cylinder engine, power enough to go from 3 to 55 miles per hour in top gear, fuel economy of 21 miles per gallon, Westinghouse electric starting, enclosed valve springs, and a multiple-disc clutch. An ever expanding list of body types followed, and a sporty new style appeared in 1922 with cycle-style fenders and step plates instead of running boards. In 1924 the Traffic Transmission appeared which was an early version of the synchromesh transmission. One-shot lubrication and four-wheel brakes came in 1926, followed by Chandler's first eight-cylinder engine in 1927. Prices for the basic open touring Chandler had dropped to $1,495.

A new financed-sale plan was introduced in 1925 in hopes of boosting sales.[12] However, the new financing plan did not produce the improvement in sales that had been hoped for. In view of the fact that Chandler and Cleveland automobiles had now become quite similar in appearance and price, management determined that operations could easily be made more economical. In 1926 Chandler and Cleveland operations were merged to form the

Chandler-Cleveland Motors Corporation, at which time the Cleveland model itself was discontinued. Prospects improved significantly, more new dealers were signed up, and the work force was increased to keep pace with ever-growing demand. In addition, a new sedan was added and priced at a very reasonable $995.[13] Sales were promising in early 1927 when the combined companies produced 15,803 automobiles in the first half of the year, a very good start.[14]

But it was now a buyers' market.[15]

Chandler sales dropped steadily. Some other automobile companies seemed to succeed where Chandler had failed and the Hupp Motor Car Corporation of Detroit (see Hupp Motor Car Corporation), in search of additional capacity for its production, acquired Chandler-Cleveland in December of 1928.[16] After the last Chandler went out the doors in 1929, the plant was converted over to the exclusive manufacture of Hupmobiles. Total Chandler production, exclusive of the Cleveland, was 131,917.[17] This put Chandler second only to Ford's Cleveland plant in total production.

---

1. Historic Architectural Engineering Record, HAER OH-11G.
2. *The Automobile*, February 2, 1913.
3. *The Automobile*, November 4, 1915.
4. *The Automobile*, March 27, May 8, August 7, 1913.
5. *The Automobile*, June 17, 1915.
6. *The Automobile*, February 17, September 28, October 25, 1916.
7. *The Automobile*, March 16, 1916.
8. *The Automobile*, February 8, 15, 1917.
9. *Horseless Age*, March 15, 1917.
10. Wager, *Golden Wheels*; *Automotive Industries*, February 14, 1918.
11. *Automotive Industries*, February 20, 1919.
12. *Automotive Industries*, October 29, 1925.
13. *Automotive Industries*, March 19, April 2, 16, 1927.
14. *Automotive Industries*, August 13, 1927.
15. *Automotive Industries*, June 18, 1927.
16. *Automotive Industries*, December 1, 22 1928.
17. Kimes and Clark, *Standard Catalog of American Cars, 1805–1942*, 3d ed.

Clark & Company (1900 to 1901)

This company appears in several rosters of early automobiles as a manufacturer of steam automobiles but the existence of any such vehicles is unsubstantiated.[1]

---

1. Kimes and Clark, *Standard Catalog of American Cars, 1805–1942*, 3d ed.

Clark-Norwalk (1910)

The Clark-Norwalk may have been nothing more than an early example of a dealer-badged vehicle—an Ohio-built Norwalk with the brass-script name "Clark" mounted on its radiator.

Such a vehicle is said to have been exhibited at the 1910 Cleveland Automobile show.[1] However, there is no evidence that the Clark-Norwalk ever made such an appearance,[2] and there is no proof that a Clark dealership even had a Cleveland presence.[3] In fact, no Norwalk automobile was exhibited at the 1910 Cleveland show, despite the Norwalk Motor Company's publicized intention to do so.[4] (See Norwalk Motor Car Company in Part II.)

The best guess regarding the Clark-Norwalk is that it was a marketing experiment which did not produce sufficient public response. The Clark-Norwalk was never heard from again.

---

1. Kimes and Clark, *Standard Catalog of American Cars, 1805–1942*, 3d ed.
2. *1910 Cleveland Automobile Show Program*, Cleveland Automobile Club.
3. *Cleveland City Directory 1910*; *Cleveland Plain Dealer*, January 15 and July 23, 1911.
4. *The Evening Herald*, Norwalk, Ohio, February 23, 1910.

Cleveland Auto Sales & Manufacturing Company (1911)

The company was capitalized with $25,000 to manufacture and deal in automobiles. It is doubtful an automobile was produced.[1]

---

1. Kimes and Clark, *Standard Catalog of American Cars, 1805–1942*, 3d ed.

Cleveland Automobile Company (1902 to 1904)

A.L. Moore, president of Cleveland Machine Screw Company, formed the Cleveland Automobile Company in 1902. The company did not undertake actual production of its automobile, but relied on a variety of Cleveland based suppliers to provide parts for and assembly of the Cleveland automobile.

The Cleveland Machine Screw Company was well positioned to build engines for the Cleveland automobile, as it had much prior experience in producing vehicles on contract for such Cleveland automobiles as Baker, Sperry, Berg, and Euclid. Bodies were supplied by Theodore Kurtz of Cleveland and the chassis were built by Automobile & Cycle Parts Company.[1] It is presumed that assembly took place at Machine Screw as was the case with the Berg automobile. The Cleveland automobile came with either a "single or a twin engine" (one or two cylinders); and prices were $750 and $1,750 respectively. The automobiles were popular with their purchasers as evidenced by a variety of testimonials. One owner, an E.H. Moulton, Jr., wrote the company June 2, 1903, to express his great pleasure with his Cleveland Roadster, its handling, performance, and speed.[2] By 1903 the company was turning out its maximum of nine vehicles per week.[3]

Clevelands were displayed at the 1904 Chicago Automobile Show and, as a result, Rothschild & Company of Chicago became a distributor offering installment financing to purchasers, a first for the automobile industry.[4] As often happened during the formative years of the automobile industry, although things initially looked extremely promising, the Cleveland company terminated production before the year was out. (See Cleveland Motor Car Company.)

1. Wager, *Golden Wheels*.
2. Letter of E.H. Moulton, Jr., June 2, 1903 to the Cleveland Automobile Co., Antique Automobile Club of America Library.
3. Wager, *Golden Wheels*.
4. *The Automobile*, February 13, 1904.

The handsome four place 1903 Cleveland touring was powered by a two cylinder opposed engine mounted in the rear. The front hood was a compartment which concealed the water and gasoline tanks.

Cycle fenders and step plates in place of the more typical running boards were new for 1922 on the Cleveland Six and gave it a sportier appearance.

Cleveland Automobile Company (1919 to 1926)

This second Cleveland Automobile Company is in no way related to the 1902–1904 company, above. Chandler Motor Car Company, which had been formed in Cleveland in 1913, elected to enter the lower-priced automobile market to augment its successful Chandler automobile. In February 1919 it organized the Cleveland Automobile Company to manufacture a new Cleveland marque automobile. The company was set up as an entirely separate operation, with all of its activities completely divorced from those of the Chandler company.[1] A new factory was built on seventeen acres of land at a location some distance from the Chandler plant and construction, which was begun in April, was completed in July.[2] When the new Cleveland automobile made its appearance it was attractively priced at $1,385.

The existing network of Chandler dealers marketed the Cleveland and 4,836 were produced during its first full year. Press announcements stated that the company had new orders on hand by the end of August 1919 for 30,000 of next year's models, and that its plant was being expanded to help handle the expected demand.[3] As with many company announcements for the trade press, actual production turned out to be substantially short of projections. This may have been due to the post–World War I economic depression. In any case, production in 1921 appears to have been only 5,318 automobiles, notwithstanding a reduction in price to stimulate sales.

The industry saw a modest improvement the following year, and the company said that during the early months, workers had been added to step up production.[4] In an effort to boost sales, relatively significant styling changes were made for 1922, which gave the Cleveland a very sporty air. Cycle-style fenders were introduced, and instead of a running board extending between the front and rear fenders, step plates were positioned below each door. Graceful wire wheels that leant a very nimble appearance to the Cleveland were featured. The 1922 Cleveland was a very attractive automobile but the base price had now crept up to $1,595. It was claimed that within the first seven months the company had shipped 6,600 automobiles, and the expectation was that 10,000 Clevelands would be sold in 1922.[5] Instead, apparently only 6,449 Clevelands passed through the factory doors that year.

In an effort to "improve momentum," as the company put it, prices were reduced and new features were added. Running boards replaced step plates, a new engine was introduced, some body styles were added for 1923, and prices were reduced to as low as $995. The company told the press that sales responded and 14,500 were

For only $1,495 one could acquire a 1923 Cleveland Six four-door sedan. The Cleveland Six featured a metal-paneled body constructed by the Fisher body plant, which was located just a few steps away from the Cleveland automobile plant on Euclid Avenue. If an open vehicle was all that was required, one could be obtained for only $1,095 (author's collection).

produced in that the year.[6] There seems to have been a credibility gap, in as much as reliable sources indicate that 8,811 was the real number.

More changes were made for 1924, including the addition of an automatic spark advance, along with a new generator, starter, and carburetor.[7] By early 1924 the factory was said to be producing an average of fifty Clevelands per day.[8] With an unusual mid-year model introduction, the company offered a new Mileage Motor Six with an automatic lubrication system and no price increase.[9]

Economic recovery at last seemed to be taking hold and production was claimed to have increased significantly in early 1925, improving as much as 300 percent month-to-month, with sales achieving a twenty-five percent advance year to year.[10] In this case, company releases more closely tracked actual production. The year 1925 was Cleveland's best ever with 12,435 having been produced.

Unfortunately the following year production dropped precipitously. Having struggled in vain to make the Cleveland automobile an independent entity, Chandler realized that the time had come to merge the two operations. The benefits derived from operating two separate and distinct companies to produce what had now become automobiles that were more and more alike finally induced Chandler to absorb its Cleveland company in March 1926. The resulting enterprise was called Chandler-Cleveland Motors Corporation.[11] Once again, putting too good a face on things, when the Cleveland brand was discontinued, it was said that 19,000 of the 1926 model Clevelands had been produced.[12] In fact, only 3,213 were manufactured in Cleveland's last year.

Up until this point in time, bodies for Cleveland automobiles had been made at the nearby Fisher Body plant. For 1926 and subsequent years, Chandler-Cleveland automobiles bodies were built in house at what had been the Cleveland automobile plant.[13]

If the company's purported production figures had been correct, the total number of Cleveland automobiles manufactured would have been something in excess of 100,000. In fact, when production ended in 1926 a total of 49,090 Cleveland automobiles appears to be closer to the actual figure.[14]

1. *Automotive Industries*, March 27, 1919.
2. *Historic Architecture Engineering Record*, HAER OH-11G.
3. *Automotive Industries*, September 4, 1919.
4. *Automotive Industries*, January 19, 1922.
5. *Automotive industries*, September 14, 1922.
6. Wager, *Golden Wheels*.
7. *Automotive Industries*, September 6, 1923.
8. *Automotive Industries*, March 1924.
9. *Automotive Industries*, June 12, 1924.
10. *Automotive Industries*, April 2, 1925.
11. Wager, *Golden Wheels*.
12. A note about production numbers. There is a wide disparity among sources for this information. Kimes and Clark, *Standard Catalog of American Cars, 1805–1942*, 3d ed. lists production as follows:
  1919 and 1920: 4,836
  1921: 5,318
  1922: 6,449
  1923: 8,811
  1924: 8,028
  1925: 12,435
  1926: 3,213
13. *Automotive Industries*, June 17, 1926
14. Kimes and Clark, *Standard Catalog of American Cars, 1805–1942*, 3d ed.

Cleveland, Beck and Lyman Motor Corporation (1909)

The Cleveland company was formed to manufacture motors, motor boats, and vehicles. With a capitalization of $8,600, this was a slim financial base for such an undertaking. Actual production of an automobile is unlikely.[1] It is interesting to note that Lyman, a family owned boat-building firm with its origins in cabinet-making, produced highly respected Great Lakes pleasure craft for nearly 100 yars, including a custom-built yacht for pioneer Cleveland automobile manufacturer Alexander Winton.

1. Kimes and Clark, *Standard Catalog of American Cars, 1805–1942*, 3d ed.

Cleveland Cycle Car Company (1914)

What possessed the founders of this company to forsake their secure positions with one of Cleveland's leading automobile manufacturers in March 1914 and enter the faddish field of cyclecars is a mystery. When they left the employ of F. B. Stearns to jump into the cycle car wading pool, W. E. Burnes, W. H. Hoyes, and Robert Clark, had extensive automobile experience. Their ambitions were as grand as the slogan for their cyclecar "The Aristocrat of Cycle Cars."[1] The vehicle was a four-place touring car with side-by-side seating. It had a sixteen horsepower water-cooled four-cylinder engine connected to a friction transmission and V-belt drive. Priced at $395, it should have been competitive, but like all other cycle car ventures at the time, it quickly succumbed to the fact that there really was no longer a viable market for such vehicles.[2]

---

1. Kimes and Clark, *Standard Catalog of American Cars, 1805–1942*, 3d ed.
2. Wager, *Golden Wheels*.

Guaranteeing the automobile for one year was assurance that a 1906 Cleveland would live up to its reputation as a high quality vehicle. Prices ranged from $2,800 to $5,000.

Cleveland Electric Company (1900)

This appears to be one of the ephemeral automobile companies of which there were many. Although it was listed in the book *Horseless Vehicles, Automobiles, Motor Cycles*, published in 1900, the Cleveland city directories of the era have no listing for this company.[1]

---

1. Kimes and Clark, *Standard Catalog of American Cars, 1805–1942*, 3d ed.

Cleveland Electric Vehicle Company

(See Cuyahoga Motor Car Company.)

Cleveland Motor Car Company (1904 to 1909)

The Cleveland Motor Car Company, successor to 1902–1904 Cleveland Automobile Company, had a rather convoluted genesis and existence. It began its life informally in 1904 but was not incorporated until 1906.[1] It took over the Worthington Automobile Company in 1904 and changed the name of Worthington's automobile from Meteor to Cleveland.[2] The Cleveland was a handsome four-cylinder vehicle of rugged construction which proved itself in numerous events and cross-country tours. As had been the case with its predecessor, components for this automobile continued to be manufactured by Federal Manufacturing Company, and the complete automobile was assembled by Cleveland Machine Screw Company.

In late 1906, Cleveland Motor Car Company moved into its new plant in the Whitney Block on East 12th between and Power Street and St. Clair where it could assemble and finish its own automobiles.[3] One year later this plant was sold to the Garford Company, and in December of 1907 the Cleveland Motor Car Company moved into larger quarters nearby.[4] At about this time the company's headquarters were moved to New York City. Chassis were shipped to New York where the finished automobile was assembled.[5] The Cleveland continued in production until 1908.

1. *The Horseless Age*, vol. 18, no. 10 (1906).
2. Kimes and Clark, *Standard Catalog of American Cars, 1805–1942*, 3d ed.
3. *The Horseless Age*, vol. 18, no. 10 (1906); *Cycle and Automobile Trade Journal*, October 1906.
4. *Cycle and Automobile Trade Journal*, September 1907; Wager, *Golden Wheels*.
5. Wager, *Golden Wheels*.

Cleveland Motor Carriage Company (1901)

Incorporated by F.D. Dorman, Charles Drabek, George W. Dunham, C.O. Ann, and John T. Morris the stated purpose of this undertaking was to build steam, gasoline, and electric vehicles at company facilities located at 66 Chestnut Street. With a capitalization of only $10,000, such an ambitious venture had little chance for survival and, although a prototype automobile was built, the effort was over by the end of the year.[1]

1. Kimes and Clark, *Standard Catalog of American Cars, 1805–1942*, 3d ed.

Crawford-Hough Garage Company (1910)

This company was organized to manufacture, rent, and repair automobiles. It was incorporated by Richard H. Lee, G.R. Gallagher, George E. Bradbury, and Henry R. Gail with a capitalization of $10,000. There is no evidence that an automobile was ever produced.[1]

1. Kimes and Clark, *Standard Catalog of American Cars, 1805–1942*, 3d ed.

Croxton Motor Company (1911 to 1912)

Herbert A. Croxton had made a major investment in the Jewel Motor Car Company of Massillon (see Forest City Motor Car Company, in Part II) in 1907, and gained control of the company's business in 1909. He then joined with Forest M. Keeton of Detroit to form the Croxton-Keeton Motor Car Company in 1910.[1] The company planned to continue production of the Jewel in Massillon, renaming it the Croxton, and to add a second vehicle with a Renault-style hood, to be named the Suburban.[2]

As of March 1910, 200 men were employed in building the Croxton. It was said that the company's entire production of 600 automobiles for that year was sold.[3] However, financial complications arose and by August the company was in receivership. Herbert Croxton characterized these proceedings as nothing more than the first step toward reorganization.[4] Production continued and sales were the best that they had ever been.

Reorganized as the Croxton Motor Company, operations and production were moved to Cleveland in early 1911, where the company occupied what had been the first Baker Motor Vehicle Company plant (see Baker Motor Vehicle Company) on the city's East Side. In March 1911, in an effort to strengthen its financial position, the company merged with Royal Motor Car Company (see Royal Motor Car Company) to form the Consolidated Motor Car Company. The combination was in trouble almost immediately, and before a few months had passed the merger was dissolved. The company was reorganized again, assuming its original name, the Croxton Motor Company, and production continued at the East Side factory.[5]

In early 1912, the company announced that arrangements to move to a newly built two-story facility in Washington, Pennsylvania, were in place. By September plant construction was completed and Croxton operations left Cleveland.[6]

Production continued in Pennsylvania until 1914, when operations were discontinued.

1. Kimes and Clark, *Standard Catalog of American Cars, 1805–1942*, 3d ed.
2. *The Horseless Age*, vol. 24, no. 16 (1910).
3. *The Automobile*, March 17, 1910.
4. *The Horseless Age*, vol. 26, no. 6 (1910).
5. Kimes and Clark, *Standard Catalog of American Cars, 1805–1942*, 3d ed.
6. *The Automobile*, January 25, April 25, May 2, May 30, 1910.

Cuyahoga Motor Car Company (1908 to 1909); Cleveland Electric Vehicle Company (1909 to 1911)

The Cuyahoga Motor Car Company seems to have spent more time changing its mind than making vehicles. The company name was changed once, the name of its automobile was changed once, and its objective was changed four times, all within the span of little more than two years' time.

The Cuyahoga Motor Car Company had been operating as an automobile dealership and garage when, in October of 1908, it decided to produce an electric automobile of its own to be named the Cuyahoga Electric. When the prototype, designed by Raymond C. Doty, actually appeared it was called the Cleveland Electric instead.[1]

In 1909 the company was reorganized as the Cleveland Electric Vehicle Company and stated that it now planned to manufacture electric powered taxicabs rather than passenger vehicles. By the end of the year however, the new company returned to its original objective of making passenger automobiles, and the Cleveland Electric automobile finally emerged the following year. Three models were offered in 1910 priced from $2,250 to $2,800 and powered by what the company refered to as a Cuyahoga 9MV battery of the company's own design and manufacture.[2]

It is not known how many Cleveland Electrics were produced during the intervening two years, but in 1911 the company decided to abandon the manufacture of electric vehicles altogether, and to concentrate instead on the development and manufacture of batteries for electric vehicles.

1. Kimes and Clark, *Standard Catalog of American Cars, 1805–1942*, 3d ed.
2. Wager, *Golden Wheels*.

Davis Motor Car Company (1911)

Organized with a $10,000 capitalization by Charles A. Rolfe, F.H. Grace, George V. Gunderman, C.A. Lemmon, and J.K. Kirkpatrick, the company intended to produce motor cars, motor car accessories and parts, and to carry on a garage business. There is no evidence that any motor vehicle was ever produced.[1]

1. Kimes and Clark, *Standard Catalog of American Cars, 1805–1942*, 3d ed.

De Gallier, E.P. (1902)

It was reported in *Automobile Motor Review*, February 1902, that Mr. DeGallier of 317 Electric Building was constructing a motor vehicle which, if actually produced, would have been one of a kind.[1]

1. Kimes and Clark, *Standard Catalog of American Cars, 1805–1942*, 3d ed.

De Luxe Motor Car Company (1910)

The De Luxe Two Wheeler was a rather unconventional vehicle. It was motorcycle-like in appearance, rode on two thirty-inch artillery wheels, had wheel steering, and came with either a one-or two-cylinder engine and the driver sat in a fully upholstered bucket seat. The two-cylinder version was said to be capable of seventy miles per hour. Two small side wheels could be let down to support the De Luxe in an upright position when moving slowly or standing still.

This rather unique creation was referred to as a two-wheeled automobile because its various appointments and overall comfort surpassed that of even the most advanced motorcycle. The steering wheel was adjustable to suit the rider and had a windshield mounted on its column. The engine was enclosed within the vehicle's body and the rear wheels were supported by half elliptical springs. The Deluxe weighed 260 pounds and was said to possess smoother riding qualities than the finest four wheeled automobile. Although it was basically

The "De Luxe" Two-Wheeled Auto.

Slightly more automobile than motorcycle, thanks to having a steering wheel and a seat, the De Luxe was one of the most unconventional vehicles to appear on the scene during the early days of self propelled transportation.

a single-place vehicle, it could accommodate packages or a second passenger on the rear baggage deck.[1]

Prototypes were built, but whether any actual production followed is not known with certainty. The company offices were at 1002–04 American Trust Building.[2]

---

1. Kimes and Clark, *Standard Catalog of American Cars, 1805–1942*, 3d ed.
2. *Cycle and Automobile Trade Journal*, August 1910, p. 270, Antique Automobile Club of America Library.

DeMars Electric Vehicle Company
(1904 to 1906)

Four virtually identical automobiles, variously named DeMars, Blakeslee, Williams, and Byrider, were produced at the same Cleveland location from 1904 to 1910. It all started with William O. DeMars, who had begun electric vehicle experimentation some time in 1902. DeMars presented his first automobile in 1904, under the auspices of the newly formed DeMars Electric Vehicle Company.

The DeMars Electric was a beautifully finished and especially attractive two-place conveyance with handsome artillery-style wheels and a large center headlight.[1] Its one and one-half horsepower motor may have been inadequate for the vehicle, but no commentary on this point exists. Sales began well but gradually diminished and in late 1905 DeMars production ceased.

In February 1906 C.J Blakeslee, the son of one of the DeMars company founders, bought out DeMars and established the Blakeslee Electric Automobile Company. An advertisement for the now renamed Blakeslee boasted that the vehicle had beaten all electric vehicle records in a test run on the East Coast, although details about the event were not given.

A few months and twenty Blakeslees later, the factory and the rights to the Blakeslee Electric were purchased by the Williams Motor Carriage Company of Akron, Ohio.[2] (See

Powered by a 1½ horsepower electric motor, this 1905 Demars had dual chain drive and an attractive body enhanced by the unusually light appearance of the spoked wheels.

Williams Motor Carriage Company.) Williams Motor Carriage had been formed in July 1906 by H.A. Williams, together with George Byrider and other members of the Byrider family, to build gasoline-powered automobiles, but the company had been unable to locate suitable facilities in Akron for its factory.[3]

The Blakeslee Electric was now renamed the Williams Electric, and a gasoline-powered Williams automobile was added to the production line. The latter vehicle, however, was produced in very limited numbers, and its manufacture was discontinued by the end of 1906. At this point, the company name was changed to the Williams Electric Vehicle Company. A new Williams Electric model was introduced in January 1907, and sales went well.

With this promising sales future in mind, the company considered relocating to Akron, where a larger factory could be built to serve the expected increased demand[4] and, in May 1907, John and William Byrider bought out H.A. Williams.[5] The company was reorganized as the Byrider Electric Automobile Company, and the automobile was renamed the Byrider. A new Victoria model was added, featuring a more powerful two-and-one-half horsepower electric motor. However, the anticipated move back to Akron never occurred, and production continued only into early 1910, when all operations ceased.[6]

1. *The Horseless Age*, vol. 16, no. 2, July 12, 1905.
2. Kimes and Clark, *Standard Catalog of American Cars, 1805–1942*, 3d ed.
3. *The Automobile*, October 25, 1906.
4. *Cycle and Automobile Trade Journal*, October 1906; *Motor Age*, November 8, 1906.
5. Kimes and Clark, *Standard Catalog of American Cars, 1805–1942*, 3d ed.
6. Ibid.

De Mooy Brothers (1900)

The Cleveland brothers De Mooy had developed and sold two- and four-stroke marine engines of their own design since the late 1890s.[1] One of these engines was installed in a carriage in 1900 with apparent success.[2] This vehicle, and any that may have followed, were constructed for the brothers' personal use, as they advised *Cycle and Automobile Trade Journal* in 1902, stating that their marine engine business was taking all of their time and effort and they had no intention of going into the manufacture of automobiles. Nothing further materialized from this undertaking. However, in 1904 De Mooy brothers were involved in the formation of the American Automobile Company which took over the defunct maker of the American Gas automobile.[3] (See American Automobile Company.)

1. *The Motor Vehicle Review*, December 6, 1900, p. 33, Antique Automobile Club of America Library.
2. *The Motor Vehicle Review*, October 4, 1900, Antique Automobile Club of America Library.
3. *The Automobile*, April 30, 1904, p. 488, Antique Automobile Club of America Library.

Derain Motor Company (1908 to 1911)

The Sherbondy brothers, William and Earl, organized the Simplex Manufacturing Company in 1906 to build a variety of automotive components, including transmissions and air-cooled engines. (See Simplex Manufacturing Company.)

In October of 1908, the brothers joined together with drug store owner A.F. May to form the Derain Motor Company, with the intention of building twenty-five automobiles to be sold at a price of $4,000 each.[1]

For the new Derain automobile, Earl designed a two-cycle 4-cylinder water-cooled engine, which produced torque equal to that of a contemporary 8-cylinder engine, and ran just as smoothly.[2] The Derain itself was a large and attractive automobile, which weighed over 3,500 pounds and rode on a 125½-inch wheelbase.

It is not known how many vehicles were ultimately produced, but a 1911 model was offered for sale. The venture did not survive beyond that year.

1. Wager, *Golden Wheels*; Kimes and Clark, *Standard Catalog of American Cars, 1805–1942*, 3d ed.
2. *Cycle and Automobile Trade Journal*, December 1909.

Disbrow Motors Corporation (1916 to 1917)

Louis A. Disbrow was a highly successful race driver who earned over $100,000 during

The Manufacturers Disbrow 55

Derain 7-passenger 2-cycle Car.

Fig. 1. Complete view, right side. Wheel base 125½ inches. Tires 36 x 4 inches front, 6 x 5 inches rear. Motor, 4 cylinders, 5 x 5½ inches, 2-cycle, crank-box pressure cylinder harge supply, with rotary crank-box intake valves. Nominal 30 H. P. Sliding gear, selective, three-forward speeds and reverse to bevelgear and divided live rear axles. Seats for even passengers. Weight about 3,600 lbs. Price, as shown in illustration, $4,000, including igh-tension magneto and dry cells and Atwater-Kent unisparker, complete double ignition, ith 5 lamps, 3 fitted with electric bulbs, Prest-O-Lite tank, wind shield, mats, horn, tools nd cape top, all ready for extended touring.

For 1911 Derain offered a large seven passenger touring with a four-cylinder 2-stroke engine. Weighing 3,600 ponds and costing $4,000, it was to be the last year for the make.

New Louis Disbrow Special.

The 1917 Disbrow had the appearance of a racecar and performance to match. Though an assembled automobile, it utilized components that met the high standards of its designer and race driver Louis Disbrow. Each purchaser's physical measurements and weight were taken, and the cockpit area was built to suit.

a career that ran from 1905 to 1914. During this time he raced in four Indianapolis 500 events and a multitude of other competitions. A serious crash in 1914 almost ended his life and, after enduring a nine month recovery, he elected to pursue more placid occupations.[1]

When Disbrow's racing exploits are reviewed it is easy to understand both his successes and his calamities. It was reported in 1912 that Disbrow and and other "knights of the wheel" got into an argument about which one could drive his race car farther out into the Gulf of Mexico before the engine stopped firing. On the day of the race, daredevils that they were, the drivers hit the water at forty miles per hour. The winner of this challenge was Louis Disbrow, who immediately predicted that it would not be long before a combination motor boat and automobile would evolve.[2] (See Hydro Motor Car Company.)

Disbrow entered 147 races in 1912, a record for any one driver, and in doing so he covered 3,500 racing miles while establishing thirteen track and road records. Disbrow made the astonishing claim that he and his Simplex Zip automobile won every one of those races.[3] Racing was not without its risks for Disbrow, who is said to have broken 36 bones during his career and once was lying in a morgue, having been taken for dead after a crash.

Disbrow often competed against another racing great, Eddie Rickenbacker. Rickenbacker was a resident of Columbus and in addition to his racing exploits is perhaps most famous for his achievements as a military "ace of aces" pilot who achieved a multitude of air combat victories in World War I. Rickenbacker, knowing Disbrow's dislike for driving behind a cloud of dust, used this knowledge to his advantage whenever possible, winning a Sioux City race against Disbrow in 1914. Rickenbacker went on to lend his name to the Rickenbacker automobile, which was manufactured from 1922 to 1927 in Detroit.[4]

When Disbrow moved to Cleveland in 1915 to begin a more pedestrian lifestyle, he planned to open an automobile sales agency. But in 1916 he decided to turn his hand to designing and building racing and race-type automobiles, and formed the Disbrow Motors Corporation.

To refer to his automobile as an "assembled vehicle" would convey the wrong impression. Although many of the major components were acquired from suppliers, he was very selective, and every part had to satisfy his exacting specifications.[5] As a result, commentators referred to the Disbrow as a custom built automobile. The engine was a Wisconsin 4-cylinder T-head type and came in 90 and 110 horsepower versions. Wire wheels were made by Houk, ignition was from Bosch, Warner Gear provided transmission and steering gear, and Borg & Beck the clutch. What was entirely of Disbrow's own design was the aluminum body which was mounted on a 114-inch wheelbase chassis built by Hydraulic Pressed Steel Company. Special mention was made of the fact that the engine's reciprocating parts and special cams made its performance especially lively, but the versatile Disbrow could be driven as slowly as 8 miles per hour in high gear.[6]

The Disbrow was not built as a race car, although it could perform this role admirably. Instead it was designed to appeal to those who wanted something truly distinctive and personal in an automobile. The body was sleek, sporty, and clearly reflected its race heritage. Each one was custom-made to suit the size of its purchaser, a consideration only a race driver would think of.[7] Cycle-type fenders added to the Disbrow's impression of speed and agility. Top speeds ranging from 87 to 95 miles per hour were guaranteed. Prices were between $2,650 and $3,500.

A Disbrow was displayed in January 1917 at the Chicago Automobile Salon and was well received. A contract was closed for 250 Disbrow Specials to be shipped to a leading East Coast dealer who had formerly handled the British Sunbeam racing automobiles with which Eddie Rickenbacker was associated.[8] It seemed that things were off to a good start and production of 2,500 Disbrows was scheduled for the year. A new factory was built and additional models were added to the lineup.

But, as was the case with many automobile companies trying to get started around the time that World War I began to consume much of the country's attention and resources, fate was unkind to Disbrow Motors Corporation. Like the competitive race driver he had always been, Disbrow did his best to make a go of it. The company developed a high-speed armored car based on Disbrow's Quad-Express model. Although it was demonstrated to the Army, nothing came of the effort.[9]

What began with such promise faded from the scene before 1917 ended, and Louis Disbrow moved on to the Moore Motor Vehicle Company in Minneapolis as chief engineer, where he stayed for only a short time before leaving to join the Victory Company of Milwaukee, a maker of spark plugs.

---

1. Wager, *Golden Wheels*.
2. *The Cleveland Motorist*, December 1912.
3. Edward V. Rickenbacker, *Rickenbacker*.
4. *The Cleveland Motorist*, January 1913.
5. Kimes and Clark, *Standard Catalog of American Cars, 1805–1942*, 3d ed.
6. *Automobile Trade Journal*, May 1917, p. 237, Antique Automobile Club of America Library.
7. *The Automobile*, February 1, 1917.
8. *The Automobile*, May 10, 1917.
9. *The Automobile*, July 23, 1917. It may be remembered that Preston Tucker did exactly the same thing some forty years later.

Downing Motor Car Company (1913 to 1915)

The Downing company had two locations. One was in Detroit and was named the Downing Cycle Car Company. The other was in Cleveland and was known as the Downing Motor Car Company. It was located in the "Industrial Spotless Town" of the Belt & Terminal Realty Co. and was devoted exclusively to the manufacture of cyclecars. The Detroit plant of the Downing company made full size automobiles as well as cyclecars.[1] The Cleveland-built Downing cyclecar was the most automobile-like of all the cyclecars manufactured in Cleveland. It had a standard tread width of 56 inches and a wheelbase of 98 inches, which compared favorably with the Model T's 100 inch wheelbase. There were two models, a twelve horsepower two-cylinder roadster and an eighteen horsepower four-cylinder roadster, with prices starting below $500. Unlike most cyclecars the seating was side-by-side rather than in-tandem.[2] The Detroit cyclecars were distinct from those made in Cleveland in several respects, including a longer wheelbase and the availability of a four passenger model.

---

1. *Automobile Topics*, July 26, 1913, p. 820, Antique Automobile Club of America Library.
2. Kimes and Clark, *Standard Catalog of American Cars, 1805–1942*, 3d ed.; Wager, *Golden Wheels*.

The Downing Cyclecar had side-by-side seating and full width 56-inch wheel tread, which made it more automobile-like than its brethren, which usually had only tandem seating and a narrower tread dimension.

E.A. Hammer Company (1912)

The Hammer company was formed with the ambitious expectation of manufacturing, buying, selling, and dealing in automobiles, which it planned to do with a modest capitalization of $15,000. It is unlikely that an automobile was produced.[1]

---

1. Kimes and Clark, *Standard Catalog of American Cars, 1805–1942*, 3d ed.

Eastman Automobile Company (1898 to 1901)

Basing his approach to the automobile on the simplicity of the bicycle, Henry F. Eastman introduced his electric-powered Eastman Electro-Cycle in 1898. It appears that the Electro-Cycle featured the automobile industry's first all-steel automobile body, which was designed by H. Jay Hayes, Eastman's business associate.[1] Eastman said that steel was easier to paint and, with its asbestos covering, muffled sound. He also felt that an inherent advantage of his vehicle's three wheels was that they could be steered out of ruts and over tracks much more readily than could four.[2]

After having said that, Eastman forthwith dropped his three-wheel Electro-Cycle in 1900 and replaced it with a four-wheel steam vehicle.[3] The steam vehicle featured an all-steel body that had removable panels which allowed the owner to change the steamer's body style. In addition to first making electric then steam vehicles, Eastman was simultaneously manufacturing steel bodies for the trade.[4]

Ever restless, Eastman sold his automobile company in 1901 to A.M. Benson of the Benson Automobile Company of Cleveland. (See Benson Automobile Company.) He then reorganized as the Eastman Metallic Body Company.[5] Upon the discontinuance of his automobile activities, Eastman moved the manufacturing activities of his steel body business from High and Sheriff Streets near downtown to a factory farther out on Cleveland's East Side.[6] The reason given was that the volume of the body business had greatly exceeded that of his automobile venture. Hayes went into business for himself, also manufacturing steel automobile bodies, but moved to Detroit.

---

1. Kimes and Clark, *Standard Catalog of American Cars, 1805–1942*, 3d ed.
2. *The Horseless Age*, July 5, 1899.
3. *The Automobile*, June 1900.

The 1900 Eastman steam car had an all-steel body which was quite advanced for the era. Earlier Eastman vehicles had been electrics with a tricycle wheel arrangement.

4. *Cycle and Automobile Trade Journal*, August 1900.
5. *The Automobile*, May 1901; Wager, *Golden Wheels*.
6. Eastman used several names interchangeably from time to time, including Eastman Automobile Company, Eastman Auto Company, and Eastman Metallic Body Company. (See also *Cycle and Automobile Trade Journal*, November 1900 and January 1902.)

Eckenroth Automobile Livery Company (1912)

Organized by brothers Rudolph H., Harry S., and Peter L. Eckenroth with the extremely modest capitalization of $5,000, the company intended to build and repair automobiles. No reports emerged as to the achievement of either of these objectives, so it is doubtful any automobiles were constructed.[1]

1. Kimes and Clark, *Standard Catalog of American Cars, 1805–1942*, 3d ed.

Elwell-Parker Electric Company (1905 to 1908)

The Elwell-Parker company manufactured everything to build a complete running chassis for an electric vehicle, and many electric automobile companies used their components. Over a period of years the company assembled several passenger automobiles of its own which were constructed to showcase company products, but none were marketed to the general public. Elwell did manufacture commercial trucks and after the components portion of the business was sold in 1909, the company focused on the manufacture of commercial electric fork-lift trucks.[1]

1. Kimes and Clark, *Standard Catalog of American Cars, 1805–1942*, 3d ed.

Euclid Avenue Automobile Company (1904)

The Euclid company was formed for the manufacture and sale of automobiles. Organizers included Wade, Benson, and Webster McIlrath, E.V.K. Hopkins, Clyde Martin, and Harry W. Orndorf. It is highly unlikely even a prototype vehicle was constructed.[1]

1. Kimes and Clark, *Standard Catalog of American Cars, 1805–1942*, 3d ed.

Euclid Motor Car Company (1907 to 1908)

Herbert R. Palmer had been working on the development of a unique three-cylinder engine since 1900. Its most unusual feature was the use of a long dual-diameter piston. The upper portion of the piston acted as a typical working piston while the larger lower portion acted as a compressor supplying the gasoline/air charge to the next cylinder in the firing order. The engine was to be mounted on a tubular chassis and power was transmitted through a disc-and-friction wheel arrangement which provided virtually infinite speed adjustment.

Palmer formed the Euclid company in May of 1907 to make automobiles utilizing his highly imaginative air-cooled two-stroke engine. The Euclid was offered in both a roadster and touring body style each priced at $1,000.[1] It is unknown how many were built, but it is likely that at least one example was constructed.[2] (See Palmer Automobile Manufacturing Company.)

1. *Cycle and Automobile Trade Journal*, March 1908, p. 134 et seq. and p. 91, Antique Automobile Club of America Library.
2. Kimes and Clark, *Standard Catalog of American Cars, 1805–1942*, 3d ed.

Falcon Cycle Car Company (1913 to 1914)

The Falcon cyclecar was a very sporty-looking vehicle with staggered seating and some rather advanced features for a conveyance that cost as little as $385. These features included an electric starter, electric lighting, and a circular shifting mechanism which was mounted on the steering wheel and looked very much like a horn ring. The front suspension, however, was a throwback to horse and buggy days. It consisted of a transverse leaf spring which also served as the front axle. This was all attached to the chassis by means of a central kingpin, and steering was controlled by cables running off of a steering column spool.[1] This was all very clever and efficient but of dubious durability, even for a vehicle which weighed only 325 pounds. Within months of its formation the company moved its operations to Staunton, Virginia, and, as part of the

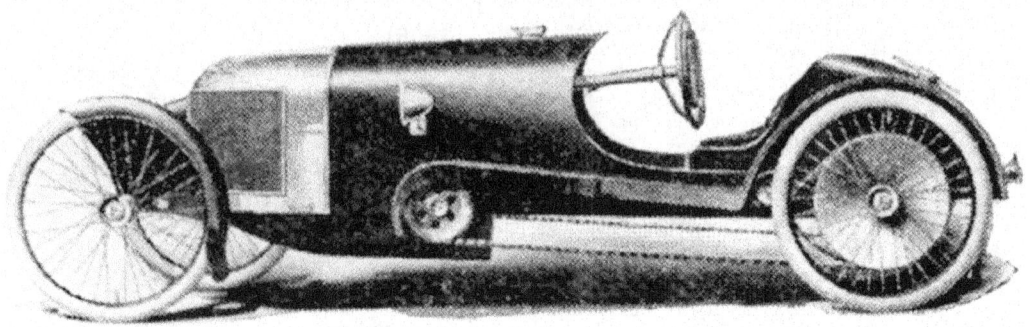

FALCON 2-PASS. ROADSTER, $385.

The 1913 Falcon had V-belt drive and a two cylinder air cooled engine. At $385 it was priced just more than a dollar a pound. Seating was staggered, tread was only 36 inches, and it came with an electric starter.

move, drove one of its cyclecars on a factory road test from Cleveland to Staunton, presumably completing the trip as planned.[2]

1. Wager, *Golden Wheels*.
2. Kimes and Clark, *Standard Catalog of American Cars, 1805–1942*, 3d ed.

Fedelia Cycle Car (1913 to 1914)

All that we have on this cyclecar indicates that it had a sporty boat-tailed body, a thirty-eight inch tread, and was powered by a Deluxe engine of unknown specifications. The point of manufacture was next door to the home of the builder, John H. Sizelan.[1]

1. Wager, *Golden Wheels*.

Ford Motor Company (1915 to 1932)

When you think Ford, you think Detroit. But the Ford Motor Company maintained a major manufacturing presence on Cleveland's

The last automobile to be produced in Cleveland was the 1932 Ford. A total of 6,638 were built, with the V-8 outselling the carried-over four cylinder two-to-one.

Ford's Cleveland branch plant on Euclid Avenue began assembling automobiles in 1915.

East Side for a number of years. Ford's Euclid Avenue assembly plant was selected as one of the company's several strategic satellite locations, because Cleveland was an important Ford sales and distribution center.

Cleveland had been America's automobile capital from 1898 until 1908, at which time Henry Ford introduced his Model T Ford, and the balance finally tipped in favor of Detroit. But, Cleveland retained its manufacturing infrastructure and an efficient rail network, which played an important part in bringing Ford to Cleveland.

In August 1913, Ford introduced the industry's first moving assembly line at its River Rouge plant in Detroit, reducing the time required to build a Model T from over twelve hours to just one hour and thirty-three minutes.[1] Ford's new facilities in Cleveland, designed by Albert Kahn, incorporated this innovative assembly line concept.

A contract for construction of the Cleveland plant was let in August 1914.[2] Work was completed in short order at a stated cost of $500,000, and by early 1915 the plant had begun producing Model Ts.[3]

Cleveland's new four-story facility was one of Ford's largest outside Detroit, and one of its most important.[4] The building's first floor contained a salesroom and offices facing the street, with a garage and service areas at the rear.[5] The upper floors were dedicated to the assembly of automobiles, and an adjacent one-story storage and distribution facility supplemented the main building.[6] One reason for selecting the Euclid Avenue plant location was its proximity to an important rail line, and Kahn made use of this, arranging for the plant to be directly served by an elevated rail spur which entered the facility on the second floor.

Model T production continued unabated in Cleveland until 1917, when it was suspended for two years during World War I. Production resumed in 1919, and in 1923 Ford updated the plant's moving assembly line, in addition to making modifications to the building to improve overall operating efficiency. By 1925 the plant was turning out 225 Model Ts per day, and employment had reached 1,600.[7] The last Model T rolled off the Cleveland assembly line on May 31, 1927, to be replaced by the Model A in 1928, and the Model B in 1932.

The last Model B, which was not only the last Cleveland-built Ford, but also the last Cleveland-built automobile of any marque, left the plant in December 1932.

During the Cleveland Ford plant's seventeen years of operation, several Cleveland parts suppliers benefited from the company's presence. One in particular was Baker-Raulang (see Baker R & L), which provided bodies for Ford, beginning with the introduction of the Model A in 1928, until 1932 when the Ford Cleveland plant ceased production.

---

1. Kimes and Clark, *Standard Catalog of American Cars, 1805–1942*, 3d ed.
2. *The Automobile*, August 13, 1914.
3. Historic American Engineering Record, HAER OH-11E: It should be noted that *Golden Wheels* states that the plant began production in 1914 but this does not appear to be correct.
4. *The Automobile*, May 21, 1914.
5. *The Automobile*, April 16, 1914.
6. *The Automobile*, May 7, 1914.
7. Ibid.

Forest City Motor Car Company (1905)

A prototype Forest City automobile was constructed by the company in 1905. When the promise of better financial prospects beckoned from Massillon, Ohio, the company moved there to commence production and the automobile was renamed the Jewell.[1] (See Forest City Motor Car Company in Part II.)

---

1. Kimes and Clark, *Standard Catalog of American Cars, 1805–1942*, 3d ed.

Freeman Motor Car Company (1920)

The Freeman company of Omaha, Nebraska declared that it would build automobiles and trucks in Cleveland, Ohio. Its address was listed as the Whitney Power Block, near downtown Cleveland, where the company had leased space for assembly of its automobile.[1]

The company intended to build its own plant on the west side in the Berea Road district along the Belt Line Railroad but material shortages postponed the effort and the company ceased operations before the year was out.[2] Apparently a prototype was constructed, but actual production was never achieved.

The 1915 Model T Ford was the first to be assembled in Cleveland at the new Ford branch plant.

1. Kimes and Clark, *Standard Catalog of American Cars, 1805–1942*, 3d ed.
2. *Automotive Industries*, April 8, 1920, p. 878, Antique Automobile Club of America Library. The company was also referred to as the Freeman Motor Company.

French-American Motor Company (1907 to 1908)

The French-American company was organized in early 1907 for the purpose of producing automobiles powered by a forty-five horsepower water-cooled engine. In January 1908 it was announced that the F.A.M. automobile would be marketed by the Auto Parts Company, which was owned and managed by two of the French-American company organizers. A prototype F.A.M. may have been constructed. However, by the end of 1908 all parties involved concluded that the parts business offered more attractive prospects and the idea of building automobiles was abandoned.[1]

1. Kimes and Clark, *Standard Catalog of American Cars, 1805–1942*, 3d ed.

Gabriel Auto Company (1910 to 1912)

One of the city's oldest companies, the W.H. Gabriel Wagon & Carriage Company began business in 1815. Sometime in early 1909 it began work on an automobile of its own design, and in 1910 the Gabriel Auto Company was incorporated to pursue the manufacture of the Gabriel automobile.[1]

Gabriel's large touring automobile entered production in April of that year. It had a 120 inch wheelbase and a 4-cylinder three-main-bearing engine of 30 horsepower. The drive shaft was contained in a torque tube. The electrical system was by Bosch, and the carburetor was Stromberg. The rear brakes were a combination internal expanding and external contracting type.[2] The Gabriel proved its merit in local competition, but production was on a limited basis. Despite the automobile's initial success, the company began to explore the possibilities of entering the commercial motor truck field, and in 1913 it elected to produce only the Gabriel truck. The Gabriel Auto Company is not to be confused with another Cleveland company, the Gabriel Manufacturing Company. The latter was formed in 1904 to produce the Gabriel automobile horn and later the Gabriel shock absorber.

THE GABRIEL IS A FOUR-CYLINDER MOTOR CAR

The first Gabriel automobile appeared in 1910. It was powered by a four-cylinder 25/30 horsepower engine and rode on a 120-inch wheel base.

1. Kimes and Clark, *Standard Catalog of American Cars, 1805–1942*, 3d ed.; the company is also referred to as the Gabriel Carriage Company.
2. *Motor Age*, March 10, 1910, p. 18, Antique Automobile Club of America Library.

Gaeth, Paul (1898 to 1902); Gaeth Automobile Company (1902 to 1910)

Paul Gaeth began work on his first automobile in 1896, but it took two years before he finally completed it. After an unsuccessful venture with another automobile inventor he opened his own shop in 1901, and formed the Gaeth Automobile Company in 1902.[1]

His early automobiles, powered by a single-cylinder engine, attracted enough buyers that by 1903 he had manufactured over twenty-four such vehicles. Gaeth was meticulous about the materials and craftsmanship that went into the production of his automobiles, and was personally involved in the construction and testing of each Gaeth that was built.[2] This of course meant that very few automobiles could be built each year, and were built only to order.

Gaeth automobiles performed extremely well in local endurance and Glidden events, usually achieving one of the highest if not the highest score of any contestant. By 1909 his automobiles had grown into large handsome vehicles priced around $3,500 which, considering the fact that they were virtually hand-built, was not an unreasonable price.

Increasing demand for his vehicles resulted in Gaeth moving in 1905 to a new plant which had a capacity for the construction of 100 automobile per year. Up to this point sales had been largely to local motorists, but in 1907 an expanded sales effort was launched. Gaeth sent a demonstration automobile on a tour of East Coast cities in 1908 in order to generate a wider interest in his vehicles.[3] The success of this effort was such that Gaeth announced plans in early 1910 to expand production to 500 per year by 1911.[4]

But, as with many of Cleveland's early automobile entrepreneurs, Gaeth was more interested in being personally involved in building a superior automobile than in devoting time to the practical aspects of running a large business enterprise. As was stated in a Gaeth sales brochure of 1909, "Mr. Gaeth ... has consistently adhered to the policy of never building more automobiles than he could personally supervise."[5] Although his vehicles could hold their own with the finest being made, Gaeth had no interest in further expanding his operations. It is instructive to note that, in 1906 when *Cycle and Automobile Trade Journal* undertook a critical evaluation and comparison of

The Gaeth Automobile Company offered three models in 1910: a seven-passenger Touring-Car, a Tourabout, and a Limousine. Whichever model was selected, it was virtually a bespoke automobile as Paul Gaeth personally oversaw the construction of each one of his company's vehicles (author's collection).

Cleveland's most prestigious automobiles, its analysis included an extensive technical examination and road test of Peerless, Stearns, and Gaeth.

Paul Gaeth left the automobile business in 1910 and the company was liquidated. The assets, including the plant, were purchased by the Stuyvesant Motor Car Company. (See Stuyvesant Motor Car Company.) But Gaeth did not abandon his automobiles and maintained a garage where he repaired and made parts for Gaeths which were still in operation.

Riding on a 78-inch wheel base powered by an 8 horsepower engine, the 1903 General cost $900. Customers who wanted flexibility could add a rear tonneau, which seated two, for $100, and a box for delivery service for $100.

1. *The Automobile and Motor Review*, 1902.
2. *The Automobile*, December 30, 1909.
3. *Cleveland Leader*, advertisements 1907 to 1908.
4. Wager, *Golden Wheels*.
5. *Cycle and Automobile Trade Journal*, October 1906; Gaeth booklet, Kathleen Gaeth-Steenstra, Western Reserve Historical Society.

Gas Engine and Appurtenance Company (1910)

Organizers of this company were Andrew B. Nichols, Edward H. Sherbourne, Florence A. Lautermilch, Rob Roy Alexander, and J.M. Bing. Its stated purpose was the manufacture of automobiles, gas engines, motor boats, and accessories. Capital stock was $10,000. There is no record of an automobile actually having been constructed.[1] This is one of the rare instances in which a woman acted as a founding member of an automobile enterprise.

1. Kimes and Clark, *Standard Catalog of American Cars, 1805–1942*, 3d ed.

General Automobile and Manufacturing Company (1902 to 1903); General Automobile Company (1903 to 1905)

New investors reorganized the Hansen Automobile Company (see Hansen Automobile Company) as the General Automobile and Manufacturing Company, and operations were moved to a new facility. Production of the General in two versions, a single-cylinder vehicle priced at $900 and a twin-cylinder automobile priced at $1,000, was commenced and things appeared to be progressing well. The General was a solidly built small automobile that, like its Hansen predecessor the Cleveland, performed well in racing events. General automobiles were displayed at shows in Cleveland, Chicago and New York City in 1903, which reputedly resulted in over 500 orders being placed. Although the company was initially on sound footing, production did not progress smoothly and as a result many orders were withdrawn due to delays on delivery of finished automobiles.[1] That and other difficulties involving the Selden patent discouraged the founding investors from putting more money into the venture, and General was forced into bankruptcy at the end of 1903.[2]

The purchaser in bankruptcy was the Studebaker Brothers Manufacturing Company, which reorganized the General company as General Automobile Company.[3] A new model General was introduced in 1904 and prices ranged between $1,100 and $1,600. Sales were slow and limited production continued at the Cleveland location until late 1905, when operations ceased and the General passed into history.[4]

1. Wager, *Golden Wheels*.
2. *Motor Age*, February 5, 1903; Kimes and Clark, *Standard Catalog of American Cars, 1805–1942*, 3d ed.
3. Wager, *Golden Wheels*.
4. *Motor Age*, August 1903.

Githens, Herbert A. (1900)

With the assistance of C.M. Raymond, Herbert Githens constructed a steam-powered vehicle which bore his name. The power plant of the Githens used a water tube boiler which the two men had designed. The boiler fed steam to a two-cylinder Mason steam engine which powered the vehicle. The Githens was an experimental effort and there was no intention of production beyond the initial prototype. At the time, Herbert Githens oversaw the operation of the American Bicycle Company's Cleveland outlet. Subsequently Githens' brother Walter organized Githens Brothers, Inc. in Chicago Illinois for the manufacture of automobiles. Herbert joined his brother in 1903 and although a prototype electric vehicle had been constructed by then, the brothers turned their attention to selling rather than manufacturing automobiles.[1]

1. Kimes and Clark, *Standard Catalog of American Cars, 1805–1942*, 3d ed.

Globe Motor Company (1920 to 1922)

Charles H. Davies was founder of the Supreme Motor Corporation in Warren, Ohio, a maker of four-cylinder engines.[1] When it came to manufacturing an automobile, he and his investors had a good idea but bad timing. They were hoping to capitalize on what was seen to be a post–World War I demand for a reasonably priced medium-sized automobile that possessed "daring lines, a touch of color, speed and snap" when they incorporated the Globe Motor Company in September 1920.[2]

Davies probably chose Cleveland over Warren for the location of the Globe Motor Company plant due to its reputation as an automotive center and possibly partly due to promotion of the city by its very active Chamber of Commerce. A site was located on Cleveland's East Side only steps from the Stearns-Knight factory. One building was quickly completed and in use, with construction of the second to be completed by December 1920 and first deliveries of Globe Four automobiles were expected before the end of the year.[3] Ambitious plans were announced for the production of 5,000 passenger cars and 1,000 ¾-ton Globe Flyer trucks during 1921.

The Globe Four was an assembled automobile, which was typical for most of the start-up companies at this time. It was powered by a Supreme four-cylinder engine and both the roadster and touring cars were to be priced between $1,800 and $2,000. Sales brochures said that the Globe Four offered the largest body to be mounted on its size wheelbase. Also, every automobile had to have its own special fillips to differentiate it from the competition. In the case of the Globe Four there was a light for under-hood illumination and inside there was a dash mounted lamp on an extension cord for the occupants.

The Globe Four was introduced in the midst of the post–World War I depression, which was fatal for its chances of success. Financing was tight and purchasers were few. Nothing ever came of the Globe Flyer trucks and what remained of the 1921 automobiles became the 1922 Globe Four models.[4] With their disposition the company quietly faded from the scene.

1. *Automotive Industries*, September 30, 1920. Kimes and Clark, *Standard Catalog of American Cars, 1805–1942*, 3d ed., lists the name as Supreme Motors Corporation.
2. Kimes and Clark, *Standard Catalog of American Cars, 1805–1942*, 3d ed.
3. *Automotive Industries*, September 30, 1920.
4. Kimes and Clark, *Standard Catalog of American Cars, 1805–1942*, 3d ed.

Goby, G.S. (1914)

In an attempt to capitalize on the cyclecar craze, G.S. Goby designed and built a three-place vehicle that featured a four-cylinder water-cooled engine of Mr. Goby's own design.[1] Apparently it was a very respectable effort, according to the April 1914 issue of *The Cyclecar Age*, and was priced very reasonably at $400. Prospects for financial backing seemed assured and it was said that the Motor Engineering Company of Cleveland was at work on the first batch of Goby cyclecars. With the exception of the prototype vehicle which had received high praise in April, no additional cyclecars seem to have been made, and nothing else was heard about the venture.[2]

1. Wager, *Golden Wheels*.
2. Kimes and Clark, *Standard Catalog of American Cars, 1805–1942*, 3d ed.

Grant, John J. (1864)

The first Cleveland automobile was a self-propelled steam powered vehicle created by John J. Grant, which made its appearance in 1864 while the country was in the midst of the Civil War. Grant's steam vehicle was also involved in the city's, if not the country's, first traffic accident involving a self-propelled conveyance. While out testing his steam vehicle John Grant managed to hit a woman and her child. The encounter was so embarrassing for Mr. Grant that he took his vehicle home and never drove it again. Mr. Grant's mechanical inclinations then drew him into working for Cleveland Machine Screw Company which ultimately became involved in the assembly of several later Cleveland automobiles. After leaving Machine Screw he opened his own shop as the Grant Machine Tool Company in Franklin, Pennsylvania. Unfortunately no details are known about his steam vehicle itself but it did exist and it did run. We have the June 27, 1901, issue of the trade publication *Motor Age*, and the *Standard Catalog of American Cars, 1805–1942*, 3d ed., to thank for this intriguing piece of Cleveland's automobile lore.

Grant-Lees Machine Company (1912 to 1913); Grant Motor Car Company (1912 to 1913)

The Grant-Lees Machine Company took over the Stuyvesant Motor Car Company in 1912. For 1912 Grant-Lees retained the Stuyvesant Motor Car Company name and continued to produce the Gaeth-based Stuyvesant Four, but the Stuyvesant Six model was dropped. It soon appeared that Grant-Lees had its own problems and, perhaps in November 1912 but at least by 1913, the company had disposed of its Stuyvesant assets to the Benton Motor Car Company of Benton, Illinois, which, after an initial promotional splash for its newly acquired Stuyvesant automobile, also vanished from the scene. (See Stiverson Motor Car Company.)

It was also in 1912 that Harry Elmer came to town. Elmer had attempted to undertake production of an automobile in Elkhart, Indiana, but having been thwarted in this effort, found brighter prospects in Cleveland with the Grant-Lees company. The company provided the necessary financial backing for Elmer's automobile and organized the Grant Motor Car Company as a division of Grant-Lees to undertake production. What had been named the Elmer Six, now called the Grant Six, entered production in April 1912 and was described as being a semi-assembled automobile. It had a fifty-horsepower engine, was very similar in appearance to its predecessor, and cost $2,750. The automobile was produced at the Grant-Lees factory while plans were being made for a new plant. But come November 1912 Harry Elmer left the organization. Although production continued for a little while longer, by early 1913, the Grant Six was gone, and the Stuyvesant along with it.[1]

1. Kimes and Clark, *Standard Catalog of American Cars, 1805–1942*, 3d ed. Confusing as it is, this Grant Six should not be confused with the Grant Six of the Grant Motor Car Company of 1916 to 1922.

Grant Motor Car Company (1916 to 1922)

Before coming to Cleveland in 1916, the Grant Motor Car Company was producing Grant automobiles in Findlay, where it had been since 1913. The Grant was an assembled automobile or, as the advertising put it, a "Standardized" automobile. The company made no bones about it, in fact it extolled the fact that being Standardized made it possible to provide the best overall value.[1] The Grant was well received and the company was growing.

In May 1916 the company announced that it had purchased seven acres of land on Cleveland's northeast side where it would build a 124,000 square foot factory which was to be in operation July 15.[2] Actual production did not begin until December, but it was still expected that automobile production for 1917 would reach 20,000, at the rate of seventy-five per day.[3] The

The Grant automobile plant opened in 1916 on Cleveland's east side.

automobiles in the new plant were assembled while being drawn along on a cable conveyor system which facilitated efficient production.[4]

The 1917 Grant Six was priced at $845 and, consistent with it being a Standardized automobile, the source of every major component was proudly listed.[5] Production began with a work force of 570 employees and the plant's rail sidings allowed for the loading of thirty finished automobiles at one time.[6] No sooner had April arrived than a plant expansion was in the works, along with the acquisition of the Cleveland based Denneen Motor Company, maker of Denmo trucks.[7] Things were indeed moving very fast for Grant, thanks to the fact that there was a record demand for automobiles selling below $1,500, and Grant was one of them.

All these moves seemed to be paying off and 1918 net earnings reflected this fact. Encouraged by these results the company projected production of 12,000 automobiles in 1919.[8] In order to protect its supply of engines, Grant company purchased the neighboring engine builder H.J. Walker Manufacturing Company in early 1920, with plans to use 80 engines per day and to release an additional 70 to the trade.[9] It was expected that the nearby location of the Walker engine company would reduce material handling costs and its ownership would give Grant company control over its engine supply. However, the post-war economy was pinching automobile manufacturers around the country and the Grant company was no exception. Pay cuts were put in place for new employees in 1921 and only 7,000 automobile were projected for the 1922 production year.[10] The

The attractive 1917 Grant Six sold well, finding 12,000 purchasers thanks to its high quality and low price.

company began scrambling to shore up its financial situation, but by the end of 1922 the company and its Walker engine subsidiary were in the hands of a bankruptcy receiver.[11] Production of automobiles was halted but Denmo truck construction continued, as demand remained strong.[12]

So ended the Grant Motor Car Corporation. Its plant was purchased by Lincoln Electric Company and the plant equipment was sold. Only the automotive repair and service departments remained in operation during the receivership.[13]

---

1. *The Automobile*, June 27, 1912, sales advertisement.
2. *The Automobile*, May 11, 1916.
3. *The Automobile*, October 19, 1916.
4. *The Automobile*, December 16, 1916.
5. *The Horseless Age*, vol. 37 (1916).
6. *The Automobile*, January 4, 1917.
7. *The Automobile and Automotive Industries*, April 26, August 23, 1917.
8. *Automotive Industries*, February 6 and 13, 1919.
9. *Automotive Industries*, April 1, 1920.
10. *Automotive Industries*, January 20, 1921, and January 12, 1922.
11. *Automotive Industries*, October 26, 1922: Perhaps the last sale of Grant company common stock was of 50 share to George Simon on June 5, 1922, Western Reserve Historical Society Library collection.
12. *Automotive Industries*, November 23, 1922.
13. *Automotive Industries*, June 7, 1923.

H & H Auto Company (1913)

Organized by F.M. Fogarty, J.O. Fordyce, A.B. Brackenridge, H.M. Reidel, and C.M. Dolan with a capitalization of $10,000, the company was to manufacture and sell automobiles. Nothing further was heard and it is unlikely that an automobile was actually produced.[1]

---

1. Kimes and Clark, *Standard Catalog of American Cars, 1805–1942*, 3d ed.

H.A. Lozier Company (1915); Hal Motor Car Company (1916 to 1918)

The story of Cleveland's Hal Motor Car Company begins with the Cleveland bicycle and its manufacturer, Clevelander Henry A. Lozier.[1] Although Lozier's company had a Cleveland sales outlet, the main bicycle factory itself was in Toledo.

But Lozier was interested in more than just two-wheelers, and the company, under his direction, designed a motorized tricycle in 1898.[2] The firm apparently also built a steam vehicle which utilized a flash boiler system, but further development of this vehicle was not pursued.

Before Lozier's tricycle was actually in production, the company was sold to Albert Pope's American Bicycle Company trust, and the sale included the tricycle rights as part of the arrangement.[3] Pope's trust went on to produce at least one hundred examples of the Lozier tricycle in 1900.[4]

After Albert Pope's American Bicycle Company purchased Lozier's bicycle interests, Lozier was finally able to pursue his long-held desire to build an automobile, forming the Lozier Motor Company in Plattsburg, New York, where one of his former Lozier bicycle plants had been located. However, before development of a Lozier automobile had gone very far, Lozier died in 1903, leaving an estate worth in excess of $5,000,000.

Upon Lozier's death, his son Henry A. Lozier, Jr., known as Harry, took over operation of the company and oversaw the manufacture of the first Lozier automobile, which was introduced in 1905.

After a reorganization and a move from Plattsburg to Detroit, competing interests within the company wished to introduce a low-priced Lozier automobile, which was very much against the wishes of Harry. When the two factions could not resolve their differences, Harry was forced out of the company in July of 1912.

Harry was not to be discouraged, and he made plans to build an exclusive V-12 automobile of his own design, along the lines of the original highly regarded Lozier which he had shepherded through its formative years from 1905 to 1912. To accomplish this objective, he formed the H.A. Lozier Company.

Details about the new vehicle were released in mid–1915, while Harry was still located in Detroit.[5] By September Harry had moved his company to Cleveland, locating temporarily on the second floor of what had been the Royal Tourist factory, now owned by F.B. Stearns.[6] (See Royal Motor Car Company.)

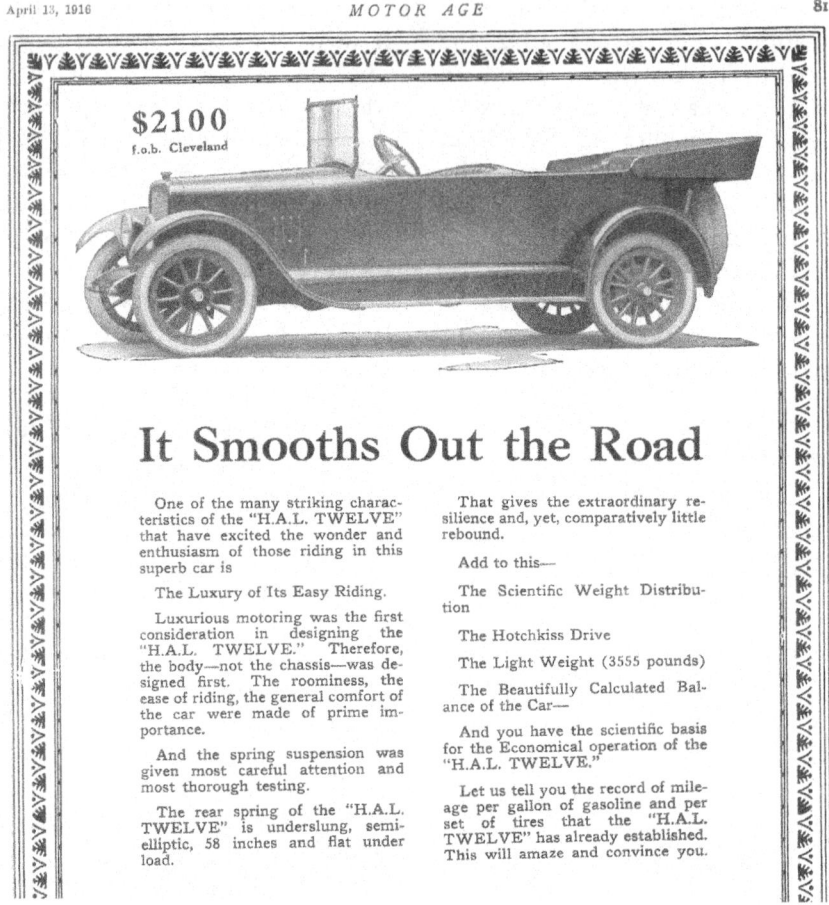

The H.A.L. TWELVE was designed with luxury motoring foremost in mind. The body of the 1916 H.A.L. was roomy and comfortable, and its ride was gentle thanks to the underslung mounting of its semi-elliptic rear springs, which were said to remain flat under load, providing extraordinary resilience with little rebound. Weighing in at 3,555 pounds, the H.A.L. was relatively light for a twelve-cylinder luxury automobile (author's collection).

The H. A. Lozier Company displayed its first H.A.L. TWELVE at the New York Automobile Show. Full production followed by May 1916.[7] The automobile rode on a 135-inch wheelbase, was powered by a Weidely V-12 engine, and was priced at $2,100. Two body styles were offered, a seven-passenger touring and a roadster. The styling of both vehicles featured an uninterrupted beltline reaching from the radiator back to the rear of the automobile, with no break at the cowl, an unusual design feature for the era.

The company was anticipating sales of 1,000 vehicles in 1916, and had optimistically ordered materials sufficient to construct 2,000 automobiles during 1917.[8] By September of 1916 production was up to four per day, and continued on schedule rising to six, all of which could easily be handled by the 300-man staff.[9] The Lozier company had also taken on upwards of forty dealers across the country, in line with expected sales demand.

In a surprise move, Harry Lozier left the enterprise in September 1916, citing ill health, and management changed the company name to the Hal Motor Car Company.[10]

Immediately after leaving the company, Harry formed a new Cleveland organization which he named Lozier Bros. Company.[11] Although the corporate purpose was not stated, a capitalization of $10 million indicated that very ambitious plans were afoot, but the ultimate outcome of this venture is unknown.

Meanwhile, back at the Hal Motor Car Company, things seemed to be going smoothly, and two hundred automobiles had been produced by October 1916. However, because of America's war effort, it became increasingly difficult to obtain the necessary material for the H.A.L. TWELVE, and demand for the automobile was not strong.

By October 1917, in an attempt to rescue the company, talks were under way for a merger between the Hal company and Cleveland's Abbott Corporation, manufacturer of the Abbott automobile (see Abbott Corporation). It was intended that after the merger each company would continue to make its own respective automobiles. However the merger did not take place.[12]

Notwithstanding these difficulties, a Hal-Twelve was displayed at the Chicago Automobile Show in late January 1918, but the following month Hal Motor Car Company was forced into involuntary bankruptcy. The company was liquidated in April with ten finished Hal-Twelve automobiles on hand, plus an assortment of accessories, machinery and office furniture, all of which was auctioned off.[13] Use of the factory building returned to the hands of F.B. Stearns (see F.B. Stearns Company), and that brought to a close the Hal-Twelve chapter of Cleveland's automobile industry story.[14]

It is of more than passing interest to note that Frederick C. Chandler, who formed the Chandler Motor Car Company in 1913, had been involved with Henry Lozier, Sr., since his bicycle manufacturing days, and had served as vice president of sales for the Lozier Motor Company of Detroit. (See Chandler Motor Car Company.)

---

1. *Cleveland City Directory*, 1890 and 1899.
2. Ibid.; Kimes and Clark, *Standard Catalog of American Cars, 1805–1942*, 3d ed.
3. Kimes and Clark, *Standard Catalog of American Cars, 1805–1942*, 3d ed.
4. *Cycle and Automobile Trade Journal*, October 1900.
5. *The Automobile*, September 30, 1915.
6. *The Automobile*, January 13, 1916.
7. *The Automobile*, September 14, 1916.
8. Ibid.
9. *The Automobile*, September 28, 1916.
10. Kimes and Clark, *Standard Catalog of American Cars, 1805–1942*, 3d ed.
11. *The Automobile*, November 16, 1916.
12. *Automotive Industries*, October 25, 1917.
13. *Automotive Industries*, May 2, 1918.
14. H.A.L Twelve was the first of many names for the vehicle:

Company Name	Vehicle Name	Year
H.A. Lozier Company 1915–1916	H.A.L. TWELVE	1916
Hal Motor Car Company 1917–1918	H-A-L- TWELVE	1917
	HAL TWELVE	1917
	Hal-Twelve	1917
	Hal-Twelve	1918

Habig, Harry (1919)

During his high school years Cleveland teenager Harry Habig assembled a speedster using the air-cooled engine, wheels, and tires from a motorcycle. *American Automobile Digest* declared in a 1921 issue that the result of his effort was "...a marvel of mechanical genius and skill." Weighing in at less than five hundred pounds and carrying a sleek racing style body, this single-place vehicle was said to be capable of sixty miles per hour and up to forty miles per gallon. It appears that the speedster was actually built in Cleveland although some sources disagree.[1]

---

1. Kimes and Clark, *Standard Catalog of American Cars, 1805–1942*, 3d ed.

Hallock Engineering Company (1915)

Formed with a capitalization of $25,000, the company was set up to manufacture automobiles and accessories. The founders were T.P. Hallock, R.H. Bosley, R.E. Kimmel, William H. Chapman, and Olga E. Schultz. It is probable that no automobile was ever produced. It is interesting to note that Olga E. Schultz is one of only a few women to have been involved in organizing a Cleveland automobile company.[1]

---

1. Kimes and Clark, *Standard Catalog of American Cars, 1805–1942*, 3d ed.

Hansen Automobile Company (1902)

The Hansen Automobile Company, founded by Rasmus Hansen, was the maker of the second automobile to be named Cleveland. Production began in the same building on E 45th Street in which Alexander Winton had built his first automobiles.[1] The Hansen was a single-cylinder gasoline powered runabout and performed quite well in local automobile events.

The company had hardly been organized when Hansen determined that he had bigger plans in mind and reorganized the company as the General Automobile and Manufacturing Company.[2] (See General Automobile Manufacturing Company.)

---

1. *The Motor Age*, May 1902.
2. Kimes and Clark, *Standard Catalog of American Cars, 1805–1942*, 3d ed.

THE HANSEN COMPANY'S CLEVELAND CARRIAGE.

Fenders were optional on the 1902 Cleveland by the Hansen Automobile Company.

Harding Motor Car Company (1915 to 1916)

When Frank I. Harding and Nathan Wyeth resigned their positions at the Peerless Motor Car Company in order to start an automobile venture in 1915, they did not have to go far to set up shop. Harding, who had been Peerless' Secretary, and Wyeth, an engineer involved in the design and testing of both Peerless V-8 and V-12 engines, merely moved across the street to a factory building at 93rd and Quincy Avenue.[1]

The first Harding Twelve automobile made its appearance in January 1916, and was an impressive vehicle with a tractable and powerful engine.[2] The engine was an L-head of the twin-six type, cast in separate six-cylinder blocks with a common crankshaft, and displacing 713 cubic inches, with a bore of 2¾ inches and a stroke of 5 inches. This powerful engine could run comfortably at 3,000 rpm, and was capable of propelling the Harding from a crawl up to 50 mph within a few hundred feet.

The Harding rode on a 132-inch wheelbase and featured a streamlined European-style touring profile with blended body lines, crowned fenders, and an impressively low stance.[3] Priced at $2,000, including a top, it received favorable comment from the automotive press, especially regarding its smooth performance and ample power.

The Harding Twelve was one of the country's earliest V-12 automobiles. Only eight other V-12-powered vehicles were offered in the mid-teens, including the Enger (see Enger Motor Car Company in Part II), the H.A.L. Twelve (see H.A. Lozier Company), the National, Haynes, Pathfinder, Austin, and Kissel.

Quick to come into being, Harding was equally quick to leave the automotive scene. After only one year of existence, and shortly after the vehicle's public debut, the venture was dissolved and ceased all operations. This speedy demise was undoubtedly facilitated by the fact that the Harding Motor Car Company had never been formally organized. The only indication of grander plans appears in a 1916 Cleveland City Directory, which lists offices for Harding at 506 Cuyahoga Building in downtown Cleveland. There also had been some talk of obtaining permanent sales and manufacturing locations, but this was never realized.

A relationship between Peerless and the start-up Harding Motor Car Company may have existed, but it is not possible to establish how much outright support was given to

Harding by Peerless. Nevertheless, facts indicate that support of one kind or another was likely.

Peerless had opted for a V-8 engine instead of a V-12, and thus would have no use for the V-12 prototype which it had been developing; thus Harding's use of such an engine type would not have been competitive. (See Peerless Motor Car Company.) In addition, it is impossible to ignore the fact that the Harding V-12 made its appearance within little more than one year after the company's formation. This was an extremely short period of time within which to design, build, and thoroughly test a new engine of any configuration. Similarly, for Harding to have also designed and built a body and chassis from scratch while developing a new V-12 engine would have been a daunting task. Support from Peerless might explain this swift progress. It is even possible that the engine which powered the Harding Twelve prototype might have in fact been the Peerless V-12 test engine.

Whatever the situation surrounding the short life of the Harding Motor Car Company might have been, it is known that only one example of the Harding Twelve was ever constructed.[4] Shortly after its completion and testing, the venture was disbanded.[5] It is also known that this vehicle passed into the hands of Nathan Wyeth, who drove it for several years.

1. Wager, *Golden Wheels*.
2. *Horseless Age*, February 15, 1916.
3. *The Automobile*, January 27, 1916; Kimes and Clark, *Standard Catalog of American Cars, 1805–1942*, 3d ed.
4. *The Automobile*, February 17, 1916.
5. Kimes and Clark, *Standard Catalog of American Cars, 1805–1942*, 3d ed.

Hines, William R. (1902 to 1908); Hines Car Company (1908 to 1911)

William R. Hines, chief plant engineer for National Screw & Tack Company of Cleveland, built his first experimental automobile in 1902 and powered it with a one-cylinder four-stroke engine. The vehicle is said to have been built for Hines by Moehlhauser Machine Company of Cleveland.[1] Other experimental automobiles followed, which utilized Brew-Hatcher chassis equipped with a Hines-designed three-cylinder two-stroke engine. (See Brew-Hatcher Company.) These automobiles proved to be very strong hill-climbers with good pulling power, although the top speed was limited to about 35 miles per hour.[2]

Convinced of the superiority of a two-stroke engine, further experimentation led Hines to build a four-cylinder two-stroke engine in 1907, which he placed in a chassis of his own design. Hines road-tested his creation for over 16,000 miles and subjected it to very hard use, during which time the engine required no repairs.

Hugh Dolnar, the lead automotive journalist for *Cycle and Automobile Trade Journal*, followed this trial and reported that the tires clearly evidenced hard use, as they were very badly worn. Dolnar also had an opportunity to drive this particular Hines for over 50 miles on Cleveland city streets, and achieved fuel economy of over 17 miles per gallon. He concluded his report by saying that the motor

The four-cylinder two-stroke water-cooled 1909 Hines sat on a 106-inch wheelbase. The five passenger touring had a three-speed transmission, Timken roller bearings on the front and rear wheels, and weighed 2,650 pounds.

was absolutely silent, performed far better than any four-stroke engine, and that the Hines was one of the best automobiles he had ever test-driven.

In order to assure himself of the superiority of his four-cylinder engine, Hines built and tested a three-cylinder version of the engine for comparison. Rigorous testing confirmed the four-cylinder engine's advantages. At last William Hines was completely confident in his vehicle, and formally created the Hines Car Company in 1908.

Between 1908 and 1910 Hines produced an unspecified number of automobiles, all of which were five-passenger touring cars with a 106-inch wheelbase and four-cylinder two-stroke engine.[3] By 1910 things were proceeding so well that Hines announced plans to build a factory of his own in Cleveland, capable of producing 500 automobiles for the 1911 model year.[4] There was even talk of renaming the vehicle the Hinescar.

Meanwhile, two Hines vehicles were successfully entered in the Cleveland-Columbus-Toledo Reliability Run conducted in July 1910. After this event, Hines sent a letter to the Diamond Rubber Company stating that their tires had performed so flawlessly during the contest that the Hines Car Company would use Diamond tires exclusively for its 1911 automobiles.[5] This was no small compliment, as Hines' experience in his 1907 road test had shown that only the highest quality tires could stand up to his automobiles' performance demands.

However, Hines' automobile efforts came to an end in late 1910 or early 1911. The only epitaph is a used car ad, placed in the *Cleveland Plain Dealer* December 17, 1911, and again on January 14, 1912, by the Winton Motor Car Company, offering a 1909 Hines for sale, no reasonable offer refused.

---

1. Kimes and Clark, *Standard Catalog of American Cars, 1805–1942*, 3d ed. It should be mentioned that the *Cleveland City Directory* shows no listing for the Moehlhauser company.
2. *Cycle and Automobile Trade Journal*, February 1908, Antique Automobile Club of America Library.
3. *Cycle and Automobile Trade Journal*, March 1908, Antique Automobile Club Library.
4. *The Automobile*, May 5, 1910, Antique Automobile Club of America Library.
5. Testimonial letter by Orion Alexander of the Hines Car Company 1910, published in advertisement by The Diamond Rubber Co., Antique Automobile Club of America Library.

Hoffman, Louis (1900 to 1902); Hoffman Automobile and Manufacturing Company (1902 to 1903)

Before becoming enamored with the automobile, Clevelander Louis E. Hoffman was president of a bicycle company, not unlike other contemporary Cleveland automobile

The 1902 Hoffman steam car, fitted with a water tube boiler which fed a double-cylinder engine, initially developed 6½ horsepower, which was soon increased to 10.

The Hoffman gasoline automobile for 1903 was instantly distinguishable from its steam counterpart by the coil radiator suspended beneath the front hood.

pioneers Alexander Winton and Otto Konigslow, who also started out as bicycle manufacturers.

It was in 1900, in his former bicycle plant, that Hoffman produced his first prototype vehicle, utilizing a flash steam generator of his own design. Production of a small number of these vehicles occurred in 1901 and, to formalize the enterprise, the Hoffman Automobile and Manufacturing Company was organized the following year.[1] By mid–1902 it was reported that twenty-five steam automobiles were ready for final assembly.

Meanwhile, Hoffman was well along in the development of a gasoline-powered version of his vehicle.[2] By the end of the year Hoffman's gasoline prototype had successfully completed testing and, in 1903, it was introduced to the public.[3]

Louis Hoffman was more attuned to the benefits of publicity than most automobile manufacturers of his era, and announcements and progress reports about the Hoffman were constantly appearing in motoring publications of the day. This publicity produced an impressive demand for Hoffman automobiles. However, the small former bicycle plant where production took place could not keep up with dealer orders, especially for the gasoline-powered version.

Adjustments were made, and production improved. By the end of the year, 102 vehicles had been sold, and the gasoline version was out-selling the steam automobile ten-to-one.[4]

In late 1903, Louis Hoffman departed the company in order to pursue other business interests. He left behind a well-equipped factory and ample financial backing.[5]

Shortly afterward, the company changed its name to the Royal Motor Car Company and introduced the Royal Tourist automobile, a much larger and more elegant offering than the Hoffman.[6] (See Royal Motor Car Company.)

1. Kimes and Clark, *Standard Catalog of American Cars, 1805–1942*, 3d ed.
2. *The Automobile and Motor Review*, June 9 and July 28, 1902.
3. *The Automobile and Motor Review*, January 10 and December 1, 1902.
4. *Motor Age*, April 19, August, and October 2, 1903.
5. *The Automobile*, October 10, 1903; *Motor Age*, October 1903.
6. *Motor Age*, November 1903. Note that *Motor Age* incorrectly stated that the name of the company was the Regal Motor Car Company.

Hoffman, William G. (1900)

Listed in *Horseless Vehicles, Automobiles, Motor Cycles* as a manufacturer of automobiles, William G. Hoffman's premises were located at 79 Bolivar Street. A contemporary *Cleveland*

City Directory, however, describes his activity as the manufacture of delivery wagons and makes no specific mention of motorized vehicles. The extent of actual automobile production is unknown.[1]

1. Kimes and Clark, *Standard Catalog of American Cars, 1805–1942*, 3d ed.

Hoyt, Francis R. (1909)

In 1913 when the cyclecar craze was in full bloom, Mr. Hoyt laid a dubious claim to having constructed, in 1909, the first cyclecar built in this country. A photograph of this vehicle shows what is most probably something on a scale fit only for children, judging from the appearance of the girl seated in the vehicle. Nevertheless, it does seem to confirm that he built a motorized vehicle albeit of diminutive proportions.[1]

1. Kimes and Clark, *Standard Catalog of American Cars, 1805–1942*, 3d ed.

Hupp Motor Car Corporation (1929 to 1931)

The Hupp Motor Car Company was organized in Detroit on November 8, 1908, and its sprightly Hupmobile was immediately popular. Founder Robert C. Hupp, after a dispute with others at the company, left the firm in 1911 to form the Hupp Corporation and produce the R.C.H., an automobile which used Hupp's initials for its name. By 1915 Hupp's endeavor had foundered, while the original Hupp Motor Car Company and its Hupmobile continued to prosper.[1]

Hupmobile annual sales had reached 65,862 automobiles by 1928, and the company was in dire need of greater production capacity. Fortunately, suitable facilities were available in

The 1929 Hupmobile was available in forty-two body and equipment combinations. Prices started at $1,345 for the Century Six model and reached $1,645 for the Century Eight. The Hupmobile assembly line illustrated in this advertisement shows that the automobiles were assembled using the "station" method whereby the vehicle moved from point to point, at each of which a variety of parts were added, as opposed to the more efficient continuously moving assembly line (author's collection).

Cleveland, and Hupp acted quickly to secure them. On January 11, 1929, Hupp Motor Car Corporation acquired the Chandler-Cleveland Motors Corporation, and its large manufacturing complex which was capable of producing 300 automobiles per day.[2] (See Chandler-Cleveland Motors Corporation.)

It was only six weeks later that the first test Hupmobile rolled off the new Cleveland assembly line.[3] What made this so remarkable was that in less than two months Hupp had installed an entirely new assembly line, which used conveyors and was totally realigned for maximum efficiency.[4] Some of the modifications involved removing walls and linking together several of the eight buildings in the old Chandler Automobile Company plant complex, to facilitate the change to conveyors for the assembly lines. One of these connecting passageways was utilized to house drying ovens for painted engine blocks, thus saving valuable floor space. All Hupmobile bodies were built two miles away in what had originally been the Cleveland Automobile Company's plant. They were then delivered to the old Chandler plant for installation and finishing.[5]

A new Model S designation was reserved for all Hupmobile Six automobiles manufactured in Cleveland. For 1929, production progressed well and over 16,000 Model S Hupmobiles were turned out. Prices started at $995 for a two-passenger business coupe and $1,175 for a four-passenger roadster.

As the Depression tightened its grip, production fell and only 8,700 Cleveland-manufactured Hupmobiles were produced for 1930. Production for 1931 was even lower. At that point, the decision was made to move all production back to Detroit. Hupp's Cleveland operations were shut down and, by October 1931, most of the plant equipment had been moved to Detroit.[6] Total Cleveland Hupmobile production probably did not exceed 30,000.

There was now only one company manufacturing automobiles in Cleveland—the Ford Motor Company. (See Ford Motor Company.)

1. Kimes and Clark, *Standard Catalog of American Cars, 1805–1942*, 3d ed.
2. *Cram's Automotive Reports*, Hupp Motor Car Corporation, February 5, 1929.
3. *Automotive Industries*, January 18, 1930: The date of the last Chandler varies depending on source as being April 15, May 1, or May 15, 1929.
4. Ibid.
5. Ibid. This is a detailed and fascinating article which gives an excellent overview of the manufacturing process at Hupp company's Cleveland operation.
6. Wager, *Golden Wheels*.

Hutchcroft & Sons Company (1912)

Organized for the purpose of manufacturing and dealing in automobiles and parts, the Hutchcroft company was capitalized at $10,000. Those responsible for its formation included William W., Thornton, and D.G. Hutchcroft, William Mertz, and S.H. Meacham. Production of an automobile is unlikely.[1]

1. Kimes and Clark, *Standard Catalog of American Cars, 1805–1942*, 3d ed.

J. Keller Electric Works (1903)

After having constructed one electric vehicle in Canton in 1899 the Keller Electric Shops moved to Cleveland in 1903 and slightly altered its name, substituting "Works" for "Shops." Construction of a prototype Keller electric runabout was begun shortly thereafter and completed in August. The vehicle was powered by a Willard battery that was said to be good for forty miles without a recharge.[1]

1. Kimes and Clark, *Standard Catalog of American Cars, 1805–1942*, 3d ed.

Jacob Hoffman Wagon Company (1902 to 1905)

A mention in *Automobile and Motor Review*, February 1902, stated that Jacob Hoffman was experimenting with an automobile at his 41 Michigan Street premises. This apparently was in reference to a prototype electric vehicle which Hoffman had constructed for Theodore A. Willard. (See Sipe & Sigler Company and Willard Storage Battery Company.)

The battery, controller, and motor for this vehicle had been designed and built by Willard. Willard's intention seems to have been to use this vehicle to test his electrical equipment, and the Hoffman-built automobile was never intended for sale.

A second Willard-powered vehicle was built by Hoffman in 1903. This was larger and had a range of seventy-five miles on a single charge. Although Willard once again expressed no interest in offering such a vehicle for sale, Jacob Hoffman was so pleased with the automobile's performance and prospects that he made an arrangement with Willard to produce and sell the vehicle on a custom-order basis.

Whether Hoffman actually did sell any of these automobiles is unknown. However, Hoffman did continue to produce Willard-powered vehicles between 1903 and 1905.[1] Throughout this period, the arrangement with Willard supplemented Hoffman's very successful automobile body and canopy business.

1. Kimes and Clark, *Standard Catalog of American Cars, 1805–1942*, 3d ed.

Johnson-Jennings Company (1902)

It was reported that a T.J. Calhoun was building an automobile at the Johnson-Jennings Company. Further details are lacking.[1]

1. Kimes and Clark, *Standard Catalog of American Cars, 1805–1942*, 3d ed.

Jordan Motor Car Company (1916 to 1919); Jordan Motor Car Company, Inc. (1919 to 1931); Jordan Motors, Inc. (1932)

Edward S. (Ned) Jordan first came to Cleveland from Wisconsin in 1906 when he took a position as a reporter for the *Cleveland Press*. Following this job, with one intermediate stop in Dayton working for the National Cash Register Company, he moved on to become public relations officer with the Thomas B. Jeffery Company of Kenosha, Wisconsin, manufacturer of the Rambler automobile. While at Jeffery, Jordan worked his way up from advertising manager, secretary, and sales manager to general manager.

Jordan left Jeffery January 13, 1916, to start an automotive venture of his own with two fellow employees who were highly skilled in automobile design and manufacture. Together they formed the Jordan Motor Car Company.[1]

From the very beginning, Ned Jordan admitted that he did not know very much about designing and manufacturing automobiles, but he did know a great deal about how to market them. In this, he was unique among early automobile entrepreneurs, who generally had prior experience in vehicle manufacture, and were inventors in their own right.

Although Jordan was primarily a marketing expert, this was not his only strength. He was also an excellent manager, who could recognize design and engineering talent, and inspire loyalty in his employees. But he never had any illusions about the type of enterprise upon which he had embarked, once stating "we never were automobile manufacturers. We were pioneers of a new technique in assembly, production, custom style sales, and advertising."[2] The Jordan was, in fact, an assembled automobile. Because of this, Ned Jordan paid as much attention to lining up suppliers as he did to arranging for a factory location. Even before deciding on a factory location, Jordan had already contracted with select suppliers for parts sufficient to produce 2,000 automobiles, while design work continued in temporary headquarters in Detroit.[3]

In June 1916 a decision was made to locate the Jordan plant on a five acre tract in Cleveland. Not only was Jordan attracted by Cleveland's automotive infrastructure, but he also received additional incentive in the form of community financial backing.[4]

Things moved along quickly. By August 14 the plant had been built, the first Jordans were completed, and 2,600 dealership applications had been received.[5] Before Jordan's first year was out, 1,788 automobiles had been produced and sold, and projected production for 1917 was 5,000 vehicles. All of this was accomplished with a staff of a little over 100 men.[6]

Ned Jordan was known for treating his employees well. From the very beginning they were given annual bonuses and offered the chance to acquire stock in the company. On one occasion, employee wives even received a bonus. Because workers were treated so generously, they were unfailingly loyal to the company, dedicated to their jobs, and far more productive than those at most other automobile companies.

The 1927 Jordan is portrayed in the simplest possible terms: A beautiful impressionistic rendering of the Jordan with simple statements about the Jordan including the phrases, "Companionable—snug—close to the ground—marvelously balanced—style—lines—looks—comfort—power—speed" and "It's different from the mass—always will be" (author's collection).

Jordan's relationship with dealers was no less noteworthy. He never forced automobiles on dealers by using the quota system which most other manufacturers employed. Instead, he delivered only the cars that the dealers wanted, when they wanted them, and in the quantities requested.

In 1917, to generate enthusiasm among his dealers, Jordan invited them to Cleveland to view the plant and the entire new lineup of seven body styles. Each dealer present at the event was given the chance to win an exclusive Jordan sport limousine that would not be available for sale to the general public, and one envied dealer was able to drive this elegant automobile home in style.[7]

Jordan's overall business approach was, as he himself described it, based on the cooperative idea. Practically all of his dealers were associated with him as stockholders, as were many of the manufacturers of the various components and accessories that went into the Jordan. In addition, a portion of the unsubscribed stock was held aside for prospective future dealers.[8]

Jordan's journalism background and marketing acumen made him the darling of automotive trade journalists. As a past newspaper reporter, he knew that journalists were always in search of interesting newsworthy items, and he relentlessly kept the press up to date on his company and its automobile developments. It also would not have hurt that some well-known advertising and newspaper men were company stockholders.

Despite Jordan's statement that his automobile was an assembled vehicle, it was far more. Its sporty appearance was complemented by impressive performance. Handling was light and supple, due in no small part to the vehicle bodies being made of aluminum rather than steel. The resulting lighter overall weight gave livelier acceleration, ease of handling, and better gasoline mileage, all of which was uniquely appealing to women.

There were also production benefits for Jordan, as aluminum bodies could be shaped using wooden forms and bucks, which were far cheaper to make than the metal dies required for forming sheet steel into body panels. As a result, changes in body styles could be made much more inexpensively and quickly with wood forms. These first aluminum-bodied Jordans had a six-cylinder engine rated at 29.4 horsepower, rode on a 127 inch wheelbase, and were priced at $1,650.

No sooner had Jordan embarked on his venture than World War I intervened, limiting availability of such war materiel as steel and aluminum, and depriving factories of their manpower.

Although the country's war involvement detrimentally affected all Cleveland automobile companies, Jordan negotiated the war period reasonably well, and emerged with its business virtually intact, with 1917 production of 1,727 vehicles—nearly equal to the previous year's production.

By 1919 things were improving rapidly and a plant expansion was needed to accommodate a 150 percent increase in production,[9] as this was the year that the most celebrated Jordan of all, the Playboy, was introduced. The Playboy, although not appreciably different from the other Jordans in terms of engine and wheelbase, had a top speed of 65 miles per hour, and a selling price of $2,175.

Ned Jordan had always displayed a talent for clever advertising, but the ads which he created for the Playboy were extraordinary for the era. His presentation of the Playboy could even be considered a watershed moment in American automobile advertising. Although the Playboy itself was a very respectable vehicle, it was the image of the automobile which made it a sales success.

By emphasizing image rather than performance, and consciously making an appeal to female purchasers, Jordan placed romantic full-page ads for the Playboy in major magazines. One of these presentations began with the arresting statement "Someday in June, when happy hours abound." But, by far, the most famous of Jordan's ads bore the caption "Somewhere west of Laramie." The Playboy was an instant hit.

That same year the Jordan company was reorganized to allow for increased financing, and a new name was adopted: Jordan Motor Car Company, Inc.

However, just at this time Jordan production slowed, something which Ned Jordan blamed on the competition from Ford, which had reduced the price of its Model T substantially.[10] In fact, a temporary slowdown was being experienced by all Cleveland automobile manufacturers at this time, regardless of vehicle price range.

Fortunately, by the end of March 1921, the market for all automobiles was recovering. During 1921 Jordan had increased production by 100 percent, and turned out over 8,000 automobiles that year.[11] The company now announced that it was free of debt and had a very substantial surplus on hand.[12]

The year 1923 proved to be a good one for Jordan, with production running at 1,000 automobiles per month during the first months of the year. To keep momentum up, prices were cut across the board in May, and sales for the year were said to have reached 10,147 vehicles.[13]

But a new factor began to affect the automobile scene. Used vehicles were flooding the market, and this caused demand to decline and prices for new vehicles to suffer. At this point Jordan instituted a program to help its dealers.

Clear standards were set for the reconditioning of used Jordans, so that purchasers of these pre-owned automobiles knew that their vehicle had achieved "The Mark of Jordan Service" standard. Trade allowances were also adjusted according to a company scale, to reflect the amount of work required to recondition the automobile. All prices and allowances were set by the Jordan company.[14]

This and other policies, along with manufacturing improvements, led to a successful 1924.

In 1925, a Jordan-designed straight-eight built by Continental was introduced, and sold well from the beginning. Also new that year were Budd-built steel car bodies, which were assembled at the Edw. G. Budd Mfg. Co. in Philadelphia and shipped to Jordan ready for trim work and installation. Previously, Jordan bodies had been built at a variety of Cleveland locations, including the predecessor of bicycle maker Murray Ohio Manufacturing Company, and at a plant which Jordan had leased from the auto body manufacturer Briggs Manufacturing Company in 1923.[15]

Even with the expenses resulting from the introduction of the steel bodies and straight-eight engines, Jordan remained free of debt and showed ever-increasing production levels, while at the same time adding 250 new dealers.[16]

The year 1926 started out strongly, but by the time 1927 was in sight, automotive sales prospects had changed. Like many other manufacturers, Jordan had over-produced during 1926 in anticipation of a favorable market.

Additionally, Jordan had chosen this year to introduce its new smaller automobile, the Little Custom. Heavy advance promotion to build up public demand had begun in December, and in January 1927 a lavish national advertising campaign accompanied the presentation of the Little Custom at the New York Automobile Show.

The Little Custom was quite different from prior Jordan models. It sported a more powerful six-cylinder engine, which delivered 60 horsepower, had a roofline only 60 inches from the ground, and rode on a compact 107-inch wheelbase. Capable of a top speed of 70 miles per hour, it was offered at a very modest price of $1,595.

However, with 4,000 1926 models on hand as the year drew to a close, Jordan was in a tight spot. The company was forced to hold back production and delivery of the Little Custom, while it worked to sell off its large inventory of 1926 models.

When the Little Custom was finally made available for sale five months after its formal introduction, the market for it had weakened.[17] As a result, Jordan was in a very bad position, with unsold prior year inventory on hand, and a new model which failed to meet sales expectations. The following year compounded Jordan's problems, as 10,000 automobiles were built, and only 6,357 were sold.[18]

Management changes were announced in March 1928, as several key people left Jordan for what they saw as more promising prospects.

The need for additional capital was resolved in September by a stock offering, the banks taking what had not been sold.

As 1928 was ushered in, press releases to the trade media announced that the pace at Jordan had reached almost frenetic levels. Production was constantly being increased. A redesigned version of the Little Custom was presented with sales of this model said to be better than any that came before, a newly designed light straight-eight was in the works, more orders were on hand for immediate shipment than at any time in the company's history, and dealer stocks were at an all-time low.[19]

However media hype did not match reality. *Cram's Automotive Reports, Inc.* issued a lengthy analysis of the Jordan company in January 1929, pointing out that Jordan's main problem was its outmoded method of manufacture, and that unless this matter was addressed, the company could not survive. The report went on to say that, if this problem were solved and volume production were instituted, the Jordan would be one of the outstanding automobiles from the sales standpoint in the industry.

Then came the stock market crash of 1929. When the economy went into a tailspin, all automobile companies scrambled to survive. At Jordan, a management shakeup soon followed, and Ned Jordan, no longer in control of the company, became a mere figurehead. Short of capital, the company was unable to pursue the recommendations of the Cram report without a substantial infusion of more new cash.

Jordan was approached by New Era Motors Inc. in early 1930 with a merger proposal to bring together the Kissel, Gardner, Moon, Stutz, and Jordan companies under one corporate umbrella.[20] Jordan passed on this venture and, instead, in October proposed a restructuring of the company to raise capital with the intention of manufacturing a new type of automobile.[21]

Nevertheless, Jordan remained aware of the benefit of cooperative ventures, and in 1931 an attempt to arrange a purchasing alliance with another automobile manufacturer was considered.

A last desperate effort for Jordan's survival was made with an imaginative proposal for an arrangement with the Brotherhood of Locomotive Engineers. This would have traded the goodwill of the BLE's 90,000 members in promoting the sale of the Jordan, for a five year BLE option to purchase new Jordan company stock at a fixed price.[22] This effort was to no avail.

Although Jordan had survived the First World War, it could not weather the Great Depression. Production ceased in March 1932, and a receiver was appointed in May. The receivers were allowed to produce 262 Jordans to fill a standing order from Felze Motor Sales, Inc., and the bankruptcy was concluded by November of that year.[23]

The purchaser in bankruptcy was a consortium of the company's management team, which organized itself as Jordan Motors, Inc. Ned Jordan was now out of the picture, but what remained of the old Jordan company had been acquired along with the rights to the name. The group intended to resume production with a new 1933 Jordan that was to retain the characteristics of the original Jordan.[24]

Unfortunately, nothing came of this venture and, after having produced 78,780 vehicles over its lifetime, a level of production that was exceeded by only one other Cleveland automobile company, Chandler, the Jordan was no more.[25]

---

1. *The Automobile*, January 20, 1916.
2. Jordan, *The Inside Story of Adam and Eve*.
3. *The Automobile*, February 10, 1916.
4. *The Automobile*, April 21, June 8, 1916.
5. *The Automobile*, August 31, 1916.
6. *The Automobile*, September 28, 1916; February 8, October 20, 1917.
7. *The Automobile*, August 30, 1917.
8. *The Automobile*, January 27, 1916.
9. *Automotive Industries*, May 15, 1919.
10. *Automotive Industries*, December 16, 1920.
11. *Automotive Industries*, March 31, 1921; October 12, 1922.
12. *Automotive Industries*, January 11, 1923.
13. *Automotive Industries*, May 24, June 7, July 19, 1923.
14. *Automotive Industries*, April 26, 1923.
15. *Automotive Industries*, November 5, 1925; March 10, October 6, 1928. Note that *Automotive Industries* incorrectly identifies the Murray company as Murray Corporation of America, a manufacturer of automobile bodies, which is located in Detroit.
16. *Automotive Industries*, March 18, December 16, 1926.

17. Lackey, *The Jordan Automobile*.
18. Kimes and Clark, *Standard Catalog of American Cars, 1805–1942*, 3d ed.
19. *Automotive Industries*, March 12, April 23, May 14, August 20, 1927; February 25, March 31, April 14, May 5, June 23, 1928.
20. *Automotive Industries*, March 29, 1930.
21. *Automotive Industries*, October 11, 1930.
22. *Automotive Industries*, April 4, 1931: Jordan company and the Brotherhood occupied adjoining offices in a downtown office building.
23. *Automotive Industries*, May 16, August 1, 1931.
24. *Automotive Industries*, November 19, 1932.
25. *Automotive Industries*, November 19, 1932; *Cars, 1805–1942*, 3d ed.

Kimple, George W. (1914)

With the assistance of a local blacksmith shop, George W. Kimple built a cyclecar of his own design. The engine was an air-cooled V-2 mounted on a 100-inch wheelbase with a 48-inch tread.[1] All the components were made by Mr. Kimple and he planned to price the cyclecar at $375. No formal organization was established to carry out this project and it is likely that only the one prototype was built.[2]

1. Kimes and Clark, *Standard Catalog of American Cars, 1805–1942*, 3d ed.
2. Wager, *Golden Wheels*.

King Cyclecar Company (1914)

The King Cyclecar Company of Cleveland announced its intention to produce a cyclecar to be named the Ambler. It is not known whether an example of the Ambler was actually produced.[1]

1. Kimes and Clark, *Standard Catalog of American Cars, 1805–1942*, 3d ed.; Wager, *Golden Wheels*.

Kirk-Latty Manufacturing Company (1903)

The Kirk-Latty company was in the business of making bolts for use in carriages, stoves, and heavy machines, as well as a variety of automobile parts. It also manufactured velocipedes, wagons, and wire-wheeled toys for children.

In November 1902 the company managers resolved to build a four-cylinder right-hand drive automobile, which was designated as Automobile No. 3.[1] Judging from this we may presume that previous automobiles had at least been attempted and there is evidence that the company in fact did build at least two automobiles.[2]

By February 1903 the company had completed Automobile No. 3 and was testing a new touring-type vehicle on city streets, with the announced intention of manufacturing the automobile on an extensive basis.[3]

It subsequently developed that although a few automobiles had been built for use by members of the company, Kirk-Latty had a change of heart and now had no intention of engaging in the regular manufacture of automobiles.[4] Kirk-Latty abandoned its automobile endeavor and returned to its core business.

1. Specifications for Automobile No. 3, November 28, 1903, Western Reserve Historical Society Library.
2. Letter, George Case, the Lamson & Sessions Co., November 7, 1944, Western Reserve Historical Society Library.
3. *Motor Age*, February 26, 1903; *The Automobile*, March 14, 1903.
4. *The Automobile*, October 3, 1903.

Kohl & Gates Motor Company (1900 to 1902)

Guided by Edward Kohl, this company built a line of gasoline-powered automobiles utilizing a four-stroke one-cylinder engine. Powered by a six horsepower engine, this 900 pound two-speed vehicle was capable of thirty-five miles per hour. Between 1900 and 1902 approximately two dozen Kohls were constructed.[1]

In late 1902 Edward Kohl left for New York where he organized the Kohl Automobile Company and constructed a new prototype vehicle which he planned to market, but his venture ended abruptly and he engaged in no further automotive endeavors.[2]

1. Kimes and Clark, *Standard Catalog of American Cars, 1805–1942*, 3d ed.
2. *The Horseless Age*, June 25, 1902, p. 767; *The Automobile and Motor Review*, October 13, 1902, Antique Automobile Club of America Library.

Krastin Automobile Manufacturing Company (1901 to 1904)

August Krastin had been experimenting with an automobile of his own design for several years before he formed the Krastin

August Krastin demonstrates his unusual steering device on the 1902 Krastin. Tilting the column left or right changed the vehicle's direction. Turning the wheel to the right disengaged the clutch and shifted the gears; turning it to the left put the car in reverse. The Krastin cost $2,500 and weighed 1,900 pounds.

company in 1901. Although an advertisement was run in the *Cleveland Leader* in 1902 announcing that the company was geared up to produce seven vehicles per week, it may not have been until 1903 that Krastin actually completed and sold his first vehicle.[1] The development of the Krastin automobile took a considerable amount of time because August was a perfectionist. It seemed that whenever he encountered a situation which he felt had not been adequately addressed by existing methodology, he embarked on an effort to improve it to his satisfaction.

As a result he received numerous patents along the way. These included such innovations as a screw-type noiseless muffler, a smokeless carburetor, and a device that appeared to be a column-mounted steering wheel, but actually controlled the clutch and shifted the transmission, while the column upon which it was mounted acted as a tiller which steered the automobile.[2]

The Krastin, a two-cylinder runabout, was priced at $2,500 which indicates that August placed considerable added value on the numerous patented innovations he had incorporated in his automobile.

Before the Krastin company gained its footing, a fire destroyed the factory and its contents. The loss was uninsured and as a result the company was bankrupt and closed its doors in 1904. It appears that only four Krastin automobiles were produced.[3]

---

1. *The Automobile*, October 3, 1903; Western Reserve Historical Society, Krastin files, newspaper article, July 20, 1960.
2. Kimes and Clark, *Standard Catalog of American Cars, 1805–1942*, 3d ed.
3. Ibid.

Kurtz, Cyrus B. (ca. 1906); Kurtz Motor Car Company (1920 to 1925)

Cyrus B. Kurtz built his first two automobiles while attending college at Cleveland's

Case School of Applied Science, from which he graduated in 1906. He built these automobiles in a chicken coop on his family's West Side Cleveland farm. Although not in as glamorous a situation as was another Case student, Frank B. Stearns, who had built his first automobile in the basement of his parents' Millionaires Row mansion, Kurtz was equally talented.[1]

His first efforts were impressive. While out road testing one of his automobiles he encountered famous race driver Barney Oldfield, who was driving the Winton Bullet No. 2, and a short race ensued. After driving in close contention for some distance, Oldfield waved Kurtz over to the side of the road and complimented Kurtz on the quality of his machine.[2]

After graduating from Case, Kurtz continued to pursue his interest in motorized vehicles, working for a variety of automobile-related companies including Spaulding, in Grinnell, Iowa. By 1916 his continual experimentation and inventiveness had brought him numerous patents and he decided to devote his full attention to automotive inventions. He returned to Cleveland to pursue this line of work and established the Kurtz Syndicate with the backing of local investors.

The most advanced of his creations was the semi-automatic transmission, an achievement years ahead of its time. Based upon this patent the syndicate decided to go into the automobile business and build a vehicle that featured the Kurtz automatic transmission. The Kurtz Motor Car Company was formed in 1920 for this purpose, and it operated separately from the syndicate, which continued to manage the other Kurtz patents.[3]

A new single-story factory was constructed on Cleveland's southwest side and the first Kurtz Automatic appeared that year. The shifting mechanism was operated by a lever on a pre-selector mounted on the steering wheel. By moving the lever to indicate the desired gear and then depressing the clutch pedal, the shift occurred instantly with no clashing of gear teeth. With the shift lever eliminated from the floor and the emergency brake handle relocated to the dashboard, the Kurtz Automatic was advertised as "The Car with a Clean Floor," as well as "The Car of Tomorrow" and "America's Most Advanced Motor Car."

The Kurtz Automatic was an assembled automobile. Herschel-Spillman furnished the six-cylinder engine and Westinghouse furnished the lighting and starter systems. For 1921 the body colors offered were Colorado Blue or Brewster Green with the hood, fenders and splash plates painted black.[4]

In January 1922 Kurtz company claimed to be making one car per day, and by April said they were up to five per day and selling every one of them.[5] This was more boosterism than reality. Over three years of existence production appears to have totaled somewhere between 250 and 600 automobiles.[6] In 1924 an eight-cylinder version was offered with engine by Lycoming and body by Bender Body Company of Cleveland. For 1925, three prototype vehicles were assembled and some sales brochures were printed.

The Kurtz Automatic was a quality automobile throughout and garnered an excellent reputation. Consideration was given to expanding production capabilities significantly, which would have required a $3 million investment. When it was found that this sum could not conveniently be raised locally it was decided to quit the automobile business and focus on the Kurtz Syndicate operations instead.

Cyrus Kurtz continued his activity as an inventor and ultimately patented what was called a "doorless lamp," the predecessor to the sealed-beam headlight.

---

1. Kimes and Clark, *Standard Catalog of American Cars, 1805–1942*, 3d ed.
2. Wager, *Golden Wheels*.
3. Kimes and Clark, *Standard Catalog of American Cars, 1805–1942*, 3d ed., notes that other sources say 1921.
4. *Motor Age*, January 27, 1921.
5. *Automotive Industries*, January 12, April 7, 1922.
6. Ibid.; *Golden Wheels* says 250 were produced. *Standard Catalog of American Cars* notes that other sources say few more than 600 were built.

LaMarne Motor Company (1919 to 1920)

The LaMarne automobile was Francois Richard's swan song. He had three prior automobile names to his credit including the Only, Metropol, and RiChard, all of which had relatively brief lives. It appears that the LaMarne had the shortest life of them all. It picked up where the RiChard had left off, taking over the manufacturing facility and equipment previously the domain of the RiChard. (See Richard Auto Manufacturing Company.)

Like the RiChard, the LaMarne was a large and imposing automobile and featured an eight-cylinder engine which was undoubtedly a carryover from its predecessor. It was modified to some extent with a reduced bore and stroke size, and a claimed increase in horsepower from forty-five to eighty-five. The LaMarne also had a shorter wheelbase of 128 inches down from 137 inches for the RiChard, and came with a hard and permanently affixed touring-style top, retractable headlights, like those on the RiChard, and a visored windshield.[1]

The LaMarne was constructed and sold on a contract basis with the prospective purchaser. It is doubtful that the LaMarne could have been built for as little as the offering price of $1,485.

It is also doubtful that more than a handful of LaMarnes were produced, although it is said that at least one was built under license in Canada by Anglo-American Motors, Ltd.[2]

By the end of 1920 the LaMarne Motor Company had ceased to exist and Francois Richard was no longer involved in the manufacture of automobiles.[3]

---

1. "LaMarne—The Great Sensation of 1920," advertisement, 1920: As with the RiChard sales brochures the automobile depicted is a rendering and not a photograph of an actual automobile.
2. Kimes and Clark, *Standard Catalog of American Cars, 1805–1942*, 3d ed.
3. Wager, *Golden Wheels*.

Levy, S.M. (1901)

S.M. Levy announced in a 1901 summer issue of *Motor Vehicle Review* that the construction of a Levy electric was under way with distribution to be by Squires Company. The effort never assumed corporate form and no more was heard.[1]

---

1. Kimes and Clark, *Standard Catalog of American Cars, 1805–1942*, 3d ed.

Lincoln Electric Company (1900)

In a proof of concept effort the Lincoln Electric Company assembled a 2½ horsepower electric vehicle that weighed 1,175 pounds and could go twenty-five percent farther without recharge than similar electric vehicles. This performance was achieved thanks to a specially designed "Lincoln Controller," which compensated for the inefficiencies of a series motor, that operated best under heavy loads but poorly when under light loads, by holding the shunt fields at a constant level whatever the voltage level on the armature may have been.[1] The vehicle utilized Cleveland-made Willard batteries as its power source. One prototype vehicle was made but it is doubtful that other examples followed. Apparently the company abandoned the project by 1901.[2]

---

1. Kimes and Clark, *Standard Catalog of American Cars, 1805–1942*, 3d ed.
2. *The Motor Age*, October 6, 1900, Antique Automobile Club of America Library.

Lohse Automobile Improvement Company (1914)

Incorporated to manufacture motors, cars, and accessories the Lohse company was capitalized at $25,000. Organizers were B. Ryder, W.G. Rauder, M. Reitz, R. Lohse, and K.C. Wehrmeyer. Actual production is unlikely.[1]

---

1. Kimes and Clark, *Standard Catalog of American Cars, 1805–1942*, 3d ed.

Maclaren Company (1911)

The Maclaren Company was formed in 1911 by Don P. Maclaren, Harry H. Hamilton, W.R. Godfey, and R.W. Sanborn to manufacture and deal in automobiles. Capitalization was set at $10,000. It is unlikely an automobile was produced.[1]

---

1. Kimes and Clark, *Standard Catalog of American Cars, 1805–1942*, 3d ed.

Marsh Motors Company (1919 to 1924)

Brothers Alonzo and William Marsh had an impressive background as engineers and automobile manufacturers before relocating to Cleveland in 1919, perhaps enticed by the

Cleveland Chamber of Commerce. While in Brockton, Massachusetts, they had produced several automobiles, including the Marsh (1905), the Eastern (1910), the Lima Roadster (1912), and the Sterling (1915). Although none of these vehicles achieved commercial success, the brothers did prosper from their World War I munitions manufacturing contracts.

In 1919, the Marsh brothers, along with Alonzo's sons David and Bennett, moved to Cleveland, where they set up business with the intention of producing an attractive alternative to Henry Ford's Model T.[1] The Marsh Motors Company was incorporated in Cleveland in 1919, and plant construction was expected to begin immediately on a one-story wood-frame structure built of timber from woodlands that Alonzo and William owned in New England.[2] This venture was entirely financed by investors from the brothers' Massachusetts home town.[3] By 1921, prototype vehicles were being assembled in the new plant, with full production expected to begin in early 1922.[4]

These prototype vehicles included four 114-inch wheelbase four-cylinder automobiles and two 117-inch wheelbase sixes. The engines were by Continental, and the bodies were hand-built of aluminum, installed over a wood frame. The final production version of the Marsh was to be priced at $1,450.[5] Deemed to be "snappy little cars" by some observers, two of these prototypes were driven to Nova Scotia and back as a demonstration of their reliability.

However, despite having struggled through the post-war depression, the Marsh company was unable to construct more than these six prototype vehicles before going into receivership in June 1923.[6] To make matters worse, in 1924, while still in receivership, a fire destroyed the main Marsh factory building, and with it several of the Marsh prototype automobiles. Nevertheless, the company managed to pay stockholders fifty cents for every dollar of their investment.

After the Marsh company was dissolved, Alonzo Marsh remained at the Marsh factory location, doing business in used machinery.

1. Kimes and Clark, *Standard Catalog of American Cars, 1805–1942*, 3d ed.
2. Wager, *Golden Wheels*.
3. *Automotive Industries*, April 8, 1920.
4. *Automotive Industries*, January 12, 1922; Wager, *Golden Wheels*.
5. Kimes and Clark, *Standard Catalog of American Cars, 1805–1942*, 3d ed.; Wager, *Golden Wheels*.
6. Kimes and Clark, *Standard Catalog of American Cars, 1805–1942*, 3d ed.; Wager, *Golden Wheels*.

Master Motor Car Company (1917 to 1918)

Organized with the substantial sum of $200,000, the Master company intended to manufacture motorcars. The vehicles were to be priced at $5,000 and powered by a 100 horsepower six-cylinder engine. Three body styles were offered including touring, runabout, and limousine. Automobile production might have taken place, but it seems more likely that the Master company only produced a limited number of commercial vehicles.[1]

1. Kimes and Clark, *Standard Catalog of American Cars, 1805–1942*, 3d ed.

McIntosh Brothers (1903)

Very little is known about this venture and it may be that no automobile was actually built. The brothers, who were machinists and built bicycles, announced in October 1903 that they had developed a gasoline-powered automobile which was characterized as being "satisfactory," a rather uninspired statement when compared to contemporary announcements by other early entrepreneurs. Nevertheless, it was said that the brothers planned to go into production the following year.[1]

That is the first and the last heard from the brothers McIntosh and their automobile.

1. *The Automobile*, October 24, 1903; Kimes and Clark, *Standard Catalog of American Cars, 1805–1942*, 3d ed.

Mercury Motor Car Company (1920)

The Mercury company intended to produce high-priced luxury automobiles using a four-cylinder 81 horsepower Rochester-Duesenberg engine. The automobiles were to have a 138-inch wheelbase, and only open-body styles would be offered. Regardless of body type, all automobiles were to be priced at an ambitious $6,750. Although advertisements were run for the Mercury, there is no solid evidence of any being produced. If any were, it would have been a very limited number.[1]

---

1. Kimes and Clark, *Standard Catalog of American Cars, 1805–1942*, 3d ed.

Merit Motor Company (1920 to 1922)

Billed as "The Finest Light Six in the World," the Merit automobile had a lot to live up to. It was an assembled automobile, as were many others of the era, but the careful selection of components resulted in a very fine vehicle.

The Merit rode on a 119-inch wheelbase and had extra-long springs to provide a smooth ride. It was powered by a Continental six-cylinder engine with a Stromberg carburetor. The two-wheel rear drum brakes were of the combination external-contracting and internal-expanding type. Delco furnished the ignition, starter, and lighting systems. The upholstery was high-grade genuine leather, provided in colors to match the body finish. Other styling highlights included one-piece fenders, an all-season top, and a slanted windshield. All of this was offered as standard for $1,985.

The Merit Motor Company had been formed in 1920 by pharmacist Bert F. Landefeld and department store owner Henry J. Berger, whose business establishments were near one another on Cleveland's West Side. The entrepreneurs set up their factory in rented quarters on Cleveland's East Side, and began construction of a prototype automobile in preparation for the 1921 New York Automobile Show, which was to take place in January.[1]

While finishing touches were being applied, the prototype was almost destroyed when a wet coat of varnish was ignited by an oil heater. Although the Merit prototype did not make it to the New York show, it did appear later that year at the 1921 Cleveland Automobile Show,[2] where it received a favorable reception.

Shortly afterwards the company announced that it had received 500 orders for its 1921 model.[3] For 1922 the company ran a clever advertisement picturing Miss Mae Murray, a "famous and charming screen artist" of the day, who "voted yes" for the new Merit.[4]

Unfortunately, like other automobile manufacturers which started up immediately after World War I, the Merit company had to contend with unfavorable economic conditions. At that time, the average annual earnings, for those fortunate enough to be employed, were $1,250, and most teachers made a mere $920. Under these circumstances, the purchase of a Merit was not an inexpensive investment.

Sales were slow, and even a 1922 price reduction to $1,895 did not improve matters. The end came quickly for Merit, and production ceased. Overall, sixty-seven 1921 Merits had been built, plus an additional eighty-two models for 1922.[5] Landefeld returned to his pharmacy and Berger to his department store, and Mae Murray returned silently to her film career.

---

1. Kimes and Clark, *Standard Catalog of American Cars, 1805–1942*, 3d ed.
2. Wager, *Golden Wheels*.
3. *Automotive Industries*, April 21, 1921.
4. *Motor Age*, The Merit, advertisement, November 3, 1921: It is intriguing that two start-up automobile entrepreneurs and small businessmen were able to secure the endorsement of one of Hollywood's silent film stars.
5. *Standard Catalog of American Cars* notes that one source states that production records had been lost and estimated no more than 75 Merits having been produced (see *Golden Wheels*).

Metropolitan Garage Company (1913)

Incorporators were C. Mulvahy, H.C. and W.I. Quigley, H. Loeb, and M. Schwab. Capitalization was a very inadequate $5,000. The company was said to be organized to manufacture and deal in automobiles and to operate a garage. It may be that a garage business was successfully undertaken, although a capitalization of $5,000 seems inadequate even for that modest objective. There is no evidence that an automobile was ever produced.[1]

---

1. Kimes and Clark, *Standard Catalog of American Cars, 1805–1942*, 3d ed.

Minch, Captain Philip J. (1909)

The *Standard Catalog of American Cars* mentions Captain Philip J. Minch under a heading for Cleveland automobiles. It is stated

The Manufacturers Monarch

that the Captain had constructed a four-passenger electric roadster and that he was in search of a location for its production. It also cites an August 1909 *Horseless Age* announcement that Minch was seriously considering Springfield as a location for a plant. In any event, nothing ever came of the Minch automobile beyond the first experimental vehicle.[1]

1. Kimes and Clark, *Standard Catalog of American Cars, 1805-1942*, 3d ed.

Monarch Motor Car Company (1906)

W.D. Drown, a Cleveland electrician and aspiring automobile enthusiast, built a large 90 horsepower automobile which he entered in the Gates Mills (Ohio) Hill Climb in 1906.[1] The vehicle's performance on that Memorial Day was impressive, even though it crashed when Drown failed to successfully negotiate a particularly challenging turn.[2] Watching from the sidelines, brothers Irwin and Bernard Gutherie thought enough of Drown's automobile that they agreed to join forces with him that October to form the Monarch Motor Car Company.[3]

Monarch planned to construct sixty vehicles based on Drown's original automobile. Fifty of them were to be 40–45 horsepower touring cars, and ten would be 90 horsepower versions of Drown's hill-climb vehicle.[4] These 120-inch wheelbase automobiles were to have many advanced features, including rear-wheel braking which employed a combination of internal-expanding and external-contracting brakes. The Monarch's valve-in-head engine was similar to the highly successful one which Walter L. Marr had designed for Buick in 1903, and employed intake and exhaust manifolds on opposite sides of the engine block. Priced at $4,500, this large automobile was offered with either a shaft or double-chain drive.[5]

By December of 1906 the company had rented a portion of the Broc Carriage Company plant on Cleveland's East Side for construction of its automobiles, and preparations were under way for the coming year's production. (See Broc Carriage & Wagon Company.) At

W. D. DROWN IN 90-HORSEPOWER MONARCH

The four cylinder 1906 Monarch provided 90 horsepower for this high-powered version of what its high-powered promoters hoped would become an entire line of automobiles.

this point, Monarch hired noted race driver Fred Crum to campaign the new Monarch automobile and act as its demonstrator and salesman.

Although it was said that a 120 horsepower version of the Monarch was under construction at the end of 1906, apparently only the first hill-climb prototype was ever built, and there the story ends.

---

1. Kimes and Clark, *Standard Catalog of American Cars, 1805–1942*, 3d ed.
2. Wager, *Golden Wheels*.
3. Kimes and Clark, *Standard Catalog of American Cars, 1805–1942*, 3d ed.
4. *The Automobile*, December 20, 1906.
5. Ibid.

Moore, Harry S. (1903 to 1904; 1906)

Harry S. Moore had been in the business of repairing automobiles on Cleveland's East Side since 1900. By 1903 Moore had also become a dealer for Shelby and Elmore automobiles (see Beardsley & Hubbs Manufacturing Company, and Elmore Manufacturing Company in Part II).

However, Moore soon began having difficulty obtaining timely delivery of automobiles and parts for his dealership, and it occurred to him that he might solve this problem by becoming an automobile manufacturer in his own right. Moore moved very quickly along these lines, and acquired the Star Automobile Company (see Star Automobile Company) of Cleveland in 1903,[1] relocating the Star manufacturing operation to his East Side repair facility.

The year 1904 was a very busy one for Moore, but unfortunately, not a very successful one. Moore began by offering Star automobiles of his own manufacture at prices ranging from $900 to $1,000.[2] Also, in order to expand his dealership offerings, he introduced the spartan Buckboard, which was made in Massachusetts by the Waltham Manufacturing Company.

The Buckboard was said to be the cheapest machine on the market and was, in many ways, hardly more than the automotive equivalent of its horse-drawn namesake, although it did have leaf springs at each of its four wheels, in contrast to the under-seat elliptical springs which provided the ride for which the horse-drawn buckboard was famous.

Despite its highly successful introduction at the Detroit Automobile Show, the Buckboard was not a profitable venture for Moore, and he ceased to offer it for sale within the year.[3] Likewise, sales of the Star did not meet expectations, and its production was discontinued by the end of 1904.

No more mention is made of any manufacturing endeavors on Moore's part. It is known that in 1906 he was still the proprietor of an automobile repair facility, and that he had enlarged his automobile dealership to include sales of Stoddard-Dayton (see Stoddard-Dayton Manufacturing Company and Dayton Motor Car Company in Part II), as well as Orient and Queen automobiles.[4]

But, the story does not end here. Although Moore had discontinued his manufacturing endeavors, he never lost interest in automotive innovation.

The Auburn-Moore Special, a custom-made vehicle built on an Auburn chassis, made its appearance at the Cleveland Automobile Show in February 1906. As described in *The Horseless Age* Vol. 17, March 1906, it was a five-passenger touring model which rode on a 94-inch wheelbase, had an opposed two-cylinder engine, and was capable of speeds ranging from 3 to 40 miles per hour. Most likely commissioned for Moore's personal use and customized based on his years of automotive experience, the vehicle may have been assembled at Moore's repair shops in Cleveland. However, the actual builder and location of its assembly are not known.

---

1. *Motor Age*, December 8, 1903.
2. Wager, *Golden Wheels*.
3. *The Automobile Review*, April 1904; Kimes and Clark, *Standard Catalog of American Cars, 1805–1942*, 3d ed.
4. Kimes and Clark, *Standard Catalog of American Cars, 1805–1942*, 3d ed.

Morrison, Fred (1902)

A trade journal reported that Fred Morrison was experimenting with construction of an automobile. Whether an automobile was actually produced is speculative and details are unavailable.[1]

1. Kimes and Clark, *Standard Catalog of American Cars, 1805–1942*, 3d ed.

Noble Automobile Manufacturing Company (1902)

Activities of the Noble company were reported in a trade publication article datelined Cleveland, September 28, 1902, wherein it was announced that the company would soon begin manufacturing an automobile. The article went on to say that the company had been working on an experimental vehicle for five months, and its success encouraged the introduction of a line of three different style gasoline-powered vehicles. The primary automobile was to be a medium-weight single-cylinder vehicle priced at $800.[1] It has been suggested that, in addition to the experimental prototype, one or two examples of the intended basic automobile were built although whether this happened is not known with certainty.[2]

The company's only known sale was of a complete chassis with running gear to a Washington, D.C., scissors grinder who intended to add a body to suit his commercial needs. His equipment was to be driven by a pulley mounted on the engine shaft, which had been specially extended for this purpose. J.C. Meader of the Noble company felt that if this commercial application of the chassis was successful it would present additional opportunities for Noble.

Unfortunately, Mr. Meader's optimism proved to be unjustified, as it was not long before the company was attached for back wages and the Noble experiment ended.[3]

1. *The Automobile and Motor Review*, October 4, 1902.
2. Kimes and Clark, *Standard Catalog of American Cars, 1805–1942*, 3d ed.
3. Ibid.

Ohio Motor Vehicle Company (1919 to 1922)

In a sort of cart-before-the-horse situation, the Ohio Trailer Company of Cleveland became the Ohio Motor Vehicle Company in 1919.[1] Its new purpose was to be the manufacturer of an automobile of "distinction with an elegant bearing that exuded character," quite a change from making two-wheel utility trailers. The company was clearly up to the task it had set for itself. Its Ferris automobile had clean elegant lines and was quite handsome. With a base price of $3,390, it was relatively expensive for a six-passenger touring model, and thus had to appeal to those who were able to afford a little luxury in their lives.[2]

Not surprisingly, production was low, with only 123 automobiles being built in 1920, its first year of production. Things were somewhat better the next year, with 214 having found owners.[3]

But midway through its second year the Ohio company placed itself in voluntary receivership to ward off claims of small creditors and to protect both the company and its engine

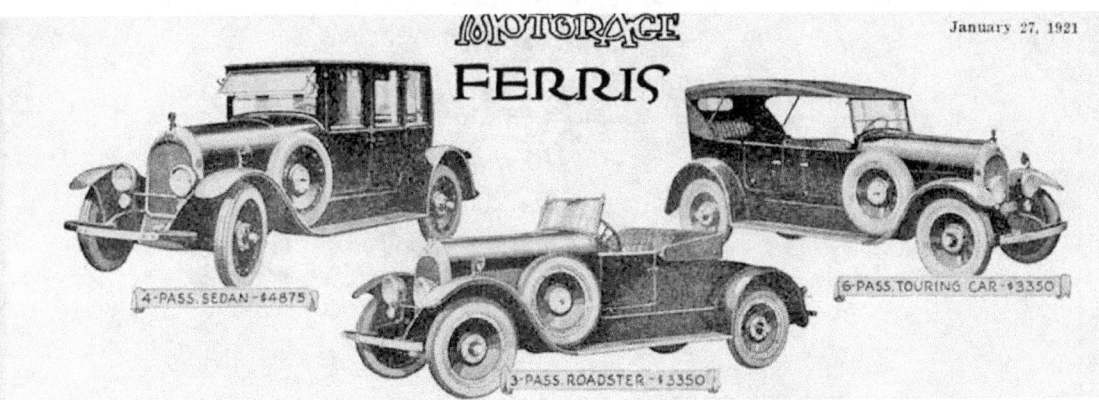

The aluminum bodied 1921 Ferris was not an inexpensive automobile, with the most expensive version, a four-passenger sedan, costing $4,875. Wire wheels were a seldom seen option.

supplier, Continental Motors Corporation. Although its assets were well in excess of its liabilities the company did not have the financial liquidity necessary to satisfy all of its claimants. Nevertheless, preferred creditors were paid off. William E. Ferris, the company treasurer and one of its receivers, successfully acted to continue production of automobiles for the balance of 1921, and new models were introduced for 1922.[4]

That was to be the last hurrah for the Ohio Motor Vehicle Company. Undoubtedly the post-war depression played a part in ending production of the Ferris, which terminated some time during 1922. During this year an additional 103 vehicles were manufactured, bringing the total number of Ferris automobiles built to 440.

---

1. Kimes and Clark, *Standard Catalog of American Cars, 1805–1942*, 3d ed.
2. *Automotive Industries*, January 8, 1920.
3. Kimes and Clark, *Standard Catalog of American Cars, 1805–1942*, 3d ed.
4. *Automotive Industries*, August 11, 1921.

Otto Konigslow Manufacturing Company (1902 to 1904)

The OttoKar was a long time in coming to fruition. Otto Konigslow had previously built thousands of "OK" brand bicycles before he began his automotive experimentations in 1898. By 1902 he was able to present a finished OttoKar automobile to the public. The OttoKar, a reasonably priced two-passenger runabout, was well-built, neat in appearance, and turned in impressive performances in a variety of endurance events, but never achieved the level of public acceptance necessary for the company to continue production beyond 1904.[1]

After building something in excess of fifty examples of the OttoKar, the Konigslow company ceased production, sold its plant and moved to new facilities, where Konigslow concentrated his efforts on the manufacture of a variety of automotive-related components.

Perhaps Konigslow deserves to be best remembered for developing an advanced rotary gasoline engine for use in an automobile.[2] A rotary engine is unusual in that the engine

A 1903 OttoKar could be had for just less than $1,000 and came with a double-opposed engine of 14 horsepower.

block, which contains the cylinders arrayed in a circular fashion, rotates around a fixed crankshaft, whereas a radial engine has a fixed block with a rotating crankshaft. The rotary engine was important in early aircraft through the World War I era, in such airplanes as the Sopwith Camel.

Konigslow never ceased to be an inventor at heart and ultimately held over twenty automobile-related patents.[3]

---

1. *Cycle and Automobile Trade Journal*, February 1903; Kimes and Clark, *Standard Catalog of American Cars, 1805–1942*, 3d ed.
2. *The Automobile*, April 2, 1904.
3. *Cycle and Automobile Trade Journal*, May 1906.

Owen Magnetic Company (1915 to 1919)

We have the ingenuity of Justin B. Entz to thank for the unique transmission that became an integral part of the Owen Magnetic automobile. Instead of a box full of gears to transmit power from engine to rear wheels, Entz relied on the principle of "magnetic attraction" to transmit power to the drive shaft. Entz's 1890 patented invention was first applied to an automobile in 1898. However, it was not until 1912, when Walter C. Baker acquired Entz's patents, that serious work on adapting the Entz transmission for production automobile use began in earnest.[1]

It was at this time that Baker joined together with Cleveland brothers Raymond M. and Ralph R. Owen (see Owen Motor Carriage Company), who had been experimenting with the Entz invention before Baker obtained the patents. The trio worked to develop an automobile using the Entz transmission, and by late 1914 they had a finished prototype which was entered in the New York Automobile Show in January 1915.[2]

Although the initial production of about 250 Owen Magnetic automobiles took place in New York City, the manufacturing operation was moved to Cleveland by the end of 1915.[3] Once relocated to Cleveland, the manufacture of the Owen Magnetic occurred at the plants of Baker R&L Company, of which Raymond M. Owen was now a vice president.

Construction of the Owen Magnetic closely paralleled that of other vehicles being assembled in the Baker R&L facilities at that time. Chassis and running gear were manufactured at Baker R&L's original Baker plant location, and the old Rauch & Lang plant produced the Owen Magnetic bodies. General Electric Company, which held three seats on the Baker R&L board of directors at this time, provided the transmissions.[4]

The Owen Magnetic was an expensive automobile, costing up to $6,500, but its quality and mystique attracted many of the well-to-do and famous. Amongst early owners were noted opera virtuosi Enrico Caruso and John McCormack.

In late 1916, to demonstrate the capabilities of the Owen Magnetic, Raymond Owen sponsored a tour of 800 miles through the challenging countryside of New England. Eleven vehicles, carrying fifty select guests, made the tour, which was proclaimed a complete success.[5]

Unfortunately, the economic situation accompanying World War I intruded on the production of Owen Magnetic automobiles and, although new models were offered in 1918, production was limited. After the war, production began again in 1919, but by mid-year it was decided to terminate the effort, and the last Cleveland-produced Owen Magnetic left the factory, with Cleveland production having reached about 700 automobiles.[6]

Not wishing to surrender to circumstances, Raymond Owen went on to form the Magnetic Motor Company, and moved production of the Owen Magnetic to Wilkes-Barre, Pennsylvania, where the company remained in business until 1921, producing a limited number of automobiles.[7]

---

1. Kimes and Clark, *Standard Catalog of American Cars, 1805–1942*, 3d ed.
2. *The Horseless Age*, vol. 34, no. 6 (1914).
3. Kimes and Clark, *Standard Catalog of American Cars, 1805–1942*, 3d ed.
4. Wager, *Golden Wheels*.
5. *The Automobile*, September 14, 1916.
6. Wager, *Golden Wheels*.
7. Kimes and Clark, *Standard Catalog of American Cars, 1805–1942*, 3d ed.

There was "no gear shifting—no clanking noises—no jerks nor lunges—just a quiet floating sensation" when you drove a 1919 Owen Magnetic. The magnetically coupled transfer of power from engine to wheels gave the Owen Magnetic what was one of the first "automatic" transmissions (author's collection).

Owen Motor Carriage Company (1899 to 1901)

The Owen brothers, Raymond M. and Ralph R., built a motor vehicle to serve as a delivery wagon for their carpet business in 1899. It was designed so that it could be easily converted to act as either a passenger automobile or a delivery vehicle.[1] The vehicle performed quite successfully in their business, and several copies were made and sold.

In 1900 the brothers formed the Phoenix Motor Vehicle and Engine Company as a subsidiary of their business, in order to build trucks. For a short time the Owen Motor Carriage Company sold automobiles using both the Owen and Phoenix names. By early 1900, the Owen and Phoenix brands had several vehicles under construction in both passenger and delivery configurations.[2]

The convertible Owen/Phoenix wagon had a 2-cylinder engine with 5-inch-by-6-inch pistons, and was capable of two speeds forward, producing 6 and 16 miles per hour. The vehicle had a load capacity of 1,200 pounds and, to compensate for this added weight, had two powerful brakes.

Where the Owen brothers actually built their early Cleveland automobiles is not known with precision. Raymond and Ralph lived next door to each other at 1701 and 1705 Russell Street in Cleveland.[3] The *Cleveland City Directory* lists the R.M. Owen Company and the R.R. Owen Machine Shop at these Russell Street addresses as well.[4] The brothers' carpet company was located at what is now 7714 Carnegie Avenue. Owen and Phoenix vehicles may have been assembled at a combination of these locations.

In 1901 the brothers abandoned automobile manufacturing for the time being and changed direction, joining up with the Olds Motor Vehicle Company. Raymond signed on to sell Olds automobiles in New York City, representing himself as the R.M. Owen Company, while Ralph relocated to Lansing, Michigan, as factory manager for Olds.[5] In 1904 when Ransom E. Olds left his eponymously named company to form REO, Raymond followed him and took on a new task as distributor of REO automobiles. Ralph subsequently formed an alliance with former Olds employees to build an Owen automobile in Detroit in 1910.[6]

No more is heard about the Owen brothers' automobile manufacturing endeavors until they reappear in Cleveland in 1915. (See Owen Magnetic Company.)

---

1. *The Horseless Age*, May 31, 1899.
2. *The Motor Review*, February 13, 1900, Antique Automobile Club of America Library.
3. *Automobile*, March 1900: photo of a freshly built Phoenix wagon in a residential back yard.
4. *Cleveland City Directory*, 1898–1902.
5. Kimes and Clark, *Standard Catalog of American Cars, 1805–1942*, 3d ed.
6. *Ibid*.

Palmer Automobile Manufacturing Company (1906)

H.R. Palmer's stated objective was to create a vehicle which would be low-priced and could be operated by an inexperienced person. However, when one considers the complexities involved in operating his automobile, it appears that Palmer may have had in mind an operator who also happened to be an engineer.

Palmer's automobile, presented at the 1906 Cleveland Automobile Show, was quite handsome, rode on an extremely compact 60-inch wheelbase, and was priced between $400 and $500.[1] It was powered by a one-cylinder two-stroke valveless engine, at a time when the typical engine was four-stroke and had valves. To achieve the effect of a differential, rods from the steering wheel were utilized to modulate driving power to the rear wheels, depending upon which direction the automobile was turning.[2]

The vehicle's drive train was the very model of creativity and almost defies description. Instead of utilizing either a shaft or chain drive to transfer power directly to the wheels, Palmer employed a series of ropes, pulleys, jackshafts, shives, and sliding collars, all of which was manipulated by the driver using a variety of hand levers. In addition, the driver had to operate a dual-function foot pedal, using the ball of his foot to engage the clutch, and his heel to place the vehicle in reverse. It is difficult to conceive of an inexperienced driver mastering all of this without lengthy practice.

In addition to his prototype, Palmer had other automotive interests, as he also claimed to have developed an engine which burned crude oil with a combustion chamber that was so designed and insulated that it required no provision for cooling.[3]

H.R. Palmer's prototype vehicle, manufactured in Cleveland, appears to have been the only automobile which he produced.[4] In late 1906, Palmer moved his operations to Ashtabula.[5] However, there is no evidence of any additional vehicles having been built at this location. (See also Euclid Motor Car Company.)

1. *Cycle and Automobile Trade Journal*, April 1906; *The Automobile*, March 1, 1906: The company was identified as the Palmer Motor Car Company.
2. *Horseless Age*, vol. 17, no. 8 (1906).
3. *The Automobile*, June 21, 1906.
4. *Cleveland City Directory*, 1904–1906; Kimes and Clark, *Standard Catalog of American Cars, 1805–1942*, 3d ed.
5. *Horseless Age*, vol. 17, no. 8 (1906): It should be noted that the Ashtabula Historical Society archives contain no record of the Palmer having been produced there.

Paragon Motor Car Company (1919 to 1921)

The Paragon Motor Car Company was formed in late 1919. Its engineering department, located at 6545 Carnegie Avenue, was headed by the former assistant chief engineer for Mercer and Templar companies, Paul F. Hackenthal. Five prototype Paragon automobiles were constructed in Cleveland in 1920 with the expectation that actual production would to take place in Connellsville, Pennsylvania, where financing for the venture had been secured.[1] After having been displayed at the February 1921 Cleveland Automobile Show the five Paragon prototypes were shipped to Connellsville, and four more prototype vehicles

Many things set the 1920 Paragon apart including its radiator shell, crowned fenders, and multi-paned windshield.

This prototype Paragon was completed in 1920 and featured a distinctive boat-tail body with nautical railings and a compartment for golf clubs.

were under construction in Cleveland. The Connellsville manufacturing arrangements seemed to be on sound footing in early to mid-1920.[2] Unfortunately, after the new factory building cornerstone was laid, the financial backing promised in Connellsville did not materialize and the Pennsylvania venture collapsed. However, an attractive offer of financial support was soon received from Cumberland, Maryland, which encouraged the Paragon promoters to relocate once again.[3] But, the Cumberland deal also collapsed. All machinery was brought back Cleveland to be used in the manufacture of Paragon automobiles there. At least nine demonstration examples were produced and it is speculated that in all around two to three dozen vehicles were ultimately turned out in Cleveland.

This very limited production Paragon was a high-quality handsome automobile with attractive styling and unusual features, including a unique prismatic windshield and a massive aluminum Packard-like radiator shell. The Paragon had laminated wood bumpers, a power tire pump and tire gauge, tilt steering wheel, and automatic brake adjustment. The bodies were all aluminum, trimmed in pebble-grain leather, and a Paragon could be painted in any color the purchaser desired.[4] The Paragon's four-cylinder engine was highly engineered with two inlet valves and one exhaust valve per cylinder, extensive use of aluminum, and finely honed reciprocating parts. Priced at $3,000, which would also buy an elegant Stearns Knight or a Peerless, the Paragon appealed to a very limited number of potential purchasers, which may be why the Paragon story came to an end before ever advancing into full scale production.

1. *Society of Automobile Historians*, October 1975, and *Automotive Industries*, January 19, 1920, p. 533, Antique Automobile Club of America Library; Kimes and Clark, *Standard Catalog of American Cars, 1805–1942*, 3d ed.
2. *Automotive Industries*, January 19, April 22, 1920, and *Automobile Trade Journal*, April 1920, p. 266, Antique Automobile Club of America Library.
3. *Automobile Topics*, May 7, 1921, p. 1116, Antique Automobile Club of America Library.
4. Sales brochure "Paragon, The Pattern of Excellence," 1920, Antique Automobile Club of America Library.

Parsons Electric Motor Carriage Company (1905 to 1906)

The Parsons company was formed in

December 1905, shortly after John G. Parsons had successfully developed an electric vehicle.[1] Two versions were produced, the first of which was a light delivery wagon that was shown at the Cleveland Automobile Show January 1906. The second was a stanhope passenger vehicle which appeared shortly thereafter.[2] Elwell-Parker Electric Company of Cleveland supplied the vehicle's eight horsepower motor, and Willard Storage Battery Company of Cleveland furnished the batteries.[3] Nothing more was heard about Parsons or his electric vehicles.

1. *The Horseless Age*, vol. 16, no. 3 (1905).
2. Kimes and Clark, *Standard Catalog of American Cars, 1805–1942*, 3d ed.
3. *The Horseless Age*, vol. 16, no. 3 (1905).

Peerless Manufacturing Company (1900 to 1902); Peerless Motor Car Company (1902 to 1931)

The Peerless Manufacturing Company, whose origins went back to 1869, had initially been in the business of making washing machine wringers, bird cages, and bicycles. The company added an automobile to the list of its products in 1900, at which time the company obtained a license to manufacture a De Dion-based Peerless-designed Motorette. This compact French-style automobile was priced at $1,300 and met with immediate acceptance. By the end of the following year the success of the Motorette made it clear that automotive ventures would ultimately prove to be more profitable than the company's existing business. As a result the De Dion license was dropped and a new automobile, entirely of the Peerless company's own design, was introduced in its stead in 1902.

This new Peerless had its sixteen horsepower one-cylinder engine mounted under a front hood, and used shaft rather than chain drive. Steering was by a wheel rather than tiller, and a three-speed sliding gear transmission provided variable speeds. The tonneau-bodied Peerless had two bucket seats up front, carried a side-mounted wicker picnic basket, and sported full fenders front and rear. A single large headlight, centered in front of the hood, was augmented by two cowl-mounted running lights. The new Peerless was capable of going quite fast, which was amply proven when a Cleveland owner received a ticket for traveling

The main offices and manufacturing plant of the Peerless Motor Car Company. Showrooms were maintained in the street corner first floor, where large windows and effective lighting displayed new automobiles to their best advantage.

Peerless production ended in 1931 with the elegant Custom Eight, which had been designed by the Russian Count A. de Sakhnoffsky, a highly regarded automobile stylist.

thirty-five miles per hour in a twenty-five mile per hour speed zone.

Production for 1902 totaled 238 automobiles. These results were so encouraging that all of the company's other ventures were discontinued and the company name was changed to Peerless Motor Car Company. From 1902 on, the company devoted itself to the manufacture of automobiles exclusively.[1]

By 1903 the Peerless company was offering automobiles ranging in price from $2,800 to $11,000, which made it the manufacturer of the

Peerless relied on its well-known reputation as an exemplary luxury automobile in this advertisement for the 1908 Peerless by saying simply, "All That the Name Implies" (author's collection).

most costly automobile in America. That such a new entrant to the automobile industry felt it could market an automobile at such a high price demonstrates that Peerless was completely confident in its ability to produce an automobile of quality and distinction. This expectation was proven to be correct with the sale of 623 vehicles that very next year.

Following the lead of other automobile pioneers, Peerless entered a variety of competitions in 1904. The most powerful of its race cars was the Green Dragon, which had two four-cylinder engines mounted in tandem and was piloted by famed race driver Barney Oldfield. The Green Dragon quickly scored numerous victories and, after setting world records for all track races from one to fifty miles in length, Peerless withdrew from competition in 1905 to focus on the production of luxury automobiles.[2]

By now Peerless had outgrown its existing facilities and a new factory was built near the company's original location on Cleveland's East Side, with sufficient acreage to allow for future expansion. The facility which Peerless moved into in 1905 consisted of a complex of four large two-story buildings, which quadrupled the space available at the previous plant.[3] Things progressed rapidly, and by 1906 the company had produced its 1,000th automobile. In one especially busy week of production at its new plant, Peerless shipped a record seventeen automobiles. To reflect its reputation for high quality luxury automobiles, the company adopted the slogan "All That the Name Implies" in 1906.

The company was especially sensitive to losses arising from waste of any kind, whether it was material or time. A system of oversights was introduced to control loss due to damaged parts and, as a result, Peerless was able to improve its in-house parts production efficiency by almost fifty percent.[4] In search of greater production cost savings, the company instituted a scrap material management plan and opened a laboratory for the analysis of metals being used in its automobiles. All of this helped significantly in the reduction of waste.

The new Peerless factory was expanded almost immediately, raising production capacity to 120 vehicles per month. Further expansion took place in 1908 and production increased to the point that automobiles were now assembled in batches of fifty. A new six-cylinder engine was introduced, in addition to the existing four-cylinder engine, and prices reached $6,000.[5] By 1911 Peerless was employing 2,200 factory workers and producing over 2,000 vehicles per year. Demand for Peerless automobiles was so great that the factory offered purchasers a discount if they would delay delivery of their order for thirty days.[6]

Pure luxury, as always, was the watchword. Peerless automobiles came with plate glass windows, carpeting of English pile, window coverings of silk, and brocade casual pillows. There were courtesy lights which came on automatically and disappeared when not in use, and the interior was graced with silver-plated appointments.

In 1912 a self-starter was introduced as standard equipment, and in 1914 Peerless automobiles came with six-cylinder engines exclusively, bearing prices as high as $7,200.

Although production for 1913 reached 3,000, the figures for 1914 were surprisingly low, with only 2,218 Peerless automobiles leaving the factory. The public's interest had now turned to lower-priced automobiles, and Peerless was quick to react to this market shift.

With an eye to capturing a part of this new and growing segment of the market, a less expensive line of automobiles was introduced in 1915. Described as being small and light but with Peerless quality, this new line was dubbed the All-Purpose, and came with four- or six-cylinder engines, and prices ranging from $2,000 to $3,350. The result of these changes was gratifying, with total Peerless sales exceeding 3,600 vehicles, making 1915 a highly profitable year.

At the same time that Peerless was developing its All-Purpose line, the company was also experimenting with prototype V-8 and V-12 engines, to make its luxury line more competitive with Cadillac and Marmon. Following extensive testing, the V-8 was selected in preference to the V-12. This experimentation had an unexpected side effect, as two Peerless employees went on, perhaps with Peerless' tacit support, to utilize just such a V-12 engine in a vehicle of their own design (see Harding Motor Car Company).

The year 1915 also saw significant changes in the company's corporate structure. Peerless Motor Car Company became a subsidiary of the newly formed Peerless Truck & Motor Company and, for the first time in the history of the company, Cleveland investors no longer held financial control. This did not mean that Cleveland people were no longer in control of actual operations. It was reported in 1919 that they held positions as president and general manager, in addition to maintaining control of over seventy percent of the board seats.

With the onset of World War I, production of trucks for the military overtook automobiles, and during that time period Peerless delivered a total of 12,000 trucks to the U.S. Government. For most of this time Peerless was still able to manufacture automobiles at the rate of up to fifty per week.

By 1920, Peerless production had reached 6,000 automobiles per year, but management was in turmoil. Richard H. Collins, who had been in charge of the Cadillac and Oldsmobile divisions of General Motors, joined with others to purchase Peerless Motor Car Company outright in 1921. Collins assumed the presidency and brought with him people from General Motors to run the company. For the time being, Cleveland interests were no longer in control.

The change of ownership did not disrupt production, and in 1922 Peerless shipped 1,009 vehicles in one month, which was a new record for the company. Total sales for the year hit a respectable 3,958.[7] Although the company showed a profit in each of the succeeding years, investors were unhappy about Collins' high salary and the royalty which he received on each six-cylinder Peerless sold. As a result, Collins was forced out at the end of 1923 and a new guard took over.

Under this new management, production in 1924 and 1925 continued to increase, and Peerless was now shipping up to 100 automobiles per day, thanks in part to a new paint-finishing process.[8] Peerless also added a line of automobiles in the so-called "popular priced" field, starting at $1,500, while retaining its luxury line with prices in the $4,000 range. For 1926 and 1927 sales came in close to 10,000 for each year.

However by 1928, harmony between management and the company's Cleveland-based investors was once again under stress, and new corporate captains were called in to displace the old. This new management team had Cleveland-approved representation in the posts of president and vice-president-in-charge-of-manufacturing.

The new team replaced Peerless' tried-and-true V-8 with a Continental-built straight eight. This change made it possible for the company to consider body style modifications, and it soon commissioned the renowned Russian automobile designer Alexis de Sakhnoffsky to create an entirely new 1930 Peerless automobile, with a modern sleek and dramatic appearance.

Unfortunately, all of this came too late for Peerless. Demand and production came to a standstill as the Depression took its toll. A slim profit was reported for 1930, but the writing was on the wall. It was time for Peerless to move in a new business direction, as the luxury automobile market was rapidly evaporating.

Peerless had expanded its plant on an almost annual basis during the heat of its on-going successes, and now it had a superb manufacturing facility, but no product demand. Although a prototype 1932 Peerless was built, the last Peerless automobile came off the Cleveland assembly line in 1931. The company ceased the manufacture of automobiles and moved on to a more profitable pursuit: the brewing of beer. After three decades, the Peerless company had manufactured a total of 108,116 luxury automobiles.[9] The number of bottles of beer produced by Peerless' successors at the old plant is not known.

1. *Motor Age*, November 16, 1903.
2. Kimes and Clark, *Standard Catalog of American Cars, 1805–1942*, 3d ed.
3. *The Automobile*, November 2, 1905.
4. *Motor Age*, April 2 and 25, October 10, 1907.
5. *The Automobile*, May 13, 1909.
6. *The Automobile*, May 13, 1913.
7. *Automotive Industries*, April 10 and 21, November 9, 1922.

8. *Automobile Trade Journal and Motor Age*, March 27, 1926.
9. Kimes and Clark, *Standard Catalog of American Cars, 1805–1942*, 3d ed.

Pennington, Edward Joel (1903 to 1904)

Edward Joel Pennington was a promoter of extraordinary zest. We first find him in Cleveland in 1893 when he formed the Motor Cycle Company in order to secure certain rights he held in an automobile patent application, the details of which are lost in the dim past. Pennington's stay in Cleveland was a short one, and he left in 1894 in quest of opportunities in a wide variety of other cities both here and abroad.

It was not until ten years later, in 1903, that Pennington once again turned his attentions to Cleveland. During the intervening years he had left a trail of disappointed investors and lawsuits. Along the way he had morphed from a promoter and supposed inventor of automobiles to a visionary of the dirigible airship which was then capturing national headlines. Before returning to Cleveland he stopped briefly in Carlisle, Pennsylvania, where he formed the Pennsylvania Steam Vehicle Company which was to manufacture the Tractobile.

Once back in Cleveland, he formed the Cleveland Motor Company. It was reported that Pennington was soon busy constructing an extravagant vehicle at the Eclipse Machine Company located at 16 Middle Street just south of Cleveland's Public Square.¹ *Motor Age* characterized this proposed vehicle as one of the most remarkable automobiles ever constructed. It was to be twenty-five feet long, powered by two engines totaling 308 horsepower, and capable of 100 miles per hour. It was said that Lewis D. Schoenberg, Vice President of the May Company, Cleveland's premier department store, was the expected purchaser of this magnificent conveyance. The price was a very ambitious $35,000, which is the equivalent of some $945,000 today. The automobile was to be equipped with three different interchangeable bodies and a set of flanged wheels for driving on railroad tracks. One of the bodies was a light aluminum racing shell, another was a park-touring body that would accommodate twenty-eight people, and the third was a long distance touring body with Pullman style berths and appointments the equal of any private railroad car. This incredible vehicle was reported to be nearing completion as of March 5, 1904.²

It should come as no surprise that at this point Pennington decamped to Toledo, Ohio, where he intended to manufacture automobile parts.³ That was the last heard of Edward Joel Pennington.

1. *The Motor Age*, February 18, 1904.
2. *The Automobile*, March 5, 1904, p. 283, Antique Automobile Club of America Library.
3. *The Automobile*, December 14, 1905.

Penton Motor Company (1927)

The Penton company declared capital stock of $50,000 when it was organized with E.W. Penton as president, H.S. Sherman as vice-president, and J.F. Potts as secretary-treasurer. The company was located at 1890 E. 40th Street and its stated purpose was "electrical goods," without specifically mentioning automobiles of any kind. It was reported in the media that the production of automobiles was intended, but there is no evidence this ever occurred.¹

1. Kimes and Clark, *Standard Catalog of American Cars, 1805–1942*, 3d ed.

People's Automobile Company (1900 to 1902)

The People's Automobile Company was formed in 1900 to manufacture and operate omnibuses engineered by Paul Gaeth, with the expectation of capitalizing on a Cleveland trolley car strike, but the plan failed when the striking workers would not let the buses operate on city streets.¹ People's then installed the omnibus engine that Gaeth had developed in a light runabout named People's. In search of the broadest possible market, the company also offered the Buckeye, which was a unique concept in turn-of-the-century motoring.

The Buckeye came either as a do-it-yourself kit or in finished form, a fact that made it unique among Cleveland automobiles. For

The People's Gasoline Vehicle.

THE PEOPLE'S AUTOMOBILE.

The Buckeye was built by the People's Automobile Company in 1901 and came with tiller steering, chain drive, and a 2¾ horsepower one-cylinder engine.

$477.50 an energetic purchaser could obtain all the parts necessary to construct a complete running chassis. Not included were a body and tires. For those less mechanically inclined, a completed Buckeye could be acquired for $1,000.[2] Neither the People's nor the Buckeye found acceptance among the motoring public, and the venture soon ceased operations and went into receivership in 1902.[3]

It is likely that the People's, and probably the Buckeye as well, were actually manufactured in Paul Gaeth's facilities at 54 Castle Street, where at that time he was building a vehicle of his own design.[4] (See Gaeth Automobile Company.)

---

1. Kimes and Clark, *Standard Catalog of American Cars, 1805–1942*, 3d ed.; *The Motor Age*, October 20, 1900, p. 77.

2. *Cycle and Automobile Trade Journal*, February 1902: Several sources indicate that the Buckeye was introduced in 1901 while an advertisement of February 1902 states that a Buckeye "has run three years in the country south of Cleveland without being in our shop."
3. Wager, *Golden Wheels*.
4. The Buckeye Auto Company, a name used by the People's company to market its Buckeye, listed an address of 87 Wade Park Avenue.

Pierce Supply Company (1915)

Organized with a minimal capitalization of $5,000 to undertake manufacturing and dealing in motor cars, it is unlikely that the Pierce company did either.[1]

---

1. Kimes and Clark, *Standard Catalog of American Cars, 1805–1942*, 3d ed.

Rauch & Lang Carriage Company (1905 to 1915)

Jacob Rauch and Charles Lang joined forces in 1884 to form the Rauch & Lang Carriage Company for the manufacture of horse drawn carriages and wagons. Rauch (pronounced to rhyme with "cow") had been a blacksmith and maker of wagons and buggies since 1853 and Lang was a successful real estate investor and financier. By the turn of the century it was apparent that the automobile promised to be the wave of the future and in 1903 Rauch & Lang company became agent for the Buffalo Electric.[1]

The success of this venture encouraged the company to develop its own electric vehicle to be called the Rauch & Lang Electric. It was immediately successful and fifty vehicles had been sold by the end of 1905. The Rauch & Lang Electrics were finished to the highest standards and were guaranteed to go 75 miles on a single charge.[2] In 1906 stanhope, closed coupe, and limousine bodies were offered.[3] The following year Rauch & Lang bought out its supplier of electric motors and controllers and initiated a plant expansion so that it would now be able to manufacture all the parts for its vehicles under one roof.[4] The company produced five hundred vehicles in 1908 thanks to its plant expansion. Although substantially more could have been sold adherence to the company's famous high standards held production down. Full utilization of the new plant's capacity in 1909 allowed the manufacture of one thousand vehicles annually.

In 1912 the company undertook a second plant expansion, adding a huge four story building which, upon its completion in 1913, made the Rauch & Lang factory the world's largest facility for the exclusive production of electric vehicles.[5] As of January 1914 Rauch & Lang had no debts, mortgages, or liabilities of any kind and declared that sales of its electric vehicles, which were now being sold in one hundred ten different cities, were steadily increasing.[6]

However the market for electric vehicles had reached its peak. On June 7, 1915, in order to achieve economies of operation, Rauch & Lang and Baker Motor Vehicle Company merged to form the Baker R & L Company.[7] (See Baker R&L Company; Owen Magnetic Company.)

---

1. Rauch & Lang. *The First Hundred Years of Rauch & Lang.*
2. *Horseless Age*, vol. 16, no. 25 (1905).
3. *The Automobile*, January 18, 1906.
4. *The Automobile*, February 14, 1907; Kimes and Clark, *Standard Catalog of American Cars, 1805–1942*, 3d ed.
5. *The Automobile*, September 19, 1912, and July 3 1913.
6. *The Automobile*, January 1, and April 23, 1914.
7. *The Automobile*, June 10, 1915.

Richard Auto Manufacturing Company (1914 to 1919)

Frenchman Francois Richard had come to America in 1904, bringing with him a well-earned reputation for being a genius with things mechanical.[1] He had already built France's first two-cycle engine, which won a gold medal at the 1900 Paris Exposition Universelle. In the United States he received similar recognition for a gasoline and kerosene carburetor at the 1904 Louisiana Purchase Exposition in St. Louis, Missouri.[2]

To better understand the automobiles Richard produced when he finally arrived in Cleveland in 1914, a look at what preceded them helps give a useful perspective.

Finding himself on the East Coast in 1905, Richard became acquainted with Alfred G. Vanderbilt, who was looking for someone to design and build a racing automobile for the upcoming 1906 Ormond-Daytona Beach races. Richard signed on to construct, within three months, a 250 horsepower racer capable of 100 miles per hour. Although he did produce a vehicle in three months, whether it achieved its objectives fully or failed miserably is a matter of dispute.[3]

Richard then resurfaced in Port Jefferson, New York, in 1909 with substantial financial backing and his oddly named Only automobile. This vehicle was a harbinger of the somewhat quirky automotive creations that would ultimately flow from Richard's endeavors in Cleveland. It was powered by a 201 cubic inch one cylinder engine with a bore of 5 inches and a stroke of 10 inches, perhaps the longest stroke automobile engine ever put into production. It

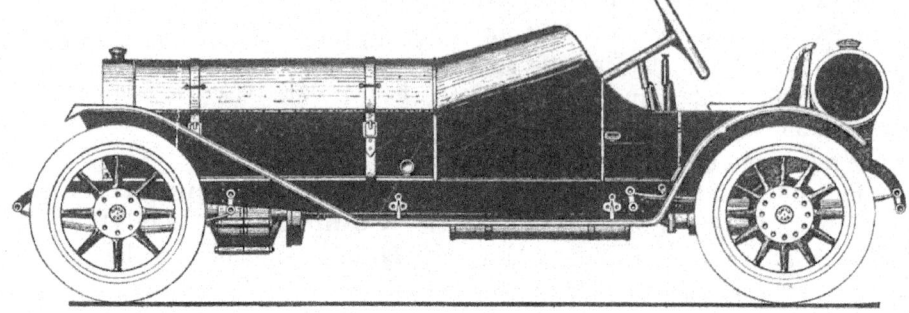

PRICE, $800

R. I. V. Ball bearings throughout.

Bosch magneto.

60 Miles per hour guaranteed.

30 Miles per gallon guaranteed.

We give a signed guarantee for twelve months to each customer.

The same workmanship and material found in any $5000 car on the market.

ONLY CAR, 1919 Broadway, New York City

DISTRIBUTERS:

| Washington, Oregon, California, Nevada | Sierra Motors Company, Inc.
834-40 South Spring St.
Los Angeles, California | New York State:
THE ONLY CAR DISTRIBUTING CO.
1919 Broadway, New York City |

We will exhibit at the Grand Central Palace Show.

Richard's very sleek two-place Only for 1913 was both economical and swift, and for a mere $800, it was also quite a bargain (author's collection).

For 1918 the RiChard's front fenders, radiator, and hood had a more streamlined appearance, enhanced by concealed headlights. Note the fringe on the top.

also had another unusual feature: a flywheel at each end of the crankshaft.[4] This bizarre engine was concealed within a very handsome race type torpedo body.

The Only was not a huge success and, in 1913, the Only Motor Car Company was reorganized as the Metropol Motors Corporation and the Only was renamed the Metropol. This effort did not succeed either, and in 1914 Francois Richard was enticed to Cleveland by a group of backers to begin making an automobile bearing his own name.[5]

Richard's Cleveland story began in early 1914 with the formation of the Richard Auto Manufacturing Company.[6] The intended Richard automobile was to use his award-winning gasoline/kerosene carburetor and to be powered by a four-cylinder engine with a 4-inch bore and $8^{15}/_{16}$-inch stroke, which was claimed to produce 96 horsepower and deliver 26 miles per gallon. The Richard was to be a seven passenger touring automobile with a 128-inch wheelbase and electric starting and lighting.[7] How many of these automobiles were produced beyond the prototype is not known, but changes were announced for each subsequent year's models. It may be that it was only his backers who were motoring around Cleveland in examples of the Richard.

A 1918 RiChard sales brochure announced that a RiChard Magnetic automobile was soon to be introduced. The magnetic transmission was to provide a smooth flow of power and serve as the vehicle's brakes as well. This RiChard was to have a nine-passenger body with an extended boat-tail, which reduced the chance of dust being drawn into the passenger areas when traveling at speed. It also featured

The 1915 Richard was a big automobile with an impossibly small price. Its tall hood housed a four cylinder engine that had a 4 inch bore and almost 9 inch stroke.

what may be the first retractable headlights and a tasseled fringe around the top. The proposed Magnetic never came to be. Instead the company focused on the new RiChard for 1918, which appeared with a conventional transmission and braking system and was mated to a 600 cubic inch V-8 engine at a price of $8,000.[8]

Over the years production of the RiChard was minimal at best and by 1919 the company was reformed as the LaMarne Motor Company. (See LaMarne Motor Company.)

---

1. Francois Richard changed the style of his automobile's name to RiChard in an attempt to encourage the more correct French-like pronunciation "ree-SHARd."
2. Wager, *Golden Wheels.*
3. Ibid.; Richard Auto Manufacturing Company, 1918 sales brochure.
4. Kimes and Clark, *Standard Catalog of American Cars, 1805–1942*, 3d ed.
5. Wager, *Golden Wheels.*
6. *The Automobile,* April 9, 1914.
7. Ibid.
8. Ibid., 1918 RiChard sales brochure.

Rogers, Frank W., and Hanford, George (1899 to 1901); Rogers & Hanford Company (1901 to 1902)

The record concerning this automotive effort is sketchy. George Hanford was an electrician living at 644 Castle Avenue and Frank W. Rogers was a machinist residing at 87 Slater.[1] When and how they initially joined forces is not known, but by 1899 the two had collaborated on a vehicle powered by a four-cylinder rotary engine, the first of its kind.[2] A rotary engine is radial in configuration but the crankshaft is stationary and the engine block and pistons rotate around the crankshaft. The engine was said to be self-starting and its high wagon-style wheels came with pneumatic tires. What had been a partnership was recast as the Rogers & Hanford Company when the automobile was presented for sale to the public in 1901. This endeavor did not last more than four years, and production was terminated sometime in 1902. It is doubtful that more than a few examples of this vehicle were built.[3]

---

1. *Cleveland City Directory,* 1898–1902.
2. Kimes and Clark, *Standard Catalog of American Cars, 1805–1942*, 3d ed.
3. Wager, *Golden Wheels.*

Rogers & Thatcher Automobile Company (1903)

Two gentlemen, George D. Rogers and A. Q. Thatcher, joined forces in February 1903 to form the Rogers & Thatcher company with the intention of producing automobiles.[1] The two men had been working on building a prototype since late 1902, and it was hoped that the automobile would be ready for display at the Cleveland Automobile Show in February 1903. Although it was reported that only the chassis was displayed, *Motor Age*[2] showed a photo of a completed Rogers & Thatcher in its February automobile show issue. The vehicle shown was neatly designed, and was said to have a body which could be adapted to carry anywhere from one to four passengers.

In mid-1903 Rogers & Thatcher entered into negotiations for the purchase of a site on Cleveland's East Side where a factory was to be built with the expectation of manufacturing one hundred automobiles for the 1904 model year.[3] A prominent Cleveland dealership that handled Peerless and General automobiles even signed on to carry the Rogers & Thatcher. However, nothing concrete came of this endeaver and the Rogers & Thatcher automobile disappeared from the scene.[4]

---

1. Kimes and Clark, *Standard Catalog of American Cars, 1805–1942*, 3d ed.
2. *Motor Age,* February 5, 1903.
3. *Motor Age,* August 3, 1903.
4. Wager, *Golden Wheels.*

Rollin Motors Company (1923 to 1926)

Before Rollin Henry White built an automobile bearing his given name, he had already experimented extensively with steam engines. These early experiments led to the construction of the first White steam automobile, which he built in his father's sewing machine factory in 1900. This White steam automobile, powered by a flash steam boiler of Rollin's own design, received international recognition. (See White Sewing Machine Company.)

In 1914 Rollin's interest turned to farm tractors, and he left his fathers' company to build a new type of tractor. Rollin's crawler-tractor was one of the earliest applications of continuous

When introduced in 1923, the Rollin had a distinctly European flare. It was said to be smaller and more agile than the typical American automobile.

The new generation of motorists discovers its ideal car

MOTORING conditions have changed in the last few years. There are more cars on the road, naturally. City and suburban driving has become a real problem. To say nothing of parking! As a result, the big, unwieldy car is on the defensive.

The new generation of motorists have demanded a smaller, more agile car that has all the smart appearance and mechanical ability of the larger car, but without its bulk. They have found their ideal in the Rollin!

Engineers have called the Rollin "The only *fine* small car being built in America." It is a fact that no car, regardless of size, price or reputation, is better built than the Rollin. Money cannot buy finer materials.

People who can afford the larger cars are turning now to Rollin. Men who love the sing of a golf-ball in full flight ... women who dress smartly and reflect good taste in everything they own. Young men and women who inherently reject the commonplace. These are the people for whom the Rollin car was designed.

It handles easily in the thickest going, and is untiring on even the longest trips. It parks in a space that automatically forbids bulkier cars.

The Rollin motor, prideful achievement of Rollin H. White, is a symphony in mechanical perfection. Quiet. Sweet-running. Powerful on the steep climb. Fleet on the straightaway. Gives 25 to 30 miles to the gallon. Good for 100,000 happy, care-free miles.

Rollin bodies are in keeping with the car's mechanical excellence. Finished in Duco, in many color combinations, they are a delight to the eye. The upholstery and fittings are the kind you associate with cars costing several times as much.

Pictures and type are inadequate indeed in attempting to convey more than an impression of this unusually fine small car. You must see the Rollin ... drive it ... sense the quality feel in every competent part. So ... *this is an invitation!*

There is still some desirable territory available for dealers of Rollin calibre. The Rollin Motors Company, Cleveland, Ohio.

Brougham, $1325   Coupe, $1325   Sedan, $1455   Phaeton, $1155
(f. o. b. Cleveland)

Proclaimed "the only fine small car being built in America today," the 1925 Rollin could be acquired for as little as $1,155. Perhaps one of the earliest "compact cars," the Rollin was nevertheless an automobile of the highest quality in construction and materials. The motor, which was capable of 30 miles per gallon, was designed by Rollin H. White, designer of the White automobile's flash-steam boiler. Although the advertisement focuses largely upon technical matters, it contains a spark of Ned Jordan's advertising genius when it rhapsodizes that the Rollin is for "Men who love the sing of a golf-ball in full flight ... women who dress smartly and reflect good taste in everything they own" (author's collection).

tracks instead of wheels, which allowed it to work in situations which would defeat a wheeled vehicle. Called the Cletrac, it was small, weighing only 2,750 pounds, and was powered by another engine of Rollin's own design. The Cletrac could plow at four miles per hour, and was priced at $985.[1] In 1916, Rollin formed the Cleveland Motor Plow Company, and constructed a new plant to build his tractor. The name of the company was changed the next year to Cleveland Tractor Company.

By 1920 the Cleveland Tractor Company was on solid ground and progressing well. Now Rollin's attention returned to building an automobile, incorporating ideas he had developed over the last several years. Rollin's new product was to be a small automobile, along the lines of those found in Europe, but it was designed to be equal in comfort and performance to the typical American automobile of the era.

To produce this automobile, Rollin joined forces with two other entrepreneurs in 1922, E.E. Allyne and Fred M. Zeder. Allyne was a director of Aluminum Manufacturers Inc. and owner of a Cleveland foundry, and Zeder had been an engineering consultant for Studebaker Corporation[2] (see Zeder Motor Company). When Zeder and his associates left in order to work for Chrysler in 1923, Rollin turned his attentions back to commercial vehicles. It was soon announced that Cleveland Tractor Company would add a 1¼-ton truck to its line, utilizing the same engine which Rollin had designed for his tractor.[3]

However, this plan was quickly abandoned, and Rollin returned once again to his earlier intention of building a compact European-style passenger automobile. In May 1923, Rollin announced the formation of his Rollin Motors Company. The company's new Rollin automobile was to be to be manufactured in a plant adjacent to the Cleveland Tractor Company.[4] The operating staff was predominantly made up of prior Studebaker people, including a former Studebaker vice president who had been in charge of that company's engineering and production.

As promised, the first Rollin automobiles were out before the end of the year. The new Rollin's rear suspension was a single transverse leaf spring. It had a four-cylinder engine with precision-balanced lightweight aluminum alloy pistons and rods, and an exhaust and intake manifold made in a single casting. Company advertising described the Rollin as "trim, alert, resourceful, and spirited," which suited its compact European proportions.

An intensive effort for export sales was launched in early 1924, with Rollin representatives sailing to Asia, South Africa, and Australia.[5] In the first three months of 1924, 1,450 Rollins were shipped.[6] Rollin White had hoped to offer his automobiles at a price below $1,000, but by 1925 they were priced between $1,155 and $1,455.

Notwithstanding some early successes, it gradually became apparent that the manufacture of Rollin automobiles would not be financially self-sustaining, and a creditors' committee assumed management of the company in June 1925.[7] By the end of the year, bankruptcy was declared, and liquidation followed on March 4, 1926.

Unfortunately, Rollin White's venture proved once again that the American motoring public preferred a full-sized automobile, regardless of how meritorious a smaller one such as the Rollin might have been. During the company's brief existence, something just short of 6,000 automobiles were produced.

After this, Rollin White focused his energies on his more successful Cleveland Tractor Company venture, where he remained for the next twenty years.[8]

---

1. *The Automobile*, June 7, 1917; *Automotive Industries*, June 29, 1916.
2. *Automotive Industries*, March 1922.
3. *Automotive Industries*, August 31, 1922.
4. *Automotive Industries*, July 12, 1923.
5. *Automotive Industries*, April 3, 1924.
6. *Automotive Industries*, April 17, 1924.
7. *Automotive Industries*, June 18, 1925, March 4, 1926.
8. Kimes and Clark, *Standard Catalog of American Cars, 1805–1942*, 3d ed.

Royal Motor Car Company (1904 to 1906); Royal Motor Car & Manufacturing Company (1906 to 1908); Royal Tourist Car Company (1908 to 1911)

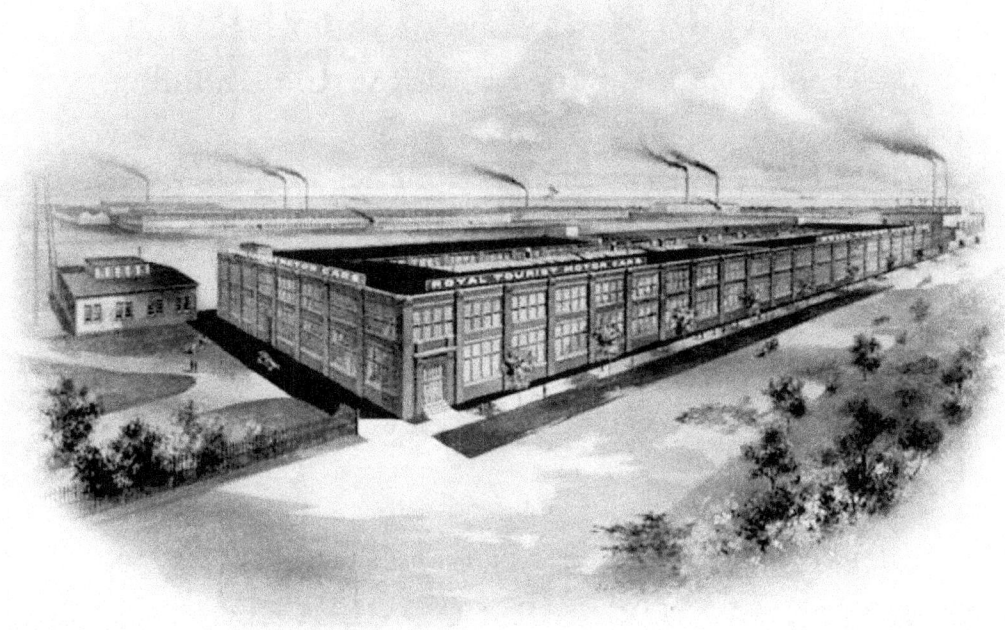

Royal Tourist plant on East 70th Street built in 1907.

Royal Tourist's modern efficient two-story plant featured direct rail access.

Edward D. Schurmer acquired ownership of the Hoffman Automobile and Manufacturing Company, of which he had been president, in late 1903. (See Hoffman Automobile and Manufacturing Company.) He reorganized the company as the Royal Motor Car Company in 1904 and began the manufacture of an elegant new automobile, the Royal Tourist. The Royal Tourist featured a stylishly rounded radiator top, hood, and dashboard, which was to become its signature profile. This highly regarded vehicle was the hit of the 1904 New York Automobile Show, and one hundred automobiles were sold that year.[1] New York automobile dealer Duerr-Ward found the Royal Tourist to be so reliable that the dealership sold each Royal Tourist with a one year guarantee, which may have been the first such warranty in the country.[2]

By 1905 Royal, flush with success, expanded its existing facility, added new equipment, and broke ground on a new assembly shop.[3] At the 1906 New York Automobile Show, more Royal Tourists were sold than any other similar make. This included a $40,000 sale of Royal Tourists to one family, which is quite impressive, given the fact that the price range for the automobile was between $3,500 and $5,000.[4]

At this time, the Royal Motor Car Company was turning out two cars per day, and the need for a completely new factory had become apparent. In November of 1906 the company was reorganized as the Royal Motor Car and Manufacturing Company, in order to facilitate financing and construction of new facilities, which were quickly completed and occupied by October of 1907. The company now had a work force of 400 men.[5]

The timing of this expansion was unfortunate, as the nationwide panic of 1907 proved to be a difficult time for Royal. Although it survived bankruptcy and reorganized as the Royal

The 1904 aluminum bodied Royal Tourist with rear entrance tonneau featured roller bearings throughout and force-feed lubrication.

Tourist Car Company in 1908, it never regained its financial stability. Despite the fact that the company was selling every automobile that it could make in 1909, overall profitability declined in 1910, and by March of 1911 the company made a last-ditch attempt at survival by merging with the Croxton Motor Company to form the Consolidated Motor Car Company. (See Croxton Motor Company.) The Consolidated merger collapsed almost immediately and, by the end of 1911, the Royal Tourist was no more.

1. *The Automobile*, July 9, 1904; Kimes and Clark, *Standard Catalog of American Cars, 1805–1942*, 3d ed.
2. *The Automobile*, June 11, 1904.
3. *The Automobile*, September 7, 1905.
4. *Cycle and Automobile Trade Journal*, March 1906.
5. *Motor Age*, October 19, 1907; Kimes and Clark, *Standard Catalog of American Cars, 1805–1942*, 3d ed.

Rubay Company (1920 to 1923)

Leon Rubay came to America from Paris, France, at the turn of the twentieth century. In 1904 he had become an importer of J. Lacoste & Cie. electrical ignition devices, which he promoted as being the best in the world. This claim may have had merit, based on unsolicited endorsements from several prominent users. Rubay continued in this line of business in New York City at least through 1906.[1] In 1908 he became associated with Rothschild & Company of New York, a builder of automobile bodies, where he was manager of the wholesale department.[2] Rubay subsequently moved on to another coach builder, Holbrook & Company. In 1915 he was hired by the White Motor Company (see White Sewing Machine Company), and brought to Cleveland to head up its Pleasure Vehicle Department.[3]

Staying at White for only one year, Rubay left and formed his own company in 1916 to build high quality luxury automobile bodies. The Leon Rubay Company attracted many prestigious clients in the automobile industry, initially including White and Lozier, and then

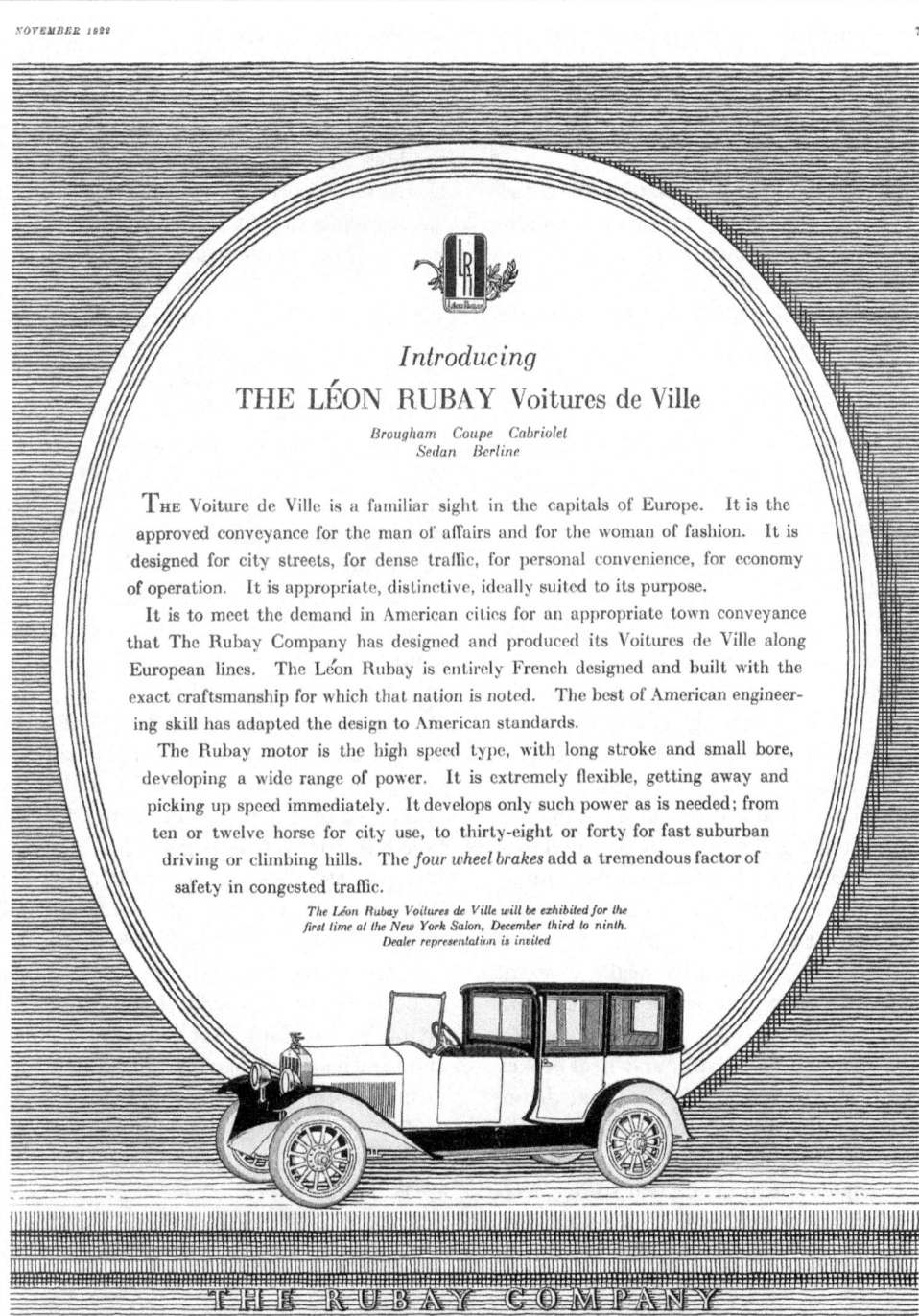

Leon Rubay was a Frenchman who came to Cleveland to seek his fortune in the automobile field. His 1923 offering, the Voitures de Ville, was portrayed as being a blend of French design and American engineering. It was remarkable in that its high-revolution engine was declared to be capable of providing just the right amount of power needed for any particular situation, from ten horsepower for city use to forty horsepower for fast suburban driving (author's collection).

later on Franklin, Duesenberg, Roamer, Locomobile, Marmon, Cole, and Pierce-Arrow. During World War I the company also manufactured airplane wings for the Army Signal Corps.[4]

In 1920 Rubay undertook plans to manufacture a vehicle of his own, which would become known as the Leon Rubay. While on a business trip to Paris, Rubay obtained the assistance of Paul Bastiens, who agreed to help design and build Rubay's vehicle. What resulted was a small town car intended especially for city use. The 118-inch wheelbase chassis was of French design, but adapted for American conditions. Arthur M. Dean, chief engineer for Templar, participated in adapting the engine for use in the Leon Rubay.[5]

The power plant was a European concept four-cylinder engine, of 124.7 cubic inch displacement, which relied on high rpm rather than torque, and therefore required a rather high 5.1 to 1 differential ratio. The engine was ingenious in its engineering. It had an overhead camshaft and valves, and the cylinders were offset ⅞ inch, rather than being set squarely above the crankshaft, to enhance torque. Air for the Stromberg carburetor was drawn over the exhaust pipe and then through the cylinder block before entering the carburetor, which created a slight vacuum in the crankcase and tended to prevent external oil leaks, a vexing problem with many automobile engines of the era.

Rubay's automobile had four-wheel brakes, which may have been a first. The brake drums were of aluminum with steel liners, and the shoes were aluminum, which reduced unsprung weight. The front and rear springs were almost flat in profile, with the outer ends mounted in conventional eye-and-bolt brackets, while the inner ends were carried between two hardened rollers mounted in cast steel spring brackets.[6]

One the most inventive features of Rubay's automobile was his design of the collapsible windows on his 1923 Cabriolet, which easily transformed a four-door fixed-roof vehicle into what we would today call a four-door hardtop. An intricate assortment of hinges and pivots worked with hidden storage pockets on each body panel to conceal the glass windows.[7]

The Leon Rubay automobile was introduced in December 1922, but production did not extend beyond 1923. The actual number of vehicles finally manufactured probably did not exceed one hundred.[8] Rubay's automobile followed the fate of other similarly conceived vehicles which, by American standards, were too small. Although the body work was excellent and the overall finished product was of the highest quality, this was not enough to entice American buyers to embrace a luxury vehicle of a smaller size. When a purchaser could obtain a larger automobile of equal quality for a similar price, the Leon Rubay with a top price of $5,000 only appealed to the most sophisticated or eccentric motorist.

During the time that the Rubay Company was manufacturing its own automobile, it continued to make bodies on contract for other manufacturers, including Sterling-Knight, Peerless, Franklin, Reo, and Wills Sainte Claire. These contracts were taken over by Baker R&L Company when Rubay's land and plant were purchased by Baker R&L on January 16, 1924.[9] (See Baker R&L Company.) The Rubay plant was only steps away from the existing Baker R&L plant at 8000 Baker Street, and the intention was to physically join the two facilities. However, this did not occur.

Leon Rubay returned to France in 1923 and abandoned the automobile business entirely, choosing instead to become an egg and chicken farmer in Villiers.[10]

---

1. *Motor*, February, March, July 1905; *Cycle and Automobile Trade Journal*, April 1906.
2. Wager, *Golden Wheels*.
3. Kimes and Clark, *Standard Catalog of American Cars, 1805–1942*, 3d ed.; Wager, *Golden Wheels*.
4. Kimes and Clark, *Standard Catalog of American Cars, 1805–1942*, 3d ed.
5. Kimes and Clark, *Standard Catalog of American Cars, 1805–1942*, 3d ed.
6. *Automotive Industries*, November 2, 1922.
7. *Automobile Trade Journal*, January 1923, p. 85, and undated brochure titled "Collapsible windows on this car pre-date hardtops!," Antique Automobile Club of America Library.
8. Production has been estimated at less than a dozen (*Standard Catalog of American Cars*), and not more than seventy-five (*Golden Wheels*).

9. *Automotive Industries*, January 17, 1924.
10. Kimes and Clark, *Standard Catalog of American Cars, 1805–1942*, 3d ed.

Russell Motor Vehicle Company (1902 to 1904)

E.L. Russell, a mechanically adept individual, incorporated the Russell Motor Vehicle Company in 1902, with the intention of manufacturing a motor vehicle of his own design.[1] A prototype of the Russell was completed in 1903 and featured numerous innovations.[2] Among its advances were the control of all functions with just two levers, and the absence of engine timing and ignition devices, which were replaced by a hot-tube ignition. A double rotary pump circulated both water and oil. An engine-driven generator provided a spark for ignition, charge for a battery and, at a time when most other automobiles relied on kerosene lamps for illumination, power for electric lights.[3]

E.L. Russell and his innovative automobile must have shown significant promise, because one of the people he attracted to his venture was C.E. Thompson of Thompson Products Company, which later became part of TRW. It is likely that Cleveland Cap Screw Company, Thompson's firm, built the Russell prototype. In early 1904 it was announced that the Russell company had purchased a large woolen mill which was to be converted into an automobile factory for Russell company.[4] From this point on nothing further was heard of Russell or his highly advanced automobile.

1. *The Horseless Age*, vol. 10, no. 24 (1902).
2. *The Automobile*, October 3, 1903.
3. *The Horseless Age*, vol. 10, no. 24 (1902).
4. *The Automobile*, January 3, 1904.

Saf-T-Cab Corporation (1926 to 1928)

The Saf-T-Cab Corporation of Cleveland was the taxi-building arm of the Auburn Automobile Company of Auburn, Indiana. No vehicles were actually produced in Cleveland, but rather in the Auburn company's Indiana factory. Why a Cleveland company was formed for this purpose is a mystery.[1]

1. Kimes and Clark, *Standard Catalog of American Cars, 1805–1942*, 3d ed.

THE RUSSELL 6 H.-P. GASOLINE MOTOR CAR.

The 1903 6 horsepower Russell had a four-cylinder horizontal engine and a steel body which was very advanced for its era.

Saur, Frank (1902)

Another short story in the panoply of automobile manufacturing endeavors is that of Frank Saur of 19 Broadway in Cleveland. It was reported in the *Automobile & Motor Review* of February 1902 that Saur was experimenting with an automobile. That is all that is known about Saur's efforts.[1]

1. Kimes and Clark, *Standard Catalog of American Cars, 1805–1942*, 3d ed.

Schmidt, J.A. (1902)

Mr. J. A. Schmidt of 286 Baker Avenue was reported in the February 1902 issue of *Automobile & Motor Review* as experimenting with an automobile. Nothing more is known.[1]

1. Kimes and Clark, *Standard Catalog of American Cars, 1805–1942*, 3d ed.

Simplex Manufacturing Company (1906 to 1911)

Brothers William E. and Earl H. Sherbondy organized their Simplex Manufacturing Company sometime between 1906 and 1908.[1] The company was situated in a small factory building on Cleveland's East Side. William was a machinist with twelve years' experience in gasoline engines and Earl, who had been educated at the University School of Cleveland, had a natural talent for designing internal combustion engines. In 1904, at the age of sixteen, he made a single-cylinder two-cycle engine that produced 16½ horsepower, the most powerful of any such engine at that time.[2]

Earl built his first four-cylinder air-cooled engine in 1905. The complete engine weighed only 260 pounds, produced 38 horsepower, and had a carburetor of the brothers' own design. Innovative features included piston tops that had a deflector to prevent the intake charge from escaping through the exhaust ports, a problem peculiar to two-cycle engines.

The brothers began building an automobile the next year and had it on the road by August of 1907. The automobile was successfully tested and shown at the 1907 Cleveland Automobile Show, but the brothers stated that they had no intention of manufacturing anything other than engines and transmissions.[3] In 1908 they joined forces with A.F. May, owner of a drug store to form the Derain Motor Company. (See Derain Motor Company.)

1. *Cycle and Automobile Trade Journal*, April 1908.
2. *Cycle and Automobile Trade Journal*, December 1909.
3. Kimes and Clark, *Standard Catalog of American Cars, 1805–1942*, 3d ed.

Sipe & Sigler Company (1900)

A prototype vehicle powered by a two horsepower Elwell-Parker electric motor with a battery designed by Theodore A. Willard was constructed for Mr. Willard with the help of the Sipe & Sigler Company. Willard had taken Sipe and Sigler in as partners in his battery manufacturing company, although their main focus was in the jewelry trade. The prototype stanhope electric which they produced was intended to demonstrate the capabilities of Willard's battery and had a range of forty miles without recharging. Although Willard continued to pursue his automotive experimentations, the April 1900 issue of *Electrical World and Engineering* confirmed that neither Willard nor Sipe & Sigler had any desire to enter into active production of an automobile.[1] (See Jacob Hoffman Wagon Company and Willard Storage Battery Company.)

1. Kimes and Clark, *Standard Catalog of American Cars, 1805–1942*, 3d ed.

Sixth City Machine Company (1913)

With a capitalization of $10,000 Ray C. Skeel, Charles M. Ringle, C.F. Bruggemeier, E.M. Becker, and A.F. Goldenbogen organized the Sixth City company, which had the stated purpose of dealing in and manufacturing automobiles. No automobiles are known to have been built.[1]

1. Kimes and Clark, *Standard Catalog of American Cars, 1805–1942*, 3d ed.

Snyder Motor & Manufacturing Company (1914)

Lasting no more than one year, the Snyder cyclecar was offered in three versions. There was a $450 four-passenger touring vehicle weighing 800 pounds that had a twelve horsepower four-cylinder L-head engine and two-speed transmission. They also offered a mid-sized and similarly powered roadster priced at $425 and finally a nine horsepower two-cylinder version for $390.[1] The largest of these cyclecars had a 100-inch wheelbase and a 50 inch tread.[2] The cyclecar had doors, 38-inch-wide seats, ample luggage space, and came fully equipped with tools, jack, and pump. The men behind this venture, G.J. Snyder and R.E. Blackwell, also produced the Snyder motorcycle.[3]

1. Kimes and Clark, *Standard Catalog of American Cars, 1805–1942*, 3d ed.
2. Wager, *Golden Wheels*.
3. *The American Cyclecar*, April 1914, Antique Automobile Club of America Library.

Special Motor Vehicle Company (1904)

Primarily acting as a Ford dealership, the company undertook to build an automobile with a 9-horsepower engine and shaft drive. The drive shaft was quite unusual, consisting of flat pieces of steel formed into a square-ended box which fit into a square socket on the transmission. The Special was built to order only. The total number produced is unknown.[1]

1. Kimes and Clark, *Standard Catalog of American Cars, 1805–1942*, 3d ed.

Sperry Engineering Company (1898 to 1902)

A genius in matters electrical, Elmer A. Sperry began to develop an electric vehicle in the late 1890s. His experiments, some of which were conducted on the premises of Walter Baker's American Ball Bearing Company plant, (see Baker, Walter C.) ultimately came to fruition October 1898.[1] At this point, he formed the Sperry company to undertake the building and marketing of his electric vehicle. Sperry immediately contracted with the Cleveland Machine Screw Company to manufacture his new electric vehicle, to be named the Cleveland, in batches of 100. The first of these batches came out in 1899.[2] The vehicle's singular and most interesting feature was its universal control which governed the vehicle's movement including direction, speed, and braking. Sperry Electrics were priced between $1,800 and $2,200.

A consortium of French businessmen involved with Cleveland Machine Screw encouraged Sperry to show his electric vehicle at the Paris Exposition in 1900, where it received a gold medal. Subsequently, manufacturing rights were sold in France for what was now named the Sperry, and in addition no fewer than 100 vehicles were exported to France.[3] However, Elmer Sperry's interests lay elsewhere and, in late 1901 or early 1902, the remaining Cleveland Machine Screw-built Sperrys, along with the patent rights, were sold to the American Bicycle Company trust of Albert A. Pope, maker of the Pope-Hartford electric vehicle.

Throughout the years Elmer Sperry had given talks designed to educate the public about electric vehicles, their maintenance, and the comparative advantages of private and motor-trade electrical charging facilities.[4] But with the sale of his electric vehicle interests Sperry went on to other pursuits, including the invention of the Sperry Gyroscope. His company eventually became the Sperry Rand Corporation. Cleveland Machine Screw continued for a number of years to build automobiles on contract for other Cleveland automobile entrepreneurs.

1. *The Automobile*, October 3, 1903
2. Kimes and Clark, *Standard Catalog of American Cars, 1805–1942*, 3d ed.
3. Wager, *Golden Wheels*.
4. *Cycle and Automobile Trade Journal*, July 1900.

Standard Automobile Company (1905)

Incorporated to manufacture, purchase, sell, and store automobiles, the Standard company had a capitalization of $100,000. The organizers were F.B. Williams, T.H. Hoggsett, M.G. McAleenan, George H. Smith, and George H. Kelly. The Standard company was agent for Autocar, Cadillac and Packard but apparently never produced an automobile of its own. If the company had built a car named the Standard, it would have found difficulty in distinguishing itself, as there were already over one dozen other "Standard" automobiles in existence or proposed at that time.[1]

1. Kimes and Clark, *Standard Catalog of American Cars, 1805–1942*, 3d ed.

Star Automobile Company (1902 to 1904)

Formed in October 1902 the Star company was off to a promising start with a vehicle designed by Gilbert Albaugh, an engineer who had worked previously for Peerless, Rambler, and Olds. The company was also soundly backed by Cleveland industrialists of considerable experience.[1]

Star occupied a very solid and eminently suitable two-story factory building on a tree-lined street and seemed poised for success. However, the vehicle was a single cylinder runabout priced at a heady $1,250, and by early 1903 only ten examples had been sold. The promoters quickly determined that the automobile business, as they had envisioned it, was not likely to be profitable.[2] The operation was sold to Harry S. Moore that year with a total of only twenty Star automobiles having been produced. (See Moore, Harry S.)

1. *The Automobile and Motor Review*, November 1902.
2. *The Automobile*, October 24, 1903.

The 1904 Star Gasoline Car.

Top: Claiming 20 miles per gallon, the 1904 Star was an eye-catcher in its bright red finish with gold pin striping. *Bottom:* Priced at $1,250, the 1903 Star had a one-cylinder 8½ horsepower engine and was claimed to be capable of delivering more than 25 miles per gallon.

Stearns, Frank B. (1896 to 1898); F.B. Stearns & Company (1898 to 1902); F.B. Stearns Company (1902 to 1929)

Fourteen-year-old Frank B. Stearns was the youngest Clevelander to address the challenge of building a self-propelled vehicle. Inspired by seeing early European automobiles at the 1893 Chicago World's Columbian Exposition, Stearns was determined to build an automobile of his own design. The lack of knowledge and

For 1904 Stearns introduced eight improvements among which were larger tires, enhanced suspension and an improved lubrication system.

In 1910 the Stearns was the product of fourteen years of experience, which its builder felt entitled the Stearns to the slogan "the Ultimate Car." A Stearns was available with either a chain or shaft drive at $4,600 for a 30–60 horsepower touring, or $3,200 for a 15–30 horsepower shaft drive version (author's collection).

experience in business, engineering, and manufacturing did not deter him. In 1896, at the age of seventeen, he successfully completed his first automobile in the basement of his parents' Euclid Avenue home.[1]

Frank Stearns had never driven a self-propelled vehicle before the day he took his creation on a test drive. This first test drive was so successful that his father advanced Frank enough money to expand his automobile operation from the family basement out into the barn behind the house.

Local Clevelanders soon became aware of young Stearns' success and began enquiring about having this teenager build a similar automobile for them. As a result, Frank's business quickly outgrew its backyard quarters. As demand for his automobiles rose, Frank joined forces in 1898 with the Owen brothers of Cleveland to form F.B. Stearns & Company. (See Owen Motor Carriage Company.) Although the Owen brothers left the company shortly thereafter to pursue other automotive interests, Frank continued on his own. By 1900 Stearns had completed and sold no fewer than twenty vehicles, and by 1901 had produced another thirty.[2]

The reliability of the Stearns single-cylinder engine had been proven in 1901 when a Stearns was driven from Cleveland to New York City, duplicating Alexander Winton's achievement of 1897. The vehicle's impressive performance on this occasion attracted investors who joined with Stearns in 1901 to build a new factory, located a little over a mile east of his parents' home. Stearns' automobile enterprise was now fully fledged and business was brisk.

In 1902 the company name was changed to F.B. Stearns Company, and the plant received its first of many expansions. The following year the plant produced a total of 147 automobiles. Up to this point, Stearns automobiles had remained single-cylinder vehicles, but the engines had gradually increased in horsepower from eight to eleven, due primarily to a larger bore and stroke. In 1902, Stearns introduced a twenty horsepower two-cylinder engine.

At this time, endurance trials and speed events were an important way for an automobile manufacturer to demonstrate the reliability of his product. Although several Cleveland automobile manufacturers entered these events with specially-built race cars, as was the custom at the time, Stearns never did so. It was his policy that any race entered by a Stearns must be with a stock automobile identical to one that could be obtained directly off the factory floor. It was especially gratifying for Stearns that his stock automobiles, raced not by professionals but by their owners, won numerous events, including a Cleveland Automobile Club race in 1904, as well as two successive local Memorial Day hill climb races and a coinciding Memorial Day race in Massachusetts. Other triumphs included the winning of a New York City hill climb in 1907, and the setting of a track speed record in Cincinnati that year. Stearns automobiles soundly beat such luminous names as Mercedes, Lozier, Thomas, Mora, and Hotchkiss in a multitude of events, and did it all with stock automobiles. Especially noteworthy was the success of Mrs. Kenneth Otis, who piloted her stock Stearns to victory in the Cleveland Automobile Club's 1908 annual hill climb. The AAA decreed that, thereafter, women could not participate in member club events.

Each Stearns vehicle was thoroughly tested before being delivered to its purchaser.[3] It was claimed in 1904 that it took the equivalent of over two thousand man-hours to produce each Stearns automobile, which included test runs of over one hundred fifty miles, with a speed test by Frank Stearns himself.[4]

Prices for Stearns automobiles at this time were above the reach of most, as an early two-cylinder touring model was set at $3,000. But this price did bring with it some exceptional features, including dual carburetors and a system for heating the engine oil.

New to the Stearns offerings for 1905 was a four-cylinder engine, which doubled the horsepower of its two-cylinder predecessor. Prices likewise increased to as high as $4,150. Improvements followed the next year, as did another price increase, to $5,200. The factory was expanded in 1907 to meet increasing sales demand, and suppliers were pressed to meet Stearns' need for timely delivery of parts. By now some Stearns models had reached their highest price ever, of $7,500.

For 1908 Stearns announced the introduction of a new six-cylinder engine, in order to "meet the demands of the more experienced motoring public," as the company explained it. This six-cylinder Stearns, priced at $6,250, was capable of the impressively high speed of 100 miles per hour.

Always in pursuit of the most advanced engineering, Stearns became the first American licensee of the Knight sleeve-valve engine technology in 1911, at which time the company acquired the nearby Royal Tourist automobile plant in order to build Knight engines in-house. (See Royal Motor Car Company.) The name of Stearns-Knight was adopted and, from this time forward, the company produced only

Silent Knight-powered automobiles, turning out over 1,500 vehicles of this type in 1912.[5]

It was a well-known fact that the Knight sleeve-valve engines actually improved with use, increasing in horsepower and smoothness of operation over the years and miles. Even when new, the Knight engines were extremely quiet when compared with the then-typical poppet valve engines. The addition of an electric starter, beginning in 1912, added to the vehicle's ease of operation. Meanwhile, the engines increased in power and size from the initial four-cylinder version to a V-8 by 1916, with almost 4,000 vehicles being sold that year.[6]

A decision was made to move the manufacture of Knight engines to the main Stearns plant on Euclid Avenue, and the plant was once again expanded for this purpose. Some of this expansion took place in 1914, when famed industrial architect Albert Kahn designed a substantial plant addition for the company. At this time, additional land was also acquired for future expansion, which was felt to be imminent.

For 1915 a new light, smaller, and less expensive vehicle appeared in response to public demand. Priced at only $1,750, it was so successful that the Albert Kahn expansion was quickly followed by yet another new building that very same year.[7]

In 1917 Frank B. Stearns departed from his company to pursue the development of diesel engines. The Stearns company, under new management, continued producing high-quality automobiles under the Stearns-Knight name. In 1917, during World War I, the company achieved a remarkable feat by producing Rolls-Royce airplane engines while still managing to turn out 3,718 automobiles.[8] After the war, full automobile production resumed with prices in the low $3,000 range.

Another plant expansion followed in 1920, at which time annual sales reached 3,627 automobiles. A test track was constructed, and further plant expansion occurred in 1923.[9] However, production dropped to 1,593 automobiles that year, and in 1925 the Stearns company was purchased by the Willys-Overland Company of Toledo, Ohio. (See Willys Overland Company in Part II.)

Optimistically, a 100 horsepower straight-eight Stearns-Knight vehicle, capable of seventy-five miles per hour, was introduced in 1927 at a price of $4,500. However, Willys' purchase of Stearns turned out to be poorly timed. Sales struggled from 1925 until the end of 1929, when the Stearns-Knight line was dropped, and Willys-Overland no longer manufactured Stearns-Knight automobiles.

The total number of Stearns and Stearns-Knight automobiles produced over the years came to 32,432.[10]

---

1. Kimes and Clark, *Standard Catalog of American Cars, 1805–1942*, 3d ed.
2. *The Automobile*, October 1903; Kimes and Clark, *Standard Catalog of American Cars, 1805–1942*, 3d ed.
3. Wager, *Golden Wheels*.
4. *Motor*, March 1906; *Automobile Quarterly*, vol. 10, no. 4 (1972).
5. *Automobile Quarterly*, vol. 10, no. 4 (1972); Wager, *Golden Wheels*.
6. Wager, *Golden Wheels*.
7. *The Automobile*, August 20, 1914.
8. *Automobile Quarterly*, vol. 10, no. 4 (1972).
9. Stearns sales brochure, 1921.
10. Kimes and Clark, *Standard Catalog of American Cars, 1805–1942*, 3d ed.

Sterling Motor Company (1920 to 1923)

J.G. Sterling, who had been the chief engineer for F. B. Stearns Co., left Stearns in 1920 to form his own company. Sterling is credited with having designed the Stearns-Knight 4- and 6-cylinder engines during his tenure between 1911 and 1914. Capitalizing on his experience with the Stearns-Knight engine, Sterling obtained his own license under the Knight patents to manufacture a 6-cylinder Knight engine for his new automobile. A temporary syndicate was formed to undertake development and experimentation and a Cleveland machine shop on Coit Road was purchased for the purpose of building the first automobile. The syndicate also made arrangements to secure a Cleveland site for a future plant, but this was never built.[1]

In late 1920 or early 1921 the Sterling Motor Co. was chartered with a capitalization of $1 million to assume the syndicate's operations. Other Clevelanders joined the company including Alonzo Snyder, Alva Bradley, W.D. Gongwer, and J.V. Thomas. By the time the company was organized, three Sterling-Knight automobiles had been built and extensively tested in addition to having been exhibited at automobile shows in both Cleveland and Chicago.[2]

In May 1923, anticipating a move to Warren, Ohio, the company was reorganized as the Sterling-Knight Company. (See Sterling-Knight Company in Part II.) The Warren plant of the Supreme Motors Corporation was purchased for use as the Sterling factory.[3] (See Supreme Motors Corporation in Part II.) It was expected that full production of both closed and open five-passenger automobiles would be under way by August with prices set at $2,000. Sterling did not entirely sever its Cleveland connections, as it entered into an order for 1,000 bodies to be built by the Rubay Co.[4] (See Rubay Company.)

Production continued into 1926 when the bank which had been underwriting the company's operations ran into financial difficulties, forcing Sterling to operate on a cash basis. The situation was not tenable and bankruptcy ensued before the year was out.[5]

1. *Automotive Industries*, April 29, 1920, p. 1033; McCarthy, *A History of the Knight Engine in America*, Antique Automobile Club of America Library.
2. *Automotive Industries*, April 21, 1921, p. 883.
3. *Automotive Industries*, May 31, 1923, p. 1197.
4. *Automotive Industries*, October 25, 1923, p. 840, and January 17, 1924, p. 149.
5. Wager, *Golden Wheels*.

Stiverson Motor Car Company (1909); Stuyvesant Motor Car Company (1909 to 1912)

Cleveland resident Frank E. Stiverson organized the Stiverson Motor Car Company in November 1909 in order to build a factory near Cleveland to produce four- and six-cylinder Stiverson automobiles.[1] The company had developed an en bloc six-cylinder engine, said to be the first in the country. In order to begin production of an automobile as soon as possible the company purchased Cleveland's Gaeth Automobile Company in November 1910. (See Gaeth, Paul.) Stiverson operations, some of which had previously been carried on in Sandusky, Ohio, were consolidated in the Gaeth plant on Cleveland's near West Side. At the same time the company name was changed to Stuyvesant Motor Car Company.[2]

For 1911 the Stuyvesant company announced the continuation of the Gaeth automobile, renamed as the Stuyvesant Four, and introduced a new Stuyvesant Six. The company intended to manufacture 200 fours and 100 sixes, but it is doubtful that anything approaching these levels was achieved. By November of 1911 Stuyvesant was in financial trouble, which forced the sale of the company's assets to Grant-Lees Machine Company of Cleveland.[3] At that time Grant-Lees was manufacturing its own six-cylinder Grant.[4] (See Grant-Lees Machine Company.)

After leaving the field of automobile production in 1911, Frank Stiverson engaged in the manufacture of automobile accessories, operating as the Hudson-Stuyvesant Company. By this time he had changed his name to Frank E. Stuyvesant, which is perhaps the only instance in automotive history where an automobile entrepreneur became the namesake of his vehicle.

1. *The Automobile*, January 29, 1910.
2. *Horseless Age*, vol. 26, no. 21 (1910).
3. Kimes and Clark, *Standard Catalog of American Cars, 1805–1942*, 3d ed.
4. Kimes and Clark: The Grant-Lees Company produced one of the Cleveland-named automobiles.

Stringer, Mel (1918 to 1920)

Mel Stringer, a dirt-track race car driver, came to Cleveland in 1918 to build Mel Special race cars of his own design. How many of these cars he built is unknown but production was to-order, and undoubtedly quite limited.[1] While in Cleveland, Stringer also built and sold non-racing sport-type automobiles, and produced automotive racing accessories. Meanwhile, he actively raced his own automobiles, which were known as The M.E.L.[2] Stringer continued with these various Cleveland-based endeavors until 1920, at which time he moved to Pottstown, Pennsylvania.[3]

1. Kimes and Clark, *Standard Catalog of American Cars, 1805–1942*, 3d ed.
2. *Motor World, June 6, 1917*, Antique Automobile Club of America Library.
3. Kimes and Clark, *Standard Catalog of American Cars, 1805–1942*, 3d ed.

Strong, Edwin L., and Rogers, Lewis H. (1900 to 1901)

Edwin L. Strong, a wholesale druggist, and Lewis H. Rogers, treasurer of a construction supply company, were members of the board of the Cleveland Automobile Club when it was formed in 1900.[1] That same year, these two gentlemen joined together in an informal venture to manufacture an electric vehicle, to be called the Strong & Rogers.[2] It is not known where the Strong & Rogers was assembled,[3] but the vehicles were built to order only, priced from $1,200 to $2,000, and delivery was generally made within three months of an order.[4]

The automobile was powered by a 40-cell battery made by the Willard Battery Company of Cleveland.[5] Under normal operation the Strong & Rogers had three speeds forward, but the electric motor fields could be shifted from series to parallel, which gave the vehicle an additional three speeds forward.[6]

The Strong & Rogers had an attractive stanhope carriage body which rode on rubber-tired wagon-style wheels. Some of the vehicle's notable features included an electric braking system, seat cushions covered in fine goatskin, a set of illuminated gauges in a goatskin case on the dashboard, and an electrically actuated odometer. Emphasizing the overall elegance of the Strong & Rogers, one model was offered with a silver-inlaid mother-of-pearl tiller handle.[7] When exhibited at the Cleveland Automobile Show of 1900, the Strong & Rogers received an award for being "the most complete and handsome in detail."[8] Later that year, a Strong & Rogers electric made an appearance at the prestigious Inter-Ocean Automobile Show in Chicago.[9]

Although prospects were promising, the venture ended abruptly in 1901, due to the ill health of Lewis Rogers.[10]

1. Wager, *Golden Wheels*.
2. Kimes and Clark, *Standard Catalog of American Cars, 1805–1942*, 3d ed.
3. *The Automobile*, October 1900.
4. *Cycle and Automobile Trade Journal*, November 1900.
5. Kimes and Clark, *Standard Catalog of American Cars, 1805–1942*, 3d ed.
6. *Electrical World and Engineer*, October 6 and November 10, 1900.
7. Kimes and Clark, *Standard Catalog of American Cars, 1805–1942*, 3d ed.
8. *Electrical World and Engineer*, October 6 and November 10, 1900.
9. *Cycle and Automobile Trade Journal*, November 1900.
10. Wager, *Golden Wheels*.

The 1900 Strong & Rogers electric stanhope had a range of 40 miles and cost $1,200.

Superior Automobile Company (1902)

I.H. Lewis is said to have built two or three one-cylinder runabouts in his shop on Clara Street. These vehicles were apparently for experimentation and for his own use, with no intention of putting the vehicles into production. Lewis's automotive endeavors did not appear to have lasted beyond the end of 1902.[1]

1. Kimes and Clark, *Standard Catalog of American Cars, 1805–1942*, 3d ed.

A 1920 ad for the Templar, of which 1,850 were built that year.

Supreme Motors Corporation (1917 to 1918)

The main focus of the Supreme company was the design and manufacture of four, six, and twelve-cylinder engines. Several automobiles were built by the company for the purpose of demonstrating its engines. None were intended for sale. The company never truly gained its footing, although the leaders of the Supreme company had brought with them a depth of experience in the automobile industry from such companies as Pierce-Arrow, Chandler, Lozier, Thomas, Saxon, and Elgin. The company moved to Ashtabula during 1918, then to Warren, and then to bankruptcy. Its Warren plant and equipment were acquired by Sterling-Knight which moved to Warren from its Cleveland location on Coit Road.[1] (See Sterling-Knight Company in Part II.)

---

1. Kimes and Clark, *Standard Catalog of American Cars, 1805–1942*, 3d ed.

Templar Motors Corporation (1916 to 1923); Templar Motor Car Company (1923 to 1924)

Templar Motors Corporation was organized in late 1916 by F. M. Bramley, president of Cleveland Trinidad Paving Company,[1] to manufacture automobiles ranging in price from $1,225 to $1,850. The company boasted an impressive list of associates from a variety of well-known automobile companies such as Mercer, Stearns, Chalmers, and Hal. Before the year 1917 was out, a factory had been built on Cleveland's western edge and the first Templar automobile had made its appearance.[2]

The Templar, bearing a Maltese cross badge, was a compact and sporty two-place vehicle which, except for its 43 horsepower engine, was an assembled automobile. The company was especially proud of its four-cylinder Top-Valve engine, which had been designed and built in-house.[3] To guarantee reliability, engines were belt-run for twenty-four hours then run on a power stand for another six hours. Each assembled Templar was then test driven before delivery. It was said that Templars received a more rigid final inspection than Winton or Peerless, two of Cleveland's highest priced automobiles.[4]

The company went to great lengths to make sure that its automobiles were of the best quality. Employees were required to take physical examinations, as it was believed that healthy workers made better automobiles. Supervisory personnel made regular reports to management, providing reviews of departmental efforts to maintain high standards. All material and parts were fully inspected in the receiving department before being passed on to plant assembly areas. Templar also made its own windshields, a rarity among automobile manufacturers of the era. Even the crating wood used for export deliveries was of the highest quality to ensure safe shipment. All of this attention to detail contributed to Templar's exemplary reputation for reliability and justified the company slogan "Templar, the Super Fine Small Car."

The Templar automobile proved itself to be a superior product. It won far more endurance events and races than many higher priced automobiles of the day. Much of Templar's racing success was attributable to famous race car driver "Cannonball" Baker, who set a multitude of records behind the wheel of a Templar. So successful was Baker that, when he challenged all comers to contests of speed, economy, or durability, there were no takers.[5] This is no wonder, as Templars had already won every competition in which they had been entered.[6]

Templar was also proud of its location. Promotional material touted the fact that having its factory located in Cleveland helped establish the company's reputation for high grade production, as the city was known the world over as the home of many successful automobile manufacturers.

During World War I the company made artillery shells for the U.S. Government. For this purpose an additional 300 men were taken on to help the 514 already on the job, and a half-million dollars' worth of new machinery was acquired.[7] By the end of 1918, war-based manufacturing represented ninety percent of the company's output,[8] while it still managed to build 150 automobiles that year.[9]

When World War I came to an end, the company returned full-time to the manufacture of automobiles. Production grew rapidly and by 1920 forty Templars per day were leaving the factory. Five body styles were now offered: touring, sportette, roadster, sedan, and coupe. Plans were also in place to construct a new factory building to meet expected production demands.[10] This decision proved to be premature, as the post-war depression was especially hard on Templar, so much so that employees agreed to accept a twenty percent reduction in wages to help keep the company afloat. Prices were also reduced in the hopes of improving sales.[11] By late 1921 sales had begun to recover and prospects for the ensuing year were good.[12]

A fire in December destroyed three of Templar's buildings, and a stock of new automobiles as well. Fortunately, the company's new factory building, which was still under construction, escaped the catastrophe, and manufacture was shifted to the partially completed building, where production continued virtually uninterrupted. It was expected that 5,000 Templars would be built in 1922, and 500 new workers were added to the payroll.[13]

However, by now, parts suppliers were owed a considerable sum of money and the company was forced into bankruptcy, while the manufacture of Templars continued under the supervision of the bankruptcy receiver.¹⁴ To satisfy creditors, the company was reorganized as the Templar Motor Car Company in 1923, and was headed up by an entirely new group of individuals, including among them the man who had been the company's bankruptcy receiver.

The reconfigured company announced the introduction of a new six-cylinder engine, and also solicited dealer input to guide its overall operations.¹⁵ It is possible that the new Templar for 1924 was too conservative and conventional in appearance to attract buyers. However, for whatever reason, before 1924 was out the company was taken over by the banks,¹⁶ and Templar production ended, with a total of 5,519 Templars having been built from 1917 to 1924.

1. *The Automobile*, January 29, 1917.
2. *The Automobile*, April 19, June 28, August 2, 1917.
3. *The Automobile*, January 29, 1917.
4. *Templar Aces*, Supplement 1920.
5. *Templar Topics*, December 1921:
   Among the records were:
   A run between New York City and Chicago of 992 miles, 540 of which were through fog, rain, and mud, in 26 hours 50 minutes, averaging 36.97 mph
   Transcontinental runs in 1920 from the Atlantic to the Pacific and Mexico to Canada
   Breaking all "Cannon Ball" Baker's motorcycle records for which he was famous
   Driving in 1921 from Akron, Ohio, to Cleveland in twenty-five minutes averaging over 60 mph
   Economy run from Los Angeles to Yosemite over 356 miles, averaging 29.9 mpg.
6. *To the Stockholders of the Templar Motor Company*, July 30, 1920.
7. *Templar News*, July 1918.
8. *Automotive Industries*, October 31, 1918.
9. *Templar News*, July 1918.
10. *Automotive Industries*, March 25, 1920; *Templar Aces*, Supplement 1920.
11. *Automotive Industries*, January 20, February 10, March 30, April 7, April 21, October 15, 1921.
12. *Templar Topics*, December 1921.
13. *Automotive industries*, January 12, February 16, 1922.
14. *Automotive Industries*, November 23, 1922; June 7, 1923.
15. *Automotive Industries*, January 3, 1924.
16. *Automotive Industries*, September 25, 1924.

United Factories Company (1909)

The United company was engaged in the business of manufacturing buggy tops when it decided to try the arena of automobile manufacturing. The resulting vehicle was the Unito, a high wheeler befitting the company's dedication to the buggy trade. Perhaps one or two were built, but before the year was out it was decided to stick with making buggy tops rather than automobiles.¹

1. Kimes and Clark, *Standard Catalog of American Cars, 1805–1942*, 3d ed.

Washburn, George A. (1896 to 1902)

George A. Washburn was listed in the Cleveland Directory at different times as an electrician and a manager at the United Motor Company.

In 1896 he had designed and was building a vehicle that combined two different systems of motive power for its propulsion.¹ These systems worked in concert, depending upon the type of driving conditions encountered. On level stretches either an internal combustion gasoline engine or a battery powered electric motor was sufficient to drive the vehicle. On steep grades the gasoline engine and the electric motor acted together to drive the automobile. When descending a grade or coasting, the gasoline engine was disengaged and the electric motor acted as a generator to recharge the battery. This hybrid version of propulsion was the very first of its kind.² It also appeared to be truly hybrid, as neither the gasoline engine nor the electric motor alone was of sufficient power to propel the vehicle when maximum effort was required.

Beyond this, nothing specific is known about Washburn's efforts although he did announce that he was experimenting with a new vehicle of unspecified type or description in 1902.³

1. *The Horseless Age*, November 1896.
2. Kimes and Clark, *Standard Catalog of American Cars, 1805–1942*, 3d ed.
3. *The Automobile & Motor Review*, 1902.

Washington Automobile Company (1921)

Since the Washington automobile, which was to have been built by the Washington company, never saw the light of day, any confusion between it and the six other automobiles named Washington was avoided. As with so many new ventures of the era, the Washington

Six was to have been an assembled automobile. Its one distinctive feature would have been its air-cooled overhead-valve six-cylinder engine. Although a prototype may have been constructed, the Washington Six never reached the production stage.[1]

---

1. Kimes and Clark, *Standard Catalog of American Cars, 1805–1942*, 3d ed.

White Sewing Machine Company (1899 to 1906); White Company (1906 to 1915); White Motor Company (1915 to 1918)

The White automobile began its life in the factory of the White Sewing Machine Company. Prior to this, the company had made not only sewing machines, but also roller skates and bicycles. Rollin H. White, a budding engineer and son of the company's founder Thomas H. White, built his first steam-powered automobile in a corner of the White plant in 1899, utilizing a flash boiler system of his own design.[1] The flash boiler had two distinct advantages. It could bring water to a boil in only a few minutes, and it was free of the risk of explosion. An additional advantage, common to all steam engines, was that each stroke of a piston, both up and down, was a power stroke.

After extensive testing, Rollin offered his steam vehicle for sale to the general public in 1900, and its immediate success carried over to 1901, when 193 were sold. The 1901 and 1902 models had the steam engine mounted under the seat of a light runabout body. In 1902 Rollin added a steam condenser, increasing the automobile's range to 100 miles, before needing to add water.

Advertisements in *The Automobile and Motor Review* for 1902 boasted that a White had won a 650-mile contest in England with a perfect score, thanks in part to the White's extended range. That same year, Rollin White drove a White steamer to new speed records for distances from two to ten miles.

Changes were made for 1903. The engine was relocated from the rear of the vehicle to a space under the front hood, and a substantial touring body with wood-spoked wheels and comfortable seating for five was introduced. The new model had shaft drive instead of chain, and a steering wheel replaced the tiller. By the end of the year, annual sales of White steamers had reached 502.

As the White steamer increased in popularity, more space for production became a pressing need, and in 1903 the White automobile operation moved to its own facilities at

A rendering (circa 1905) of the new White company complex at East 79th and St. Clair, which combined both the sewing machine business, housed in the buildings to the left of the central administration offices, and the automobile business on the right.

The last White automobiles were produced in 1918 as the White Company changed to the exclusive manufacture of trucks and commercial vehicles.

Champlain and Canal Streets in Cleveland's Flats district, not far from the White Sewing Machine plant. Automobile frames and drive trains were built at this new plant, while bodies and trim were obtained from local suppliers. These components all came together and were assembled into a finished automobile at a White dealership and garage in downtown Cleveland.[2]

The White steamer steadily grew in size and elegance and, in 1905, it received its famous "White Curve" style hood which appeared on all White automobiles thereafter.

The first White steam car factory, 1903, on Canal Street in the Flats.

At this time, White was making its broadest marketing effort ever. While making a clear appeal to female motorists by touting the non-crank ease of starting a White steamer, the company was also paying attention to its performance image. Like most other early automobile companies, White took part in competitive racing, and campaigned its "Whistling Billy" race car around the country. Both the race car and White company's standard passenger automobiles competed successfully in numerous events against all types of automobiles. When a White set a world speed record in 1905 for one mile at 73.75 miles per hour, commentators applauded the event as having clearly demonstrated the White's superiority.[3]

Perhaps most impressive was White's ability to appeal to the luxury market. This was most clearly demonstrated when, in 1905, John D. Rockefeller purchased a White, and President Theodore Roosevelt rode in one at his inaugural parade.

White sales increased from just over 1,000 vehicles in 1905 to more than 1,500 in 1906, the highest yearly level ever reached for the White steamer.[4] In 1906 White's automobile business had advanced to the point where it was necessary to totally separate it from the sewing machine company. Accordingly, the White steamer operation was reorganized under a new corporate identity as the White Company.

In 1907 the White Company and the White Sewing Machine Company moved to newly built adjacent factories on Cleveland's East Side.[5] Both plants were single story sawtooth-roofed structures built over raised basements. Bringing all automobile production entirely under one roof was a boon to the efficiency of White's operations. The new automobile plant was arranged around a central transit corridor flanked by bays in which various component parts were manufactured. Finished parts were then delivered along the corridor to an assembly area where the automobiles were completed.

Automobile manufacturing at the new

facility proceeded apace, while at the same time production was expanded to include fire trucks, buses, and ambulances. This latter capability proved to be instrumental in the U.S. Government's selection of White for World War I military vehicle contracts.

Meanwhile, White was not neglecting the luxury market. A chauffeur-driven landaulette was introduced in 1907, the same year that the price for a White Pullman limousine reached $4,900.

The year 1907 was also an impressive one for the company's competition performance, as a White steamer completed the prestigious 1,570-mile Glidden Tour with a perfect score of 1,000. However, many of White's most serious competitors were gasoline-powered vehicles. And, toward the end of the first decade of the 20th century it was becoming apparent that the days of the steam-powered vehicle were numbered.

Fortunately, Rollin White had written his college thesis on the internal combustion engine, and he now decided to revisit the potential this might hold for the future of White automobiles.[6] He began experiments with a gasoline-powered vehicle and, in 1909, produced an operating example. Intensive performance comparisons between a White steam automobile and the new gasoline-powered version convinced him that the latter was the route to follow. Accordingly, White Company introduced two gasoline models in 1910, alongside its steam vehicles.

This decision proved to be a wise one. In 1910, White sold an equal number of gasoline- and steam-powered vehicles. It was becoming increasingly clear that the market for gasoline-powered vehicles was thriving. Therefore, in 1911, the company converted totally to the manufacture of internal combustion automobiles. As a growing company, White was now the employer of no fewer than 1,500 people.

The 1910 White gasoline-powered automobiles came with a four-cylinder engine available in either a 30 or 40 horsepower version, and prices ranged from $2,500 to $5,000. By 1912 a new six-cylinder engine was introduced which boasted 60 horsepower. It was mated to a 132-inch wheelbase chassis, while the original four rode on a 120-inch wheelbase. Prices for the six were as high as $6,500. By 1913 all White models had electric self-starters and modern left-hand drive.

The year 1914 was marked by a major change for the company. Rollin's father Thomas White, who was a major stockholder, died. Then Rollin himself left the company, to form the Cleveland Tractor Company and, later, Rollin Motors Company (see Rollin Motors Company). As a result, it became necessary to restructure the company. The White Motor Company was organized, and a smooth transition to new management was effected, with Rollin's brother Windsor acting as president, and his brother Walter taking on the office of vice president.

Ever greater demand for White automobiles made it necessary for the company to expand its facilities. However, as the war in Europe escalated, the White company was increasingly called upon to provide trucks for France and its allies. Just over 600 trucks were delivered overseas in 1914, and by the end of World War I, 18,000 White trucks had been sent into war service.

Meanwhile, the company not only continued automobile production, but also expanded its offerings. A broad range of body styles was now available: roadster, coupe, touring, semi-touring, town car, and limousine. One roadster was even offered with oversized 40" wheels, for travel in desert conditions. Most impressive was the fashionable White limousine, which came with a rakishly slanted windshield. And, for 1917, the White four was improved, having sixteen valves instead of eight.

Although the company had not initially intended to abandon automobile manufacturing once war-time truck production ended, the shift from personal to commercial vehicles offered more attractive opportunities. In 1918, White ceased the manufacture of automobiles completely to focus exclusively on the production of trucks.

By 1918, White had produced a very impressive number of vehicles, including some 18,000 military trucks for the U.S. war effort. The company had also manufactured 21,134 automobiles, of which 9,122 were steam-powered, and another 12,012 were gasoline-powered.[7]

White continued to manufacture commercial vehicles well into the latter part of the 20th century.

---

1. *Automobile Quarterly*, vol. 3, no. 4 (1993).
2. *The Automobile and Motor Review*, October 11, 1902; *The Automobile*, October 3, 1903.
3. Kimes and Clark, *Standard Catalog of American Cars, 1805–1942*, 3d ed.
4. Ibid.
5. *The Automobile*, September 17, 1907.
6. Wager, *Golden Wheels*.
7. Kimes and Clark, *Standard Catalog of American Cars, 1805–1942*, 3d ed.

Willard Storage Battery Company (1902 to 1903)

Theodore A. Willard had several prototype vehicles constructed to test his various designs for electric vehicle devices. The first was built with the help of Sipe & Sigler Company, and the next two were constructed by Jacob Hoffman Wagon Company. Willard had no intention of placing any of his experimental vehicles into production.[1] However, Willard did agree to produce copies of Hoffman's vehicle on a custom order basis for the years 1903 and 1905.[2] (See Jacob Hoffman Wagon Company and Sipe & Sigler Company.)

---

1. Kimes and Clark, *Standard Catalog of American Cars, 1805–1942*, 3d ed.
2. Willard Storage Battery Company supplied batteries for a variety of Cleveland automobiles including Strong & Rogers, Sipe & Sigler, Lincoln Electric, Hoffman, and Parsons.

Williams Motor Carriage Company (1906); Williams Electric Vehicle Company (1906 to 1907)

H.A. Williams began experimenting with a gasoline-powered automobile in Akron, Ohio, in 1906, but it was not until he moved to Cleveland and joined with backers to form the Williams Motor Carriage Company that he was able to build his automobile. Williams' automobile was an instant failure.[1] This may have been due to the vehicle's price range of $3,500 to $5,000, or perhaps it was due to the vehicle's hefty cast iron body.[2]

Meanwhile, the Williams company purchased the rights to manufacture the Blakeslee Electric automobile, which was renamed the Williams Electric. As a result, the company also changed its name to reflect this new focus, and became the Williams Electric Vehicle Company.

Williams soon sold his interest in the company, most likely as a result of unsatisfactory business relations with his investors, and departed in early 1907.[3] (See Demars Electric Vehicle Company.)

---

1. Kimes and Clark, *Standard Catalog of American Cars, 1805–1942*, 3d ed.
2. *The Automobile*, April 18, 1907.
3. Wager, *Golden Wheels*.

Winton, Alexander (1895 to 1897); Winton Motor Carriage Company (1897 to 1915); Winton Motor Car Company (1915 to 1924)

Henry Ford is often given credit for being the father of the modern American automobile industry. Because he employed the assembly line method of production, he was able to offer automobiles at affordable prices for the average American. However, the American automobile industry was not born with the assembly line. It, in fact, came into being in the late 19th century, at the hands of Clevelander Alexander Winton. If the American automobile industry can be best described as providing mass-produced vehicles offered for sale to the general public, then Alexander Winton should be credited as the father of this nascent industry.

It all began in 1891, when Winton founded what became the highly successful Winton Bicycle Company. By 1895, Winton had become so entranced by the new field of self-propelled vehicles that he left his bicycle company in order to concentrate full time on the development of an automobile of his own design.

Winton began his automobile experiments at home, but by 1896 his prospects for a commercial enterprise appeared so promising that he rented manufacturing space in the Brush Electric Company factory on East 45th Street,

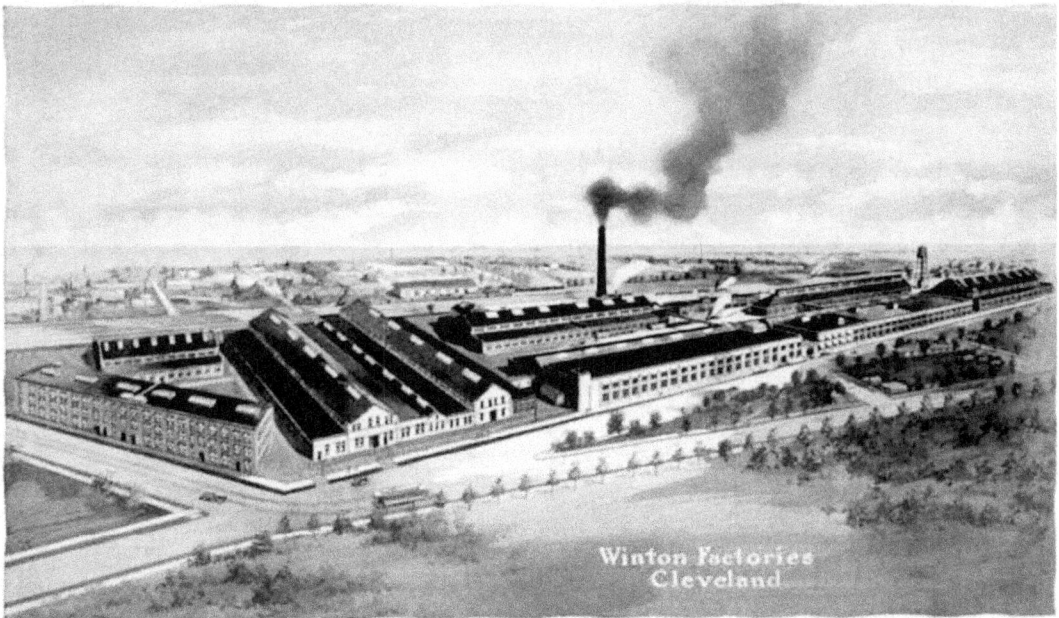

Top: Alexander Winton has his hand on the tiller of his second prototype vehicle, which is parked in front of his factory on East 45th Street in Cleveland in 1897. *Bottom:* Rendering of the new 1902 Winton factory complex on Berea Road.

January 18, 1911. THE HORSELESS AGE. 37

This Test Covered 800,000 Miles

If you were to cross the continent from New York to San Francisco some 246 times, your distance traveled would be about 800,000 miles.

And even then you would not have equaled the distance traveled by 74 Winton Sixes in the Upkeep Contest of 1910.

* * *

Last week we told you about the records of the best cars in that test. Now we want to tell you about all the cars.

In the table we have divided the records into three classes.

The best class (10 cars) traveled 165,901.9 miles, and averaged for repair expense 4.2 cents per 1000 miles.

The worst class (eleven cars having $25 or more repair expense each) traveled 132,181.6 miles, and averaged for repair expense $6.594 per 1000 miles.

The remaining cars (53 of them) traveled 503,148.2 miles, and averaged for repair expense 42 cents per 1000 miles.

And all the cars taken together (74 in number) traveled 801,231.7 miles (more than 246 times across the continent), and averaged for repair expense $1.36 per 1000 miles.

* * *

Every mile of this distance was traveled by regular stock model Winton Six cars in the service of their individual owners.

And all these figures are compiled from the monthly reports of these owners, supported by affidavits.

* * *

This was the most tremendous test ever given to any make of automobile.

And it goes to prove that for ability to deliver the greatest possible service at the lowest possible repair expense the Winton Six is without an equal.

* * *

Our catalog tells all about the Winton Six. Also it gives the full reasons why so many manufacturers are beginning to make six-cylinder cars. With the catalog we will send our Upkeep Book, which presents in detail the figures that make the Winton Six the holder of the World's Lowest Repair Expense Record.

Clip the coupon and mail it today.

The Winton Motor Car. Co.
Cleveland, O., U. S. A.

WINTON BRANCH HOUSES:

NEW YORK..............Broadway at 70th St.
CHICAGO..........Michigan Avenue at 13th St.
BOSTON..............Berkeley at Stanhope St.
PHILADELPHIA........246-248 No. Broad St.
BALTIMORE..............209 North Liberty St.
PITTSBURGH..............Baum at Beatty St.
CLEVELAND.......Huron Road at Euclid Ave.
DETROIT....................998 Woodward Ave.
KANSAS CITY..............3328-3330 Main St.
MINNEAPOLIS............16-22 Eighth St. N.
SAN FRANCISCO..........300 Van Ness Ave.
SEATTLE..................1000-1006 Pike St.

COMPLETE RECORD OF THE 1910 WINTON SIX UPKEEP CONTEST				
Class.	No. of Cars.	Total Miles.	Total Repairs.	Average Repairs Per 1000 Miles.
1—Best performances...........	10	165,901.9	$6.96	$0.04
2—Worst performances..........	11	132,181.6	871.58	6.59
3—Remainder	53	503,148.2	210.62	.42
Totals	74	801,231.7	$1,089.16	$1.36

| The Winton Motor Car. Co. |
| 425 Berea Road, Cleveland, Ohio. |
| Please send Winton Six literature to |
| .... |
| .... |
| .... |
| .... |

In writing to advertisers please mention THE HORSELESS AGE.

This advertisement for the 1911 Winton Six lays claim to the "World's Lowest Repair Expense Record," which was achieved by its predecessor, the 1910 Winton Six. Repair costs for that vehicle were, on average, just $1.36 for every one thousand miles driven (author's collection).

which was just a few steps away from the Winton Bicycle Company plant.[1]

By the end of that year Winton had completed his first prototype vehicle, which had a rather tall and box-like appearance, as the body barely extended beyond the front and rear axles. Weighing just over 1,000 pounds, it was powered by a single-cylinder eight-horsepower engine, and was geared for a top speed of thirty-five miles per hour. It had tiller steering, and featured "dos-a-dos" seating, with the front seat facing forward and the back seat facing to the rear. The prototype rode on four pneumatic tires which were mounted on large wire-spoked wheels. The gasoline tank was located on the dashboard, and the engine and water tank were positioned underneath the seats.

Winton's experiments continued until a second, and significantly different, prototype was produced in 1897. This two-cylinder ten-horsepower vehicle hit the then-amazing speed of 33.64 miles per hour on Cleveland's Glenville race track.

Pleased with his progress, and anticipating that his venture would prove commercially successful, Winton incorporated the Winton Motor Carriage Company in March of 1897 and, in early 1898, built a third and final version of his automobile.

It was a two-place four-wheeled vehicle powered by a horizontal one-cylinder six-horsepower gasoline engine located in a compartment over the rear axle. The engine had a bore and stroke of five inches by six inches, and was governed to run between 200 and 1000 revolutions per minute, limiting its top speed to 20 miles per hour. It rode on wire-spoked bicycle-style wheels which were fitted with pneumatic tires. The front wheels were 32 inches in diameter, and the rear wheels had a diameter of 36 inches. Right-hand steering was by tiller, and chain drive connected the engine to a differential at the rear axle. The vehicle's phaeton body was finished in Brewster Green, with leather cushions and dash, and all trimmings were nickel-plated. Amenities included a top, storm apron, headlight, fenders, and a gong.

Winton constructed four of these vehicles, and offered them for sale to the general public through an advertisement in *Scientific American* magazine. The advertisement was immediately successful; on March 24, 1898, Alexander Winton sold his first automobile to Robert Allison of Port Carbon, Pennsylvania.

It had been Winton's intention from the very beginning to produce a vehicle of unsurpassed quality and engineering. As a result, his automobiles were, of necessity, very expensive, and appealed to a limited market of well-to-do individuals. Consequently, to initiate sales by means of national advertising, without ever having made any prior custom sales, was a very bold move. But this is exactly what Alexander Winton did. He offered the general public a selection of automobiles from a standing inventory of vehicles which were available for demonstration, immediate sale, and delivery. Winton took quite a risk, but it paid off.

Winton's achievement received special recognition in the April 2, 1908, issue of *The Automobile*. It was noted that two of Winton's vehicles had been sold to distant purchasers (Allison was from Pennsylvania and H.C. Sargent, the second purchaser, lived in Westfield, New Jersey), but a third sale was made to Jon Moody of Ontario, Canada. Winton thus had also made the automobile industry's first international sale.

Racing and endurance events were a very important part of proving a new vehicle's capabilities to the buying public, and Alexander Winton was keenly aware of the importance of publicity in this regard.

In 1897 he made the first long distance endurance run from Cleveland to New York City, managing the feat in just seventy-eight hours. He repeated the trip in 1899, when he drove one of his automobiles from Cleveland to New York City in just forty-seven hours, this time taking along a *Cleveland Plain Dealer* reporter as a passenger. Prior to this time, Winton sales had been primarily to individuals with a technical bent, but now the general public had been attracted to the automobile, and publicity from this adventure caused sales to leap, with 100 Winton automobiles being sold that year.

In 1900 Alexander Winton made a third trip to New York City, this time to display his new vehicle at the New York City Automobile Show. Cutting his driving time to just over thirty-eight hours, which was less than half the time of his first trip, he drove his mud-splattered automobile directly onto the display floor, creating one of the show's most unusual exhibits.

Capping the success of Winton's early promotional endurance runs was a totally private venture, undertaken in 1903 by Dr. H. Nelson Jackson and his chauffeur Sewell K. Croker. Setting off on a whim, the two adventurers left San Francisco, California, just three days after the notion had occurred to them that they could become the first to cross the continent by automobile.

Starting out driving their two-cylinder 1903 Winton with no more than a compass to guide them, they surmounted unimaginable challenges just to reach the Mississippi River. From there, things were more civilized, and the pair arrived in New York City just sixty-four days after beginning their journey, having covered over 5,500 miles. So dedicated to their venture were the two gentlemen that, when passing through Cleveland, they declined an offer from Alexander Winton to give their automobile a check-up and a wash job.

Racing performance, as well as endurance runs, generated publicity and resulted in increased sales for Winton. In 1901 a Winton automobile set a world speed record for the ten mile distance, averaging just short of 54 miles per hour, which Winton bested in a similar event just weeks later, reaching 57.8 miles per hour. The famous Winton Bullet race car then picked up the speed mantle in 1902. Powered by a four-cylinder engine that had a massive six-inch bore and seven-inch stroke, the Bullet hit over 70 miles per hour on a one-mile course and, in 1904, with famed race driver Barney Oldfield at the wheel, achieved a speed of 83.7 miles per hour.

The success of these trials and the publicity they generated kept the factory busy filling orders. Winton sales were brisk, and in 1902 the company moved from its modest leased quarters on East 45th Street to a new eleven-acre complex on Cleveland's West side.

According to the March 28, 1903, issue of *The Automobile*, Winton's new factory was the largest plant in the world devoted exclusively to the manufacture of automobiles. This new purpose-built complex, located at Berea Road and Madison Avenue, extended for a quarter mile along the Lake Shore & Michigan railroad tracks, and had direct rail access for receipt of materials and for shipment of automobiles. The factory was entirely self-contained, having its own foundry, power plant, and the capacity for manufacturing everything necessary to construct new automobiles, with the exception of tires, batteries, and glass. It even had its own test track.[2]

Winton automobiles steadily became heavier, more powerful, more luxurious, and more popular. By 1904 Wintons were being offered at over $3,500, and the new plant had to be expanded to meet sales demand.[3] Winton now had over 1,500 employees and once shipped 300 automobiles in a single month. This was a far cry from the 300 men who had previously produced sixty automobiles per month at the original East 45th Street facility.[4] Throughout this time the company maintained a complete inventory of replacement parts for all of the automobiles which it had produced.[5] By 1905, annual sales had hit the 1,000 mark.[6]

Innovation was a Winton hallmark, and by 1908 Winton was the only automobile company to offer six-cylinder engines exclusively. Most impressive, however, is the fact that Alexander Winton is credited with over one hundred patents. Many of his inventions were quite advanced, including the use of compressed air to operate a variable-lift inlet valve, and a compressed air self-starter that could also be used to pump up tires. Both of these features were introduced in 1909.

Meanwhile, Alexander Winton's creative talents had been attracted by another area of transport. When Winton could not find a suitable marine engine for his personal yacht, he began experimenting with the diesel engine, which was gaining popularity in Europe at that time. He was so pleased with the results of these experiments that he soon added a diesel engine manufacturing section to his automobile plant, and in 1913 it produced the first all-American-built diesel engine. Shortly afterwards this division was formally organized as the Winton Gas Engine and Manufacturing Company, which focused on the production of quality marine and railroad engines.

The year 1915 was a busy one, with sales continuing apace, and the company being reorganized as the Winton Motor Car Company. Sales continued to climb and, even though Winton employed 2,000 people and was operating two shifts per day in 1915, the company was running as much as six months behind on deliveries.[7]

Bowing to a new industry trend toward smaller automobiles, Winton introduced a new lighter vehicle for 1916, the Six-33, which had a 33.75 horsepower engine and rode on a 128-inch wheelbase. This smaller Winton was still a premium automobile, with prices as high as $3,500. Winton offered only one other basic model in 1916, the larger and more powerful Six-48, which had a 138-inch wheelbase and sported a 48.6 horsepower engine.

A stunning array of ten body styles was available on the two models, including five- and seven-passenger tourings, a runabout, a three-quarter limousine, a full four-door limousine, a limousine landaulet, a sedan, and a coupe. An electric starter replaced the compressed-air starter this year, primarily at the insistence of Winton dealers.

With sales now projected at 4,000 automobiles, another plant expansion was undertaken in 1917. However, America's involvement in World War I was making heavy demands upon manufacturers, especially those in the automobile trade. Winton was no exception, and the company reduced its production of automobiles to provide the U.S. government with a variety of war materiel and limousines for high-ranking military officials.

After the war, sales were sluggish. In 1921 Winton reported having sold only 325 automobiles, down from a pre-war figure of 2,458 in 1916.[8] Production efficiencies were introduced to counter the downturn in sales,[9] and production was even halted for a few months in early 1921.[10] But it was too little, and too late. Winton had always built only expensive, high-quality automobiles, but in the 1920s the market for such an automobile had shrunk significantly. Winton produced fewer than 700 cars in 1922, and when the Winton Motor Car Company ceased operations in 1924, only 129 automobiles had been produced that year.

Winton was not one to lower his standards in order to adapt to the new market. He half-heartedly sought a merger with the Haynes Automobile Company of Indiana and the Dorris Motors Corporation of Missouri, but the deal never materialized. Rather than sell his company, Winton closed it down, sold off the assets, and focused his energies on the diesel engine.

Between 1898 and 1924, a total of 28,492 Winton automobiles were produced.[11]

---

1. Saal and Golias, *Famous but Forgotten*.
2. Ibid.
3. *The Auto Era*, vol. III, no. 5 (1904).
4. *The Auto Era*, April 1902.
5. Saal and Golias, *Famous but Forgotten*.
6. Kimes and Clark, *Standard Catalog of American Cars, 1805–1942*, 3d ed.
7. *The Automobile*, April 15, 1915.
8. Wager, *Golden Wheels*.
9. *Automotive Industries*, April 12, 1923.
10. Van Tassel and Grabowski, *The Encyclopedia of Cleveland History*.
11. Kimes and Clark, *Standard Catalog of American Cars, 1805–1942*, 3d ed.

Wissman Auto Repair Company (1911)

Organized for the purpose of manufacturing, repairing, and dealing in automobiles, the company was formed with a modest capitalization of $5,000. Its organizers were Joseph H. Wissman, William J. Cerma, and Joseph Kocian. It is unlikely that an automobile was produced.[1]

---

1. Kimes and Clark, *Standard Catalog of American Cars, 1805–1942*, 3d ed.

Woodland Motor Car Company (1909)

Like many early automobile pioneers, Frank J. Moore had a background which gave no indication that he would develop a marketable automobile. All that is known of his early years in Cleveland is that he served as general baggage agent for the New York Central & St. Louis Railway in 1901.¹ However, by 1909 his automotive experiments had been successful enough to attract the attention of local residents, for whom he created four custom-made automobiles.

These Woodland automobiles were large and imposing touring vehicles, priced at $2,300 and powered by relatively uncommon three-cylinder two-stroke engines. The bodies for the Woodland were built by Patterson Body Company of Cleveland. One Woodland body style was unique, as it offered four doors. This was at a time when front doors or, as they were then known, "fore-doors," were not common.² The Woodland was apparently a reliable vehicle, as one reportedly traveled over 70,000 miles in just six years.³

Although he seems to have manufactured no more automobiles after the four produced in 1909, Moore did continue to work in the automotive field under the name of Woodland Motor Car & Repair Company.

1. *Cleveland City Directory*, 1909.
2. Kimes and Clark, *Standard Catalog of American Cars, 1805–1942*, 3d ed.
3. Wager, *Golden Wheels*.

Worthington Automobile Company (1904)

Charles Campbell Worthington was a New Yorker with a minimal Cleveland presence. He was an inventor and entrepreneur who came from a family of creative engineers. His father, Henry R. Worthington, had invented the first direct-acting steam pump in 1840, and its success led to the creation of the Worthington Pump and Machinery Corporation. After his father's death, C.C. Worthington took over the company, making many engineering improvements during his tenure, and increasing the company's worldwide presence. His expertise even led to a British knighthood.¹

Sometime in the early 1900s Worthington formed the Worthington Automobile Company, to sell several types of steam- and gasoline-powered pleasure cars which he had designed.

Early in 1904, Worthington acquired the Berg Automobile Company of Cleveland from fellow New Yorker Hart Berg (see Berg Automobile Company). Worthington then made arrangements with the Federal Manufacturing Company of Cleveland to produce his own Meteor automobile as well and, by July 1904, Federal was turning out both Berg and Meteor automobiles.²

The Meteor was a substantial touring automobile with a four-cylinder engine and a price that varied from $2,500 to $2,950. It employed an 18-horsepower engine, as did one model of the Berg automobile, which was manufactured at the same facility.

Worthington left the company in December 1904. Shortly thereafter, William Colt, who had been with Federal Manufacturing Company, took over the Worthington company and merged it into his Cleveland Motor Car Company. The Meteor was renamed the Cleveland, and production of the Berg was discontinued. (See Cleveland Motor Car Company.)

1. "Charles Campbell Worthington," retrieved January 15, 2016, from Wikipedia, https://en.wikipedia.org/wiki/Charles_Campbell_Worthington; "History of Early American Automobiles, 1861–1929," Chapter 12, retrieved January 15, 2016, from http://www.earlyamericanautomobiles.com/americanautomobiles12.htm; and "Charles C. Worthington Dies, Inventor and Golf Pioneer," retrieved January 15, 2016, from archive.lib.msu.edu/tic/golfd/article/1945jan30.pdf.
2. *The Automobile*, July 9, 1904.

Zeder Motor Company (1922)

The Zeder company is an excellent example of an enterprise which was all promise and no product.

The public was first introduced to the plans of the Zeder Motor Company in March 1922, when the company announced its intention to build an automobile in the Cleveland Tractor Company plant of Rollin White. The individuals involved were well known. They included E.B. Wilson, former sales manager of the Willys Corporation; R.T. Hodgkins, vice president of Cleveland Tractor Company; J.C. Hahn, former branch manager of Studebaker, and Rollin H. White himself.¹

The Zeder automobile was to be designed

by F.M. Zeder, of the Zeder-Skelton-Breer Engineering Corporation of Newark, New Jersey. It was to have a six-cylinder engine, use aluminum extensively, and bear a $2,000 price tag. It was expected that the prototype would be completed in nine months.[2]

Things seemed to be progressing well, and financial backing was solidified by April.[3] In May it was even announced that the Cleveland Tractor Company would be reorganized as the Allyne-Zeder Motors Company, with the specific purpose of manufacturing the new Zeder automobile. Having capitalization of $5 million in hand, and Rollin White as president, the corporation was poised for success.[4]

However, in 1923 the Zeder-Skelton-Breer group accepted an offer to work for Chrysler in Detroit, and the Cleveland Zeder plans collapsed. Rollin White subsequently formed the Rollin Motors Company, and moved on to produce a Zeder-based vehicle, which would now be named the Rollin[5] (see Rollin Motors Company).

1. *Automotive Industries*, March 23, 1922, p. 688, Antique Automobile Club of America Library.
2. *Automotive Industries*, March 30, 1922, p. 734, Antique Automobile Club of America Library.
3. *Automotive Industries*, April 20, 1922, p. 892, Antique Automobile Club of America Library.
4. *Motor World*, May 10, 1922, p. 39, and *Motor Age*, May 11, 1922, Antique Automobile Club of America Library.
5. Wager, *Golden Wheels*.

Part II.
The Automobiles of Ohio

An Overview

Although Cleveland clearly shines as the premiere city in Ohio's early decades of automotive history, the rest of the state also produced an impressive number of self-propelled vehicles from the last half of the 19th century through the first four decades of the 20th century.

It was not long after Clevelander John J. Grant had designed and driven a steam vehicle in 1864 (see Grant, John J., in Part I), that other steam-powered vehicles began to appear elsewhere in Ohio. One of the most remarkable was produced by Oliver Burdette of New Athens in 1870. Burdette's creation was gigantic. It was eighteen feet long, and towed a huge trailing fuel tender.

Other steamers followed in quick succession. A. B. Coe of Lima constructed one in 1883, and Caleb Healy built another in New London in 1888. That same year M. Schworm of Massillon followed suit with a one-cylinder steam-powered horseless carriage. The preference for steam power in these early experimental vehicles may have been due to its familiarity as reliable motive power for everything from transcontinental railroads to local farm tractors.

By 1889, eighteen Ohioans outside of Cleveland had built and driven self-propelled vehicles. By the turn of the century, thirty-nine more had entered this quest, and Ohio had over twice as many experimenters and entrepreneurs engaged in developing motorized vehicles as did neighboring Michigan. Most impressive is the fact that many of these early automobile pioneers were located in small communities and rural settings, away from the traditional industrial support network of large urban areas.

As a result of the confluence of the state's industrial might and its enterprising inventors, Ohio became the nation's most prolific incubator for the automobile industry from the late 19th century until 1906, by which time it could lay claim to no fewer than 170 automobile ventures, ranging from lone individuals at work in dimly lit sheds to highly successful companies exporting automobiles around the world. Between 1900 and 1920, Ohio generated, on average, anywhere from ten to twenty new automobile ventures each year. From the late 1800s through 1942 there were 408 Ohio individuals and enterprises outside of Cleveland that had announced their intent to produce an automobile.

However, regardless of the size of the undertaking, be it individual or corporative, the vast majority of early Ohio automotive ventures lasted for no more than one year. Fifty-four lasted only two years, and just twenty-eight were still around beyond the five year mark.

The number of vehicles produced by most endeavors was quite small. Clearly, there was a large gap between the dream of making one's own vehicle and the reality of managing a commercial manufacturing operation. Forty efforts to build an automobile produced not a single motorized vehicle, and many of these never went beyond merely announcing the intention to manufacture a prototype. Of those ventures which did produce a vehicle, at least 100 built only one example before expiring. Those that made up to five automobiles numbered a mere eighteen.

Surprisingly, the success of any particular venture was not related to its size. The sole inventor was just as likely to produce a viable motorized conveyance as was a corporation formed for the purpose of making a profit through the manufacture of automobiles. Even those companies which were organized with high expectations and various levels of capitalization, ranging from $5,000 to $10 million, were no more likely to achieve their objectives than a sole proprietor with limited means. Despite their grand-scale expectations, many of these never even assembled a single prototype vehicle.

A handful of individuals became especially significant figures in Ohio automotive history. Among these was Frederick Douglas Patterson, who must have seemed at the time to be one of the unlikeliest of men to succeed in the automobile business. Patterson, the son of a former slave, lived in Greenfield, forty miles southwest of Columbus. From 1916 to 1919 Patterson built and sold at least thirty Patterson-Greenfield automobiles before moving on to the motor bus business and building the first buses that ran on the streets of Cincinnati.

At the other end of the spectrum were three very well-known Ohio entrepreneurs, John North Willys, Powel Crosley, Jr., and James W. Packard.

John N. Willys was a successful automobile dealer who assumed control of the Overland Auto Company in 1907 to assure himself a constant supply of automobiles to sell. After having relocated Overland's manufacturing operations from Indianapolis, Indiana, to Toledo, Ohio, in 1909, Willys was soon producing thousands of automobiles. In 1928 Willys's annual output exceeded 230,000, and by the time that World War II put an end to the company's automobile manufacturing efforts, a total of 2,100,000 automobiles had been built. It was at this time that the Willys company created and produced the world-famous Jeep for the military.

Powel Crosley, Jr., like John Willys, was a successful businessman before he ventured into the making of automobiles in Cincinnati. Having become the world's largest manufacturer of radios in the 1920s, he followed this success with the highly regarded Shelvador refrigerator. In 1939 he tried his hand in the automobile industry, introducing the Lilliputian Crosley, which sold for as little as $888. When Crosley automobile production ended in the early 1950s, over 70,000 of these diminutive vehicles had been built.

James Ward Packard, an engineer and businessman living in Warren, accepted a challenge made by Clevelander Alexander Winton to build a better automobile than the 1898 Winton. By 1900 Packard had produced his first automobile and was actively engaged in its manufacture and sale. The Packard proved to be one of the longest-lived and most respected of America's earliest automobile marques, continuing in production well into the middle of the 20th century.

Throughout the early years of the 20th century, Ohio steadily grew to become a dominant automobile manufacturing location as well as an internationally significant supplier of automobile parts and accessories. By the mid-1920s the state was home to the world's largest automobile body plant, the Fisher Body Company facility on Cleveland's East Side. Ohio also had the world's greatest concentration of tire factories. Goodyear, Goodrich, Firestone, General, and Seiberling were all headquartered in Akron.

Well into the 21st century, 82 of Ohio's 88 counties still boasted active automotive industry manufacturing facilities, and the state continued to be the nation's second most significant manufacturer of automobiles and automobile parts, producing an impressive array of automotive components for manufacturing, assembly, and export. The primary source for Part II is Kimes and Clark, *Standard Catalog of American Cars, 1805–1942*, 3d edition, unless otherwise noted.

The Manufacturers

Acorn Automobile Company (Cincinnati, 1910 to 1912)

For a short while, an unknown number of runabouts and touring vehicles were made to special order by Acorn. However, before the end of 1912 the company had abandoned making automobiles in favor of producing motorized delivery wagons.

Adams Brothers (Findlay, 1910 to 1911)

After initially producing a few passenger automobiles in 1910 Adams Brothers switched to the manufacture of commercial vehicles in 1911.

Advance Manufacturing Company (Hamilton, 1899)

The Ritchie family oversaw operations of this company. William Ritchie announced his completion of a gasoline-powered motorized vehicle in 1899, although details about its construction are lacking. It appears to have been the only vehicle Ritchie or the company built. The Advance company did continue in business, building gasoline engines for the trade.

Advance Motor Vehicle Company (Miamisburg, 1909 to 1912); Kauffman Motor Car Company (Miamisburg, 1912)

The Advance company was the product of a merger between the Kauffman Buggy Company and the Hatfield Motor Vehicle Company, both of Miamisburg. (See Hatfield Motor Vehicle Company.) Production at the new company was changed from the Hatfield, a buggy-like highwheeler, to a standard automobile which was named the Kauffman. It met with moderate success but by the end of 1912 operations had ceased. Shortly before its termination the company name was changed to Kauffman Motor Car Company.

Ahrens-Fox Fire Engine Company (Cincinnati, 1913)

Ahrens-Fox made a Battalion Roadster which was intended as a fire chief's automobile. Produced for only one year, it came equipped with limited firefighting equipment and other amenities to accommodate its specialized use. Sales were negligible.

Akron Machine Company (Akron, 1899); Akron Motor Carriage Company (Akron, 1900 to circa 1904); York Machinery Company, Akron, (1904 to 1905)

Akron Machine built a prototype vehicle in 1899. After successful tests it was decided to enter full production of the vehicle, and the following year the Akron Motor Carriage Company was formed for this purpose. A limited number of automobiles was built, after which the company was sold to the York Machinery Company. York built at least one two-stroke engine automobile, also named the Akron, but in 1905 York ceased automobile operations, opting to produce only engines.

Allen, E. W., and W. O. Allen (Fostoria and Columbus, 1913 to 1922)

With plants in Fostoria and Columbus, the Allen brothers had sufficient facilities for the production of their Allen automobiles. The Allen was a smart-looking touring-style vehicle with a four-cylinder L-head engine and Neverleak roof. By 1916 a total of 3,436 automobiles had been produced, at which time the brothers acquired the manufacturer of the Allens' engines. During World War I the brothers manufactured both automobiles and military supplies, but the post-war economy was not kind to the firm. Although sales of Allen automobiles from 1917 to 1922 came to 7,595, insolvency could not be avoided, largely because the government's payment for war work did not arrive until after bankruptcy in 1922. The company's largest asset, its Fostoria factory, went to Willys. (See Willys-Overland Company.)

Alliance (Garfield, 1910)

One Alliance automobile was built by a Garfield machine shop and miraculously it has survived, reportedly still in the hands of a local collector as late as the mid–1990s.

Alliance Carriage Company (Cincinnati, 1895)

One automobile was built by the company to the design of British mechanical engineer Walter MacLeod.

Alliance Motor Car Company (Alliance, 1913)

The Alliance company was formed with a capitalization of $50,000, to manufacture automobiles and other vehicles. Apparently none were produced.

Altenberg, George P. (Cincinnati, 1906)

Mr. Altenberg produced one prototype automobile but his announced intentions to go into the full manufacture of a line of vehicles came to naught.

American Hydromobile Company (Winchester, 1902)

Joe Smith built his gasoline-powered highwheel automobile at the facilities of the American Hydromobile Company. He used it to give rides to residents of Winchester. However, Smith soon dropped the idea of building automobiles and began building gasoline engines instead, under the name O.K. Gas Engine Company. Smith was very community-minded. His O.K. factory was served by a dam that provided the factory its power and also powered the city lighting system. If he was notified of an event or party that would last beyond the usual time the city lights were turned off, he would leave them on until the party was over.

American Metal Wheel and Auto Company (Toledo, 1906 to 1907)

American built a prototype juvenile electric vehicle on a forty-one inch wheelbase. It was shown at the New York Automobile Show in 1906 but it is believed only one copy was built.

American Motor Car Company (Canton, 1917)

The company was incorporated with the stated purpose of manufacturing automobiles. Apparently nothing came of this venture.

American Motor Company (Lima, 1912)

American built a prototype of the Lima Roadster for William Marsh of Brocton, Massachusetts who was hopeful that the Lima Progressive Association would help finance its manufacture in Lima, Ohio. Hence the name of the car. Lima declined and nothing beyond a prototype came of the venture. Whether Mr. Marsh obtained financial backing elsewhere is unknown.

Anchor Motor Car Company (Cincinnati, 1910 to 1911)

Only one vehicle was built by this subsidiary company of a manufacturer of horse-drawn wagons and carriages. Although the automobile was handsome and conformed to styling trends of the day, prospects were not attractive enough to justify full scale production.

Anderson, Leonard (Painesville, 1873)

It may be that Leonard Anderson build a steam car but this fact cannot be confirmed.

Apple Motor Car Company (Dayton, 1915 to 1917)

A prototype of the Apple eight-cylinder automobile was introduced at the Dayton Automobile Show in 1915. For an eight-cylinder vehicle it was priced at a very reasonable $1,150. How many were actually produced is unknown. The company seems to have ceased operations by 1917.

ArBenz Car Company (Chillicothe, 1911 to 1918)

The ArBenz company, initially known as the Scioto Car Company, built an unknown number of four-cylinder ArBenz automobiles. When the company's chief engineer resigned in 1915, the automobile was downsized and the following year's automobiles were smaller and priced accordingly. National United Service Company acquired the ArBenz company in 1916 in an effort to assemble a General Motors–like consortium. Production may have continued into 1917 but certainly had come to an end no later than 1918.

Armstrong, Wayne (Laurelville, 1910)

An informal venture was formed in 1910 by Mr. Armstrong with a stated capitalization of $150,000. Its purpose was to manufacture gasoline motor cars. Apparently nothing further came of this undertaking and it is doubtful that an automobile was actually produced.

Arnstein, Harry (Dayton, 1908)

After having constructed a few prototypes of his Big Four Flyer automobile, it was reported that Arnstein was preparing to go into the business of manufacturing his automobile for sale to the public. Plans to form a company and construct a factory were never realized.

Aultman, Henry (Canton, 1898); Aultman Company (Canton, 1901 to 1905)

Henry Aultman built a very snappy looking steam carriage in 1898 and established a company in 1901 to carry on its production. At least ten examples were known to have been produced. After experimenting with a gasoline-powered version of his vehicle he decided to stick with steam power. His Aultman Company began encountering financial difficulties in 1902 but managed to carry on until 1905, producing an unknown number of steam vehicles, after which the company was dissolved.

Auto-Bug Company (Norwalk, 1909 to 1910)

This was an ill-timed and short-lived attempt to offer a highwheel vehicle. Although company founder Arthur E. Skadden presented three examples at the Cleveland Automobile Show in 1910 it was apparent that the public wanted a more standard type vehicle. The Auto-Bug was a very well-engineered and handsome buggy style conveyance with a "fat-man" steering wheel, an air-cooled opposed two-cylinder engine with a fan-blade flywheel, which was capable of 30 miles per hour. It also sported an impractical one-horse shaft across the front to go with a whip socket and whip. (See *Horseless Carriage Gazette*, July-August 1971.) Something short of forty were produced before Skadden changed the company name to the Norwalk Motor Car Company and offered the more conventional Norwalk automobile. (See Norwalk Motor Car Company.)

Automobile Equipment Company (Cincinnati, 1914)

Boasting a capital stock of $100,000, the company was formed to manufacture automobiles and operate a garage. A rarity among all early automobile ventures, it included a woman, Alice DeCharmes, among its formative members. However, it appears that no automobiles were forthcoming.

Automotive Corporation (Toledo, 1921 to 1922)

The Sun automobile was introduced in 1921 at a price of $375. "Not a cyclecar but a smaller automobile" was the way the company liked to describe its vehicle in sales brochures. The two-passenger Sun automobile came with a twelve horsepower engine which it was claimed could reach fifty miles per hour and deliver fifty miles per gallon. The Sun automobile was in fact attractive and smart looking, but that was not enough. The Sun did not rise in 1923.

Baker, J. L. (Dayton, circa 1917)

J. L. Baker, a carriage maker, claimed to be engaged in the manufacture of automobiles. There is no evidence that this claim was actually realized.

Baldner, Jacob, and Fred Baldner (Xenia 1900); Baldner Motor Vehicle Company (Xenia, 1900 to 1903)

Jacob Baldner was introduced to the newly emerging automobile in 1896 when he went to work for the legendary Charles Duryea who had built one of the country's earliest gasoline-powered vehicles in 1893. Jacob Baldner and his brother Fred were both mechanically talented and, utilizing much of what Jacob had learned working for Duryea, built their first automobile which they successfully drove on the streets of Xenia in 1900. The brothers began offering a handsome but unusually powered three-cylinder version of their creation in 1902. Although they discontinued manufacturing automobiles in 1903, nine examples had been assembled and sold. Subsequently Jacob unsuccessfully sued Henry Ford for infringement on a transmission patent which Jacob had secured. Brother Fred went on to become associated with the Hawkins Cyclecar Company. (See Hawkins Cyclecar Company.)

Barcus, Nemo (Columbus, 1895)

Barcus entered an automobile in the 54-mile Chicago Times-Herald Endurance Race, which was the first automobile race held in America. A vehicle seems to have been assembled but, although Barcus was willing, his entry never made it to the starting line.

Barnes Manufacturing Company (Sandusky, 1907)

The Barnes company took the unusual step of introducing two automobiles, the Barnes and the Servitor, for 1907, the first year of production. The Servitor was a runabout on a 90-inch wheelbase powered by a 20 horsepower four-cylinder engine. The vehicles were quite similar and utilized the same air-cooled engine. Though production of the Servitor did not go beyond 1907, a few Barnes vehicles were produced until 1910. It is not known how many of either automobile were built.

Beardsley & Hubbs Manufacturing Company, aka Mansfield Motor Vehicle Company (Mansfield, 1901 to 1902); Shelby Motor Car Company (Shelby, 1902 to 1903)

Mr. R. R. Darling arranged for a carriage-style vehicle named the Darling to be manufactured by Beardsley & Hubbs Co. of Mansfield. After producing a number of automobiles, the company moved to Shelby in 1902, where it reorganized as the Shelby Motor Car Company and continued to manufacture the Darling. With the financial assistance of the town of Shelby, the factory was expanded and the company's new Shelby automobile was introduced at the New York Automobile Show in 1903. It came with either a one-cylinder engine at a price of $1,200 or a two-cylinder with a price of $2,500. As a demonstration of its quality, a Shelby automobile was driven from Ohio to California with little difficulty. However, bankruptcy intervened and the venture was forced to close its doors. The assets were sold at auction and the machinery was acquired by Thomas B. Jeffery who moved it to Wisconsin where he was manufacturing the Rambler automobile. By this time R. R. Darling left for Cleveland, intending to produce automobiles of his own design, but nothing came of it.

Bellaire Automobile Company (Bellaire, 1913)

Organized with a capital stock of $65,000 and the intention of manufacturing automobiles, the Bellaire company and its venture appear to have come to nothing.

Bellefontaine Automobile Company (Bellefontaine, 1908 and 1916)

The Bellefontaine automobile was successor to the Traveler which had previously been built in what became the Bellefontaine plant. (See Zent Automobile Manufacturing Company.) The Bellefontaine had a four-cylinder engine, 104 inch wheelbase, and three-speed transmission. A purchaser could have either an air- or water-cooled engine. After one year, automobile manufacturing was abandoned. However, in 1916 the company announced plans to once again produce an automobile. It is possible that a new Bellefontaine prototype was built but, rather than build an automobile on its own, the company joined forces with the Economy Motor Car Company of Tiffin, which was already producing the Economy Car. (See Economy Motor Company.)

Bellefontaine Carriage Body Company (Columbus, 1900)

Details as to actual production of an automobile are sketchy, but the company announced intentions to produce several prototype vehicles and at least one example of a Bellefontaine automobile was actually built. Shortly afterward the company was purchased by local interests with the stated purpose of making automobiles. The extent of their success is unknown.

Belmont Motor Company (Toledo, 1917)

Two prototype Belmont Six vehicles were built and tested. Powered by Buda engines, the production models were to be priced at $1,750. Press releases stated that final selection of component manufacturers was under way and dealerships were being sought. No more was heard of the Belmont Six.

Ben Hur Motor Company (Willoughby, 1916 to 1918)

The Ben Hur company seems to have burst onto the scene full-blown when it presented four variations of its first automobile at a show in New York City in 1917. Its distinctive racy style and special colors gave it a very advanced appearance. Chair-like individual front seats allowed for easy access to the rear seat. The Ben Hur was powered by a six-cylinder 60 horsepower Buda engine and included such bonus features as a power-driven tire pump, anti-theft lock, and electric horn and clock. By 1918 the company announced that it had sold forty automobiles and planned to continue production at a rate of five to ten a week. A stockholders' meeting to expand capitalization was in the works but by May the company was in receivership and the Ben Hur was no more.

Bennett, Harry (Findlay, 1898)

In addition to having built a motorized bicycle in 1896, Harry Bennett built a four-wheeled vehicle in 1898. Although he did not pursue the manufacture of automobiles, he remained in automobile-related businesses thereafter, operating an Elmore dealership in Toledo and a magneto and battery service in Norwalk.

Berger, J. A. (Canton, 1899); Berger Manufacturing Company (Canton, 1899)

The company's founder, J. A. Berger, built one prototype automobile but never went into production as planned. The company's primary business was making sheet metal items and parts for automobiles. Although thoughts were given to starting a formal automobile manufacturing activity, this did not occur. Eventually the company became a part of Republic Steel.

The 1917 Ben Hur seven-passenger sedan came in the latest streamline cowl design, with a self-starter, transmission-driven tire pump, and a full set of tools. An L-head six-cylinder Buda engine provided 60 horsepower and had a combination splash and force-feed lubrication system. A Bosch magneto provided electricity for the ignition and lighting systems.

Bimel Buggy Company (Sidney, 1916 to 1917)

The Bimel company acquired the rights to the Elco automobile when its manufacturer, the Elwood Iron Works of Indiana, was forced into receivership. Manufacture of both the Bimel and the Elco was continued until 1917. Total production is unknown.

Bissell Electric Company (Toledo, 1909)

Having acquired patterns for an electric vehicle, the Bissell company produced one prototype based on the purchased design. Initial intentions were to go into the manufacture and marketing of a Bissell electric, but nothing came of the plan. The Bissell company stuck with its electrical equipment business instead.

Blackiston, G. P. (Canton, 1912)

One of the more bizarre automotive creations of the time was assembled by Mr. Blackiston for his own personal use with no intention of going into the business of manufacturing automobiles. The Blackiston had a ninety horsepower engine of unknown origins situated under a hood that was over seven feet long and five and one-half feet high. Two radiators were also housed under the hood. This arrangement completely obstructed the driver's view of the road ahead, but the intrepid Mr. Blackiston said the vehicle was capable of 137 miles per hour. When asked how he would overcome the inconvenience of not being able to view the road directly ahead of the automobile, he suggested that the difficulty could be solved by an ingenious placement of mirrors. That this vehicle actually existed is confirmed by the Library of Congress which is in possession of a photograph of Blackiston's automobile.

Blair Manufacturing Company (Newark, 1911)

Organized with a capital stock of $100,000, its original intention to manufacture automobiles was changed to the manufacture of trucks.

Blair Motor Company (Cincinnati, 1911)

Incorporated in 1911 with a capital stock of $25,000 the company appears never to have produced an automobile.

Bolender, F. P. (Dayton, 1914)

Caught for speeding at the breakneck speed of thirty-two miles per hour, Mr. Bolender happily paid the city of Dayton a $10 fine. The fact that his vehicle could attain such a speed is evidence that it was a reasonably creditable machine. However, Bolender's homemade creation never went any further.

Booth, Dr. Carlos C. (Youngstown, 1895 and 1898)

Dr. Booth used the facilities of the Fredonia Carriage and Manufacturing Company of Youngstown to undertake the design and construction of an automobile. (See Fredonia Manufacturing Company.) Only five months after beginning his effort, the doctor was test-driving his new conveyance on the streets of Youngstown. His vehicle was propelled by a 4 horsepower one-cylinder engine that weighed only 134 pounds. The light carriage construction allowed for speeds of up to 18 miles per hour and the automobile was used for several years by the doctor in his medical practice. After having sold his first automobile, Dr. Booth engaged the Fredonia company to build a second one for him in 1898, which he continued to use for many years thereafter.

Bowling Green Motor Car Company (Bowling Green, 1911 to 1919)

This company is sometimes incorrectly listed as a manufacturer of passenger automobiles while, in fact, it made only commercial vehicles.

Bowman, John, and Paul Bowman (Bellefontaine, 1900)

The brothers Bowman built two vehicles on special order. Visions of greater automotive manufacturing achievements in the distant city of Chicago, Illinois, danced through their heads as a result of this commission. But nothing came of it and the brothers lowered their sights to continuing their trade as machinists in Bellefontaine.

Bremac Motor Car Company (Sidney, 1932)

The people involved with the Bremac company were recognized names in the automobile industry. Most well-known among them was

Amos Northup, designer for the Murray Corporation. The intended vehicle was to have a revolutionary monocoque frameless body with the engine and drivetrain at the rear. The body sat on a 146-inch wheelbase and was to be a teardrop-streamline design with seating for three in front and two in the back. Construction was on a custom order basis and accordingly it was possible to order the automobile with a specific wheelbase depending on the customer's preferences. The company reported that three prototype examples were under construction for display at the 1933 New York Automobile Show. Although vehicles may have been built, none appeared at the show.

Brenenstul & Carpenter (Wakeman, 1900)

The enterprise of Mr. Brenenstul and Mr. Carpenter assembled a five-hundred-pound vehicle with a unique self-starter mechanism which could be operated from the driver's seat by simply lifting a lever mounted by the step sill. The engine was shut off by pushing the lever back down. The automobile was to be sold for $800 and the power plant was available for an extra $200. Apparently the undertaking was not a success.

Brenning Brothers (Springfield, 1900 to 1901)

The Brenning brothers came to Springfield from Salem, Massachusetts to continue their electrical business and undertake the manufacture of an electric automobile under a patented design of Dr. Russell of Springfield, Ohio. A prototype appears to have been produced but the venture into automobile manufacture ended there. However, Dr. Russell went on to attempt making a gasoline-powered vehicle named the Russell-Springfield. (See Russell, Dr. C. W., and McNutt, John.)

Brice Motor Car Company (Warrensville, 1911)

The Brice company was organized with a capital stock of $200,000 and the purpose of manufacturing motorized vehicles but nothing seems to have come of this undertaking.

Brockshire & Robinson Company (Saint Paris, 1911)

Organized in 1911 with a capitalization of $20,000 and the intention of manufacturing automobiles, nothing more was heard of the venture.

Brown Carriage Company (Cincinnati, 1916)

The Brown company built both a passenger automobile and what was termed a commercial vehicle, both of conventional appearance. The five-passenger touring automobile was powered by a Le Roi engine. The commercial offering was actually a salesman's style automobile rather than a truck. The passenger car was priced at a very reasonable $750 and the commercial version was $675. Total production is unknown but was certainly limited.

Buckeye Engine Company (Salem, 1914)

Although listed in a trade journal as manufacturer of a Salem cyclecar, no evidence of actual production has been found.

Buckeye Wagon & Motor Car Company (Dayton, 1911)

This producer of horse-drawn wagons ventured briefly into automobiles, making highwheel motorized carriages. The experiment did not last, and by 1912 the company had returned to its original business exclusively, serving the horse-drawn transportation trade.

Buggy Car Company (Cincinnati, 1908 to 1909)

Rather than invent an automobile of its own design the Buggy Car Company purchased an Indiana firm that was making a highwheel motorized carriage. Two models were available, differing only in the type of drive train. The outdated vehicles proved to be unsuccessful and production ceased within a year.

Bullock Electric Manufacturing Company (Cincinnati, 1900)

Although trade publications stated that the Bullock company was producing an automobile, details regarding it are unknown.

Burdette, Oliver (New Athens, 1870)

Oliver Burdette was the creator of a gigantic steam-powered vehicle of imposing proportions. More a road locomotive than a passenger vehicle, it was almost twenty feet long and was trailed by a wagon-sized fuel tender along with a water tank of equal size. It was a big attraction at county fairs but its appetite for water was a problem on journeys of any length. One drawback was that it could not be reversed and was difficult to control. After having crashed through a building and caused a fatality, because it could not be stopped, the conveyance was permanently retired. Illustrations of this monster are apparently lost to history, but it would seem to have been a version of steam tractor adapted to road use.

Burwell, George (Toledo, 1899)

Mr. Burwell was in charge of Henry Lozier's bicycle factory, and pursuant to Mr. Lozier's request, created a three-wheel motorized conveyance. It was successfully driven on the streets of Toledo but before production went into full swing, Lozier sold his bicycle company and the motorized tricycle rights went to Pope's American Bicycle company. Lozier went on to build a quality four-wheel vehicle under the Lozier name outside Ohio.

C. R. Patterson & Sons (Greenfield, 1916 to 1919)

The Patterson automobile is perhaps the only one to have been successfully designed, built, and manufactured by an African American. The founder of the company, C. R. Patterson, was born as a slave in 1833. After the Civil War he moved from his Virginia home to Greenfield, where he opened a blacksmith shop in 1865. By the time the automobile was beginning to arrive on the scene, his business had evolved into the manufacture of carriages. One of his sons, Fred, joined the company after graduating from college, and his natural mechanical talents ultimately led Fred to try his hand at building an automobile. The result of this experiment was a prototype Patterson-Greenfield automobile which appeared in 1916. The vehicle was so satisfactory that it was immediately offered for sale on order. The Patterson-Greenfield came with either a touring or roadster body, featured a 30 horsepower four-cylinder Continental engine, and rode on de-mountable rims. Priced at $850, it was a very competitive offering. One of the company's slogans was "If it's a Patterson, it's a good one." Total production is believed to be anywhere from 30 to as high as 150. Production ended in 1919 when the company decided to concentrate on building bodies for commercial vehicles, and the first buses to appear on the streets of Cincinnati had Patterson bodies. Unfortunately, as with so many ventures of the era, the depression of the 1930s ended this well-established company after almost seventy-five years in operation.

Canton Buggy Company (Canton, 1909 to 1910)

Although the Canton company intended to focus on producing commercial motorized wagons it did turn out a limited number of automobiles during 1910.

Carl Electric Vehicle Company (Toledo, 1913)

With the purchase of machinery belonging to a Chicago motor vehicle company, the Carl company intended to produce delivery-type vehicles in Toledo. It is doubtful that either passenger or commercial electric machines were ever manufactured.

Carrico Motor Company (Cincinnati, 1908 to 1909)

Mr. Carrico assembled a few chassis-only vehicles utilizing a two cylinder air-cooled engine of his own design. Some of his engines were also used in the De Tamble automobile produced in Indiana. The affairs of the Carrico company were wound up in 1909.

Carroll Automobile Company (Lorain, 1921 to 1922)

The Carroll Six featured as standard equipment accessories that were usually optional on most other automobiles. It was claimed that these items would cost a new owner at least

$1,000 if purchased separately. Handsome as the Carroll was, this fact along with the included accessory items did not seem to persuade many that the Carroll Six, an assembled automobile, was a good value at almost $4,000. Failure to attend to details may also have played a part in the company's demise. A shipment of automobiles made to the West Coast during wintertime arrived with all the engine blocks cracked due to lack of anti-freeze. Having produced 183 examples of this expensive automobile, the company went out of business in 1922.

Carthage Motor Car Company (Carthage, 1914 to 1915)

In existence for only one year, the company manufactured an unknown number of Carthage automobiles. The company was bought out by a Detroit machine company in 1915 which continued to supply parts to Carthage owners although no more automobiles were produced.

Case Motor Car Company (New Bremen, 1910)

The Case company was formed in 1910 to make motor vehicles, and a steel plow factory was modified to produce them. It appears that only commercial trucks were actually produced.

Caswell, Myron, and Harold Caswell (Sandusky, 1901 and 1905)

In 1901 Myron Caswell built a steam engine and installed it in a horse-drawn stanhope carriage for its owner in 1901. The vehicle ran successfully without the horse. Myron's son Harold built a vehicle of his own design in 1905, which was said to run but looked rather odd.

Catrow, Herbert (Miamisburg, 1899)

It was reported in a trade publication that Mr. Catrow intended to build an automobile factory and produce automobiles, but whether this actually came to pass is unknown.

Chandler, P. J. (Akron, 1902)

Mr. Chandler, a mechanic, built at least one steam automobile with the stated intention of going into the automobile business. It seems he never did.

Charles Behlen Sons Company (Cincinnati, 1909)

Already a well-established builder of carriages, the company announced the addition of a four-cylinder automobile to its offerings, to be priced at $1,500. Although reports of substantial progress on its construction were made, it appears that a finished example never materialized.

Charles Eckert Manufacturing Company (Cincinnati, 1900)

Several sources list the Eckert company as an automobile manufacturer, but it only produced bicycles.

Charles Hanauer Cycle Company (Cincinnati, 1901 to 1902)

The Hanauer company built motorcycles and steam cars beginning in 1901, in addition to the company's repair service. During that year the company name changed to Hanauer Automobile Company and it operated as a dealer for Winton and Oldsmobile. It also continued to assemble steam automobiles to order as late as 1902. The number of automobiles produced is unknown.

Chester Rubber Tire & Tool Company (East Liverpool, 1913)

Established to manufacture both tires and automobiles, the company was organized with a capitalization of $250,000. It is doubtful that an automobile was actually produced.

Church, F. S. (Cincinnati, 1920)

Quitting his job at a Chevrolet dealership, Mr. Church announced his intentions to build an automobile of his own design. The vehicle was to have four-wheel steering, braking, and drive. This combination of features was unique at the time. All of this was to be achieved in an automobile weighing only 500 pounds. In addition it was to have no metal springs and sell for $500. It is doubtful that anything came of Mr. Church's intentions.

Cincinnati Automobile Company
(Cincinnati, 1903 to 1904)

The Cincinnati Steamer was a small compact runabout vehicle with a ten horsepower engine. At least one example was produced, but operations did not last beyond 1904.

Cincinnati Automotive Trades Association (Cincinnati, 1923)

The association assembled an automobile from a collection of standard parts available through exhibitors at the Automotive Accessory and Radio Exposition in November of 1923. One-eighth of the vehicle was completed each day of the show and the finished vehicle was donated to charity at the end of the exhibition. This imaginative promotional event was the idea of John Behle, the association's general manager.

Cincinnati Motor Car Company
(Cincinnati, 1912)

The company was organized with a $10,000 capitalization and the purpose of building automobiles for pleasure and commercial purposes. It is doubtful that anything developed along these lines.

Cincinnati Motors Company
(Cincinnati, 1912)

With a capital stock of $10,000 the company hoped to manufacture automobiles and motor trucks. It appears that only trucks were produced.

Circleville Automobile Company
(Circleville, 1914)

A cyclecar was to have been produced by the Circleville company, and one prototype was in fact assembled. It was powered by an engine invented by Walker Lee Crouch and came with electric lights and a self-starter. The price of this very good-looking vehicle was to be a bargain basement $425. How many copies of the prototype followed is not known.

Cleveland Auto Cab Company
(Geneva, 1908)

Cleveland Auto Cab built one prototype Ewing automobile in 1908 and exhibited it to the public at an automobile show in New York City that December. The Ewing was a chauffeur-driven town car, which could also serve as a taxicab. Levi E. Ewing, a major investor, took over the company in early 1909 and renamed it after himself. (See Ewing Automobile Company.)

Clyde Cars Company (Clyde, 1919)

The Clyde company constructed a custom automobile for Hal Holtom whose expertise lay in the field of commercial vehicles. It possessed many unusual features including lighting behind the radiator and a rearview mirror that was periscope-like. The Holtom may have been intended for taxi service, but nothing further came of this one-off prototype experiment. The Clyde company was builder of Clydesdale trucks and Holtom was a consultant to the company at the time the vehicle was built.

Coats Steam Car Company (Bowling Green and Columbus, 1921 to 1924)

The earliest significant announcement of a Coats steam car was made by the Coats Company of Indianapolis, March 24, 1921. (See *Motor Age*, March 24, 1921.) The automobile's engineering was unique. A fire tube boiler was mounted under the front hood and a steam line, which looked much like a torque tube, ran to the rear axle. In place of a differential was a steam engine of very compact proportions with three cylinders fixed to each axle. There was no transmission or clutch.

As things progressed the Coats Steam Car Company announced that Y. F. Stewart Mfg. Company of Bowling Green would manufacture the bodies, boilers, and engines for the Stewart-Coats steam cars, and perform final assembly as well. Only one month later it was announced that the Stewart Motor Car Mfg. Company would take over the Coats Steam Car Company which it would operate as a stand-alone entity. (See *Motor Age*, June 30, 1922.) Then less than a year later a reorganization occurred, receivership followed, and ultimately bankruptcy. The Stewart company had apparently moved operations to a plant in Columbus at some time during these developments, as a plant on High Street in Columbus was part of

COATS STEAM CAR COMPANY
1675 South High Street　　　　　　　　　　　　　　　Columbus, Ohio

Model 1923 Coats Steamer—$1085—the perfect application of steam. The smoothest, simplest, safest, most economical of all powers.

The 1923 Coats Steamer was available in touring, roadster, and sedan body styles, all of which rode on a 115-inch wheel base. It was powered by a three-cylinder single-expansion engine with water tube boiler.

the bankruptcy sale. (See *Motor Age*, March 31, July 28, August 18, September 15, 1923, and June 16, 1924.)

Officially put on the market in 1923, the new Coats steam car was acclaimed by motor journalists as the most advanced steamer of the time. Its mechanical and appearance features differed significantly from the original concept, as it now had a three-cylinder engine mounted up front directly behind the boiler, which was connected to the rear wheels through a conventional clutch and transmission. The radiator acted as a condenser and two flat water tanks rode beneath the floor behind the driver's position. The steamer required no more than two minutes to start and build a pressure of 150 psi, and within five minutes pressure would rise to 600 psi. An auxiliary pedal, when depressed, allowed steam to enter the cylinders during the full piston stroke, for more power.

Priced at $1,085 it offered the purchaser a choice between roadster, touring, and sedan models. In all, a total of twelve Coats steam cars were manufactured, including at least one which was known to have been produced at the Stewart Motor Car Company facility in Bowling Green. (See Stewart Motor Car Company.) But time and money soon ran out. The company closed its doors in 1923 and disappeared entirely in 1924.

Coe, Adelbert Brown (Lima, 1883)

Mr. Coe built a steam-powered vehicle which he ran on the streets of Lima in 1883, a fact confirmed by several people who saw it in operation. It had a three-cylinder engine and was capable of twelve miles per hour. Nothing more was recorded.

Colonial Carriage Company (Circleville, 1902)

One electric vehicle was built on special

order and the vehicle proved to be a success. Although there were rumors that the company would enter full time production of similar vehicles, nothing further came of the idea.

Colonial Motors (Warren, 1922)

The Colonial Motors Company came to an end after producing one prototype Colonial automobile in Warren.

Columbia Carriage Company (Hamilton, 1909)

The prototype Columbia Motor Buggy was a totally conventional highwheeler utilizing a two-cylinder sixteen horsepower engine. An additional twenty-five examples were constructed before the company returned to the business of manufacturing horse-drawn vehicles.

Columbia Vehicle Company (Hamilton, 1911)

Although formed to manufacture automobiles, nothing seems to have come of this venture.

Columbus Automobile Company (Columbus, 1900)

This maker of a version of the German Benz existed for no more than one year. How many examples of its Benz Spirit were produced is unknown. The vehicle had a five horsepower engine and was priced at $1,700 for delivery within sixty days of an order.

Columbus Brass Company (Columbus, 1913 to 1914)

After completing a prototype of its cyclecar and testing it on the road, this company seems to have abandoned the automotive field.

Columbus Buggy Company (Columbus, 1903 to 1909); New Columbus Buggy Company (Columbus, 1910 to 1915)

Entering the automobile arena with an electric vehicle, the earliest Columbus Electric was assembled in 1903. Activity seems to have then gone into suspended animation until April

A Group of 1911 Firestone-Columbus Cars.
A feature of these cars is the left hand steering, with center placing of the control levers. In the upper left hand corner is seen the light 5-passenger fore-door car; underneath it is the limousine, while in the lower right hand corner is the torpedo roadster, the 5-passenger fore-door family car being above it.

The four 1911 Firestone-Columbus automobiles pictured are the light five passenger fore-door touring, top left; a five passenger family car with side lights, top right; the formal limousine, lower left; and a torpedo roadster. The company slogan was "The Car Complete," perhaps alluding to the fact that electric and gasoline models were available. Prices began at $1,800.

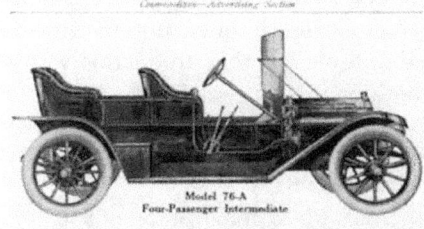

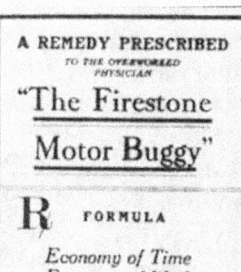

Top: The Columbus Buggy Company made two distinctly different vehicles. One was a light motor buggy, "a remedy prescribed for the overworked physician," and the other an intermediate-size four-passenger Firestone-Columbus automobile which for 1910 was advertised as being a Mechanical Greyhound, because it was speedy, graceful, and handsome. *Bottom:* For 1907 the Columbus Buggy Company offered this Columbus Station Wagon, which was intended to be driven by a chauffeur while the owner rode in weather-tight enclosed comfort.

1905 when the Columbus company introduced a stanhope electric powered by Willard batteries and priced at $1,000. Later that year the company bought control of the Springfield Automobile Company of Springfield, which had been manufacturing the Bramwell gasoline automobile. (See Springfield Automobile Company.) Production of electric vehicles continued, to be joined by a gasoline-powered Columbus in 1907, which grew in size and became the Firestone-Columbus in 1909.

The Firestone-Columbus, a full-size conventional automobile, was well received and five hundred were produced the first year. Thereafter, improvements were made continually rather than waiting to do so every model year. Promising as things appeared to be, financial problems arose. The company went into bankruptcy in 1913 and was taken over by the newly formed New Columbus Buggy Company in 1914. The Firestone-Columbus along with the Columbus Electric continued in production until 1915 when the New Columbus company closed its doors, leaving an inventory of 35 new Columbus electrics, 12 new Firestone-Columbus automobiles and a handful of used cars.

An early employee of the Columbus company, who would later become world famous, signed on in 1907 at the age of seventeen. His name was Eddie Rickenbacker, the well-known World War I flying ace. Young Rickenbacker quickly became the company's engineer and trouble-shooter. Adept with anything mechanical he was dispatched to assist Columbus automobile owners whenever they had a problem. On one occasion he was sent to help a stranded owner whose highwheel Columbus had become stuck in sand. As Rickenbacker related in his autobiography, *Rickenbacker*, he solved the problem of a badly slipping clutch by replacing the standard clutch friction plate material with brake lining instead. From then on no Columbus ever got stuck in sand and the vehicle gained a reputation for its unstopability.

Columbus Carriage & Harness Company (Columbus, 1903)

The Columbus company built a prototype motor vehicle featuring a two-cylinder engine with a shaft drive. Although announcements followed to the effect that production would begin, nothing further transpired.

Commercial Motor Car Company (Cincinnati, 1913)

Organized with a capitalization of $50,000, this undertaking is believed to have come to nothing.

Conklin, Oliver F. (Dayton, 1895)

Mr. Conklin built one example of his motorized tricycle which weighed 160 pounds. He intended to enter it in the Chicago Times Herald Endurance Race, but made no appearance.

Consolidated Manufacturing Company (Toledo, 1908)

Consolidated offered a motor-trike with interchangeable attachments that made it useful as either a passenger or commercial conveyance. The number produced is unknown.

Consolidated Motor Car Company (Columbus, 1910)

Capitalized at $4 million to manufacture gasoline and electric cars, boats, and other motor-propelled vehicles, Consolidated is another example of a company where nothing tangible transpired.

Cook, C. E. (Delaware, 1900 to 1901)

Mr. Cook demonstrated a conveyance of unknown design to motor journalists who felt that it had some attractive features but was under-powered. After building three examples for the Columbus Buggy Company in 1901, Cook dropped the idea of a motor vehicle and went into the business of making engines, as related in the book *Lyman Boats: Legend of the Lakes*, by Tom Koroknay (self-published, 2004). (See Columbus Buggy Company.)

Cook, James M. (Mount Gilead, 1896)

The Cook was a six-place motor vehicle powered by a two-cylinder engine using a friction clutch to control the gears. Cook only produced one example, never intending to go into production.

Cooney & Company (Toledo, 1906 to 1907)

A working prototype of the Cooney Electric was produced, featuring a chassis and drive line that was not mounted to the body. This allowed for installation of any body by the manufacturer or sale of the running chassis to others for their own application. The extent of production is unknown.

Coshocton Motor Car Company (Coshocton, 1913)

Although Coshocton is identified on some rosters as a producer of automobiles, no substantiation of this fact is available.

Courier Car Company (Dayton, 1910 to 1912)

The Courier of Dayton was a smaller and less expensive version of the Stoddard-Dayton. The Courier company was established as a subsidiary of Dayton Company specifically to produce and sell the Courier. The Courier roadster had a mother-in-law seat and very handsome appearance. When the United States Motor Company collapsed, so did its Dayton division and along with it the Courier. (See Stoddard Motor Car Company.)

Courier Motors (Sandusky, 1922 to 1923)

The Courier was a reincarnation of the Maibohm which had been produced by the Maibohm Motors Company from 1919 to 1922. (See Maibohm Motors Company.) It was not related to the 1904 Courier produced by the Sandusky Automobile Manufacturing Company. The Courier Motors automobile bodies were unusually well-built and relatively rattle-free. Similar in appearance to like-priced vehicles of the era, Couriers came in touring and phaeton body styles, boasted 20 miles per gallon, and could go 15,000 miles on a set of tires. But this, along with a long list of optional accessories, was not enough to attract a sufficient number of purchasers, and the company and car faded from the scene in 1923 after 373 vehicles had been manufactured. J. J. Hinde, the company's founder, was invited by Henry Ford to form a partnership to manufacture automobiles in 1902, but Hinde lacked sufficient capital to do so (Hinde obituary, *Motor*, April 1931).

Craig-Toledo Motor Company (Toledo, 1907)

The Craig shipbuilding family of Toledo financed this venture. The automobile was designed by Frank Blair, who had worked for such automobile firms as Wood, Jackson, Yale, and

This sporty 1910 Courier could be had for $1,075 f.o.b. Dayton, Ohio. It was righthand drive, had a mother-in-law seat, and a bulb horn. The auxiliary side lights were mounted on the seats rather than the more conventional location on the cowl. This Model 10-A-2 was powered by a 22–25 horsepower engine.

COURIER DOES COMBINE BEAUTY WITH POWER

The Five Passenger Phaeton

The Coupe

Advertised as being "Custom Built in the Courier Shops," the 1923 Courier Phaeton and Coupe illustrated were the epitome of the company's offerings for that year.

Ford. He designed a runabout with a three-point suspension system, which was intended to allow driving on rough roads at relatively high speeds. His invention was very effective, enabling the prototype vehicle to complete 18,000 miles of road testing and demonstrate its capability of traveling at 65 miles per hour with ease. To be priced at $4,000, the Craig-Toledo was introduced in 1907, but financial difficulties ensued and only eight examples were on hand when bankruptcy was declared.

Crane & Breed Manufacturing Company (Cincinnati, 1912)

Having already succeeded in the business of making carriages since 1850 and dabbling in professional and commercial vehicles as well, the Crane company introduced a large, expensive automobile which was offered in eight

February 7, 1907.   THE AUTOMOBILE.

1907

$4,000 F. O. B. Factory

¶ A car of such manifest and extraordinary excellence—a chassis so costly—that it will upset all your previous notions of which is really the finest car made in America. We urge upon you nothing but this: ride in the Craig-Toledo. We will abide by the results.

THE CRAIG-TOLEDO MOTOR CO., Toledo, Ohio

The Craig-Toledo Motor Company believed that it had built the finest automobile made in America and invited all comers to take a ride in its 1907 Craig Toledo and decide for themselves.

different body styles. How many were produced is unknown, but before a year had passed the company ceased manufacture of automobiles and returned to professional and commercial vehicle manufacture, not closing its doors until 1924.

Credlebaugh, H. S. (New Carlisle, 1900)

Mr. Credlebaugh made an engine of the simplest design featuring the lowest possible number of moving parts. He intended to install it in an automobile but it appears his plan never reached fruition.

Crock Motor Company (Cuyahoga Falls, 1920)

Primarily a dealership, the company was listed by a trade publication as an automobile manufacturer. Nothing more is known about its activities along those lines.

Cron & Sons Company (Columbus, 1910)

Cron was incorporated to manufacture automobiles and capitalization was set at $35,000. Actual production is doubtful.

Crosley Corporation (Cincinnati, 1939 to 1952)

Powel Crosley, Jr., was an intrepid entrepreneur. His first foray into the automotive world was in 1909 (some say 1907) with the Marathon, a six-cylinder vehicle of which only one was built. His second effort, in 1913 was the De Cross cyclecar, but this venture ended inconclusively. That same year Crosley built another prototype automobile, the Hermes, which had a 124-inch wheelbase, six-cylinder engine, and electric starter. But like the cyclecar, it did not advance beyond the prototype stage. (See Marathon Automobile Company, De Cross Cy-Car, and Hermes Motor Car Company.)

Moving on to the field of home radios, Powel hit pay dirt. By the early 1920s he was the world's largest producer of radios. Crosley followed this success with the Shelvador refrigerator which featured shelves in the door, an entirely new concept when it appeared. Like his radios, the Shelvador refrigerator proved to be a very popular product.

In 1934 Crosley was ready to return to his first love, personal transportation, and to introduce an automobile for the masses. Five years in the planning, his small inexpensive Crosley was priced at under $300 and weighed only 924 pounds when introduced in 1939. Some considered it to be a modern day cyclecar. Its motive power was a two-cylinder air-cooled 12 horsepower Waukesha engine and it had a wheelbase of only 80 inches. The Crosley Corporation already had a built-in dealership network in the form of stores that were selling other highly successful Crosley products, although after the initial sale, customer service would be problematical.

The Crosley automobile proved to be not nearly as successful as Crosley radios and refrigerators. Early mechanical problems caused sales to plummet from a high of 2,000 vehicles in 1939 to as few as 422 in 1940. In an effort to revitalize sales, race car driver "Cannonball" Baker was hired to drive a Crosley Covered Wagon (a soft-top station wagon) cross country. Baker averaged over 50 miles per gallon for the entire 6,500 mile trip but this did not seem to help sales.

In 1942 the onset of World War II cut off Crosley production. During the war Crosley built light, compact, 26.5 horsepower four-cylinder Cobra engines for the military. This was fortuitous, as the engine proved to be perfectly suited for use as motive power in the post-war automobile that Powel Crosley had in mind.

Crosley production commenced as soon as possible after the end of the war and the unprecedented post-war demand for new automobiles benefited the company. Between mid–1945 and early 1946, 16,000 Crosley automobiles were built and all of them were sold by mid–1947, at prices as low as $905. In 1948 alone 30,000 Crosleys were sold, the best year ever. However, once post-war automobile demand had been met, Crosley sales dropped precipitously, hovering around 6,000 per year from 1949 through 1951, then fell again to just over 2,000 in 1952 by which time the price of a Crosley had risen to $1,355. It was now evident that the end had come. Crosley production

The 1941 ~~CROSLEY~~ CAR
WITH NEW MOTOR FEATURES, NEW BODY STYLES, STURDIER CHASSIS AND IMPROVED PERFORMANCE

Revolutionizes Modern Transportation Costs!

RUNS MORE THAN 50 MILES ON A GALLON OF GAS — EASY!
OPERATES FOR ONE-FOURTH LARGE-CAR EXPENSE!
AND PRICES START AT $299.00* f. o. b. FACTORY!

PANEL DELIVERY $435.00*
A completely enclosed model, panelled in natural maple finish. Distinctive in design, sturdily constructed and operates at the same low cost as the pleasure cars. Quick in traffic — parks easily where larger trucks can't find room.

The Greatest Money-Saver on Wheels for Those Who Have a Delivery-Cost Problem — or for All-Around Light Hauling Service

With over 200 improvements in motor and chassis over original models, the new Crosley Commercial Cars are ruggedly constructed, have astonishing speed and power, and are capable of day-in and day-out performance at a cost so low it's actually difficult to believe! In many cases, any one of these models is capable of reducing operating expenses by *as much as three-fourth the present cost of running conventional-sized units!* And their surprising comfort, ease of handling and ease of parking make them highly desirable for use instead of motorcycles with sidecars!

Druggists, florists, printers, radio service shops, appliance service shops, telephone companies, battery and tire services, fleet operators, typographers, engravers, and scores of other businesses with delivery and hauling problems will find a Crosley commercial model that's ideal for the purpose — *that will cut operating expenses as much as three-quarters* — that will give dependable service and complete satisfaction for years to come.

Learn how this great money-saver will save *you* money — in *your* business — today!

Here's Proof!

"Cannon-ball" Baker in Stock Model Covers First 2,454 Miles of 2-Way Transcontinental Run with Average of 50.59 Miles per Gallon — Total Gas and Oil Cost, Cincinnati to Los Angeles, Only $9.14!

As this goes to press, "Cannon-ball" Baker, driving a stock model Crosley "Covered Wagon," nears the climax of his sensational transcontinental run from Cincinnati to Los Angeles and thence to the New York Automobile Show. Reports received to date furnish undeniable *proof* of the almost unbelievable economy of the 1941 Crosley Car. As this goes to press; 4,639.4 miles on 90 gallons of gasoline averaging 51.54 miles per gallon!

PARKWAY DELIVERY $375.00*
The smartest delivery car in town! Continental in appearance, it has the plus advantage of advertising value — it'll attract favorable attention and comment wherever it goes! Easy to handle, parks "on a dime" — quickly pays for itself.

CONVERTIBLE COUPE $299.00*
The "baby" of the Crosley Car family — at a price that thousands can easily pay. Provides ample leg room and storage space with up to 500 pounds capacity. Ideal for salesmen and those who must cover a large territory at minimum cost.

PICKUP DELIVERY $385.00*
Here's the answer to the general delivery problem — an all-purpose truck model with 500 pounds capacity. Rugged construction for spots where the going is tougher. Operates for less than 1c a mile and goes 50 miles on a gallon of gasoline — easy!

STATION WAGON $450.00*
The all-around body style that has "crashed society" — at its most economical in a Crosley. Sturdy, stylish, smart and *useful*. Rear seat may be easily removed for maximum carrying space. A great "knock-about" car for town or country.

COVERED WAGON $399.00*
This unique model seats four persons comfortably or the rear may be quickly converted into carrying space by removing the seat. Heavy waterproof canvas top rolls up easily and fastens to the ridge pole, letting "all outdoors" in.

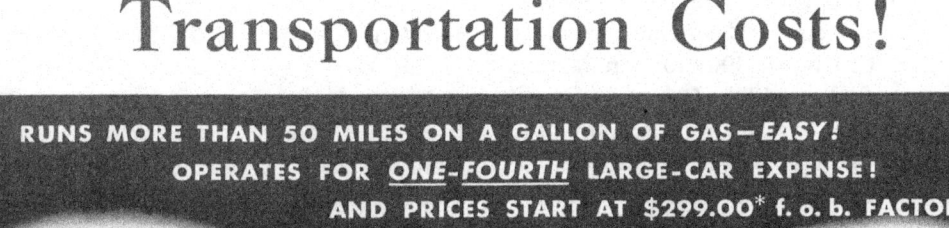

NEW CONVERTIBLE SEDAN $349.00*
New Convertible Sedan illustrated. The ideal all-purpose family car. Seats up to four people comfortably. Top can be raised or lowered in a jiffy. Three-position adjustable seat provides ample leg room. Rear seat may be removed to provide extra storage space, if desired.

Pleasure Models That Run for Less Than a Penny per Mile! Important to Those Operating a Car in Their Own Business!

The new Crosley line offers a choice of two pleasure models for the family that needs an extra car — or for those who drive a car in business, where operating costs are an important item. Think of it! — these new and greatly improved Crosleys give you 50 miles on a gallon of gas — easy! And get you there as surely, as dependably and as comfortably as cars costing four times as much to run!

In addition, the attractive Station Wagon and unique Covered Wagon are ideal for estates, for those living in suburban or rural communities — or on farms. There's a model for every possible need, every one capable of completely revolutionizing the cost of owning and operating a car — of giving lasting satisfaction and a new thrill in motoring pleasure.

Ask your nearest Crosley Car dealer for a demonstration. If there is none near you, write us direct and we will gladly arrange to have a representative call — without obligation, of course.

Automotive Distributors and Dealers!

Certain Territories Still Open — Write, Wire or Telephone Today for Complete Information About Amazing Market and Profit Opportunities in the Crosley Car Franchise!

Automotive Distributors and Dealers, in accordance with the new distribution policy recently announced, have been quick to realize the opportunity provided by the Crosley Car to add volume and profits without increasing overhead or manpower — and without competing or interfering in any way with the established business. Some territories are still open. If you are in business and can qualify, or if you want to start in business and are properly financed, communicate immediately with the factory.

All prices shown are factory-delivered prices. Excise tax additional. Transportation based on rail rate, state and local taxes (if any) are extra.

THE CROSLEY CORPORATION • CINCINNATI, OHIO • Powel Crosley, Jr., President

---

Priced for as little as $299 f.o.b., the Lilliputian 1941 Crosley was a transportation bargain. "Cannonball" Baker drove a Crosley from coast-to-coast averaging 50.59 miles per gallon for the 2,454 mile venture with a fuel cost of only $9.14 (author's collection).

ceased in July 1952 and the company was bought out by General Tire and Rubber Company in early 1953.

Croxton-Keeton Motor Car Company (Massillon, 1909 to 1910)

This Massillon-based company was formed by Forest M. Keeton and Massillon resident Herbert A. Croxton in 1909 to manufacture two types of automobiles. One was to be a French-like vehicle featuring a Renault-style hood. The other was to be more conventional and German in appearance. Before many of these four-cylinder 115½-inch wheelbased automobiles had been produced the firm was dissolved and Croxton moved to Cleveland where he organized the Croxton Motor Company in 1910. (See Croxton Motor Company in Part I.)

Cummins-Monitor Company (Columbus, 1916 to 1922)

The company produced the Monitor automobile and in 1916 the name was changed to the Monitor Motor Car Company. (See Monitor Motor Car Company.)

Curtin & Schille (Columbus, 1899)

The partnership of Curtin and Schille, which ran a carriage manufacturing business, constructed an electric vehicle at the request of a local company for use in its factory to transport material between departments. It is possible other similar vehicles were also built.

Custer Specialty Company (Dayton, 1920 to 1942)

Custer engaged in the production of a wide variety of motorized vehicles including an electric wheelchair, a factory truck, a miniature two-person city car, and an electric and gasoline powered juvenile car named the Cootie. Although designed as a juvenile car, this diminutive vehicle was licensed by several adults both in the United States and Great Britain as a road vehicle. At its introduction the price was $95.

Cyriacks Motor Company (Eaton, 1910)

Cyriacks was formed to manufacture automobiles and accessories. Actual production of an automobile is unlikely.

D. T. Williams Valve Company (Cincinnati, 1904)

The Williams company was organized for the production of automobiles and automobile valves. No automobile production followed although valves were made.

Darling Motor Company (Dayton, 1917)

The Darling company was formed by men from the National Cash Register Company who had become infatuated with an automobile designed by James Guthrie. The proposed Darling was a good-looking automobile and was to be priced at $1,600. However, the venture ended just as production of the Darling was to begin. It appears that the participants simply lost interest and decided to pursue other endeavors.

Davis, D. L. (Salem, 1900)

Mr. Davis was reported to have built an automobile, although this fact cannot be substantiated.

Dayton Automobile Company (Dayton, 1906)

This Dayton Automobile Company, one of two that bore this name, was organized in 1906 to manufacture automobiles. Although it is unlikely that any were actually produced, one of its organizers, John L. Baker, went on to form the Dayton Electric Car Company in 1911. (See Dayton Electric Car Company below.)

Dayton Automobile Company (Dayton, 1911)

Organized with a capitalization of $30,000 to manufacture, repair and deal in automobiles, it is unknown whether an automobile was actually produced.

Dayton Electric Car Company (Dayton, 1911 to 1914)

The Dayton company manufactured an electric automobile of rather standard appearance from 1911 to 1914. The end came when creditor demands resulted in dissolution of the company and sale of its assets to satisfy claims. Afterward a company was set up to complete

The Darling automobile rode on a low-hung chassis and came equipped with a Willard battery, Houk wheels, and Stromberg carburetor. The body incorporated smooth rounded contours and a slanted windshield for 1917, which helped it stand apart from most of the competition.

unfinished vehicles on hand and to supply parts for older Dayton electrics. Production numbers are unknown but were probably limited.

Dayton Motor Vehicle Company (Dayton, 1900 to 1902)

The Dayton company declared that it was in the design process for a steam-powered vehicle which it intended to put into production. The vehicle was to utilize a double boiler system which, it was purported, would provide complete steam condensation. Even before a prototype was constructed, the company redirected its efforts to the manufacture of parts for steam vehicles rather than completed automobiles. However it appears that the company offered a complete line of patterns and designs for steam vehicles utilizing its steam engines and running gear.

De Cross Cy-Car (Dayton, 1913 to 1914)

The most enduring thing about the De Cross Cy-Car is the name of one of its developers, Powel Crosley, Jr. It appears the endeavor was never formalized although at least a prototype vehicle was built and extensively tested. The prototype was of very light construction with tandem seating, the driver occupying the rear seat. An unusual feature for the era was a bulb horn mounted at the driver's left elbow. It may be that Crosley and his associate Mr. Doeller determined that the cyclecar craze was a fleeting phenomenon, and accordingly decided to end their experiment after only one was built. (See Crosley Corporation.)

De Luxe Motor Car Company (Toledo, 1906 to 1907)

How many examples of the Car De Luxe, as it was named, were manufactured in Toledo is uncertain. The company occupied what was referred to as the old Toledo Yale Lock Company plant in 1906, but management negotiated a merger with the Detroit-based makers of the Queen and Blostrom automobiles late that year. As a result, operations were moved to Detroit where the 1907 and 1908 models were produced. No further production occurred in Toledo.

Dennis Motor Company (Toledo, 1912)

It is doubtful that this company, organized with a capitalization of $25,000, actually produced an automobile.

Differential Steel Car Company (Findlay, 1930)

Often listed as a manufacturer of automobiles, the company only made railroad cars.

Ditwiler Manufacturing Company (Galion, 1914)

The Ditwiler company, a manufacturer of steering gears, built a prototype shaft-drive cyclecar mounted on a 100-inch wheelbase and priced at only $400. It is doubtful that there were many produced.

Drury-Wells Motor Company (Youngstown, 1912)

Drury-Wells was organized with a modest $10,000 capitalization and the stated purpose of manufacturing automobiles and parts, but it is doubted that any production took place.

Dum, Ed, and Harley Dum (Lancaster, 1902)

The Dum brothers built an automobile for their own use, the existence of which was recorded in a period trade journal. Details about the vehicle are lacking.

Dunkle, Ralph W. (Greenville, 1910)

Mr. Dunkle constructed a belt-drive vehicle with a two-horsepower engine mounted on a buckboard-like chassis. A trade publication journalist confirmed that it was unlike anything else on the market. This single experiment was the extent of Dunkle's automotive endeavors.

Dusseau Fore and Rear Drive Automobile Company (Toledo, 1910 to 1911)

A prototype of the Dusseau was displayed at the Detroit Automobile Show in 1911. It featured a front-wheel drive, but was in all other respects quite conventional. No manufacture of the Dusseau followed and the company founders went on to other things.

Eagle & Vincent Automobile Company (Mansfield, 1912)

Organized with a $15,000 capitalization to build automobiles, the Eagle & Vincent company was not successful in producing any.

Eagle-Macomber Motor Car Company (Sandusky, 1914 to 1918)

Eagle-Macomber moved its operations from Chicago, Illinois, to Sandusky and a larger plant, in 1914. Production evolved from a cyclecar in 1914 to a more standard small vehicle in 1918. Both vehicle types were powered by a five-cylinder rotary engine. Prices jumped from $700 for the cyclecar to a high of $1,850 for the larger automobile. As prices increased, the Eagle-Macomber found fewer takers. Production ended in 1918.

Early Motor Car Company (Columbus, 1911)

This company has been erroneously identified in some sources as being in the automobile manufacturing business. It was only a sales agency for several early automobile makes.

Eastern Automobile Company (Columbus, 1911)

Eastern was organized with a $10,000 capitalization and the stated purpose of manufacturing automobiles, but it is doubtful that the company ever produced one.

Eckert, Charles (Cincinnati, 1900)

Mr. Eckert, who built bicycles, is listed as an automobile manufacturer in period automotive journals, but it is doubtful he produced an automobile.

Eclipse Manufacturing Company (Columbus, 1904)

Fitting an air-cooled engine of its own design to standard carriages was the extent of the Eclipse company's automobile production. A few examples were turned out on a custom order basis.

Economy Motor Car Company; (Tiffin, 1916 to 1917); Bellefontaine Automobile Company (Bellefontaine, 1917 to 1919); Vogue Motor Car Company (Tiffin, 1919 to 1923)

The initial Economy automobile was an assembled car, one model of which was named the Thre-Dor. It seated five and had a third door for rear seat access. To enhance production potential, a merger was entered into with the Bellefontaine Automobile Company in 1917. (See Bellefontaine Automobile Company.) Some manufacturing operations were moved to Bellefontaine and the Thre-Dor was renamed the Chummy, incorporating a Ferro V-8 in the standard Economy line. The Bellefontaine operation folded in 1919 and the company was reorganized as the Vogue Motor Car Company, with full production returning to Tiffin. The automobile was renamed the Economy-Vogue for 1919. In 1921 the name changed again to simply the Vogue, which was now a larger automobile with a six-cylinder engine. But after all of that, it was not enough and the end finally came in 1923.

Elliott & Lang (Dayton, 1925)

H. E. Elliott and C. W. Lang collaborated on an automobile with an air-cooled engine. A prototype was said to have been built, but actual production of an automobile was not achieved.

Elmore Manufacturing Company (Clyde, 1899 to 1912)

Having built ten automobiles as an adjunct to their bicycle business, which was founded in 1899, H. V. Becker and his two sons formed the Elmore company in 1902 to produce motorized vehicles. The 1902 model had a one-cylinder engine, but the 1903 Elmore was equipped with a two-cylinder two-stroke engine located under the seat, which could be started without a crank. In 1906 Elmore stepped up to a four-cylinder engine which was now under the hood up front. Its best sales year was 1907 when 400 were produced. William C. Durant purchased the Elmore company in 1909 to add to his General Motors holdings, but by 1912 production ceased.

The Elmore two-cycle engine had only three moving parts and far more low-speed torque than any other four-cylinder four-cycle engine. A 1910 five-passenger touring model cost $1,750 and was capable of 50 miles per hour.

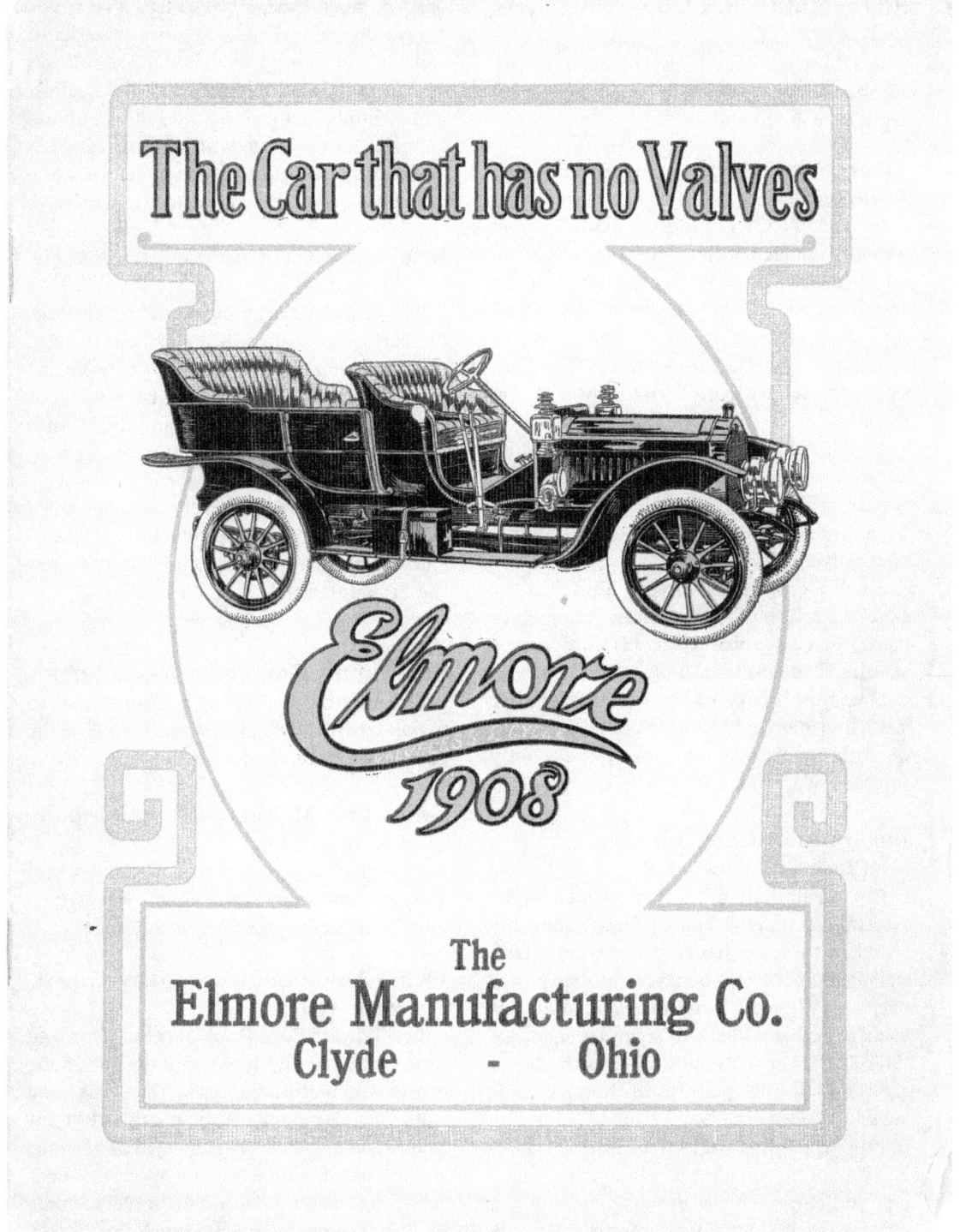

Advertised as "The car that has no valves," the 1908 Elmore was powered by a two-stroke engine, a power plant the Elmore Manufacturing Company championed as long as it made Elmore automobiles.

Elyria Auto Sales Company (Elyria, 1912)

It is doubted that the Elyria company actually manufactured automobiles although it was capitalized at $10,000.

Emerson, Victor L. (Cincinnati, 1885, 1896, 1907)

In 1885, Victor L. Emerson built a three-wheeled vehicle which ran on vaporized coal oil. He drove it as far as 30 miles on primitive country roads which, as he put it, was "a very rough sort of sport" in the days before pneumatic tires. After the novelty wore off, he consigned the vehicle to his barn to power a grain elevator.

In 1896, while associated with the Emerson & Fischer Company, Emerson produced his second vehicle, this time utilizing a Duryea-King motor. When completed, it was reportedly delivered to a circus.

Finally, in 1907, while styling himself as the general manager of the American Motor Company, Emerson embarked on his third vehicle venture. The result was a prototype which he dubbed the Military, with a 60/70 horsepower six-cylinder engine, a touring body which rode on a ninety-six inch wheelbase, and a hefty price tag of $8,000.

Enger Motor Car Company (Cincinnati, 1909 to 1917)

Having started with a two-cylinder high-wheel vehicle in 1909, Frank J. Enger's company switched to manufacturing a conventionally styled automobile the next year. Motive power over the following years changed to an advanced four- and then a six-cylinder engine in 1915. The Enger was boldly billed as the "ideal car." Frank J. Enger, a forward-thinking individual, introduced a 227 cubic inch V-12 engine in 1916, which was one of the earliest V-12s. It had one of the smallest displacements for its type and came with dual exhausts and mufflers for more silent operation. It was priced at only $1,095.

Innovation was Enger's driving force and this was amply demonstrated by the fact that his 1917 twelve could be run on just one bank of six cylinders by simply moving a lever which cut the flow of fuel and held open the exhaust valves of the unused six cylinder bank. It was said that this mode of operation would deliver up to 35 miles per gallon at 20 miles per hour. (See *The Automobile Journal*, October 25, 1916.) The factory was reorganized for war work and the Enger automobile was discontinued.

Erie Motor Car Company (Painseville, 1916 to 1919)

The Erie company bought out Vulcan Manufacturing Company which had made the Vulcan automobile from 1913 to 1915. (See Vulcan Manufacturing Company.) The company continued to service the Vulcan, and in 1917 also introduced its own automobile, the Erie, in both touring and roadster form. Prices were $795 in 1917 and $850 in 1918. During World War I it switched to the production of E.M.C. trucks. Few Eries were sold and after the war the Erie automobile was not successfully revived.

Erie Supply Company (Toledo, 1912)

Organized with a capital stock of $10,000 to manufacture automobiles and supplies, the company apparently did neither.

Evans-Eich Manufacturing Company (Cincinnati, 1911)

Organized to manufacture automobiles with a capitalization of a scant $5,000, Evans-Eich most likely never produced an automobile.

Ewing Automobile Company (Geneva, 1909 to 1911)

Levi Edward Ewing took over the Cleveland Auto Cab Company in 1909 and renamed it the Ewing Automobile Company. (See Cleveland Auto Cab Company.) A town car, selling for $3,000 and powered by a four-cylinder engine, was produced. A total of 30 town cars and taxicabs were built in 1908 and 47 in 1909. Amazingly, the company was marginally profitable. However, Geneva was a small town and it was difficult to keep a qualified work force. A move to Erie, Pennsylvania, was considered, but instead the company was sold to William C.

The Manufacturers   Falcon   171

Durant to add to his General Motors empire. The Ewing company was not profitable for Durant and was dissolved in 1911.

Falcon Motors Corporation (Elyria, 1927 to 1929)

The Falcon corporation was organized as an arm of the Willys-Knight Company to

The year 1917 was the last one for the Enger and its V-12 engine. The engine was dubbed the "Twin-Unit Twelve." The Enger Twelve achieved a world record 35 miles per gallon thanks to its ability to run on just one 6-cylinder bank at the driver's command.

For the second year of its production in Elyria, the 1928 Falcon-Knight was available in five body styles. It was powered exclusively by a 6-cylinder sleeve-valve engine.

manufacture an automobile powered by a six-cylinder sleeve-valve engine with seven main bearings. At $1,000 it was priced between the Whippet and the Willys-Knight. Falcon-Knight production commenced in 1927 at what had been the Garford plant. (See Garford Company.) Sales were strong in both 1927 and 1928 and it initially appeared that the Falcon-Knight would be a success. However, the economics of the operation proved not to justify continuing its production. The Falcon-Knight was discontinued in 1929 and the plant was turned over to the manufacture of Willys-Knight bodies. (See Willys-Overland Company.)

Falls Garage Company (Chagrin Falls, 1912)

The Falls Garage Company was formed with a capitalization of $10,000 to manufacture and deal in automobiles. Certain trade publications indicated that the company was manufacturing automobiles but facts evidencing actual production, or even the existence of a prototype, are lacking.

Farmobile Manufacturing Company (Columbus, 1908 to 1909)

A subsidiary of the Oscar Lear Automobile Company (see Oscar Lear Automobile Company), the Farmobile company may have produced the Farmobile for up to two years, but facts are in conflict and it may be that only a prototype was built.

Fetzger Automobile Manufacturing Company (Galion, 1910)

Some sources list the Fetzger company as producing an automobile, but this fact cannot be confirmed.

Findlay Carriage Company (Findlay, 1910 to 1916)

Findlay was a builder of horse-drawn carriages. In 1910 it assembled a prototype five-passenger touring automobile, powered by a four-cylinder 40 horsepower engine, which was capable of reaching a speed of 60 miles per hour. The Findlay was priced at $2,500 and the company professed to have assembled 10 automobiles, and to be proceeding on production for an order for an additional 150 in 1910. Beyond the prototype and the construction of some funeral cars for local undertakers in 1913, it is not known how long production lasted or how many Findlays were actually built. When a fire destroyed the factory in 1916 the company ceased business altogether.

Findlay Motor Car Company (Findlay, 1910 to 1914)

The Findlay company is often erroneously listed as an automobile manufacturer, whereas in fact, it was only involved with the manufacture of trucks. In 1914, shortly after Findlay went into bankruptcy, its plant was taken over by Grant Motor Company for producing the Grant automobile. (See Grant Motor Company.)

Flynn, Walter F. (Youngstown, 1905)

Flynn was initially in the business of running a local garage and electric vehicle charging station. In 1905 he assembled a prototype gasoline-powered touring automobile, which he named the Falcon. This is the earliest appearance of what became an often-used automobile name. It was a handsome and substantial vehicle for which he had great hopes. But things did not go as anticipated financially, and efforts to form a company failed. Flynn decamped to Bay City, Michigan, in search of better luck the following year. Ultimately he had to abandon his automobile venture and only the one prototype was produced.

Foley & Williams Manufacturing Company (Cincinnati, 1904)

Foley & Williams built a single Goodrich automobile which came into the hands of its first purchaser, Robert Cavender, as a used car. It was powered by an air-cooled opposed two-cylinder engine with an ignition that obtained its electricity from four telephone batteries. It was still in the Cavender family of Aurora, Indiana, as of the mid–1990s.

Foos Gas Engine Company (Springfield, 1901 to 1906)

Foos claimed to be the world's largest maker of gas engines. It apparently built a limited number of automobiles to demonstrate its

The four-cylinder 40 horsepower Jewel for 1908 rode on a 120-inch wheelbase with thirty-six inch wheels. It was advertised as the "Non-Skidding" car thanks to its Hedgeland Equalizer device.

engines, but actual production was not contemplated.

Forest City Motor Car Company (Massillon, 1906 to 1908); Jewel Motor Car Company (Massillon, 1909)

Having built and demonstrated a prototype vehicle in Cleveland, the company found a group of Massillon investors to underwrite the company's operations and it moved to Massillon. (See Forest City Motor Car Company in Part I.) The automobile was named the Jewell and featured a one-cylinder engine with rope drive. This highwheel automobile did not sell. The company changed its name to the Jewel Motor Car Company and in late 1909 added a non-highwheel automobile to its line-up. But that year the company faded from the scene when one of its formative members entered into a new automobile manufacturing enterprise based in Washington, Pennsylvania.

Forth, Clarence R. (Mansfield, 1909); Forth Motor Car Company (Mansfield, 1910)

Having successfully assembled an automobile with parts from a variety of automobile trade suppliers, Clarence R. Forth, with backing acquired through the auspices of the Mansfield Chamber of Commerce, formed the Forth Motor Car Company. The company then acquired the Bucyrus Steam Shovel Company plant, with plans to produce automobiles. At this point hoped-for financing evaporated and the Forth company went into bankruptcy, holding assets consisting of one automobile and miscellaneous parts.

Fostoria Foundry and Machine Company (Fostoria, 1904)

This manufacturer of gasoline engines appears to have built a demonstration automobile utilizing its engine, but did not pursue actual production. It stuck with the manufacture of engines instead.

Fostoria Light Car Company (Fostoria, 1915 to 1916)

The incorporators, all from Fostoria, intended to build four versions of an inexpensive assembled automobile. By 1916, 293 vehicles had been made but the company was experiencing problems with the Sterling engines purchased from a supplier. Le Roi engines replaced Sterling engines in the hopes of improving the automobile's reputation. At this point the company reorganized as the Seneca Motor Company. (See Seneca Motor Company.)

Fostoria Motor Car Company (Fostoria, 1906 to 1907)

William H. Radford, designer of the Oxford automobile of Detroit, moved to Fostoria when the Oxford company went broke, bringing his Oxford design with him and forming the Fostoria company. The automobile was renamed Fostoria and with local backing, it went into production. Manufacture of Radford's automobile lasted no more than one year.

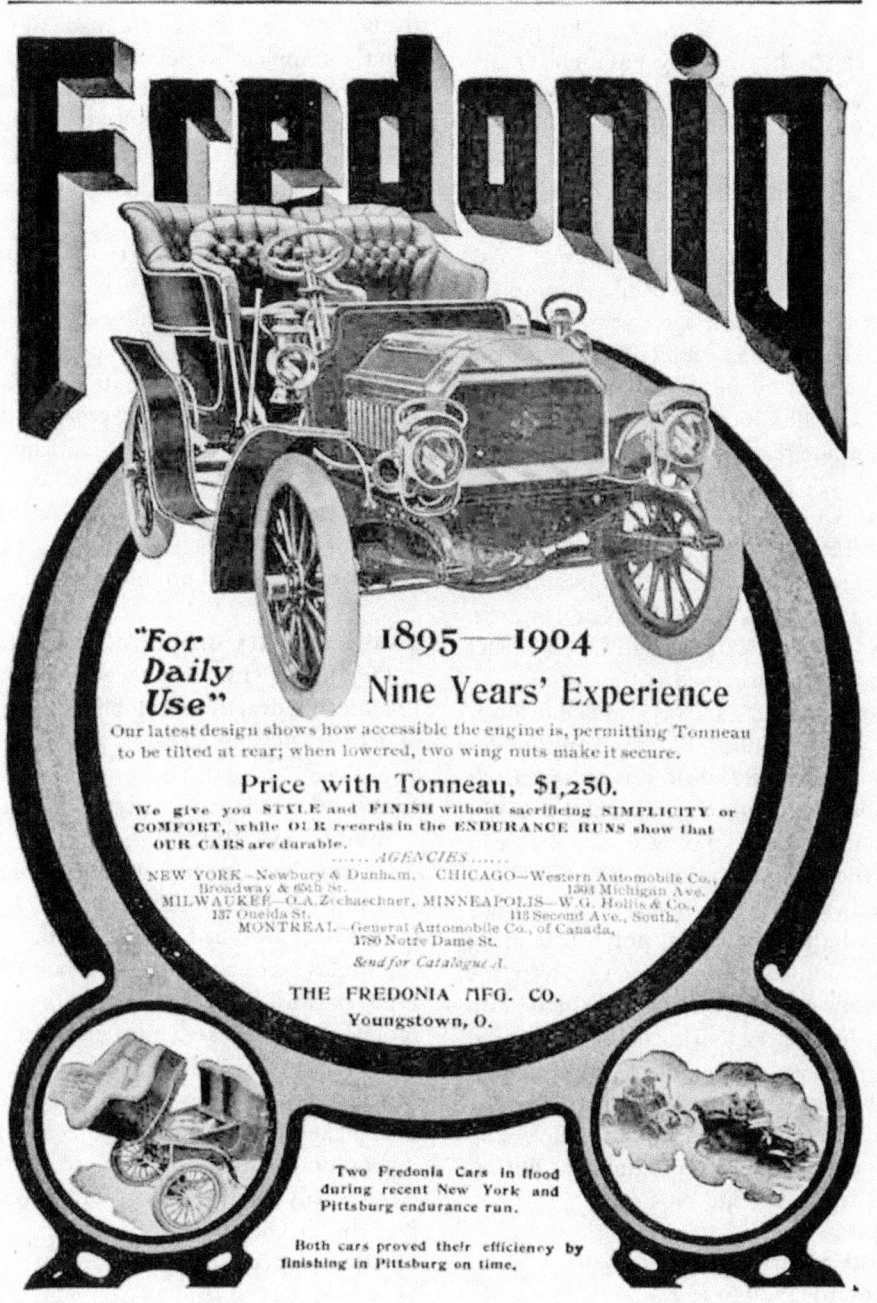

Although the first experimental Fredonia prototype was built in 1895, it was not until 1902 that actual manufacture of automobiles for sale began. The Fredonia was a capable automobile which achieved success in a reliability event through flood-swollen terrain that halted rail travel for up to three days. It was powered by a 12 horsepower engine.

Fredonia Manufacturing Company (Youngstown, 1895 to 1904)

In 1895 and 1898, Fredonia built two automobiles for Dr. Carlos C. Booth. This piqued their interest in the emerging automobile manufacturing business. The company began sporadic automotive experiments of its own and sold some of the resulting prototypes. It was probably at this time that the handsome French-style hood, which became a defining characteristic of the Fredonia, was first adopted. Actual production of the Fredonia automobile commenced in 1902, the same year that one of Fredonia's automobiles achieved a perfect score and won a gold medal in the New York–to–Boston Reliability Run.

One unique feature of the Fredonia's one-cylinder engine was the compression of the fuel-air mixture before it entered the combustion chamber. This was said to promote longer valve life and reduce cylinder temperatures, in addition to ameliorating disagreeable odors. Another unusual feature was an exhaust relief port, which was uncovered by the piston at the bottom of its stroke. This was also said to lower operating temperatures, as well as prevent deterioration of cylinder lubricating oil. (See *Cycle and Automobile Trade Journal*, October 1903.)

Fredonias once again proved their mettle in a 1903 reliability run between New York and Pittsburgh, where both of the company's entrants had a perfect score, notwithstanding having encountered what some said were the worst floods ever. Production continued into 1904, at which time a touring model was priced at $1,100, and a runabout at $1,000. However, financial strains brought a close to the business, and the company was forced into receivership after having produced approximately 200 vehicles between 1901 and 1904.

Fremont Motors Corporation (Fremont, 1920 to 1922)

Organized with a $2 million capitalization, the Fremont company was controlled by people with backgrounds in the automobile business. After spending $50,000 to perfect the prototype Fremont automobile, the company was ready to begin production in 1920 with a six-cylinder assembled automobile priced at $1,895. Due to the fact that the main focus of the company was on the manufacture of trucks, relatively few automobiles were made. It was said that the complete output for 1920 was destined for export. In an attempt to improve sales, prices were reduced to $1,685 in 1921, and $1,450 in 1922. The company discontinued all operations in late 1922 and closed its doors entirely in 1924.

Frey-Shecker Company (Bucyrus, 1896 to 1899)

A manufacturer of gasoline engines for marine and stationary use, the company built an automobile to demonstrate its engine's adaptability for use in motorized vehicles. The engine, which was named the American Vehicle Motor, had a single cylinder with two opposed pistons. Its operation was uncommonly smooth and vibration free. However, the vehicle did not advance beyond prototype stage.

Gaither Auto Company (Columbus, 1913)

Organized with a capitalization of $10,000 to build and deal in automobiles, the company apparently never realized its goals.

Garford Company (Elyria, 1907 to 1908 and 1911 to 1914)

Garford had supplied chassis to Studebaker in South Bend, Indiana, since 1904. There, bodies were installed and the Studebaker automobiles were completed. In late 1907 and 1908, Garford began producing its own automobile. At Studebaker's insistence, Garford discontinued its own automobile and concentrated its efforts solely on supplying chassis to Studebaker during the years 1909 and 1910. In recognition of its having done so, Studebaker temporarily re-badged its automobile the Studebaker-Garford.

After Studebaker acquired control of the Everitt-Metzger-Flanders Company in 1911, it produced Studebaker automobiles entirely on its own. Its relationship with Garford was terminated, and Garford resumed building automobiles independently in its own name. The Garford came on wheelbases ranging from 117 inches to 138 inches, was powered by either a four- or six-cylinder engine, and was offered in a variety of body styles, including standard touring as well as limousine.

With Studebaker's departure, the Garford company was in need of an established distribution and sales network. To solve this problem it joined with the well-established Willys-Overland Company of Toledo to form the Willys-Garford Sales Company. Each company continued to manufacture its own automobiles independently. John N. Willys was in the process of bringing together the elements of a huge automotive conglomerate and, in 1912, bought control of the Garford Company. Nevertheless, production of the Garford continued in 1913 with a $3,750 six-cylinder model featuring a centrally-located headlight, which earned it the unfortunate appellation the "one-eyed Garford." This would be the last of the Garford automobiles and Willys converted the Garford plant to the production of the 1914 Willys-Knight, which featured a sleeve valve engine. (See Willys-Overland Company.) Thereafter the Garford name

Top: The Garford Berlin was the epitome of the brand's offerings. Designed to be chauffer-driven, its $6,000 price was indicative of its elegance. *Bottom:* The 1909 Garford had a 40 horsepower four-cylinder engine, four-speed transmission, shaft drive and cost $4,000.

Public Approval of This New Six

We announced this new Six last month. On the day of its announcement we had telegraphic requests, for information on deliveries, from practically every important city in America.

It attracted more attention at the National Automobile Show than any other Six on exhibition.

The first car sold on the opening night of the Show was a new Garford Six. This sale took place just five minutes after the Garden had opened.

In seven days we had bona-fide contracts for over fourteen hundred cars—which is more cars than most six cylinder producers make in a year.

There were more of the new Garford Sixes sold at the New York show than any other high grade Six represented there.

One of our dealers alone made twenty-six retail sales the first week this car was put on the market.

$2750—Completely Equipped

We believe the new Garford Six to be the lowest priced, high grade, six cylinder car made. In it are embodied all of the very latest six cylinder developments, refinements and designs—both American and European. We are the first in the industry to build six cylinder cars in lots of ten thousand—which makes possible this exceptionally reasonable price.

This car is of brand new treatment in every single respect. The motor, the electrical equipment, the front axle, the rear axle, the control, the brakes, the transmission, the frame, the speedometer—which is driven from the transmission—the big, single electric parabolic headlight, sunk flush with the radiator and the one-piece all-steel body is new. In fact, the whole car is an entirely new development in design, treatment, style and finish, based on the very latest European and American six cylinder practice.

The new Garford Six is a five passenger touring car. It is electrically started, all lights are electric, the horn is electric; it has a sixty horsepower, long-stroke motor—the measurements of which are 3¼ in. by 6 in.—the wheelbase is 128 inches, the tires are 36 in. by 4½ in.; it has demountable rims; it has the very practical and popular left-hand drive and center control. It is, of course, completely equipped with the very best and very finest accessories. The price, complete, is $2750.

Full information from us or our nearest dealer.

Catalogue on request. Please address Dept. 5

The Garford Company, Elyria, Ohio

The 1915 "one-eyed Garford" six, as it had quickly become nicknamed, was built in batches of ten thousand, a first for the automobile industry. It seems to have been popular as the advertisement states that more than 1,400 were sold within seven days of the automobile's introduction (author's collection).

existed only on Garford company-produced trucks.

Garrison Machine Works (Dayton, 1914)

This maker of tools and dies made a prototype cyclecar to evaluate the potential for going into its manufacture. The company decided against the venture and remained in the tool and die business instead.

Gatts, Alfred Palmer (Hamersville, 1905)

There is a letter signed by Alfred P. Gatts of Bethel, Ohio, dated June 23, 1959, and addressed to William Goodwin, who owned a Gatts highwheeler. In the letter, Gatts confirms his manufacture of five vehicles. Gatts had run a machine shop in Hamersville where the vehicles were assembled, the first being a highwheel buggy with a one-cylinder engine. He sold this and two others locally and kept the remaining two for himself. (See *Horseless Carriage Gazette*, September-October 1959.) The last surviving Gatts automobile was in the possession of William Burkel of America, Ohio, as of the mid–1990s.

Geneva Automobile & Manufacturing Company (Geneva, 1901 to 1904)

The first Geneva steam car appeared in 1901. At a race in 1902 a Geneva was pitted against a White steam car and finished a respectable second. In other races where it was pitted against Winton automobiles, it usually prevailed. The Geneva's success attracted investors and a new Geneva steam car was presented in 1903 with prices ranging from $1,000 to $1,750. But by 1904 the end was near. Although Geneva made an appearance at the New York City Automobile Show that year, the marque was not heard from again. However, a Geneva steam car survives at the Henry Ford Museum in Dearborn, Michigan. Total production is unknown. The Geneva plant was taken over in 1908 by the Cleveland Auto Cab Company (see Cleveland Auto Cab Company) and then in 1909 by the Ewing Automobile Company for the manufacture of taxicabs and chauffeur-driven town cars. (See Ewing Automobile Company.)

George C. Miller Sons' Carriage Company (Cincinnati, 1900)

Miller built a motorized vehicle for one of its customers but there was no intention of going into production.

Geyer Sales Company (Dayton, 1911)

The Geyer company was organized to manufacture and deal in automobiles, aeroplanes, and accessories, with a capitalization of $75,000. That any of these aspirations were realized is doubtful.

Gilford, George (Findlay, 1903)

A trade publication stated that George Gilford was going into the manufacture of automobiles. That he did cannot be confirmed.

Glenwood Motor Car Company (Youngstown, 1922)

Backed by Cleveland interests with a rather healthy capitalization of $5 million, Glenwood seems not to have realized the expectation that it would manufacture an automobile. The only thing heard from the company was that it had made some progress on an engine for the vehicle.

Goddard, Wilford, and Winfred Goddard (Conneaut, 1908)

The enterprising Goddard brothers, both aged fifteen years, took it upon themselves to build a motorized vehicle. They bought a one-cylinder engine from their savings, added some carriage wheels and a wood frame and hit the road. A trade journal of the day confessed that the boys had done a rather creditable job of it.

Grane Brothers (Cincinnati, circa 1917)

A trade journal listed the Grane brothers as builders of automobiles. Confirming evidence is lacking.

Grant Motor Company (Findlay, 1913 to 1916)

The Grant company moved from Detroit to Findlay in late 1913. Occupying the plant of the bankrupt Findlay Motor Car Company, Grant built 2,000 of its popular cyclecars in 1914. In 1915, as the cyclecar fad faded, a six-cylinder

automobile was introduced and met with immediate success, realizing sales of 2,100. A larger six followed in 1916. It was at this point that the company left for Cleveland and a new larger plant which would allow for its production to increase substantially. (See Grant Motor Car Corporation, Part I.)

Green Engineering Company (Dayton, 1920)

A maker of engine parts since 1912, the Green company built an automobile on special order which was named the C.R.G. Special. It had a 120-inch wheelbase and a four-cylinder engine which used Green company parts. Its performance was declared to be excellent by automobile trade publications.

Both images: **The 1914 Grant four cylinder delivered 30 miles per gallon and 100 miles to a pint of oil. For $495 it came with a plate glass windshield, mohair top, gauges, five lamps, horn, jack, and full set of tools. A self starter was available at extra cost.**

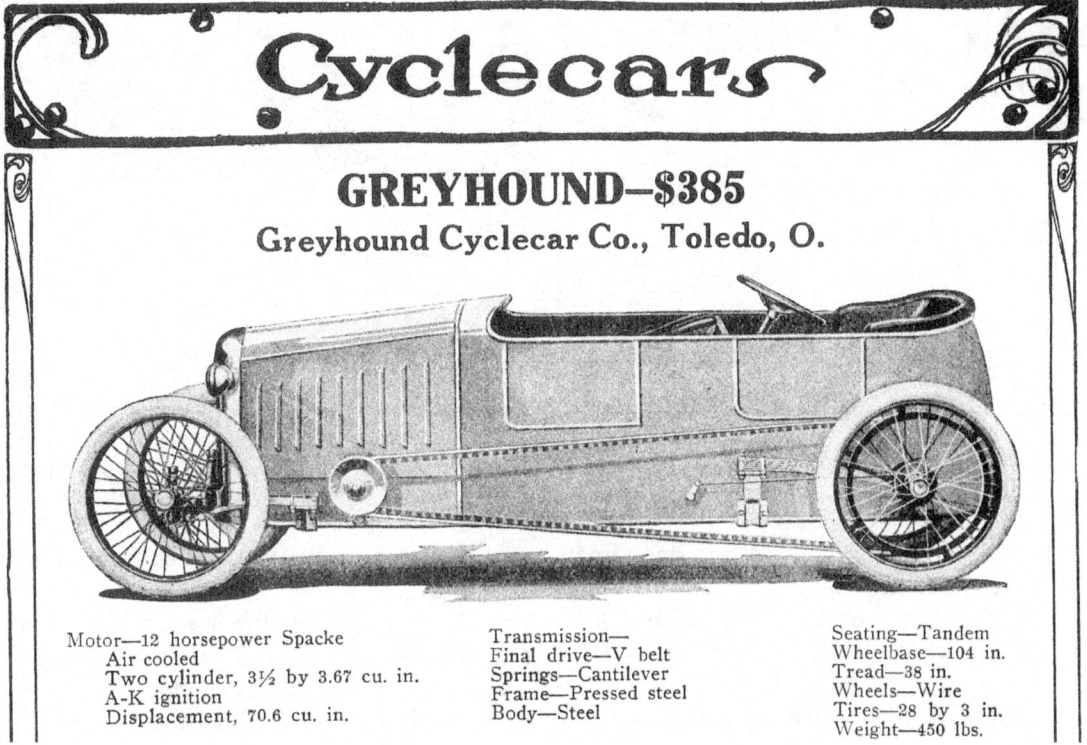

The driver of a 1914 Greyhound Cyclecar was seated at the rear of the vehicle while the passengers were treated to the front seat. Power was conveyed by an externally-mounted V-belt and the cyclecar was fenderless. Powered by a twelve horsepower air-cooled engine, it was priced at $385.

The company may have offered copies of the C.R.G. to the general market thereafter but this is not known with certainty.

Greyhound Cyclecar Company
(Toledo, 1914 to 1915)

The "Aristocrat of Cyclecars" was very unlike most cyclecars. It featured an 18 horsepower water-cooled engine, cone clutch, sliding gear transmission, shaft drive, electric starter, and a 104-inch wheelbase. Most cyclecars had friction drive, air-cooled engines, and belt or chain drive, and few had electric starting. The Greyhound at a price of $385 would have been a real bargain. However, for some reason, perhaps its appearance, it did not do well. After 1914 production was completed, the organizers thought things would go better in Kalamazoo, Michigan, and the operation was moved there. The Greyhound continued to be produced into at least 1916, with the organization passing through a withering array of iterations. Things finally closed down for good in 1918. Total production is unknown.

Groff-Runkle Motor Vehicle Company (Columbus, 1901); Columbus Motor Vehicle Company (Columbus, 1902 to 1904)

Beginning life in 1901 Groff-Runkle produced a prototype automobile that year which successfully completed a 200-mile test drive. When production began in 1902 the company name had been changed to the Columbus Motor Vehicle Company and the automobile was named the Santos-Dumont, after a famous Brazilian balloonist living in Paris. The automobile was offered with a two-cylinder engine and was priced at $1,500. A one-cylinder version appeared in 1903 for $1,250. The 1904

The 12 horsepower one-cylinder engine was mounted under the front seat of this 1903 Santos-Dumont. Named for the famous French-based balloonist Santos-Dumont, it could be had for $1,500.

model was entirely different, featuring a front-mounted twenty horsepower engine and a roomy five-passenger body. The name fluctuated between Santos-Dumont and Dumont but to no avail. Bankruptcy followed. Although virtually 100 percent of the claimants were satisfied, the company did not survive.

Gulliford, George (Findlay, 1903)

It was reported in a period automotive journal that George Gulliford was to open an automobile manufacturing plant in Findlay. Neither this fact nor production of an automobile can be confirmed.

H. B. Wick & Company (Youngstown, 1902)

Considering the prospects of manufacturing an automobile, Mr. Wick had an extravagant prototype built to his order by L. B. Smyser & Company of New York City. Sponsored by his company, it was shown at the New York, Cleveland, and Chicago automobile shows, but production of a Wick automobile did not follow.

H. W. Fenker Company (Cincinnati, 1916)

The Fenker company was organized to manufacture automobiles and capitalized at $250,000, but it is doubtful that the company actually produced an automobile.

Haberer & Company (Cincinnati, 1910 to 1913)

The Cino was a well-built sporty two-place automobile. Although it had only relatively conventional performance specifications, it was successfully campaigned at dirt track races, garnering 32 awards out of 44 starts. The automobile was well-received by the public but production ended abruptly in 1913 when the Ohio River flooded the factory.

Halladay Motor Car Company (Mansfield, Warren, Lexington, Attica and Newark, 1917 to 1919); Halladay Motors Corporation (Newark, 1920 to 1922)

The Halladay Car Company moved from Illinois to Ohio in 1917. Constantly on a quest for financial support, it passed through Mansfield, Warren, Lexington, and Attica before finally coming to rest in Newark. A limited number of demonstration vehicles had been built along the way, in the hopes of securing backing. When the company arrived in Newark it was reorganized as the Halladay Motors Corporation, which introduced its modest-size Falcon automobile at New York City's Grand Palace in 1922. Unfortunately there was a better-known Falcon, built by the Moller Company of Pennsylvania, already in existence. The

Hallady "Car of Class Built for the Mass" did not appear to have survived beyond its introduction.

Hamel, Charles D. (Toledo, 1917); Cyclomobile Manufacturing Company (Toledo, 1920 to 1921)

Despite the fact that the cyclecar fad had ended five years before, Charles D. Hamel was not deterred from introducing his own version, the Cyclomobile, in 1920. Hamel had previously experimented with a similar three-wheeler, a motorized tricycle, which he manufactured in 1917. This predecessor, however, could not be considered an automobile. Although it sported a steering wheel and was modestly propelled by a Smith Motor Wheel, it was merely an open, three-wheeled extended tricycle which seated only one person. (See *Motorcycle and Bicycle Illustrated*, November 22, 1917.) Hamel's 1920 Cyclomobile, on the other hand, was a true cyclecar with all the same primitive underpinnings of its forerunners—chain drive, friction clutch, and an air-cooled "twin-V" engine. It was also more handsome in design and featured a clever false radiator in front which was actually a gasoline tank. Production of the Cyclomobile reached 206 in 1920, and 181 in 1921, a relatively good result for a cyclecar, especially one arriving on the scene so late.

Hamilton Vehicle Company (Hamilton, 1912)

With a capital stock of $50,000, the Hamilton company was formed to manufacture automobiles. It is doubtful that any were built.

Harmer, Frederick S. (Columbus, 1907); Harmer Automobile Company (Columbus, 1907)

Frederick S. Harmer had worked as a designer on the Frayer-Miller automobile while employed at the Oscar Lear Automobile Company in Columbus. Harmer designed an overhead-valve air-cooled engine, built a successful prototype, and formed the Harmer Automobile Company to undertake production. However, production never occurred. Lawsuits by Oscar Lear and delayed granting of Harmer's patent until 1911 may have been at the heart of the failure. (See Oscar Lear Automobile Company.)

Harris Automatic Press Company (Niles, 1901)

It was reported that the Harris company intended to manufacture an automobile although there seems to be no evidence that this occurred.

Harruff, J. W. (Toledo, 1930)

Mr. Harruff built a small "one-man" automobile for his own use. It had an 80-inch wheelbase and was 60 inches tall. Except for

The 1920 Cyclomobile was a very late entry in the cyclecar field. It came in three models and was priced at a very modest $395 F.O.B. the factory.

its diminutive size and odd proportions it resembled the style of automobiles of the era.

Hatfield Motor Vehicle Company (Miamisburg, 1907 to 1908)

The Hatfield company produced a high-wheel buggy-type vehicle called Buggyabout or Unique. It had an air-cooled two-cylinder engine and double chain drive. Power was transferred from the engine to the rear wheels through a friction disc which contacted the flywheel at a ninety-degree angle. A lever moved the disc from dead center against the flywheel to its outer perimeter; the farther out the disc, the faster the vehicle went. Neutral was at dead center and reverse was to the opposite side of the flywheel. (See *Cycle and Automobile Trade Journal*, May 1907.) The company was absorbed in 1908 by Kauffman Buggy Company, also of Miamisburg, which had been its body supplier. The highwheeler was continued as the Kauffman and the resulting firm was named Advance Motor Vehicle Company. (See Advance Motor Vehicle Company.)

Hawkins Cyclecar Company (Xenia, 1914)

Built in Fred Baldner's machine shop, the Xenia cyclecar was superior to most others. One of his cyclecars was driven from Ohio to San Francisco without trouble and another defeated competing cyclecars at a Columbus, Ohio, race. Although the Xenia was well built and the company well managed, it experienced the fate of all cyclecars of the era, and the undertaking ended before the year was out.

Haydock Motor Car Company (Cincinnati, 1915 to 1916)

Haydock company was reported to be producing a four-cylinder automobile priced at $750, but no confirming information is available.

Healy, Caleb E. (New London, 1888)

Mr. Healy constructed a steam engine of his own design and mounted it on a carriage. He attached several wagons in tow and gave rides to townspeople. The powerful little engine hauled its load at about 3 miles per hour. The experiment was for Healy's own edification and he never intended to enter the business of manufacturing and selling vehicles. His vehicle had a wheelbase of perhaps six or seven feet. The rear wheels appeared to be iron tractor wheels with cleated treads.

Heatherman-Solliday Motor Company (Dayton, 1911)

Heatherman and two members of the Solliday family organized the Heatherman-Solliday company intending to manufacture automobiles and parts. It is unlikely an automobile was realized.

Heilman, John C. (Cincinnati, 1907)

Mr. Heilman built a small runabout powered by a gasoline engine. Production did not appear to have followed, although he subsequently engaged in business as an automobile dealer.

Herman Motor Company (Cincinnati, 1913)

Organized with a capitalization of $30,000 to manufacture automobiles, Herman probably did not produce any automobiles.

Hermes Motor Car Company (Cincinnati, 1913)

Joining Albert Kleybolts in organizing the Hermes company was Powel Crosley, Jr., who later presented the world with his small Crosley automobiles. The prototype Hermes was built and successfully tested on Cincinnati streets shortly after the company was formed. The vehicle rode on a 124-inch wheelbase and had wire wheels and a six-cylinder engine with electric starter. The Hermes was to be priced at $1,700 but manufacture of the vehicle did not take place. (See Crosley Corporation.)

Highway Motors Company (Defiance, 1920)

The Highway company was formed with a stated capitalization of a comfortable $1.5 million for the purpose of manufacturing passenger automobiles. One of the organizers was none other than Charles "Boss" Kettering, who would become world-famous as the founder of Delco and for his other engineering accomplishments in the automotive field. It appears, however, that the company never manufactured an automobile, but engaged solely in the manufacture of gasoline engines after it acquired engine manufacturer Belknap & Schwartz Company.

Hitchcock Motor Car Company (Warren, 1907 to 1908)

Hitchcock began work on a prototype vehicle in 1907 and announced completion of its first car in 1908. The vehicle featured a two-cylinder two-stroke air-cooled engine and friction drive. If any were put into production, the number was undoubtedly small.

Hollis Tractor Company (Tiffin, 1921 to 1922)

The Hollis company, underwritten by Tiffin investors, was to build an automobile in that city. However, actual construction and testing of what became the Hollis Electric took place outside Ohio. It appears that no Hollis vehicle was actually produced at the Tiffin plant which had initially been secured for the manufacture of the automobile.

Holmes Automobile Company (Canton, 1918 to 1923)

Arthur Holmes had been a vice-president and chief engineer for the H. H. Franklin Company of Syracuse, New York, when he left its employ to start his own automobile company. The Holmes was a six-cylinder air-cooled automobile of slightly larger proportions than the

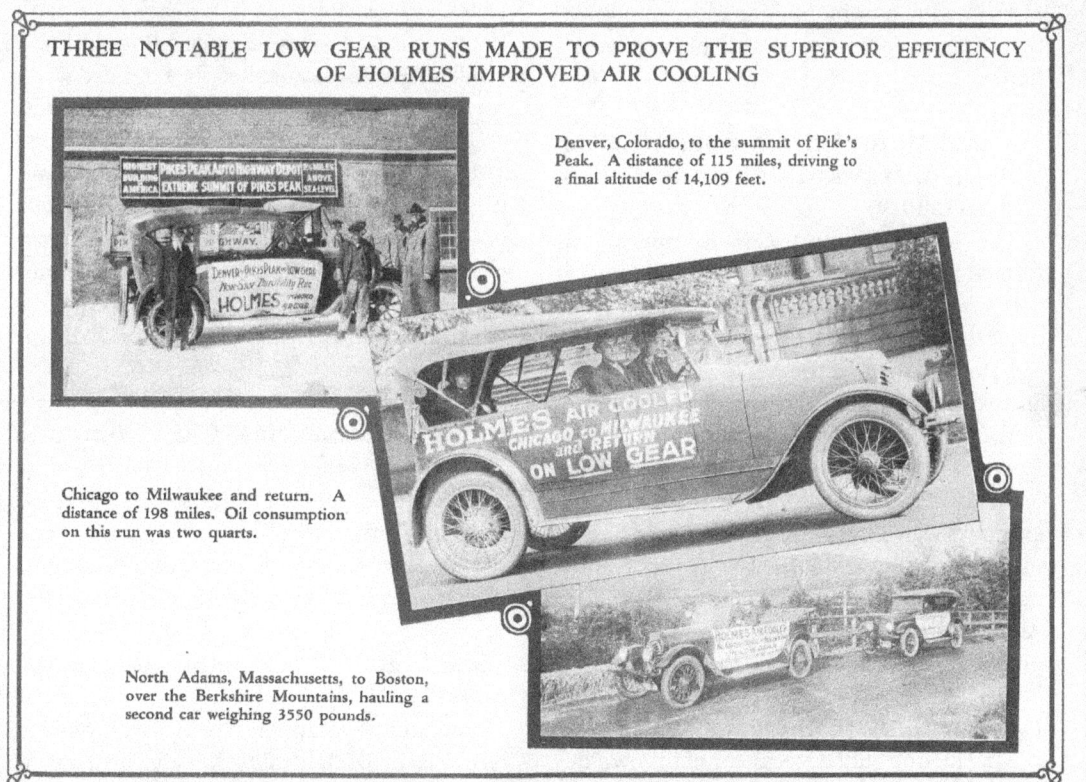

Endurance runs were still popular in 1921 when this air-cooled Holmes was driven to Pikes Peak in Colorado. On other trips it pulled a 3,550-pound vehicle behind it over the Berkshire Mountains in Massachusetts and made a round-trip from Chicago to Milwaukee and back in low gear to prove the durability and power of its six-cylinder engine.

Franklin. Advertising boasted that it was "America's Most Comfortable Car" thanks to its 124-inch wheelbase, flexible chassis, and full-elliptic springs. Some commentators added that it might have been America's ugliest as well. Apparently many people did not agree, and production ran for six years, ultimately reaching a total of 4,000 automobiles.

Horseless Carriage Company (Barberton, 1901)

Although the company is listed in compilations of automobile manufacturers as having built an automobile in 1901, no such company appears in the city directories of the era. The company may have been the alter ego of E. A. Huehne. (See Huehne, E. A.)

Houser, Orville E. (Chillicothe, 1906)

Houser operated a repair shop and built an experimental automobile for his own edification with no intention of going into production.

Howard Motor Car Company (Galion, 1911); A. Howard Company (Galion, 1916 to 1919)

The Howard Motor Car Company was formed in 1911 by Adam Howard to manufacture automobiles. Nothing came of this effort other than disgruntled investors. Then, in 1916 Mr. Howard formed the A. Howard Company and, with $500,000 in the bank, began production of an automobile almost immediately. Priced at $1,800, the six-cylinder Howard rode on a 120-inch wheelbase. However, only a few examples were built before the Howard passed into history. But in 1919 a touring-style automobile was built and shown at the New York Automobile Show. It is believed that this automobile remains in existence today.

Huehne, E. A. (Barberton, 1901)

Mr. Huehne built a steam car of his own design which had a unique propulsion system consisting of direct gear drives for each of its four wheels. His hopes to gain financing and enter production were not realized.

Hydro Engineering Company (Cincinnati, 1919)

The Hydro company planned to manufacture a $1,000 steam vehicle to be named the Hydro. Although handsomely endowed by a $1 million capitalization, production did not occur. Intentions to build a plant with worker housing may have diverted attention from the main objective of automobile manufacture.

Hydro Motor Car Company (Canton, 1917)

George Monnot was the genius behind the Hydrocar, which was capable of traveling on both land and water. It had two steering wheels because it traveled forward on land and backward in water. Two prototypes were built by his company and demonstration runs proved that the vehicle could reach twenty-five miles per hour on land and nine miles per hour in water. Presumably this latter speed was with the wheels and axles in place, although their removal was recommended for extended water travel. Attempts to interest the military in its abilities immediately before the end of World War I did not succeed. However, it may have ultimately given birth to the idea for the Duck of World War II fame, although the Duck traveled the same direction on land or sea. Financial considerations and the failure to interest the military brought an end to the Hydrocar venture.

Ideal Commercial Car Company (Akron, 1912)

Although organized with the stated purpose of manufacturing motor cars, engines, and trucks, the company focused on building its Akron brand trucks rather than automobiles.

Ideal Light Car Company (Columbus, 1915 to 1916)

Intending to manufacture an automobile to be priced at $750, Ideal had to give up its plans when the reality of material and parts costs came into play. A prototype was built before things came to an end.

Ideal Manufacturing Company (Portsmouth, 1907)

The company was organized to build automobiles, but only a single prototype truck was built.

Independence Motor Car Company (Lima, 1915)

The prototype of the Independence automobile was built at the Gramm-Bernstein truck plant in Lima. But Mr. W. A. Williams' intention to build a "cheaper and better Buick" concluded with the prototype.

Indian Motor Car Company (Upper Sandusky, 1911)

Indian was organized with a $10,000 capitalization to manufacture automobiles, trucks, and accessories. However, this seems to be another venture that came to nothing.

International Harvester Company (Akron, 1907 to 1911 and 1930)

After having built its first prototype highwheel automobile and an initial batch of one hundred in the company's McCormick facilities in Chicago in early 1907, International Harvester operations were transferred to Akron. The company purchased the plant of the Aultman and Miller Company, which had manufactured farm machinery. Between that time and 1911, approximately 4,500 highwheeler Auto Buggy automobiles were produced. The early Auto Buggy models were powered by a two-cylinder air-cooled engine with a five-inch bore and stroke configuration. The buggy-like wheels were forty inches in diameter and quite narrow so as to facilitate travel on even the most rutted and muddy country roads. Prices started at $600. By 1910 four-cylinder models were offered with either air- or water-cooled

International Auto Wagon. Two seats with top up

Although high-wheeled vehicles had largely disappeared by the end of the first decade of the twentieth century, International Harvester still found a market for its Auto Wagon, selling a total of 4,500 from 1907 to 1911. This 1910 IHC was available with either a water- or air-cooled four-cylinder engine.

engines, at which time the vehicle received the I.H.C. designation. Automobile production was discontinued in 1911 after 1,250 units had been manufactured, and the Akron plant was relegated to the manufacture of trucks. However, sometime in 1930 a few special-order highwheel automobiles were built on the small truck chassis.

International Motor Car Company (Toledo, 1901 to 1903)

The International company was formed by American Bicycle Company to manufacture the Billings steam vehicle. Two models were introduced, the Toledo and the Westchester, but the Westchester name was immediately dropped. In 1902, a three-cylinder gasoline-powered Toledo was an added offering and fifty of these were built that year. Two more gasoline-powered vehicles joined the Billings line in 1903. Later that year the Toledo name was dropped, shortly after which the operations were taken over by the Pope Motor Car Company. The vehicles then bore the name Pope-Toledo. (See Pope Motor Car Company.)

Interstate Supply Company (Toledo, 1911)

Interstate was capitalized at $10,000 to manufacture automobiles, but it appears nothing resulted along those lines.

J. H. Louis Automobile Company (Cincinnati, 1911)

Incorporated to manufacture and repair automobiles, the company's $75,000 capitalization was apparently not adequate, as evidence of an automobile having been built is lacking.

Jewel Carriage Company (Carthage, 1910)

The Breeze highwheel motor carriage with its air-cooled engine and chain drive was a re-branded copy of the DeTamble, which had been built by the DeTamble Motor Company of Indiana. The vehicle was anachronistic and not favored by the motoring public of 1910. Production was minimal. Jewel was unrelated to the Jewell Carriage Company, below.

Jewell Carriage Company (Carthage, 1909 to 1911); Ohio Motor Car Company (Carthage, 1912); Crescent Motor Company (Carthage, 1912 to 1914)

The Jewell manufacturing plant in Carthage produced the OhiO, a relatively conventional large touring automobile. The company encountered financial headwinds early on and was in trouble by 1910. Reorganized in 1912 as the Ohio Motor Car Company, it carried on production of the OhiO in the same factory as before. Ralph Northway, a manufacturer of automobile engines, had been involved with the OhiO from its beginning. He was fortunate enough to sell his engine company to General Motors in 1912, whereupon Northway acquired control of the Ohio Motor Car Company, which he reconstructed as the Cresent Motor Company. The OhiO then became a model designation for the Cresent four-cylinder automobile, and a six-cylinder model was named the Royal. Neither vehicle attracted a sufficient number of purchasers and production ended in 1914.

Jewett Motor Carriage Company (Columbus, 1901)

Organized with a capital stock of $25,000, the Jewett company intended to manufacture automobiles of an unknown type. It is unlikely that production followed.

John Kohl Carriage & Automobile Company (Mason, 1912)

Capitalized at $10,000, the company intended to build horse-drawn and horseless vehicles. No horseless vehicles followed.

John Schilito Company (Cincinnati, 1901)

A steam carriage of unknown description was built for the Schilito company on special order and was probably used for delivery purposes. Its builder is not known.

Jones, C. H. (Columbus Grove, 1899)

Mr. Jones was reported in a trade journal as organizing a company to produce automobiles. None were built.

Jones, Isaac B. (Xenia, 1899)

Isaac Jones was a successful inventor, but not when it came to automobiles. His gasoline-powered experiment ran into difficulties on its first test drive. Power was transmitted from the engine to the rear wheels by way of two cones and a leather belt, which was designed to ride up and down on the cones allowing for infinite and smoothly changed speeds. The engine turned out to be under-powered and the belts slipped badly. His more successful inventions were in the fields of cultivators, riding plows, power ditching machines, potato diggers, and buck saws.

Keller Electrical Shops (Canton, 1899)

The Keller shops built a single prototype electric vehicle in 1899 but appear to have gone no further. In 1903 they had moved to Cleveland as the J. Keller Electric Works. (See J. Keller Electric Works in Part I.)

Kent, A. W. (Marietta, 1901)

Mr. A. W. Kent is believed to have built a steam carriage in Marietta in 1901 but this fact cannot be confirmed. It may have been the steam carriage he built in Boston, which he brought with him when he moved to Ohio.

Kepler-Beery Motor Car Company (Dayton, 1903 to 1904)

Kepler-Beery built several experimental one-cylinder touring

The Ohio Motor Car Company (see Jewell Carriage Company) maintained in this 1910 advertisement that its low production level permitted more thorough inspection. It also points out that low production, high quality automobiles benefit from this fact as well.

The Crescent automobile (1913–14) was successor to Jewell's earlier OhiO automobile (1909–12). Crescent produced several models, one of which was named the Royal or Royal-Ohio, promoted in this ad. This advertisement is offering dealerships but dissolution of the company was imminent.

vehicles, but production did not take place. By 1904 even the company's engine building attempts seem to have ceased.

Kero-Car Motor Company (Dayton, 1909)

A prototype Kero-Car was powered by an engine that could burn kerosene, gasoline, or alcohol. Although it was successfully tested, nothing came of plans to enter actual production.

Kessell, Frank E. (Massillon, 1899)

The machine built by Frank Kessell traveled only five feet on its first test drive. After he put some more work into his invention and refined some of its operations, however, the vehicle performed significantly better and achieved a speed of fifteen miles per hour. Only one prototype was built.

Keystone Vehicle Company (Columbus, 1914)

Formed to manufacture and deal in automobiles, the Keystone company was capitalized at $15,000 but failed to produce an automobile.

Kinnear Manufacturing Company (Columbus, 1913)

Kinnear built a front-drive touring car which it entered in a local race. The vehicle crashed and fatally injured the company's driver. This ended the automobile's prospects and nothing further was heard about its possible production.

Kirk-Hall Company (Toledo, 1903)

With capital stock of $10,000 the company was formed to manufacture automobiles and to deal in, store, and repair them. No automobile was forthcoming.

Kirk Manufacturing Company (Toledo, 1902 to 1903); Consolidated Manufacturing Company (Toledo, 1903 to 1905)

Built in its entirety by the Kirk company, the Yale automobile was a runabout with a two-cylinder water-cooled engine, chain drive, and a price of $1,500. An order for fifty Yales was delivered to a Chicago dealer in the automobile's second year. Kirk reorganized as the Consolidated Manufacturing Company in 1903, expansion was planned, and new models were added to the line-up, with prices rising to as high as $2,500. But in 1905 it was abruptly announced that the Yale would be discontinued despite its apparent popularity. Perhaps the Consolidated company wished to pursue what it viewed as more lucrative fields. Be that as it may, bankruptcy followed in 1906.

Kitto, A. W. (Kent and Lisbon, 1907 to 1910)

A. W. Kitto bounced from state to state promoting his automobile ventures. Arriving in Kent in 1907 he successfully enticed residents to invest in his Criterion Motor Company. He then moved to Lisbon where he promoted his Lisbon Auto Truck Company with similar results. In both cases no automobile ever appeared. Unhappy investors sued for redress but were unsuccessful.

Koeb-Thompson (Springfield, 1901 to 1902); Koeb-Thompson Motor Company (Springfield, 1910 to 1911)

Partners Emil Koeb and Ralph P. Thompson were in the automobile repair business when they built their first automobile in 1902. It had a gasoline-powered two-stroke engine, chain drive, and came with a touring body. The automobile was raced actively and changes were made to its design over the ensuing years. In 1910 the partners developed a lever type suspension system, and a prototype vehicle using this system was built for them by the American Foundry Company in Leipsig, Ohio. The foundry people were so impressed with the vehicle that they helped form the Koeb-Thompson Motor Company to build the automobile. Production did not last beyond 1911.

Krebs, Mr. (Ottawa, 1901)

It was reported in a trade publication that Krebs, who had a machine shop, had built an automobile. Confirmation of this fact is not available.

Krotz, Alvaro S. (Springfield, 1903); Krotz Manufacturing Company (Springfield, 1903 to 1904)

Alvaro S. Krotz built two experimental electric vehicles which were followed by several others. Although the storage battery and tires appeared to be of Krotz design, the balance of the vehicle used conventional electric systems. The venture ended in 1904 and Krotz moved to Defiance. (See Krotz-Defiance Auto Buggy Company.)

Krotz-Defiance Auto Buggy Company (Defiance, 1908 to 1911)

This company offered an inexpensive motorized buggy intended for the farm trade. The Krotz Electric Buggy actually went into limited production and was marketed without fanfare. The number produced was small and things came to a halt in 1911. (See Krotz, Alvaro S.)

Kuqua & Son (Springfield, 1901)

Originally carriage makers, the firm ventured into the automobile arena to build steam and electric vehicles. Production if any was undoubtedly limited.

Lambert, John William (Ohio City, 1891)

Mr. Lambert owned several businesses including a hardware store, lumber yard and grain elevator in Ohio City, but apparently lived in Anderson, Indiana, just across the border. He designed, built, and by 1891, tested a three-wheeled gasoline-powered vehicle. Whether it was built in Ohio City or Anderson is not clear. In any event, although his vehicle was priced at only $550, he was not successful in marketing his creation and only the one example was built.

Landmann-Griffith (Toledo, 1914)

A cyclecar bearing the Landmann-Griffith name was exhibited at the Toledo automobile show, but no further information has been found.

Lawrence Stamping Company (Toledo, 1915)

Apparently already on sound financial footing, Lawrence built its Odelot automobile with intentions of entering full production. The rather strange name is Toledo spelled backwards. The Odelot was a two-seat raceabout with a sporty appearance. The hood and fenders were black, but a choice of colors was offered for the remainder of the body: yellow, green, or red. A leather strap hold-down over the hood added a certain flair to the raceabout's character. Whatever ultimately became of the Odelot, their number was small.

Leach Automobile Company (Lima, 1909)

The Leach company was formed to manufacture automobiles to be powered by a two-cylinder air-cooled engine. No such vehicle was ever offered for sale, although it is possible that a prototype was built.

Lecklider, A. E. (Toledo, 1898 to 1902 and 1906)

It took Mr. Lecklider from 1898 to 1902 to complete building a drivable motorized vehicle. Unfortunately, the automobile was lost in a fire. Undaunted, Lecklider built a second improved version, which he completed in 1906. This one had a six-horsepower engine, two-speed sliding gear transmission, and thermosyphon cooling. After numerous test drives, he boasted that the only repair it required was replacement of "a rattled out bolt" from time to time. He said it cost him two dollars a month to operate, while his horse cost him at least fifteen.

Lehr Agricultural Company (Fremont, 1905 to 1908)

Although the company professed to be planning to manufacture automobiles, prototype examples of the planned touring cars were the only outcome. The vehicles were developed over a span of three years.

Lepp Brothers (Belleville, 1895)

The Lepp brothers announced their having entered a race along Lake Michigan between Chicago and Evanston, Illinois. Nothing further is known about their automobile except that the brothers and their automobile did not appear at the race.

Lima Light Car Company (Lima, 1915)

The Lima company proposed building what was a typical cyclecar in three body styles: speedster, roadster, and light delivery, each to be priced at $500. The company did field a few prototype examples but never went to market with their automobile.

Logan Construction Company (Chillicothe, 1904 to 1908)

Benjamin A. Gramm's first automobile was the Buckeye. (See Motor Storage and Manufacturing Company.) He followed this in 1904 with the Logan, which was offered with either a water- or air-cooled engine. It was boasted that the Logan ran so smoothly that you could write a letter while seated in it. In addition the Blue Streak, a semi-race car, was produced from 1907 to 1908 and priced at $1,750. The automobile business did not survive and Mr. Logan moved to Bowling Green, where he built trucks under the Gramm-Logan Motor Car Company name.

Long-Crawford Automobile Company (Massillon, 1904 to 1905)

Named the Boss by its inventors, J. E. Long and John Crawford, this vehicle was never in command. The prototype had an air-cooled engine and a side-entrance touring body. The Long-Crawford company and the Boss automobile were unsuccessful.

Lorain Motor Carriage Company (Lorain, 1900)

Although listed in trade journals as being a manufacturer of automobiles, there is no evidence that the company even built a prototype.

Lunken, Edmund (Cincinnati, 1902); Lunkenheimer Motor Vehicle Company (Cincinnati, 1902)

Edmund Lunken custom built several experimental vehicles. The first was a buckboard-type conveyance, which was followed by a large handsome touring automobile powered by a two-cylinder engine. It is said that the steering wheel was a cast iron handle from a large gate valve. Since the ancestral Lunkenheimers were in the industrial valve business, this application of one of their products was a practical measure. The vehicle was not placed into production.

Lutz, Henry (Logan, 1898)

With spare time on his hands, fireman Lutz undertook building a steam car of his own design, having been inspired by seeing a steam vehicle pass through town. The Lutz steam vehicle was a snappy looking four-wheel carriage with tiller steering. Lutz drove it around town for years and it is now in the collection of the Hocking County Historical Society.

M. C. Witmore Company (Dayton, 1914)

Whitmore produced the Arrow cyclecar offering body styles with either single or two-place seating. Its 100-inch wheelbase and thirty-six inch tread were unusually generous for a cyclecar. Triple transverse springs were used and there was no front axle, the traverse spring serving the purpose. Production lasted only one year.

MacDonald Steam Automobile Company (Garfield, 1920 to 1923)

A prototype Bob-Cat steamer was built by Duncan MacDonald, utilizing a three-cylinder engine and a 106-inch wheelbase chassis. At least one prototype was assembled. McDonald's grandiose claims to have almost unlimited financial backing were proven false when he was convicted of stock fraud. No automobiles were put into production but kits for converting gasoline powered vehicles to steam were actually manufactured and offered for sale.

MacInnis Brothers (Toledo, 1909 to 1910)

The MacInnis brothers produced a small electric vehicle priced at a heady $2,400 until sometime during late 1910. They then switched to updating older automobile bodies by adding a "fore-door" which allowed for direct entrance to the front seat of an automobile.

Your Chance to Save $625

Fully equipped with top, wind shield, 5 gas and oil lamps, horn and tools
Regular price (complete) $2125. Special offer $1500

Logan "That Car of Quality"

The unusual demand this year for the LOGAN COMMERCIAL CARS has decided us to devote ourselves exclusively to them in the future. In order to clear the decks at once for this new policy, we are going to sell the last few of our 1906 five-passenger touring cars direct to the user at more than 25% discount. We have eight of these on hand, just through the factory, and ready for immediate shipment.

We could, no doubt, dispose of them through our agents, but we propose to give you the benefit of the dealers' commission, to get them off our hands at once.

The Logan is one of the best cars built and is
The Easiest Riding Car in the World

It is particularly simple, accessible and easy to drive and is a powerful hill-climber. It is well designed and well built and will not be "out-of-date" for several years, as it is of the standard pattern and contains several 1907 improvements we have added during the season.

GENERAL SPECIFICATIONS

30 H. P. water-cooled, double opposed motor; sliding gear transmission; 100 inch wheelbase; five-passenger body; double side entrance tonneau; regular price (with top and wind shield) $2125. Present price, $1500. complete. Guaranteed fully for one year.

If you have been considering buying an automobile either this fall or next spring, you cannot afford to pass up this opportunity to save $625.00 on a high grade car.

We expect to receive a large number of replies to this offer and it will be to your interest to act at once. Don't fail to *write us today*. Address Department "D."

The Logan Construction Company
Chillicothe, Ohio

"That Car of Quality" is how the 1907 Logan was described. The company was promoting a close-out sale of in-stock Logans as it was turning to the exclusive manufacture of commercial vehicles. Originally priced at $2,125, the car could now be had direct from the manufacturer for $1,500, including a one year guarantee.

The MacDonald was a conversion unit which could be installed in any gasoline-powered automobile to change it into a steam car. A prototype was built for demonstration purposes, but only the conversion unit itself was offered for sale.

Mahoning Motor Car Company
(Youngstown, 1904 to 1905)

Unlike most companies capitalized at only $25,000, the Mahoning company actually produced not only a prototype, but went into actual production, all within a year's time. The Mahoning was an attractive four-place one-cylinder vehicle that came in three body styles with prices starting at $950. Production continued for only one year. Labor difficulties were blamed, but it may have had something to do with the automobile itself. It had been reported that to ascend a hill all the passengers had to disembark and let the driver and the vehicle go up the hill unaccompanied.

Maibohm Motors Company
(Sandusky, 1919 to 1922)

Maibohm moved operations from Racine, Wisconsin, to Sandusky in 1919 after having suffered a fire at its Wisconsin plant. The Maibohm automobile was a conventionally-styled vehicle, but of uncommonly light weight at 2,395 pounds. It had leather upholstery, a six-cylinder engine which was rated at 23 horsepower, and rode on a 116-inch wheelbase. Production levels rose, and by 1920 the factory was turning out thirty vehicles a day. However, the post–World War I economic depression was not kind to the Maibohm company, and prices were dropped significantly in hopes of sustaining sales. The company struggled along but bankruptcy brought an end to the operation after approximately 14,000 Maibohms were built. Also, Peter C. Maibohm had become distracted by his involvement in the East Coast Biddle automobile venture, and his Sandusky operation suffered for it. The Maibohm business was sold to what became Courier Motors of Sandusky. Mr. Maibohm moved on to manufacturing radios instead. (See Courier Motors Company.)

Marathon Automobile Company
(Cincinnati, 1909)

Powel Crosley, Jr., and his associates established the Marathon company to build the Marathon Six automobile. This was the first

The year 1922 was the last for the Maibohm automobile. Advertised as having "willowy springs, balanced to a feather weight" and deep cushioned seats in real leather that carried you in the comfort of an old rocking chair, it was not enough to save the marque.

motor vehicle built by Crosley, and orders were taken for a half-dozen copies, but whether they were produced is a matter of conjecture. In 1913 Crosley made a second attempt at manufacturing an automobile, the De Cross cyclecar, but it too failed. (See Crosley Corporation.)

Marion Automobile Company
(Marion, 1901)

Marion ambitiously embarked on an effort to build one gasoline, one electric and two steam vehicles. Assuming that this was accomplished, it appears that none of the prototypes proved to be satisfactory, as the company never took any of them into production.

Markert, F. G. R. (Mount Healthy, 1906)

A trade journal listed F. G. R. Markert as a manufacturer of motorized vehicles. Confirmation is lacking.

Marysville Motor Car Company
(Marysville, 1905)

A prototype Marysville vehicle was built by H. Tarkington and his Marysville company in 1905. His 20 horsepower vehicle performed satisfactorily, but details about its construction are unavailable. Tarkington's search for financial backing failed, although the good citizens of Marysville were encouraged by local newspapers to help the venture along for the good of the community. (See Tarkington, H.)

Massillon Developing Company
(Massillon, 1917)

Capitalized at only $5,000 for the manufacture of automobiles in Massillon, this company most likely never realized its ambitions.

McAdams, John (Middletown, 1903)

Mr. McAdams built an automobile for his own use with no intention of going into production. It operated successfully and McAdams drove it around town regularly, using it to commute to his job.

McNutt, John (Springfield, 1902)

Mr. McNutt purchased the Brenning Bros. machine shop in Springfield, stating as his intention the production of automobiles. None were produced.

Mead Engine Company (Dayton, 1912)

A prototype vehicle was built by the Mead company but production did not follow.

Meeker Manufacturing Company (Dayton, 1900)

Listed in a trade journal as a manufacturer of automobiles, it appears that this company's only product was, in fact, tires.

Merkel, Joseph F. (Middletown, 1914)

Mr. Merkel had designed and manufactured the "Flying Merkel" motorcycle with great success. In 1914 he elected to try the automobile business. He built two prototype cyclecars in the basement of his residence, but was unable to convince investors to go into business with him. Therefore, he returned full-time to the manufacture of motorcycles and bicycles in association with the Miami Cycle and Manufacturing Company. He produced tens of thousands of bicycles and motorcycles until the factory was turned over to war work during World War I.

Meteor Motor Car Company (Piqua, 1914 to 1930)

Maurice Wolfe brought his automobile manufacturing company to Piqua from Shelbyville, Indiana, in 1914. The company moved into the old Sprague-Smith Furniture Company plant which had sufficient space to accommodate production of fourteen vehicles a day. Production focused on Meteor hearses, but passenger cars were also built on the Meteor chassis. In 1916 a V-12 automobile was offered, powered by a Weidely engine, although few were probably built. The company continued to produce automobiles on a limited special-order basis until 1930. Wolfe had a wry sense of humor which is demonstrated by his naming one of his smaller hearses the Mort (French for "dead.") He also went into the phonograph and record business selling "music that kills 'em." All of that aside, the Meteor automobile was a good-looking

The Meteor came in two models for 1915. A Model 60 with a 40 horsepower 6-cylinder engine for $1,275 and a Model 50 with a 45 horsepower version of the engine for $1,475. Both came with an electric starter.

large vehicle with gently curved fender and body lines, and an attractive radiator shell similar to the pointed Mercedes radiator.

Miami Cycle and Manufacturing Company (Middletown, 1901 to 1902)

Already a manufacturer of bicycles, Miami's first and only vehicle was a huge steam car which bore the Indian name Ramapaugh. It weighed over 4,000 pounds and had a boiler located under its front hood. Speeds of up to forty miles per hour were possible. To keep it going the Ramapaugh had a twenty-four gallon gasoline tank and a sixty-eight gallon water tank. The steamer operated on the streets of Middletown from time to time but may not have ventured farther. The last that was heard of the Ramapaugh in Middletown was in mid–1902.

Middletown Buggy Company (Middletown, 1909 to 1911)

The New Decatur Buggy Company's business was exceptionally good and stood at the head of a list of American buggy companies until it went bankrupt as a result of its leaders failing to comprehend the significance of the burgeoning automobile industry. Its owner, Harry H. Elwood, then became manager of the Middletown Buggy Company, which, under his direction, produced a vehicle based on the New Decatur buggies. The vehicle was not successful and the company went bankrupt shortly thereafter.

Middletown Machine Company (Middletown, 1905)

A manufacturer of the Miami and Woodpecker engines, Middletown Machine is believed to also have assembled a limited number of vehicles on special order for its engine customers. It seems that the engines were not especially noteworthy, which may have contributed to the company going out of business in 1906 without having gone into actual production of an automobile.

Midgley Manufacturing Company (Columbus, 1901 to 1905)

Midgley was a very successful manufacturer of automobile wheels. Between 1901 and 1905 it assembled several demonstration automobiles utilizing its wheels. None of the prototypes was destined for production.

Milburn Wagon Company (Toledo, 1915 to 1923)

Starting rather late in the electric vehicle era, the Milburn company introduced its first electric vehicle in 1915 and, perhaps surprisingly, met with immediate success. It was lightweight, capable of a speed of fifteen miles per hour, and had a range of seventy odd miles, which would have made it attractive for in-town use. In 1918 the Milburn was offered with a slide-out

Standard Model 27-L Milburn Light Electric

The Milburn was a relative latecomer to the field of electric vehicles. Normal range without recharging was 60 miles, but the Milburn Wagon Company offered a roll-out battery tray that permitted freshly charged batteries to be installed, avoiding the delay of a normal recharging. Milburns were priced about $1,885.

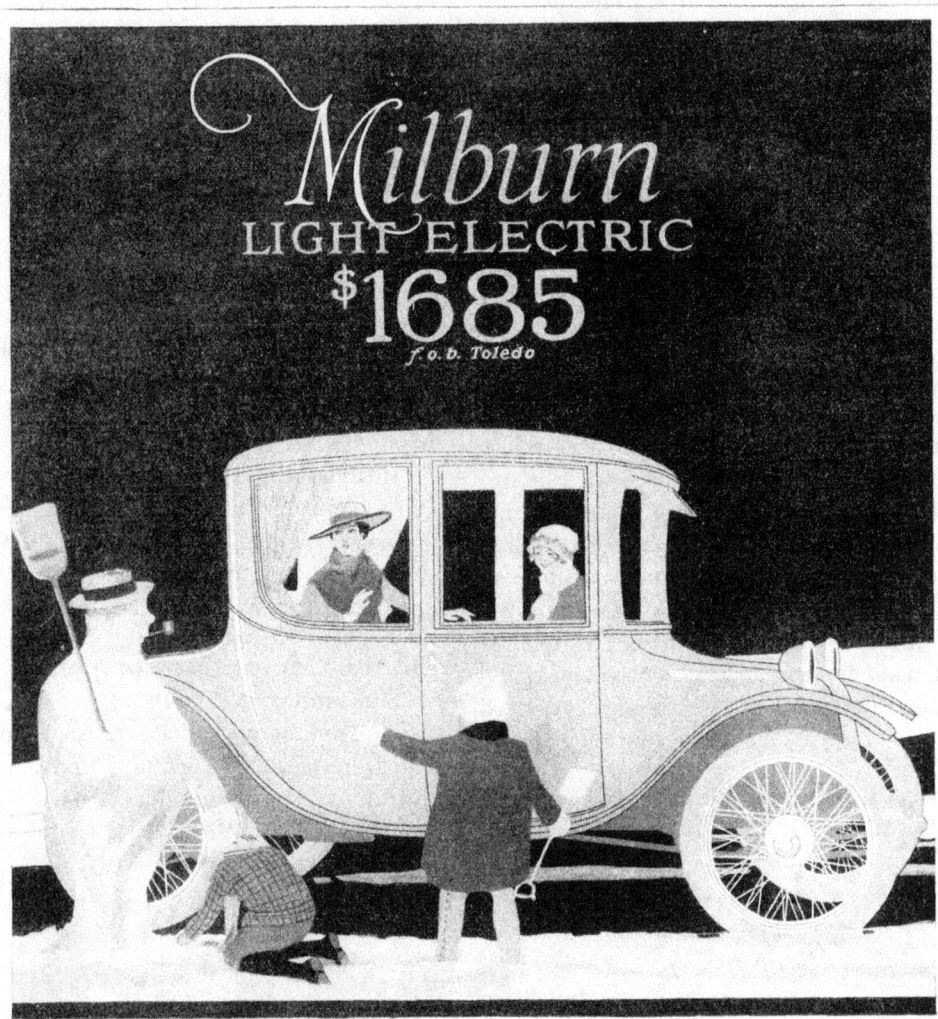

As electric vehicles went, the 1916 Milburn was one of the more attractive examples. It had a relatively low profile and a price that was the most affordable in its field. Although the majority of its models had a decidedly "electric vehicle appearance," its 1918 limousine was indistinguishable from a standard gasoline-powered automobile. The lightest Milburn, a roadster, was capable of a sustained speed of 19 miles per hour.

battery rack, permitting easy replacement of run-down batteries with a fresh set. The Milburn company did considerable export business and President Wilson chose to use the Milburn Light Electric in preference to the much noisier gasoline automobiles which were usually at his disposal. (See *Amps*, vol. II, no. 1, The Milburn Wagon Company, 1920.) Production continued until 1923, when the Milburn plant was purchased by General Motors for use by its Buick division. In the interim, from 1915 to 1923, thousands of Milburn electrics were produced.

Miller, George J. (Kenton, 1900 and 1902)

Mr. Miller was an inventor with a penchant for things electrical. He designed a dry battery and an electric motor, both of which he installed in a vehicle in 1900. After obtaining patents on his two inventions, he built another experimental electric vehicle and was successful in securing financing from investors in Bellefontaine for its manufacture. For some reason his electric vehicle never went into production, although his Miller Storage Battery & Electric Company made and sold batteries.

Miller, J. W. (Trail, 1901 to 1902)

Mr. Miller built a small number of experimental gasoline-powered vehicles on his own in 1901. Some investors from Orville seemed to have had an interest in manufacturing Miller's vehicle, but nothing came of it.

Miller Machine Company (Defiance, 1909)

Announcing the impending manufacture of its Defiance "40" automobile, the Miller company stated that the bodies would be built by the Defiance Carriage Company and the automobile assembled in a vacant Defiance bicycle factory. If a prototype was built, it probably was the only result of this undertaking.

Millersville Machine Company (Millersville, 1910)

The company announced that it was building a runabout named the Millersville. A new factory was supposedly underway but nothing more was heard about the venture.

Monitor Motor Car Company (Columbus, 1915 to 1922)

The Monitor automobile was an assembled vehicle initially utilizing four-cylinder engines from a variety of suppliers. A six-cylinder engine was added in 1916 and a public stock

The 1921 Monitor was the last of the line. An assembled automobile, it had disc steel wheels, which was not a common feature on vehicles of the era.

offering was announced in 1917. Production ranged wildly from 373 in 1915 to 1,630 in 1918 then down to 81 in its final year 1922. In all, something short of a total of 6,000 were produced. The Monitor was conventional in appearance but was spiced up in 1921 when disc steel wheels were featured. The four was last offered in 1918. The end came when the company was sued by suppliers and others, which led to the venture's liquidation in 1922.

Motor Storage and Manufacturing Company (Chillicothe, 1903)

The Buckeye was a surrey-style vehicle on a 90-inch wheelbase with seating for eight, a fringed top as standard equipment and a heady price of $2,000. After being in production for only one year, the company turned to manufacturing the Logan automobile. (See Logan Construction Company.)

Motz, Charles A. (Akron, 1899)

Charles Motz, a blacksmith, built a motorized vehicle based on a one-cylinder engine with an unusually large 6½-inch by 7-inch bore and stroke. On a pleasure trip from Akron to Wadsworth the engine overheated and refused to stop running. Motz finally resorted to throwing dirt into the carburetor which did the job. Apparently the vehicle never ran well after that. It was the only automobile Motz built.

Moyea Automobile Company (Middletown, 1903)

Although Moyea company offices were located in New York City, the first Moyea automobile was built in Middletown, while the company awaited construction of its Rye, New York, manufacturing plant. The Moyea was a copy of the French Rochet-Schneider automobile and was built under license from the French manufacturer. Subsequent examples of the Moyea were built in New York.

Napoleon Motor Car Company (Napoleon, 1916 to 1917)

The Napoleon company assembled and demonstrated its first automobile to the residents of Napoleon in the summer of 1916. It was a small touring automobile with a thirty horsepower engine and a proposed price of $795. When local investors failed to come forward with financial support by 1917, the company moved to Traverse City, Michigan. Traverse City had offered the company free use of a vacant plant and $75,000 in capital. (See Reya Motor Company.)

National Juvenile Auto Company (Toledo, 1913 to 1917)

Already in production of a child-size motorized car, National announced in 1917 that it would also produce a full-size cyclecar boasting expected gas mileage of eighty to ninety miles per gallon. Whether even a prototype was built is unknown.

Neil, Ed (Columbus, 1909)

Ed Neil, while a college student, built an automobile for his own use from miscellaneous parts and materials he had on hand. He claimed a speed of forty miles per hour for his creation.

New Concord Automobile Company (New Concord, 1902)

The company was capitalized with $50,000 and by August of 1902 reports were heard to the effect that a plant construction contract had been secured. All this before construction of a prototype vehicle had been undertaken. Actual manufacture of the New Concord is doubtful.

Niles Auto & Machine Company (Niles, 1913)

The Niles company was formed to build and repair automobiles. Actual manufacture of an automobile is doubted.

Niswender, Roman (Trotwood, 1903)

Mr. Niswender built an automobile in mid-1903, which apparently showed some promise. However, he failed to find sufficient financing to realize his hopes of actual manufacture.

Norwalk Motor Car Company (Norwalk, 1910 to 1911)

Although the Norwalk company, successor to the Auto-Bug Company, successfully constructed three prototype vehicles and a demonstrator automobile, ultimately it was not successful in obtaining adequate financing and found itself in bankruptcy in 1911, after having produced 371 additional vehicles. Its largest creditor, an Indiana engine manufacturer, acquired all the plant equipment and four remaining automobiles. The company's founder, Arthur E. Skadden, then left for Martinsburg, West Virginia, where the Norwalk continued in production from 1912 to 1922, thanks to a crop of new investors. (See Auto-Bug Company.)

Norwood Automobile Company (Cincinnati, 1905)

Organized to manufacture, sell, and repair automobiles, the Norwood company was capitalized at $25,000, but it is doubtful an automobile was produced. The company did open a dealership selling Wayne automobiles.

O. S. Kelly Corporation (Springfield, 1901 to 1902)

O. S. Kelly built a steam carriage to test a rotary steam valve system which proved to be quite satisfactory in operation. Further tests followed but production of a steam carriage was not pursued.

Ogontz Motor Car Company (Sandusky, 1916)

Taking the defunct Wolverine automobile under its wing, the Ogontz company must have hoped that it would be an easier way to get into the automobile manufacturing business than starting from scratch. It was wrong. Within a year's time Ogontz Motor Car Company was back to the basics, operating merely as a motor car service garage.

Ohio Electric Car Company (Toledo, 1910 to 1918)

The Ohio Electric was designed and marketed with the woman squarely in mind. It was a refined vehicle that catered to female preferences in motoring. Ease and smoothness of operation were paramount. The Ohio Electric was driven by a patented magnetic control device which, with a mere touch, could control the vehicle's operation and braking. Production of 950 electrics occurred between 1915 and 1916. As popularity of electric vehicles waned, the company shifted half of its operation to the manufacture of automobile bodies for the trade. The business was dissolved in 1918.

Priced at $4,000, an Ohio Electric had some of the most sumptuous interiors of any vehicle. French broadcloths, deeply-tufted upholstery, and imported goat skins were lavishly applied. The 1915 Ohio body was constructed of hand-hammered aluminum, and fenders were formed from a single piece of metal. Mechanically, its magnetic brakes and controls provided for smooth operation, which was the hallmark of electric vehicles.

THIS is the only five passenger electric made that can be driven from *both* the front and rear seats. All passengers face forward.

When riding alone with your wife sit *beside* her and drive from the *rear* seat. Don't sit in front and look like a hired chauffeur.

When riding with three or four people drive from the *front* seat and have an unobstructed view.

OHIO ELECTRIC

THIS car, in its fourth successful year, has more exclusive patented features than any other electric in America — magnetic control, chainless shaft drive.

We have some very desirable territory open for established and responsible dealers. Write for full particulars at once.

Our handsome 1913 catalogue illustrates and explains in detail our complete line.

The Ohio Electric Car Company, Toledo, Ohio

The Ohio Electric had driving positions at the front and rear seats. In addition, the Ohio featured more exclusive patented features than any other electric in America. This example was the company's most luxurious offering for 1913.

Ohio Universal Truck Company (Warren, 1911)

Professing to be entering the business of manufacturing trucks and pleasure vehicles, this company seems to have done neither. At least it did not produce an automobile.

Okey, Perry (Columbus, 1896 to 1907); Okey Motor Car Company (Columbus, 1907)

In 1896, with the creation of his first vehicle, a tricycle powered by a one-cylinder four-stroke engine to his credit, sixteen-year-old Perry Okey began actively building automobiles. In 1901 he built and sold a one-cylinder vehicle and another in 1902, which went to a doctor for $750. By the end of 1904 he had built and sold his fifth motor car, and in 1905 five more were sold. Okey was probably the first to use titanium iron and manganese bronze in automobiles, and his 1905 model was powered by a three-cylinder two-stroke engine cast en bloc. Renowned automotive journalist Hugh Dolnar was so impressed with the 1906 Okey Runabout that he encouraged investors to look into it. Some did, and the Okey Motor Car Company was formed in 1907 to produce the Okey Runabout, which was to be priced at $1,400. Unfortunately the financing was inadequate and receivership quickly followed.

Oscar Lear Automobile Company (Columbus, 1904 to 1907, and Springfield, 1907 to 1909)

Lee A. Frayer, William J. Miller and Oscar Lear collaborated on the design of an air-cooled engine which powered the company's Frayer-Miller automobile. Unique among air-cooled engines was the use of a rotary blower which sent air through an aluminum jacket

A 1905 Okey on police patrol. The company name was changed in 1907 to the Okey Motor Car Company, but that was to be the Okey's last year.

The Oscar Lear Company's 1906 Frayer-Miller six-cylinder touring, priced at $4,000, catered to the more well-to-do motorists. A four-cylinder version was available at a more affordable $3,000. In either case a Cape Top was an extra $150.

that surrounded the cylinders. Another Frayer-Miller achievement was the introduction of America's first six-cylinder engine. The Frayer-Miller was a handsome automobile and well received by the public.

Columbus resident Eddie Rickenbacker, World War I flying ace, worked for the Oscar Lear company as a young man sweeping floors. He later moved on to become an engineer and trouble-shooter with the Columbus Buggy Company before joining the U.S. Army Air Service, where he became commander of the legendary Hat-in-the-Ring squadron. (See Columbus Buggy Company.)

Frayer-Miller operations were moved to Springfield in 1907. The automobile retained its air-cooled six engine and rotary blower. Automobile production ended in 1909 and the company, now named the Buckeye National Motor Car Company, focused exclusively on production of commercial vehicles.

Owens, H. E. (Springfield, 1900)

Mr. Owens built a steam carriage in the shops of his employer, the Thomas Manufacturing Company. A trade journal reported favorably on the vehicle's characteristics but Owens decided against putting his steamer into production.

Packard & Weiss (Warren, 1899 to 1900); Ohio Automobile Company (Warren, 1900 to 1902); Packard Motor Car Company (Warren, 1902 to 1903)

The prestigious Packard automobile resulted from a partnership formed in Warren as the result of a challenge. When James Ward Packard was dissatisfied with the Winton automobile he had purchased in 1898, Alexander Winton dared Packard to do better. And many people agreed that he did, indeed, do better.

James Ward Packard, commonly known as Ward, was the perfect man to respond to such a challenge. In many ways typical of American automobile pioneers, Ward was an engineer and tinkerer by nature, who excelled at transforming raw ideas into finished products of quality and reliability.

By the time he had graduated from Lehigh

This 1901 Packard is one of 81 built in its second year of production. Horsepower was increased to 12 and, with an optional third gear, the Packard was capable of 30 miles per hour. Three body styles were offered at $1,500 each. Four 1901 Packards received First Class Certificates in the 1901 New York City to Buffalo race.

University in 1884 with a mechanical engineering degree, Ward had become enthralled by the possibilities of electricity in daily life, and in 1890 he and his brother William formed the Packard Electric Company, to supply light bulbs for this emerging market (Stacy Perman, *A Grand Complication: The Race to Build the World's Most Legendary Watch*, New York: Atria, 2013).

Packard Electric was an unqualified success, with Ward guiding production development, and William tending to the management aspects of the business. However, it was not long before the sedate nature of an established company could no longer hold Ward's attention.

What did attract Ward's attention at this time was the horseless carriage. While on business trips for Packard Electric, William Packard collected information about these popular new vehicles for his brother. At the 1893 World's Columbian Exposition in Chicago, William studied the examples on view there, as did Henry Ford and other aspiring automotive entrepreneurs. During a European trip, William purchased and brought back a three-wheeled 1896 De Dion-Bouton with a single-cylinder engine. It was this vehicle, which Ward modified and reassembled as a four-wheel version, that gave him his first hands-on acquaintance with an automobile.

Shortly thereafter, Ward bought Winton #13.

After purchasing his Winton, Ward carried on correspondence with George Weiss, a Winton investor and the man who had accompanied William Packard when he first test-drove a Winton. The three men shared an enthusiasm

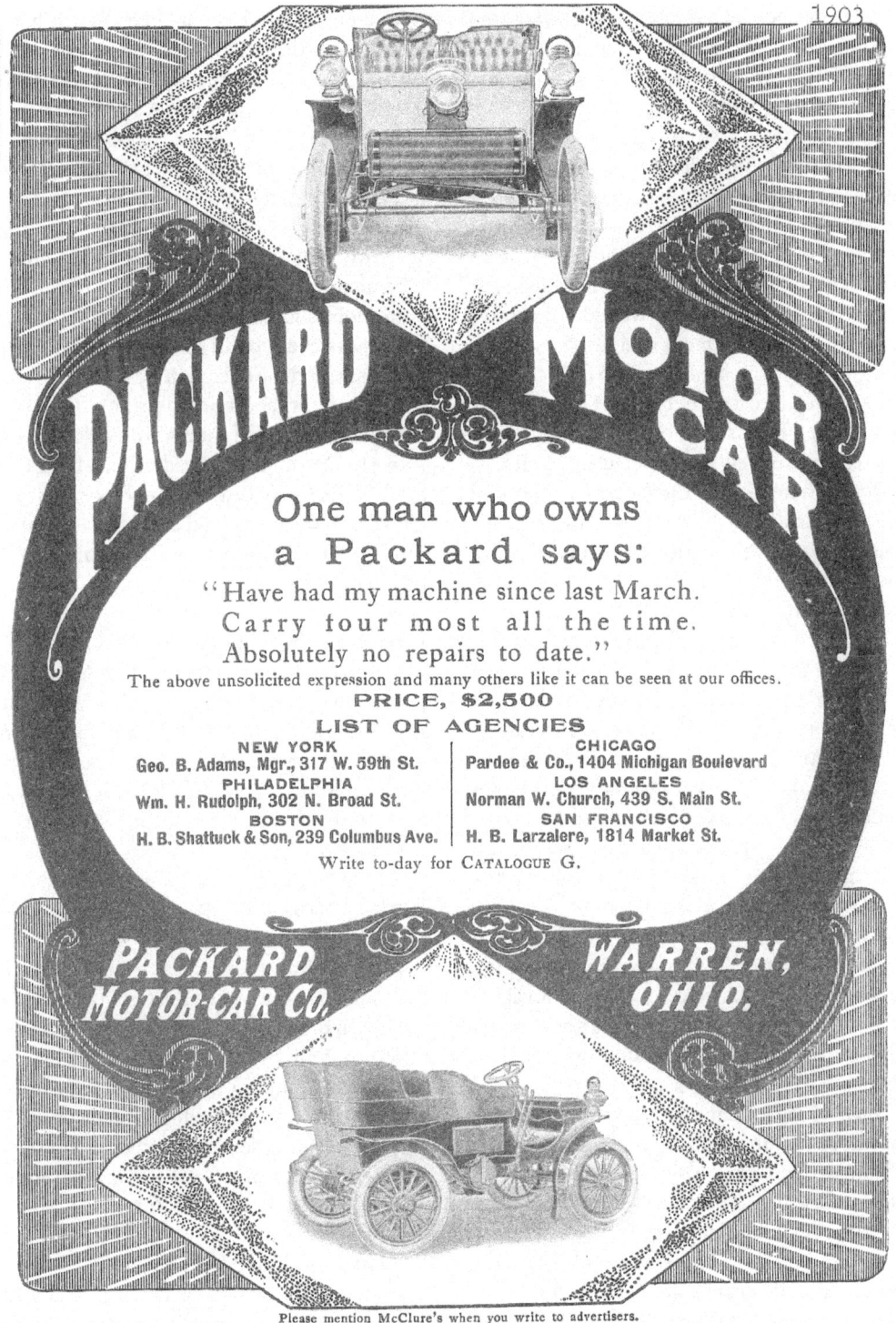

A 1903 Packard was driven from San Francisco to New York City in 61 days. This achievement beat the Winton's record, which had been set just one month before, by two days. The year 1903 was to be the last for Packard production in Ohio.

for the prospects of the horseless carriage, so when the brothers asked Weiss to join them in a new venture, with the intention of producing the finest quality vehicle possible, Weiss quickly accepted. Also joining forces with the three men was Bert Hatcher, a Winton employee who had helped Ward keep his Winton operable. Hatcher proved to be a skilled draftsman and he assumed responsibility as Ward's aide for the mechanical side of the business, while William and George Weiss looked after the venture's management and finances.

The newly formed partnership of Packard & Weiss moved into a corner of the Packard Electric facilities. In less than one year, things were progressing so well that a separate shop was constructed nearby for the specific purpose of building Packard & Weiss' first prototype automobile named the Ohio. The prototype had a nine horsepower engine and a buggy-style body which rode on a seventy-one inch wheelbase, and sported fine leather upholstery. It also carried a whip stock, in case the vehicle needed to be towed by a horse which required encouragement, but this turned out to be unnecessary.

The partners were so pleased with the prototype that they elected to immediately begin producing automobiles for sale, and by September 1900 they had sold eleven vehicles, and reorganized their venture as the Ohio Automobile Company.

During the initial production run, a Packard tradition was born: all improvements were incorporated into each vehicle, as the innovation became available, rather than waiting to implement them with the introduction of a new model.

The 1900 Packard made its appearance at the Automobile Club of America's show at Madison Square Garden in New York that year. The vehicle cost $1,750 and was equipped with a one-cylinder 12-horsepower engine, a three speed transmission, and water and fuel sight gauges. Three Packards were sold at the show, including two to William Rockefeller, previously a Winton owner, and brother of Cleveland oil magnate John D. Rockefeller.

Packard innovations during these early years included the H-pattern gear shift and the use of a steering wheel instead of a tiller. What became one of the automotive industry's most enduring slogans, "Ask the Man Who Owns One," originated with the Ohio Automobile Company in 1901, and followed Packard throughout most of its long and storied existence.

Packard's early success and impressive operating performance attracted the attention of wealthy Detroit businessman Henry B. Joy, who acquired controlling interest in the Ohio Automobile Company in 1902. The company name was changed to the Packard Motor Car Company, and the operation was moved to a new purpose-built factory in Detroit in late 1903.

Joy had expected that Ward Packard would move to Detroit after the last Ohio-built Packard left the factory in Warren, but Packard declined to relocate. He did continue as president until 1909, and remained chairman of the board until 1915.

Paine, H. S. (Westerville, 1914)

Joining the cyclecar craze, Mr. Paine built a prototype vehicle which rode on a 100-inch wheelbase and was powered by a four-cylinder engine. Efforts to secure financing for its manufacture were unsuccessful and the project was abandoned. (See Scharf Gearless Motor Car Company.)

Park Motors Company (Columbus, 1912 to 1913)

After gaining experience repairing and maintaining a variety of electric vehicles, Scott Van Etten organized the Park company to manufacture Van Etten electric- and gasoline-powered automobiles. The gasoline prototype was powered by a six-cylinder engine and capable of carrying seven passengers. No electric vehicle was built, and the prototype automobile was the only result of his efforts.

Philion, Achille (Akron, 1892)

Achille Philion was a French circus performer who built a coal-fired steam vehicle to promote his act. He began work on the steamer in 1887. It first appeared on Akron streets in 1892 and then at the Chicago World's Fair in 1893. When Philion died, his steam vehicle was acquired by a movie studio and used in films including *The Magnificent Ambersons* with Orson Welles and *Excuse My Dust* with Red Skelton. It was then acquired by Harrah's Automobile Collection.

Pilliod Motor Company (Toledo, 1915 to 1916)

Introduced as the first sleeve-valve V-8 powered automobile in America, the Pilliod made its appearance at the Toledo Automobile Show in 1915. The engine was designed by Charles J. Pilliod and made extensive use of aluminum in its construction. When Pilliod's touring car went into production it was powered by a four-cylinder sleeve-valve engine that provided 27 horsepower. The relatively conventional-appearing Pilliod was priced at $1,485. Another short-lived venture, the company was in bankruptcy before its second year was out.

Pioneer Motor Car Company (Marietta, 1911)

With a capital stock of $18,000, the Pioneer company was formed to manufacture automobiles, but it is doubtful that any were produced.

Piqua Motor Company (Piqua, 1911)

Organized with a capitalization of $50,000 to manufacture automobiles, this company appears to be another of the many that never realized their objective.

Plymouth Motor Truck Company (Plymouth, 1910)

The first of four Plymouth automobiles was presented in 1910. It was a large touring car with a 40 horsepower Wisconsin engine, a 112-inch wheelbase, and chain drive. Although a Plymouth automobile was successfully driven from Plymouth to New York City in 1911, production did not follow. Its most unusual feature was a large dome on the top of the hood beneath which was a gasoline tank. A wide-

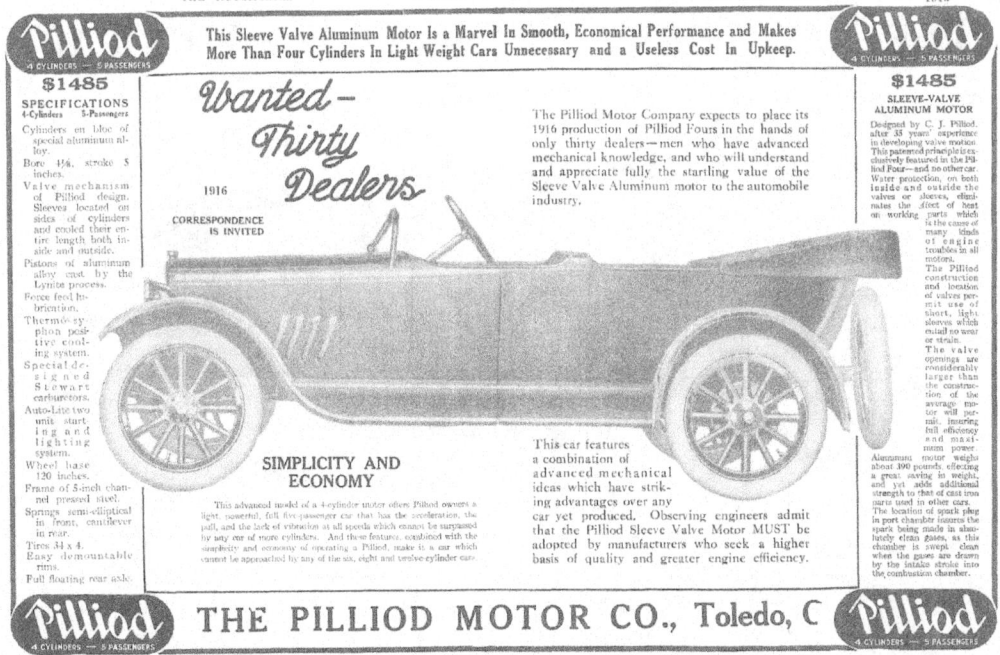

The Pilliod was powered by an aluminum 4-cylinder sleeve-valve engine which weighed only 390 pounds and was designed by C.J. Pilliod. The only model offered was a five-passenger touring priced at $1,485. This 1916 ad is from the Pilliod's second and last year of production.

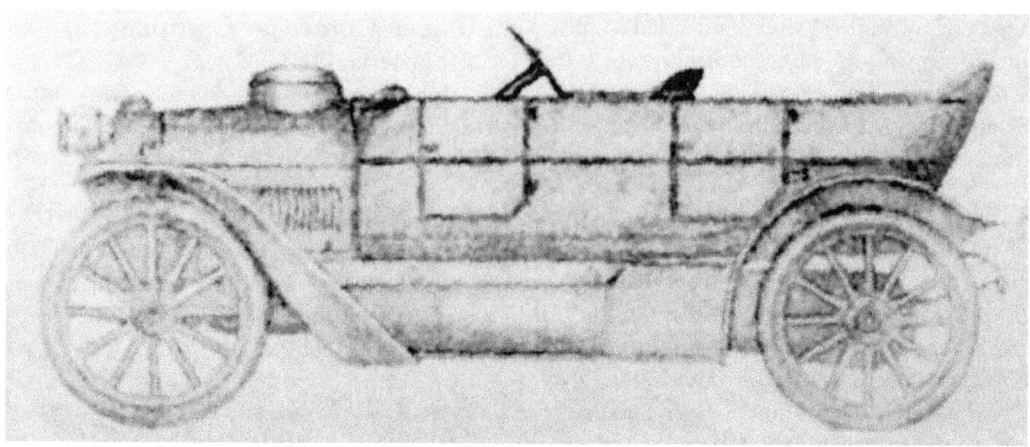

The most unusual feature of the 1909 Plymouth was the large dome on its hood which allowed gasoline to be poured from an ordinary bucket into the gasoline tank. Its headlight, which was centrally mounted in front of the radiator tank, was another identifying characteristic.

mouth filler neck allowed for pouring gasoline directly into the tank from a bucket, something which the Plymouth Company apparently considered helpful during the early days of motoring. Subsequently three other prototype vehicles were turned out, but none went into production. In 1912 the company turned its attention to the manufacture of industrial locomotives which it continued to build until 2002 when it closed its doors forever.

Pope Motor Car Company (Toledo, 1903 to 1909)

In an auspicious introduction, a prototype

A tilting front passenger seat gave access to the rear seats of this 1905 Pope-Toledo. A 30 horsepower engine was motive power for the 2,350 pound vehicle, which was priced at $3,200. A Victoria or Canopy top cost an extra $250.

Pope-Toledo automobile was entered in a 1903 West Coast race competition against such famous names as Mercedes and Mors. The Pope-Toledo was victorious and even achieved a speed of 60 miles per hour in the process. As a result the company adopted the slogan "The Mile-a-Minute Car." It was also victorious in an 800 mile New York-Cleveland-Pittsburgh endurance run which took place under the worst imaginable rain-soaked weather conditions (see "A Story of the Memorable Endurance Test of 1903," Pope Motor Car Co., 1903).

A luxurious Pope-Toledo four-cylinder touring car was priced at $3,500, and a two-cylinder vehicle was offered for $2,000. Prices remained high in subsequent years but a purchaser got a refined, extremely handsome, well-built and well-equipped automobile. Features included copper water jackets, suction intake valves, double chain drive, sliding gear transmission, and a body and chassis of all-steel alloy. Excellent as the Pope-Toledo was, the company fell into financial difficulties in 1909. Receivership followed, and it was bought out by the Overland Auto Company. (See Willys-Overland Company.)

Portsmouth Automobile & Machine Company (Portsmouth, 1911)

Formed to manufacture automobiles with a capitalization of $10,000, Portsmouth most likely never succeeded in manufacturing an automobile.

Post, Charles Bushnell (New London, 1909)

Mr. Post built a highwheel vehicle for his own use, using an air-cooled gasoline engine for power. It could accommodate four people and rode on rubber tires. Nothing more is known.

Poste Brothers Buggy Company (Columbus, 1899)

The Poste company was formed with a stated capitalization of $25,000 and the purpose of building automobiles. It was listed in trade publications as being in that business in 1900, but there is no evidence of a vehicle having been produced.

Powercar Automobile Company (Cincinnati, 1909 to 1911)

The Powercar company offered a five-passenger touring automobile with a 30 horsepower engine and three-speed transmission. Production of an unknown number of automobiles continued through most of 1911, but by the end of that year the company had discontinued business.

Prince Motor Car Company (Warrensville, 1911)

Intending to manufacture and sell automobiles, the Prince company was formed with a substantial capitalization of $200,000, but no automobile was manufactured.

Ragan, Brown & Lange Company (Napoleon, 1910)

Intending to manufacture motors and all kinds of vehicles including motor cars, the company was capitalized at $40,000. It appears no automobiles were manufactured.

Rees Motor Company (Attica, 1921)

The Rees company, formed by John Howard Rees, was capitalized at $300,000. The old Halladay Motors Corporation plant in Attica, where no Halladay automobiles were actually built (see Halladay Car Company), was purchased by the Rees company and at least six Rees automobiles were produced there. These automobiles were standard touring vehicles powered by a four-cylinder engine designed by Mr. Rees. Wheelbase was 112 inches. Nothing further seems to have transpired.

Reive-Thompson Motor Company (Columbus, 1900)

Although not listed in the Columbus city directories of the era, the Reive company does appear as a manufacturer of automobiles in a trade journal compendium of motor vehicle manufacturers. Actual production is doubtful.

Relay Motors Corporation (Lima, 1927 to 1928)

A single prototype Worldmobile was, as a trade journal put it, "cobbled together." The vehicle was of the most ordinary style four-door sedan with disc wheels and a 133-inch wheelbase. Power was furnished by a Lycoming eight-cylinder engine. The intended price was to be $1,700. The Relay company was an amalgamation of three truck-building firms including Garford of Lima. No automobile production occurred, although the Worldmobile prototype survives.

Republic Motor Car Company (Hamilton, 1910 to 1916)

The Republic company was formed by a group of successful Hamilton businessmen, none of whom had any familiarity with the automobile industry. Upon the company's formation, two large factories were purchased and production began in earnest on the first batch of Republic automobiles. The Republic was well-built and good looking touring automobile with a four-cylinder T-head engine and offset crankshaft. Republic changed over to a six-cylinder engine in 1914 and production continued into 1916 but then ended due to material shortages caused by World War I. Production was not resumed after the war. Total production is unknown.

Research Engineering Company (Dayton, 1921 to 1922)

The Spencer, a five-passenger touring automobile with an overhead valve engine and a 103-inch wheelbase, weighed 1,500 pounds and was priced at $1,200. For the second year's offerings the price was reduced to $850 in the hopes of enlivening sales, but to no avail. Only a few Spencers were ever built and the company was heard of no more.

Reya Motor Company (Napoleon, 1917)

Organized as an adjunct to the Napoleon Motor Car Company, Reya's purpose was to

Powered by a 40 horsepower T-head 4-cylinder engine, the 1912 Republic rode on a 120-inch wheelbase. The Republic succumbed to material shortages in 1917 due to the country's involvement in World War I.

build trucks. Nevertheless the company did build a few Reya automobiles in 1917, and one example has survived. (See Napoleon Motor Car Company.)

Richland Buggy Company (Mansfield, 1899)

Trade publications of the era announced that the Richland company was building a motor vehicle. Whether a prototype was built or an automobile actually went into production is speculation.

Riddle Manufacturing Company (Ravenna, 1919 to 1920)

With a lineage that went back to 1831, this long-established and well-known maker of funeral vehicles, two of which carried presidents McKinley and Harding to their final resting places, offered a limited number of passenger vehicles on special order between 1919 and 1920. Seven-passenger sedans and limousines able to accommodate up to nine people were built. A unique feature among the Riddle's other attributes was the absence of a center post on the right side of the automobile which facilitated access for wheel chair passengers. Priced between $4,850 and $5,500, these large automobiles were powered by six-cylinder engines. However, manufacture of automobiles was a sideline, and the company's primary products continued to be hearses and ambulances.

Ritchie, William (Hamilton, 1899)

In 1899 William Ritchie stated that he had completed construction of a gasoline-powered vehicle. None were to follow this initial example, although his Advance Manufacturing Company subsequently became a builder of gasoline engines.

Roberts, O. G. (Columbus, 1904)

Mr. Roberts was reported in a local newspaper as having built an automobile, but this cannot be conclusively verified.

Roberts Motor Manufacturing Company (Sandusky, 1915)

The Roberts company's main business was building engines for marine and aircraft use. In 1915 the company introduced a vehicle, powered by a Roberts six-cylinder 60 horsepower engine. The automobile endeavor did not last beyond its first year.

Rodgers & Company (Columbus, 1903 to 1905)

The Imperial, aka Columbus, automobile was designed by company superintendent T. W. Picard. It was a small runabout on a 78-inch wheelbase powered by an air-cooled two-cylinder opposed engine. Other body styles followed but its limited production ended by 1905.

Rossel Motor Car Company (Toledo, 1910)

Although formed to manufacture and deal in automobiles and backed by a capitalization of $120,000, this company was another one which seems to have come to nothing.

Ruse, Cordy (Dayton, 1896)

Cordy Ruse built a motor vehicle for himself with helpful suggestions made by Orville and Wilbur Wright. Orville was enamored with Ruse's efforts, while Wilbur suggested tying a bedsheet under the vehicle to catch parts that fell off. Whether Ruse returned the favor of a similar compliment when the brothers Wright undertook construction of their historic aeroplane is not recorded.

Russell, Dr. C. W. (Springfield, circa 1900 and 1903)

The first experimental vehicle of Dr. Russell's design was an electric which appeared at the turn of the century. A second, this one gasoline-powered and capable of thirty miles per hour, was offered for sale in 1903. It was a two-passenger runabout with a nine horsepower one-cylinder engine, chain drive, and three-speed transmission. The body was painted a deep maroon and had hand-buffed red leather upholstered seats. The price of the doctor's Russell-Springfield automobile was $1,250. How many were built is unknown.

Russell & Company (Massillon, 1900)

A trade journal reported that Russell & Company was to build an automobile. It is doubtful a vehicle resulted.

S. Toomey Company (Canal Dover, 1912)

Formed for the manufacture and sale of automobiles, the company had a capitalization of $60,000. It appears that Toomey never achieved its goal.

Sandusky Auto Parts & Motor Truck Company (Sandusky, 1911 to 1914)

Although focused on manufacturing trucks, the company did produce a small number of prototype passenger vehicles. Actual production never occurred.

Sandusky Automobile Manufacturing Company (Sandusky, 1900 to 1902); Sandusky Automobile Company (Sandusky, 1902 to 1904)

The Sandusky Automobile Manufacturing Company announced its intention of manufacturing automobiles in 1900, but none were built immediately as a result of disagreement among the company's owners. Problems continued to plague the venture and new interests soon joined the company. Prototype electric- and gasoline-powered vehicles were finally built in 1902. But dissension once again brought activity to a halt, and control of the company was assumed by a new group of investors toward the end of that year, at which time the company was reorganized as the Sandusky Automobile Company, and new factory and worker housing was planned. In 1903, actual assembly of 10 Sandusky automobiles was at last under way in temporary quarters.

The Sandusky was a light runabout priced at $700 and powered by a one-cylinder 5 horsepower engine employing chain drive. Alongside the Sandusky, a somewhat larger automobile named the Courier was introduced in 1904.

The Courier of Sandusky, Ohio, boasted that it was the only runabout for 1904 equipped with a sliding gear transmission. Priced at $700, this 1,000 pound vehicle was said to be a model of simplicity, so much so that any member of the family could run it.

Advertised as a 1901 model, this Sandusky light runabout weighed in at 600 pounds and cost about $700. Power was provided by a one-cylinder 5 horsepower engine.

However, bankruptcy soon ensued, and when business came to a halt, only Courier automobiles had been manufactured during the final year. Total production may have reached 225 automobiles.

Sayers & Scoville Company
(Cincinnati, 1917 to 1929)

A manufacturer of horse-drawn hearses, the Sayers company ventured into the self-propelled vehicle arena in 1906 with a prototype automobile that morphed into a motorized hearse and ambulance, both of which were produced. In 1917 the company added a line of passenger vehicles. Although basically an assembled automobile insofar as the mechanics were concerned, its body was built by highly regarded company craftsmen and was of the highest quality. Sayers automobiles changed hardly at all during their eight year run, although prices crept up from $1,295 to over $2,000. The long 118-inch wheelbase and six-cylinder engine were well suited to the luxurious Sayers automobile. Although annual production ranged between 100 and 200, the Sayers automobile was dropped in 1924 and replaced by the S&S automobile.

The S&S was an adaptation of the company's professional vehicle line to a passenger automobile. The marketing department might have been more imaginative in the selection of a name for this car, as the S&S designation was also used on their funeral vehicles. The S&S passenger automobile grew from a 118-inch wheelbase in 1924 to a 140-inch wheelbase in 1927. The new model name for 1927, Gotham, reflected this growth. Growth did not stop there. The 1928 wheelbase went to 141 inches and an 85 horsepower eight-cylinder engine was added. This was apparently still not enough, as in 1929 the Gotham had 143-inch wheelbase at which time it was rechristened the Lakewood. Sales never were adequate, perhaps because the passenger vehicles were so similar to the funeral limousines which were being sold to the professional trade. It must be said on the behalf of the 1929 S&S Lakewood that it was an imposing and relatively attractive vehicle. However, Sayers ended passenger automobile offerings that year and concentrated on professional trade vehicles.

Schacht Manufacturing Company (Cincinnati, 1904 to 1909); Schacht Motor Car Company (Cincinnati, 1909 to 1913)

Originally a maker of carriages and buggies, the Schacht company turned to automobiles in 1904. Perhaps the only automobile company to begin by making standard-style automobiles before changing to highwheelers, its move was surprisingly successful. Built between 1907 and 1909, the highwheelers were said to have made the company famous. The highwheeler was simplicity itself and converted readily to various uses. The company reorganized in 1909 and returned to making conventionally styled automobiles. In all, over 9,000 Schachts were produced at which point the company abandoned automobiles for trucks.

Scharf Gearless Motor Car Company (Westerville, 1914)

In the heat of the cyclecar craze, H. S. Paine designed a cyclecar which was exhibited at the 1914 Columbus Ohio automobile show. The vehicle had a 100-inch wheelbase and a four-cylinder engine. The prototype vehicle was probably built for Paine by the Scharf company. Paine's efforts to secure financial backing went unrewarded and only the prototype was produced. (See Paine, H.S.)

Known as "the Thoroughbred Car," only twenty-five examples were produced between 1910 and 1912. This 1910 Sebring was powered by a 6-cylinder engine and cost $2,750.

Schworm, Melville F. (Massillon, 1888)

Mr. Schworm built a steam-powered vehicle for his own use. During a test drive his new creation was damaged when one of its wooden wheels cracked, whereupon Mr. Schworm abandoned his automotive venture.

Scott, R. P. (Cadiz, 1897)

Mr. Scott built a 275-pound steam vehicle that he claimed was capable of thirty miles per hour on smooth roads. The outcome of a planned trip to Baltimore, Maryland, is not known.

Seagrave Company (Columbus, 1914)

Designed as a fire chief's automobile, the Seagrave featured accommodation for passengers along with certain fire-fighting gear. The automobile could be fitted with either a four- or six-cylinder engine. However, within one year the Seagrave company discontinued the venture and returned to its fire engine business exclusively.

Sebring Motor Car Company (Sebring, 1909 to 1912)

A prototype of the Sebring was completed and successfully road-tested in 1909. It was a touring-style automobile and had a decidedly sporty character. Sportier yet was the runabout model which could be ordered with a monocle windscreen. Both Sebrings were powered by a six-cylinder engine. Production in total was approximately twenty-five vehicles.

Seneca Motor Company (Fostoria, 1917 to 1924)

The Seneca company was the successor to the Fostoria Light Car Company. The Fostoria was renamed the Seneca and continued as a four-cylinder assembled automobile for its entire life. The 1919 Seneca was conventional in appearance, rode on a 108-inch wheelbase, and was priced

The Seneca was an assembled automobile and had a four-cylinder engine during all the years of its production. This 1920 five-passenger model was said to get 25 miles per gallon, and had a price of $1,185.

at $990 f.o.b. Fostoria (*Automobile Trade Journal*, February 1919). Production each year hovered around several hundred vehicles. Although some of its production was sent overseas, the market for Senecas was mostly local. Production finally ceased in 1924, but the company remained in business making replacement parts for the Seneca automobile. (See Fostoria Light Car Company.)

Shelby Stove & Manufacturing Company (Shelby, 1901)

In the late 19th century, long before he became famous as the manufacturer of Jeffery and Rambler automobiles, Thomas B. Jeffery was in the bicycle manufacturing business. With partner Philip Gormully, Jeffery operated bicycle plants in Chicago, Illinois, and Shelby. Jeffery began experimenting with automobiles at his Chicago plant, and his first example appeared there in 1897.

As the Shelby location seemed more favorable for automobile manufacture, Jeffery helped to organize the Shelby Stove and Manufacturing Company in 1901. With the stated purpose of manufacturing stoves, engines, and automobiles, and to deal in the same, the company was capitalized at $70,000. Soon after this new company was formed, however, Jeffery sold his bicycle business to American Bicycle Company and used the proceeds to purchase a huge manufacturing plant in Kenosha, Wisconsin, where he intended to build his Jeffery automobile. The Shelby Stove Company never produced an automobile.

Shrum, J. (Columbus, 1909)

Mr. Shrum built his Skiddoodler automobile for his own use. Details about its appearance are vague. He also built a motorized sleigh with a third runner for steering and a powered circular saw for propulsion.

Shunk Plow Company (Bucyrus, 1908)

The Shunk company built a highwheeler powered by a two-stroke engine. The prototype was probably the only example produced.

Sly, Ethan E. (Norwalk, 1902)

Mr. Sly was working for the Wheeling & Lake Erie Railroad when he built a steam vehicle for his own use, based on a boiler he had designed and built himself. This steamer consumed seven gallons of water while traveling eighteen miles but took only five minutes to build up a head of steam. Mr. Sly continued to use his steamer around town for several years.

Smelser, Luther W. (Akron, 1904)

Mr. Smelser built a 30 horsepower touring automobile to special order for C. C. Goodrich of the B.F. Goodrich tire company. Other special orders may have followed, but this is not known with certainty.

Smith Bicycle, Automobile & Light Machinery Company (Massillon, 1902)

This company has been listed in period trade journals as a manufacturer of automobiles. Corroborative evidence is lacking.

Smith-Eggers Company (Cincinnati, 1900)

This carriage company is listed as a manufacturer of automobiles in period trade journals. Further evidence of this fact is not available.

Sommer Motor Company (Bucyrus, 1910 to 1911)

Capitalized at $125,000, the Sommer company built an unknown number of automobiles for only a few months before returning to its main business of building engines.

Spahr, Otto (Millersburg, 1895)

The Spahr runabout was a highwheeler with a water-cooled engine of Mr. Spahr's own design. It had a differential, which was unusual for this early era automobile. Only one example was produced.

Specialty Carriage Company (Cincinnati, 1898)

Specialty built fifty broughams and fifty hansoms for the Electric Vehicle Company of New York City. No vehicles were offered on the open market by the Specialty company, and apparently the only vehicles produced were for this order.

Speedwell Motor Car Company (Dayton, 1907 to 1914)

Purchasers of the first Speedwell automobiles had a choice of either a 116-inch or a 132-inch wheelbase, and either a four- or a six-

Four thousand Speedwell automobiles were built during the company's nine years, and 1914 was to be its penultimate year. The 1914 Speedwell was powered by a unique 6-cylinder 41 horsepower engine with rotary valves, and rode on a very long 135-inch wheelbase.

cylinder engine. Switching in 1908 to a 120-inch wheelbase for all of its automobiles, the company sold twenty-five vehicles that year and 100 more in 1909. By 1909, plant capacity exceeded needs and one of the firm's buildings was leased to the Wright brothers, who used it to build an aeroplane.

The Speedwell was a carefully-designed automobile, well built, and especially handsome. This was particularly true of the 1909 and 1910 models whose base price was $2,500. Attention to detail was a credo. The horn was placed out of sight under the hood and the transmission was leak-free, unlike almost all others of the era. During the later years of its production the Speedwell offered engines with either poppet valves or rotary valves, an industry first.

Management problems began to plague the company and then a massive flood swamped the factory in 1913. The resulting inability to fill orders disrupted what had been an excellent dealer network. This combination of circumstances forced the company into bankruptcy in 1915. During its eight years of existence a grand total of over 4,000 Speedwells were built. Finally, a liquidator by the name of A. O. Dunk, who had a practice of buying up automobile companies immediately upon their failing, made the Speedwell company his sixty-first acquisition.

Spencer Manufacturing Company (Spencer, 1914)

Formed to produce automobiles of all kinds, and with a capitalization of $50,000, the Spencer company seems not to have progressed beyond the paper stage and it is doubtful that an automobile resulted.

Springfield Automobile & Industrial Company (Springfield, 1899 to 1904); Springfield Automobile Company (Springfield, 1904 to 1905)

In 1899 the Springfield Automobile & Industrial Company announced its intentions to build a small gasoline-powered automobile, but nothing came of this. In 1903 the company was approached by W. C. and C. C. Bramwell, father and son, to build their Bramwell-Robinson automobile, which at the time was being manufactured in Massachusetts. The company agreed, and took the Bramwells on as managers to assist in the operation. By mutual agreement the vehicle was renamed the Springfield. Production reached three automobiles per week by mid-year. Before the end of the year the Bramwells purchased what was now named the Springfield Automobile Company and changed the automobile model name to the Bramwell. The Bramwell sold for $800, and featured a 72-inch wheelbase and a laminated steel-reinforced wood frame. The vehicle was not a success. Subsequently, C. C. Bramwell moved on to become the designer of the Firestone-Columbus highwheel automobile for the Columbus Buggy Company in 1909. (See Columbus Buggy Company.)

Springfield Machine & Tool Company (Springfield, 1904)

The Springfield company announced construction of a motor vehicle designed by the head of the company. A trade journal reported that if the result was successful, the company would enter production of an automobile. Production of an automobile did not occur.

Standard Automobile Company (Columbus, 1902)

Capitalized at only $5,000, the company may have actually built a prototype automobile in the form of a two-passenger runabout with a body by the Columbus Body and Seat Company. Company plans for a factory probably never materialized.

Standard Motive Power Company (Canal Dover, 1902)

Organized with an astounding capital stock of $10 million for the manufacture of locomotives and automobiles, this enterprise's ultimate fate is unknown.

Star Motor Car Company (Cincinnati, 1916)

A vehicle of unknown description was the result of this company's efforts, but nothing beyond a prototype was produced before the venture succumbed.

Sterling-Knight Company (Warren, 1923 to 1926)

Leaving its original location in Cleveland, the reorganized Sterling-Knight Company moved to its newly acquired plant in Warren. Production commenced immediately on its automobile and the first Sterling-Knight rolled out of the plant in mid–1923. Powered by a six-cylinder Knight sleeve-valve engine and offering five body styles, the automobile's prices

The 1924 Sterling-Knight with its sleeve-valve engine was smoother and quieter than automobiles powered by conventional poppet-valve engines. Unlike most other engines, a sleeve-valve engine was known to improve in performance as time went by (author's collection).

ranged from $1,985 to $2,800. Unique features for the era included "automatic windshield cleaners" and a Perfection heater. During 1923 and 1924, something short of 500 automobiles were built. A new sporty body style was added to the line-up for 1925, but was quite pricey at $3,200. Financial problems not entirely of the company's making intervened in 1925, but it soldiered on until things came to an end in late 1926. (See Sterling Motor Company in Part I.)

Stewart Motor Car Company (Bowling Green, 1921 to 1922)

Organized with a capital stock of $500,000 this company should have had no financial or working capital problems. A founding member, Irene Barringer, was one of only a few women to have participated in the formation of an Ohio automobile company outside Cleveland in the early years of the automobile industry. A single prototype Stewart gasoline-powered touring automobile was the grand total production for this undertaking, which might make it the most expensive automobile ever produced in Ohio. The company was subsequently contracted to build a single steam vehicle for George A. Coats. (See Coats Steam Car Company.) Only a prototype Stewart-Coats was built. The company apparently disappeared without the formal necessity of a receivership or bankruptcy.

Stoddard Manufacturing Company (Dayton, 1904); Dayton Motor Car Company (Dayton, 1904 to 1913)

The Stoddard Manufacturing Company, which had been a maker of agricultural implements, turned its attention exclusively to the

The 1911 Stoddard-Dayton was a formidable automobile with a price to match at $3,125. Its four-cylinder engine had a high-tension magneto ignition system, and Hartford shock absorbers eased the ride.

manufacture of an automobile in 1904. Brothers John W. and Charles G. Stoddard, with the help of Englishman H. J. Edwards, built a prototype vehicle that was successfully road-tested that year. The Stoddard-Dayton was a large, luxurious, handsome, and exceedingly well-built automobile. It came with a four-cylinder engine and a shift lever mounted on the steering column. The company name was changed to Dayton Motor Car Company in 1904 and production began in earnest. The Stoddard-Dayton realized instant popularity and production grew rapidly. The company manufactured the four-cylinder engines which appeared in its 1907 models and sales soared to 2,000 that year. An overhead valve engine of the company's own design was offered in 1908. In 1909 the Dayton company formed the Courier Car Company (see Courier Car Company) for the purpose of manufacturing a lower-priced automobile at a separate facility in Dayton, and a Knight sleeve-valve engine was added in 1912. However, a fateful decision in 1911 to join Benjamin Briscoe's United States Motor Company ended the Dayton company's good fortune, when the conglomerate failed in 1913.

Stover Motor Car Company (Cincinnati, 1910)

Organized to manufacture and sell automobiles and other vehicles, the Stover company was capitalized at $25,000. Manufacture is unlikely.

Stringer Automobile Company (Marion, 1899 to 1902)

John W. Stringer completed construction of both electric- and gasoline-powered experimental vehicles in 1899 and obtained financial backing from local investors in 1900. A factory was purchased and the first conveyance to emerge was a steam vehicle with an enclosed chain drive and a four-cylinder engine, which would have been extremely powerful because each stroke was a power stroke. The 1902 steamer was a perky and attractive two-place four-wheeled vehicle, but money ran out and production ceased that year.

Stutz, Harry C. (Dayton, 1898 to 1902); Stutz Manufacturing Company (Dayton, 1902)

Young men raised on farms around the turn of the century were creative, resourceful, efficient, and economical. Think Henry Ford. In Ohio think Harry C. Stutz. Stutz, who had been raised on a farm, was smitten by the new automobiles that were suddenly popping up around the country. Inspired, he cobbled together one of his own in 1898 out of a stationary gasoline engine and a chain from a corn binder. Happy with his success, he built another in 1900. Anointing himself as the Stutz Manufacturing Company in 1902, he engaged in building similar examples of his invention, powered by an engine of his own design, for local inhabitants. The next year Stutz sold the rights for his engine to the Lindsay Automobile Parts Company of Indianapolis and moved there in 1903 to oversee its manufacture. Although he did not remain with the Lindsay, Stutz did stay in Indianapolis. In 1911 he catapulted to the top of the automobile world with "The Car that Made Good in a Day" when an automobile Stutz built won the Indianapolis 500 race in May that year.

Summit Automobile Company (Akron, 1913)

Organized to manufacture and deal in automobiles, the Summit company was capitalized at $10,000. Production of an automobile is doubtful.

Sumner, Harry (Cincinnati, 1901 to 1902)

Harry Sumner built several automobile on special order. One of the first was a six-passenger gasoline-powered touring automobile that apparently performed to the purchaser's satisfaction, as he ordered a second automobile, which was the last built by Sumner.

Sweney, Busby P. (Marion, 1901)

It was reported that Mr. Sweney, having built a prototype automobile for his own use, took it on a test drive. After having driven it into a ditch without damage, he concluded that it was a very sturdy vehicle. Finding nothing amiss

The Manufacturers   Toledo

with his vehicle, he dusted himself off and drove home. Details about its construction are unavailable. Most likely, only this single prototype was assembled.

Swope Garage and Machine Company (Washington Courthouse, 1911)

The Swope company was organized with a capitalization of $10,000 to manufacture automobiles but it is doubtful that an automobile resulted.

Sypher Manufacturing Company (Toledo, 1917 to 1922)

"Oh Boy! Build This Car!" exclaimed an ad in *Popular Mechanics*. At least one prototype of the Junior juvenile vehicle was built in Toledo but it is not known if others followed. This kit car was initially priced at $125 but ultimately rose to $152 by 1922. The car was powered by a three-horsepower engine in 1917 and a four by 1920. It is unknown how many of these kit cars were sold.

Tanner-Hower Manufacturing Company (Akron, 1913)

Capitalized at $50,000, the company intended to manufacture and sell automobiles and parts. Nothing came of the venture.

Tarkington, H. (Marysville, 1906)

A trade journal reported that Mr. Tarkington had built a 20-horsepower vehicle and was searching for financial backing, but he apparently had no success. (See Marysville Motor Car Company.)

Taylor, Will (Niles, 1899)

It was reported that Will Taylor "has invented a motor carriage." No more is known about Will or his invention.

Thomas Manufacturing Company (Springfield, 1900)

H. E. Owens is said to have built an automobile using the facilities of his employer, the Thomas company, in 1900.

Thresher Electric Company (Dayton, 1900)

The Thresher company manufactured electric motors for the trade. Using one of its motors for motive power, Thresher constructed a vehicle with what was referred to as a break-style body. One commentator stated that the vehicle looked like it had been designed specifically as a motorized conveyance, which was a compliment since most attempts at building an automobile at the time had the appearance of being converted horse-drawn carriages. Although Thresher maintained that it would be building a variety of body styles for sale, it is likely that only the prototype was completed.

Tillotson, Harry (Toledo, 1912)

Inspired by the newly introduced Knight sleeve-valve engine, Mr. Tillotson built a prototype automobile using a Knight engine to power his vehicle. Things went no further than that and no other details are known about the automobile. More is known about Mr. Tillotson, however. He subsequently formed the Tillotson Carburetor Company, which became a large supplier to the Willys-Overland Company.

Todd Manufacturing Company (Toledo, 1903)

The Todd company was a manufacturer of gasoline engines. Late in 1903 it announced intentions to build an automobile of its own design and it did, in fact, secure facilities for the purpose. If actual production took place, it was undoubtedly limited.

Toledo Auto and Garage Company (Toledo, 1910)

Acting as agents for Stearns, Franklin, and Jackson automobiles, the company claimed to be planning to build an electric vehicle of its own. Nothing further was heard of this enterprise.

Toledo Auto-Cycle Car Company (Toledo, 1913 to 1914)

Professing to be entering the automobile business with a conventional cyclecar, the company's touted "surprise" for the buying public never occurred. Perhaps a prototype was built, but details are absent.

Toledo Electric Vehicle Company (Toledo, 1908)

After several failed attempts to organize a company to develop and manufacture his proposed Clark Electric vehicle, Albert F. Clark finally organized the Toledo Electric Vehicle Company to produce and market his creation. It was claimed that the Clark Electric would go thirty miles per hour and that the battery invented by Albert F. Clark would carry an electric vehicle farther than any other battery available. Premises and equipment for building the Clark Electric were procured and some vehicles may actually have been assembled, but the venture lasted no more than one year.

Toledo Motor Car Company (Toledo, 1904)

After having been organized with a capitalization of $20,000 to manufacture automobiles, the venture seems to have gone nowhere.

Toledo Steam and Air Motor Company (Toledo, 1900)

Although a trade journal listed the Toledo company as a manufacturer of automobiles, it is doubtful that any were in fact produced.

Troxel Manufacturing Company (Elyria, 1902)

A prototype Troxel gasoline-powered automobile was built and tested, but plans to place it in production were not realized.

Troy Auto & Buggy Company (Troy, 1908 to 1910)

James Stanley of Mooreland, Indiana, announced his intention to build a car for the masses, which he said was to be priced at $350. An automobile was actually built in 1908, and soon Stanley decided to join his company with the Troy Buggy Company and move production to Troy. The new Troy-built automobile would retain the Stanley name. It was to be priced at $575, ride on an 86-inch wheelbase, and be powered by a 20 horsepower engine. Production commenced in 1909, but the endeavor ended in 1910 when the company was purchased by a wire fence manufacturer, which supposedly intended to build automobiles. No more was heard of the venture.

Trumbull Manufacturing Company (Warren, 1899 to 1905)

Two automobiles were born in Warren in 1899, the Pendleton and the Packard. At the same time as James Ward Packard was building his contribution to the country's automobile industry, William C. Pendleton was constructing a vehicle of his own on the other side of town. Pendleton's version was a one-cylinder vehicle that ran, but not with a high degree of reliability. A steam car followed in 1901, and a second gasoline-powered vehicle in 1902. The latter was a handsome, large, and luxurious automobile with a four-cylinder engine, which proved to be much more reliable than its 1899 predecessor.

The 1905 model, variously named the Trumbull or the Pendleton, was an attractive automobile, sporting deeply tufted leather seats which accommodated two people up front and three more in back. The most advanced model yet, it had a feature that prevented gears from being shifted when the clutch was engaged, and a spark cut-out which allowed the engine to provide significant braking power.

William Pendleton had always considered automobile manufacture to be a mere diversion, and before 1905 was out his interests changed and the company moved on to other pursuits. When all was said and done, total production probably did not exceed a dozen automobiles.

Turner, Robert S. (Marysville, 1900)

Mr. Turner built a gasoline-powered automobile for his own use which served him well for at least ten years. The two-cylinder engine was water-cooled and the vehicle rode on wood wheels shod with solid rubber tires. Steering was by wheel rather than tiller. The vehicle was donated by his family to the Union County Historical Society.

Twyman Motor Car Company (Columbus, 1911)

Formed with a capitalization of $20,000, the Twyman company stated its purpose as the manufacture and sale of automobiles and accessories. Production of an automobile is doubtful.

Underwood Motor Company (Sandusky, 1900)

The Underwood firm specialized in building engines for the trade. It also assembled automobiles on special order. An Underwood was the first automobile to run on the streets of Sandusky, but production was undoubtedly limited.

Union Motor Company (Eaton, 1920)

Manufacture of the Washington automobile was taken over by the Delaware-incorporated Union Motor Company in 1920. By the end of the year, the endeavor was known as the Washington Motor Company. (See Washington Motor Company.)

Union Sales Company (Columbus, 1911 to 1912)

The Union Sales Company hired Dunlap Engineering Company to build its prototype Union 24 automobile. The vehicle was to be a sporty two-seat runabout with a four-cylinder engine and sliding-gear transmission. The intention of the Union company was to market a Union 25 at $650. However, the promoter of the venture, J. W. O'Brian, after having secured deposits on the new Union 25, skipped town with the money. At this point, the Dunlap company attached the prototype for unpaid debts, and completed the vehicle on its own.

United States Carriage Company (Columbus, 1910 to 1915)

In late 1909 the company announced its intention to manufacture touring and runabout automobiles. Appropriately named the Great Eagle, these large automobiles rode on a 140-inch wheelbase, but were initially powered by only four-cylinder engines until a six was introduced in 1912.

Operations continued with some success until 1915, when the wife of company president Fred C. Myers called in her $6,000 note in advance of a potential creditor effort to foreclose on claims against the company. The company went into receivership that year and so ended the flight of the Great Eagle.

U.S. Motor Car Company (Upper Sandusky, 1907 to 1908)

The U.S. Runabout was an attractive two-place automobile with an air-cooled four-cylinder engine, three-speed transmission, and hickory frame. It rode on a 96-inch wheelbase and was priced at $900. Several examples were manufactured and sold but production lasted less than one year.

Valley Automobile Company (Warren, 1908)

Having invented a four-cylinder air-cooled rotary engine, Newell Allyn organized the Valley company for its production and installation in an automobile. Trade journal commentators were not impressed with the engine or the automobile, but at least eight examples were sold to some who thought otherwise.

Vickers Auto Car Company (Conneaut, 1910 to 1911)

The Vickers had a four-cylinder two-stroke air-cooled engine with sliding-gear transmission and rode on a 96-inch wheelbase. After one year and limited production, the company was in receivership.

Vulcan Manufacturing Company (Painesville, 1913 to 1915)

Alonzo Marsh moved from New England to Painesville in 1912 where he established a factory for the manufacture of automobile parts and accessories. Expanding operations, the company introduced its Vulcan automobile in 1913. The Vulcan was a sprightly-looking vehicle which was powered by a four-cylinder L-head 27 horsepower engine, rode on either a 105- or 115-inch wheelbase, and came with a complete electrical system. The first Vulcans carried price tags between $750 and $850 and were considered by many to be quite a bargain.

It is not entirely clear whether the Vulcan was actually built in Painesville. There is evidence that parts manufactured at the Vulcan

Painesville plant, including the engine, were instead shipped to the Driggs-Seabury Ordnance Company plant in Sharon, Pennsylvania, for assembly into the finished automobile.

In any event, the 1914 models appeared at automobile shows in New York, Cleveland and Chicago. When the 1915 Vulcans were introduced, the wheelbase had increased to 120 inches and prices rose to a still very affordable $975. Unfortunately, internal business problems interfered with operations and threatened the viability of the company and its 200-employee plant. The concerned Painesville community stepped up with financial backing but it was not enough, and in 1915 bankruptcy was declared. The company was taken over by the Erie Motor Company. (See Erie Motor Car Company.) Notwithstanding this setback, Alonzo Marsh did not give up on the idea of building his own automobile and moved to Cleveland, where he ultimately produced the Marsh automobile. (See Marsh Motors Company, Part I.)

W. B. Robe & Company (Portsmouth, 1914 to 1915)

After having constructed three prototype cyclecars, W. B. Robe's company offered the Robe cyclecar to the buying public for as low as $325. It had a 100-inch wheelbase, four-cylinder water-cooled engine, and sliding-gear transmission. A model equipped with electric starter and other features was priced at $375. Like all cyclecars, the Robe lasted only briefly.

W. S. Reed Company (Massillon, 1909)

The Massillon Six roadster was a large vehicle with an appealing appearance. It had a mother-in-law seat, a six-cylinder engine, shaft drive, 118-inch wheelbase, and a price of $1,750. A 124-inch wheelbase touring model was offered at $2,000. With a capitalization of only $10,000 it is hard to imagine how the company was able to produce even a prototype, but it did, after which the venture quickly collapsed. The company sold out to a C. P. Munch who ultimately produced the Keystone, a renamed version of the Massillon Six, in Pennsylvania and New York.

Wagenhal, W. G. (Cincinnati, 1900)

It was reported that Mr. Wagenhal was constructing a motorized vehicle with the expectation that it would achieve 30 miles per hour. Since he was manager of the Mill Creek Valley Railroad, it is possible the vehicle was steam powered. Further information about the vehicle is unknown.

Washington Motor Company (Eaton and Middletown, 1920 to 1924)

Otto M. Shipley persuaded a number of fellow Eatonites to join him in the automobile manufacturing business. The company, formerly known as Union Motor Company (see Union Motor Company), moved ahead quickly and two prototype automobiles were on the road by the end of the venture's first year. The Washington was introduced to the public on that President's birthday in February 1921, and the first production vehicle was sold later that year. Missing an opportunity to take full advantage of the Washington name, the Washington automobile was priced at $1,785 rather than $1,776. Although the Washington was an assembled automobile, it was powered by a Continental six-cylinder engine and was very well built. The line was expanded in 1922 to include four open and closed body styles, all on the same 119-inch wheelbase, and all featuring a beveled plate glass windshield and wood-spoked wheels. Only thirty-eight Washingtons were sold that year. No further production occurred in 1923 although a prototype steam car was built that year. Even though things were not going well, the company constructed a larger factory in Middletown, a decision that proved unwise. Three steam Washingtons were built as well, but the end had come. Bankruptcy was declared, due in large part to the cost of building the new plant.

Webb, W. H. (Conneaut, 1902)

It was reported in a trade journal that Mr. Webb was completing construction of a steam vehicle. Details are lacking.

Welbon Motor Car Company (Cincinnati, 1912)

The Welbon company was capitalized at

$25,000 with the declared purpose of building automobiles. Nothing further is known about the venture.

Weller Engineering Company (Elyria, 1902)

Weller built two prototype vehicles and received a limited number of orders, but it appears that, although these orders may have been satisfied, production did not follow.

Wells-Meeker Motor Vehicle Company (Columbus, 1900)

A prototype electric vehicle was constructed using a motor designed by brothers W. E. and Frank E. Wells. Actual production was not intended, as the purpose of the prototype was merely to test the motor for eventual use in street cars.

West Side Motor Company (Hamilton, 1906)

West Side Motor Company was incorporated with $10,000 capital stock. Intentions were to produce automobiles, among other things. It is doubtful that any vehicles were made.

Westcott Motor Car Company (Springfield, 1916 to 1925)

The Westcott Carriage Company was founded in Richmond, Indiana, in 1896. Burton J. Westcott, son of founder John Westcott, assumed control of the company upon his father's death in 1907. Although his father had no love for the automobile, which was a threat to the carriage business, son Burton was an enthusiastic advocate. Although Burton had been living in Springfield since 1903 where he was Treasurer of the American Seeding Machine Company, he actively managed the Richmond company, redirecting its focus to the manufacture of automobiles in 1909. The company was renamed the Westcott Motor Car Company in 1910 and ceased making carriages.

From then until 1916 the company remained in Richmond, Indiana, where a total of 4,266 automobiles were produced with orders increasing steadily each year. In 1916 the company operations were moved to Springfield, Ohio. It purchased plant facilities from the Seeding company in which the Westcott company began production of its automobiles, bringing with it a large number of its Richmond employees, so many that the area of Springfield they moved into became known as "Richmond Row."

The Westcott automobile was known for its high quality construction and excellent durability which fairly earned it the slogan "The Car with a Longer Life." Although it was an assembled automobile many innovations were offered, including four-wheel brakes, automatic spark advance, disappearing auxiliary seats, and in 1921 a "Closure" model sedan, a touring-style automobile with hard side panels with sliding glass windows, all of which could be removed for summertime motoring. All Springfield Westcotts were powered by Continental six-cylinder engines. Prices ranged from $1,585 to $2,000.

From 1916 through the Westcott's last year of production in 1925, 10,799 automobiles were sold. The company experienced its best year ever in 1921 when 1,710 Westcotts found homes. But things began to go downhill from that point and 1925 would be the company's last year notwithstanding Burton's best efforts to keep it afloat. On April 4, 1925, the company assets were acquired by its suppliers and Burton, exhausted from his efforts, died the following year.

In addition to having been one of Springfield's leading manufacturer families, the Westcotts were also famous for their 1908 Frank Lloyd Wright Prairie style home, the first house Wright had built in Ohio and one of which he was especially proud. The 4,000 square foot home featured two of the largest decorative urns to ever grace a residential property and garden themed landscaping. The Westcott house has been fully restored by the Westcott House Foundation of Springfield and is open for tours.

Western Reserve Motor Car Company (Leavittsburg, 1921)

With offices in Warren and its factory in

Leavittsburg, the Western Reserve company hoped to manufacture a touring-bodied vehicle with a six-cylinder engine of its own design and manufacture. The wheelbase was to be 121 inches. It is believed that only a prototype was built.

Wick, Henry (Youngstown, 1902)

Wick, a wealthy steel manufacturer, commissioned the construction of a custom automobile in 1902. Accounts differ as to where it was actually built. One account maintains it was designed and built in Youngstown by a local mechanical engineer; another holds that it was designed and built by L. B. Smyser & Company of New York City. In any case, the coachwork was by J. M. Quinby & Company of Newark, New Jersey. The aluminum-bodied "Blue Goose" undoubtedly earned its name as a result of its stunning Royal Blue paint work. At a cost of $8,000 it was the most expensive American-made automobile up to that time. Handsome and imposing, Wick's automobile weighed 3,100 pounds, had a plate glass windshield, four-cylinder 30 horsepower engine, three-speed sliding-gear transmission, a nineteen-gallon gasoline tank, and was capable of forty miles per hour. Consideration was given to going into production, and the "Blue Goose" was shown at the 1903 Chicago, Cleveland, and New York automobile shows, but no orders were forthcoming. In 1904 the "Blue Goose, which had been damaged in a street car accident, was auctioned off to a Cleveland bidder for $765.

Willys-Overland Company (Toledo, 1910 to 1954); Kaiser-Willys Company (Toledo, 1954 to 1955)

John North Willys of Elmira, New York, began selling and then manufacturing bicycles in the 1890s. On a visit to Cleveland in 1899, Willys saw an automobile for the first time, and quickly concluded that automobiles would replace horse-drawn carriages as the most practical mode of personal transportation in the country. Upon returning home to Elmira, he opened an automobile dealership selling Pierce-Arrow and Rambler automobiles. By 1904 his dealership was so successful that he was unable to obtain enough vehicles to meet customer demand.

In order to ensure an adequate supply of vehicles for his dealership, he contracted with the Overland Automobile Company of Indianapolis to provide him with its entire 1906 production of two-and four-cylinder runabouts. The arrangement worked so well for Willys that, in

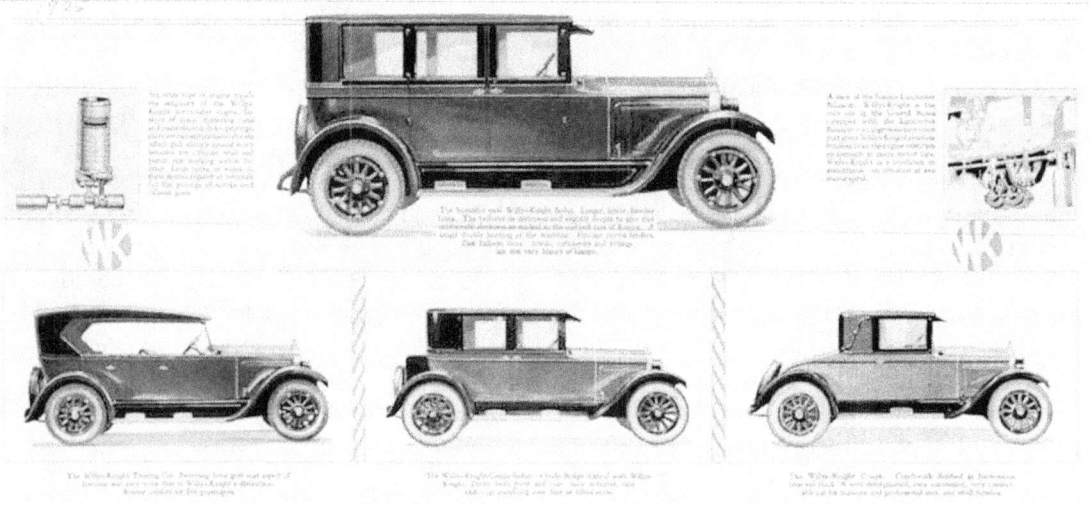

Famous for its Knight sleeve-valve engines, the 1925 Willys-Knight automobiles were the only ones to come with the Lanchester Balancer that claimed to completely eliminate engine vibrations.

WILLYS-KNIGHT

MILEAGE

BIG MILEAGE! Smooth mileage! Economical mileage! The beautiful Willys-Knight gives you more satisfying mileage than you ever dreamed you could get from a car.

This fine car keeps youth in your veins and age out of mileage. Its beauty keeps you proud. Its action keeps you happy. Mileage makes your heart grow fonder.

The wonderful Willys-Knight sleeve-valve engine is utterly free from the woes of ordinary poppet-valve engines. It *actually improves with use!* No valve-grinding or carbon-cleaning. Owners report 50,000 miles and more without a single engine adjustment. As to total mileage — no Willys-Knight engine has ever been known to wear out!

WILLYS-OVERLAND, Inc., TOLEDO, OHIO
Willys-Overland Sales Co. Ltd., Toronto, Can.

The Day of the Knight is Here!

5 Passenger Touring
$1175 f.o.b. Toledo

The Willys-Overland company's first Knight sleeve-valve engine made its appearance in the 1914 Willys-Knight automobile. The company would go on to produce more Knight engines than all other automobile manufacturers in the world combined. Knight engines were well known for actually improving in performance with use, and the advertisement says that no Willys-Knight engine was ever known to wear out.

This 1918 advertisement illustrates the elegance of a chauffeur-driven Model 88–8, which rode on a 125 inch wheelbase and was powered by a 65-horsepower 8-cylinder sleeve-valve engine.

1907, he ordered 500 four-cylinder Overlands, for which he sent a $10,000 deposit.

When no Overlands appeared in Elmira as promised, Willys went to Indianapolis to see what the problem was. He found that plant operations were at a standstill, the company was in financial distress, and the owner himself was on the verge of bankruptcy. In order to save the situation, the owner agreed to turn over the management of the company to Willys. Under Willys' guidance, production of four-cylinder Overlands was resumed and reached 465 in 1908, by which time Willys had purchased the Overland company and renamed it the Willys-Overland Company. New facilities were added to accommodate increased production, and 4,907 four- and six-cylinder vehicles were turned out in 1909.

The Indianapolis facilities proved to be inadequate to meet ever rising demand. As further expansion on site was not feasible, Willys began a search for a larger plant, setting his sights on the nearby Marion Motor Car Company of Indianapolis which he acquired in 1909. Just before purchasing Marion, Willys became aware that the much larger Pope Motor Car Company factory in Toledo was in the hands of a bankruptcy receiver and was available for sale. The Pope facilities were ideal for Willys' needs, and were large enough to serve any foreseeable future expansion. Willys purchased the Pope plant in 1910. As a result, the Marion plant was never turned over to production of Overland automobiles but continued to build Marions which were sold by Willys-Overland dealers. This arrangement continued until the end of 1910 when Willys divested himself of ownership in the Marion company. The Toledo plant quickly proved its worth and 15,598 automobiles were produced in 1910.

In 1913, eager to improve his vehicles by fitting them with the extraordinarily quiet Knight sleeve-valve engines, Willys purchased control of the Edwards Motor Car Company of New York, one of little more than two-dozen companies worldwide which were licensed to produce the Knight engine. Willys moved the Edwards company and its equipment to the Elyria plant of the former Garford automobile company. From that point on Willys continued to build automobiles powered by Knight engines until 1933, in addition to building automobiles powered by conventional engines. By 1933 the company had produced more Knight engines than all other manufacturers.

From 1912 through 1919, Willys-Overland production was second only to Ford. Business continued to improve and Willys decided to challenge Henry Ford's Model T head-on. In 1917, the company announced that it intended to produce a new Willys, equipped with a four-cylinder Knight sleeve-valve engine, self-starter, and electric lights, which was to be priced at less than $500, just slightly below the price of a Model T. Due to the country's involvement in World War I, actual production was delayed until 1919, by which time the price had risen to $845, substantially higher than the price of a Model T. But John Willys never lost sight of his intention to sell an automobile below the price of a Ford, which he finally achieved with his 1927 Whippet.

John Willys was always on the lookout for opportunities to expand his business. However, a 1917 acquisition of the Curtiss aircraft company, and his 1919 purchase of the huge former Duesenberg aircraft engine plant in Elizabeth, New Jersey, began to threaten the Willys company's well-being. When the post-war economy hit a slump, so did the company's financial health. Banks were willing to help, but only if Willys would take on Walter P. Chrysler to oversee operations. Chrysler's cost-cutting measures helped Willys to survive and, when Chrysler departed, John Willys was once again back in control of his company. The Duesenberg plant and interest in Curtiss were disposed of, and the consolidated operations in Toledo and Elyria were recovering strongly, so much so that sales hit 150,000 in 1925.

The Overland model name was dropped when the all-new 1927 Whippet was introduced. The Whippet was touted as America's smallest automobile, rode on a 100¼-inch wheelbase, and was powered by a 30 horsepower four-cylinder engine. The European-style Whippet had four-wheel brakes, a

The Coupe

A ROOMY Coupe with wide doors and windows and full vision body. The interior is luxuriously upholstered in Baker Green Velour and appointments are unusually complete. Under the rear deck is a generous luggage compartment.

The Landau

A DISTINCTIVE, dignified example of the advanced mode in fine body design, with low, level lines, wide windows, graceful roof and rear quarter set off by landau arms. Interior upholstery in Shelton Looms fabric of Grey-Green Mohair Plush.

The Sedan

$1,118.00

A SEDAN of generous proportions for five, with wide, deeply upholstered seats. The interior of the full vision body is finished in Baker Slate Velour. Cowl ventilator, automatic windshield wiper and dome light are standard equipment. The Whippet Six Sedan is a lively, powerful, smart-looking car, sturdily built to give satisfactory service.

Whippet prices were at or below $1,000, exceptional for an automobile of its quality. Automatic windshield wipers and dome light were nice touches to this European styled automobile. (Note salesman's penciled-in price.)

seven-main-bearing crankshaft, and was priced at only $545, $5 less than a Ford. The year 1927 also saw the introduction of the Falcon-Knight which was built in Elyria by an Overland-Willys subsidiary, the Falcon Motors Corporation. (See Falcon Motors Corporation.) Along with the 110,000 Whippets produced in 1928, total company output was behind only Chevrolet and Ford that year.

But once again the company fell on bad times and the subsequent Depression demanded strong measures, as total sales by 1932 had fallen to only 26,444 automobiles. Willys reluctantly decided to discontinue its Whippet and Willys-Knight models and focused all of its resources on the manufacture of one automobile, the new 1933 Willys '77, a reworked version of the Whippet which, at $500, was the least expensive American automobile on the market. The '77 was deservedly popular with sports and race enthusiasts, as it was capable of 30 miles per gallon, and had a top speed of 75 miles per hour.

Despite the '77's good showing, overall sales were down drastically, and the company was forced into receivership in 1933. As described in *By One and One* by Doreen Canaday Spitzer, John Willys called in his longtime friend Ward Canaday to help him right the company. Because Canaday had handled the Willys advertising account for United States Advertising Corporation since 1921, he was familiar with company operations. Together with Willys-Overland executive Dave Wilson, he was able to restore the company's financial footing and guide it through the introduction of the new 1937 Willys, which proved to be a sales success. The Willys continued in production until 1942, while the Overland made a brief reappearance for 1939 and was re-named the American for 1941. Unfortunately, shortly before the company emerged from receivership in early 1936, John North Willys died, and was unable to witness his company's rebirth.

Willys passenger automobile production ended shortly after the country entered World War II, but at that time a new chapter was opened in the company's life story. Anticipating the possibility of American involvement in the European war, the U.S. Army invited bids for the design and production of a small four-wheeled personnel carrier. Only two companies responded, American Bantam Car Company and Willys-Overland. Willys proved to be the low bidder, but Bantam was selected because it promised to deliver a prototype model in 49 days. The Army reconsidered its position and invited Ford and Willys to submit prototypes based on the Bantam design. All three entrants were put through grueling tests at the hands of GIs who would be using them. The Willys entry won high praise for its overall performance and especially for its "Go Devil" four-cylinder engine. No one company could possibly meet production demand, and contracts were awarded to both Ford and Willys for a unified version of what became known as the Jeep. (The name "Jeep" seems to have derived from the government designation of "General Purpose" or "GP" vehicle.) Ford would ultimately build 280,000 Jeeps, and Willys provided 363,000.

When the war ended, the Willys company did not immediately re-enter the passenger car field. Instead, it offered a line of civilian vehicles based on the military Jeep. These Willys Jeeps initially included sturdy station wagons and trucks. The Willys Jeepster, a two-door convertible version derived from the Jeep line, first appeared in 1948. It was not until 1952 that Willys again introduced a passenger automobile line, the compact Aero sedans, which included the Lark and Wing two- and four-door models, all powered by a 75 horsepower L-head six. After a short run, the Aero made its last appearance in 1955.

By 1954, it was evident that something had to be done to assure the survival of the now struggling Willys-Overland company. Not alone in this predicament, Willys combined forces with fellow independent automobile company Kaiser Motors, to form Kaiser-Willys Company.

Henry Kaiser had earlier joined with former Graham-Paige automobile executive Joseph Frazer to form Kaiser Motors out of the remains of Graham-Paige. This venture had brought forth the Kaiser and Frazer automobiles in 1946. Innovative and original in design, these automobile met with initial success, but sales began to wane by the mid–1950s, as had those of Willys.

Kaiser's founder, Henry J. Kaiser, after whom the Henry J automobile would be named, was a leading industrialist who was a prime contractor on the Hoover Dam project in the 1930s, and had mass-produced Liberty ships during World War II. He also formed the Kaiser Aluminum Company and Kaiser Steel Company, and established Kaiser Permanente Foundation to provide health care for his employees.

The new combination did not save passenger automobile production for long, as it all ended rather abruptly in 1955, leaving only the Willys Jeep line. The company was renamed Kaiser Jeep in 1963. It was sold to American Motors in 1970, which was in turn absorbed by Chrysler in 1987.

Williams Foundry & Machine Company (Akron, 1904)

Williams Foundry built a motorized vehicle on an order from Frank Goddard. Mr. Goddard declared it a failure. The only people to benefit were lawyers who were hired for a series of lawsuits that followed.

Winder, John E. (Cincinnati, 1904)

Mr. Winder built a steam automobile for his own use, to accommodate his limited freedom of movement caused by an accident to his legs. All vehicle operations were controlled by hand levers. The vehicle, capable of twelve miles per hour, served him well.

Witter, E. E. (Granville, 1900)

Mr. Witter built a six-passenger automobile for his own use, powered by a seven horsepower engine. Nothing more is known about Mr. Witter's automobile.

Woodruff Automobile Company (Akron, 1902 to 1904)

The Woodruff brothers, George and Albert, built their automobiles at the former plant of the Akron Bicycle Company. After prototypes were tested, a runabout with semi-elliptical springs was produced. Powered by a one-cylinder 6-horsepower engine, it had a top speed of twenty-five miles per hour. A later model Woodruff is said to have made the trip between Akron and Cleveland, a sixty mile drive, in less than two hours. Total production, which was only to order, was perhaps thirty in all.

Worthington Manufacturing Company (Elyria, 1902)

The Worthington company was formed to take over the operations of a wheelchair and auto parts company. The intention to manufacture an automobile was stated, but no vehicle was ever built.

Wottring Brothers (Prospect, 1902); Wottring & Son Automobile Works (Prospect, 1907 to 1908)

In 1902 the Wottring brothers produced a spritely six horsepower runabout which they named the Prospect. A top speed of thirty miles per hour was claimed for this 1,050 pound vehicle. From 1902 to 1907 the family appears to have concentrated on its carriage-building business but in 1907 an automobile was offered once again, now under the Wottring & Son Automobile Works name. Vehicles were built on an as-ordered basis only, and may also have been named the Prospect.

Wright, Fred, and Ralph Wright (Defiance, 1904)

Assembling parts gathered from a variety of extant automobiles, the brothers Wright built a touring automobile for their own use. No production was intended.

Yaple, Luther P. (Chillicothe, 1906)

Mr. Yaple announced the pending organization of a company to be capitalized at $250,000 for the manufacture of a four-cylinder automobile. Realization of this venture is doubted.

Zent Automobile Manufacturing Company (Bellefontaine, 1904 to 1906)

Capitalized at $25,000, Zent successfully

produced an automobile in 1905. This initial vehicle with a three-cylinder engine and shaft drive was followed in 1906 by a four-cylinder model. The company was superseded by the Bellefontaine Automobile Company in 1907, during which year the vehicle bore the name Traveler. (See Bellefontaine Automobile Company.)

Appendix 1: Cleveland Automobile Manufacturers by Year

1864: John J. Grant
1886: Charles F. Brush
1895 to 1924: Alexander Winton
1896 to 1902: George A. Washburn
1896 to 1929: Frank B. Stearns
1897 to 1916: Walter C. Baker
1898 to 1910: Paul Gaeth
1898 to 1901: Eastman Automobile Company
1898 to 1901: Sperry Engineering Company
1899 to 1901: Owen Motor Carriage Company
1899 to 1902: Frank W. Rogers & George Hanford
1899 to 1918: White Sewing Machine Company
1900 to 1931: Peerless Manufacturing Company
1900 to 1901: Edwin L. Strong & Lewis H. Rogers
1900 to 1902: People's Automobile Company
1900 to 1904: Louis E. Hoffman
1900: Cleveland Electric Company
1900 to 1901: Clark & Company
1900: DeMooy Brothers
1900: Herbert A. Githens
1900: William G. Hoffman
1900 to 1902: Kohl & Gates Motor Company
1900: Lincoln Electric Company
1900: Sipe & Sigler Company
1900: Automobile Carriage Supply Company
1901 to 1904: American Motor Carriage Company
1901 to 1904: Krastin Automobile Manufacturing Company
1901: Henry J. Altman
1901: Cleveland Motor Carriage Company
1901: Benson Automobile Company
1901: S.M. Levy
1902: Amstutz-Osborne Company
1902: Hansen Automobile Company
1902 to 1905: General Automobile and Manufacturing Company
1902 to 1904: Otto Konigslow Machine Company
1902 to 1904: Berg Automobile Company
1902 to 1904: Star Automobile Company
1902 to 1904: Cleveland Automobile Company
1902: E.P. De Gallier
1902 to 1905: Jacob Hoffman Wagon Company
1902: Noble Automobile Manufacturing Company
1902: Frank Saur
1902: J.A. Schmidt
1902: Superior Automobile Company
1902 to 1903: Willard Storage Battery Company
1902: Johnson-Jennings Company
1902: Fred Morrison
1903 to 1904: Edward Joel Pennington
1903: J. Keller Electric Works
1903 to 1904: Russell Motor Vehicle Company
1903: Rogers & Thatcher Automobile Company
1903: The Kirk-Latty Manufacturing Company
1903: Central Automobile Company
1903: McIntosh Brothers
1904: Harry S. Moore
1904: Worthington Automobile Company
1904 to 1909: Cleveland Motor Car Company

1904 to 1905: Brew-Hatcher Company
1904 to 1906: Demars Electric Vehicle Company
1904 to 1911: Royal Motor Car Company
1904: Euclid Avenue Automobile Company
1904: American Automobile Company
1904: Special Motor Vehicle Company
1905 to 1915: Rauch & Lang Carriage Company
1905 to 1906: Parsons Electric Motor Carriage Company
1905 to 1908: Elwell-Parker Electric Company
1905: Forest City Motor Car Company
1905: Standard Automobile Company
1906: Blakeslee Electric Vehicle Company
1906 to 1907: Williams Motor Carriage Company
1906: Monarch Motor Car Company
1906: Cyrus B. Kurtz
1906: Palmer Automobile Manufacturing Company
1906 to 1911: Simplex Manufacturing Company
1906: Harry S. Moore (Auburn-Moore)
1906: Aerocar Company
1906: Williams Motor Carriage Company
1907 to 1910: Byrider Electric Automobile Company
1907 to 1908: Euclid Motor Car Company
1907 to 1908: French-American Motor Company
1908 to 1911: Derain Motor Company
1908 to 1910: Hines Car Company
1908 to 1911: Cuyahoga Motor Car Company
1909 to 1914: Broc Carriage and Wagon Company
1909: Woodland Motor Car Company
1909 to 1912: Stiverson Motor Car Company
1909: Francis R. Hoyt
1909: Captain Philip J. Minch
1909: United Factories Company
1909: Cleveland, Beck and Lyman Corporation
1910 to 1912: Gabriel Auto Company
1910: Crawford-Hough Garage Company
1910: De-Luxe Motor Car Company
1910: Clark-Norwalk
1910: Gas Engine and Appurtenance Company
1911 to 1912: Croxton Motor Company
1911 to 1912: Bingham Manufacturing Company
1911: Davis Motor Car Company
1911: Maclaren Company

1911: Wissman Auto Repair Company
1911: Cleveland Auto Sales & Manufacturing Company
1912 to 1913: Grant Lees Machine Company
1912: Arter Auto Carriage Company
1912: Eckenroth Automobile Livery Company
1912: Hutchcroft & Sons Company
1912: E.A. Hammer Company
1913 to 1929: Chandler Motor Car Company
1913: H & H Auto Company
1913: Metropolitan Garage Company
1913: Sixth City Machine Company
1913 to 1915: Downing Motor Car Company
1913 to 1914: Falcon Cycle Car Company
1913 to 1914: Fedelia Cycle Car
1914: Snyder Motor & Manufacturing Company
1914: Cleveland Cycle Car Company
1914: G.S. Goby
1914: George W. Kimple
1914: King Cyclecar Company
1914 to 1919: Richard Auto Manufacturing Company
1914: Lohse Automobile Improvement Company
1915 to 1932: Ford Motor Company
1915: Hallock Engineering Company
1915 to 1919: Owen Magnetic Company
1915 to 1916: Harding Motor Car Company
1915 to 1918: H.A. Lozier & Company
1915 to 1920: Baker R&L Company
1915: Pierce Supply Company
1916 to 1922: Grant Motor Car Company
1916 to 1917: Disbrow Motors Company
1916 to 1932: Jordan Motor Car Company
1917 to 1924: Templar Motors Company
1917 to 1918: Abbott Corporation
1917 to 1918: Master Motor Car Company
1917 to 1918: Supreme Motors Corporation
1918 to 1920: Mel Stringer
1919 to 1922: Ohio Motor Vehicle Company
1919 to 1926: Cleveland Automobile Company
1919 to 1920: LaMarne Motor Company
1919 to 1921: Paragon Motor Car Company
1919 to 1922: Aluminum Manufacturers, Inc.
1919 to 1924: Marsh Motors Company
1919: Harry Habig
1920 to 1923: Rubay Company
1920 to 1925: Kurtz Motor Car Company
1920 to 1922: Globe Motor Company
1920 to 1922: Merit Motor Company

Cleveland Automobile Manufacturers by Year

1920 to 1923: Sterling Motor Company
1920: Champion Motor Car Company
1920: Freeman Motor Car Company
1920: Mercury Motor Car Company
1921: Washington Automobile Company
1922: Zeder Motor Company
1922: Forrest F. Cameron

1923 to 1926: Rollin Motors Company
1925 to 1928: Baker Motors, Inc.
1926 to 1928: Saf-T-Cab Corporation
1927: Penton Motor Company
1929 to 1931: Hupp Motor Car Company
1931: Canzol

Appendix 2: Leading Cleveland Automobile Marques by Name and Address

Chronological by First Year of Appearance

Winton: 1895 to 1902, 1814 E. 45th Street; 1902 to 1924, 10601 Berea Road.
Washburn: 1896 to 1902, address unknown.
Stearns: 1896 to 1901, Euclid Avenue & E. 101st Street; 1901 to 1929, 12401 Euclid Avenue.
Baker: 1898 to 1905, 2260 E. 69th Street; 1905 to 1915, 8000 Baker Street.
Gaeth: 1898 to 1904, 54 Castle Street; 1905 to 1911, 2553 E. 25th Street.
Eastman: 1898 to 1901, Corner of High and Sheriff Streets.
Sperry: 1898 to 1901, Mason & Beldon.
Cleveland Tricycle: 1898 to 1901, address unknown.
Owen: 1899 to 1901, 1701–05 Russell.
Rogers & Hanford: 1899 to 1902, 644 Castle.
White: 1899 to 1907, Canal Street in the Flats; 1907 to 1918, 79th Street & St. Clair.
Peerless: 1900 to 1906, 2654 Lisbon Road S.E.; 1907 to 1931, Quincy & E 93rd Street.
Phoenix: 1900 to 1901, 1701–05 Russell.
Strong & Rogers: 1900 to 1901, address unknown.
People's: 1900 to 1902, 54 Castle Street.
Buckeye: 1901, 54 Castle Street.
Marr: 1901, 8000 Carnegie Avenue.
American Gas: 1901 to 1904, 8000 Carnegie Avenue.
Krastin: 1901 to 1904, 4209 Clark Street/1251 Clark Street.
Benson: 1901, 102 Canal Street.
Hansen: 1902, E 45th Street & Mason.
General: 1902 to 1904, 1312–30 Hamilton at E 40th Street.
OttoKar: 1902 to 1904, 328 Prospect Avenue.
Berg: 1902 to 1904, 2269 Ashland Avenue (Cleveland Machine Screw Company); 393-99 Perkins (Federal Manufacturing Company).
Star: 1902 to 1903, 6300 Kinsman Avenue; 1903 to 1904, 1761 Crawford Road.
Cleveland (Moore): 1902 to 1904, 16–20 Lake Street.
Durabile: 1902: E 40th Street & Kelly Avenue.
Noble: 1902, 4800 Hamilton N.E.
Hoffman: 1902 to 1904, Lake Street & Marquette.

Leading Cleveland Automobile Marques by Name and Address

Rogers & Thacher: 1903, 2692 St. Clair Avenue N.E.
Kirk-Latty: 1903:W 85th Street between Madison & Detroit.
McIntosh: 1903, 50 Wright Street.
Pennington: 1903 to 1904, 16 Middle Street.
Russell: 1903 to 1904, 2216 Clarkwood Avenue.
Euclid: 1903 to 1904, 2269 Ashland Avenue.
Buckboard: 1904, Crawford Road.
Meteor: 1904, 393–99 Perkins (Federal Manufacturing Company).
Worthington Automobile Company: 1904, 393–99 Perkins (Federal Manufacturing Company).
Cleveland (Garford): 1904 to 1909, E. 12th Street between Power Street & St Clair.
Studebaker: 1904 to 1905, 1312 Hamilton at E 40th Street.
Brew-Hatcher: 1904 to 1905, Winter Street near Cuyahoga River.
DeMars: 1904 to 1906, 1948 E 55th Street.
Royal Tourist: 1904 to 1911, 1909 E 72nd Street.
Rauch & Lang: 1905 to 1915, 2180 W 25th Street.
Parsons: 1905 to 1906, address unknown.
Monarch: 1906, 1675 E 40th Street.
Palmer: 1906, 1835 E 87th Street.
Blakeslee: 1906, 1948 E 55th Street.
Williams: 1906 to 1907, 1948 E 55th Street.
Byrider: 1907 to 1910, 1948 E 55th Street.
Simplex: 1906 to 1911, 7500 Quincy Avenue S.E.
Derain: 1908 to 1911, 7500 Quincy Avenue S.E.
Hines: 1908 to 1911, 7413 Stanton Road.
Broc: 1909 to 1914, 1673 E 40th Street.
Cleveland (Cuyahoga): 1908 to 1911, 10547 Euclid Avenue.
Woodland: 1909, 2552 E 55th Street.
Stuyvesant: 1909 to 1912, 2553 W 25th Street.
Gabriel: 1910 to 1912, 1674 W 3rd Street.
Croxton: 1911 to 1912, 2260 E 69th Street.
Chandler: 1913 to 1929, 300 E 131st Street near St. Clair.
Downing: 1913 to 1915, address unknown.
Fedelia: 1913 to 1914, 1869 Penrose Avenue, East Cleveland.
Falcon: 1913 to 1914, E 105th Street near Quincy.
Cleveland (Barnes): 1914, address unknown.
Snyder: 1914, address unknown.
RiChard: 1914 to 1919, 7800 Finney Avenue.
Ford: 1915 to 1932, 11620 Euclid Avenue.
Owen Magnetic: 1915 to 1919, 8000 Baker Street.
Harding Twelve: 1915, E 93rd Street and Quincy Avenue.
Baker-R&L: 1916 to 1920, 2180 W 25th Street; 8000 Baker Street.
Grant: 1916 to 1922, Coit Road and Kirby Avenue.
H.A.L. TWELVE: 1916 to 1918, 864 E 72nd Street.
Disbrow: 1916 to 1917, E 30th Street and Chester Avenue.
Jordan: 1916 to 1931, 1070 E 152nd Street.
Templar: 1917 to 1924, 1300 Athens.
Abbott: 1917 to 1918, 1175 E 152nd Street.
Ferris: 1919 to 1922, 18222 Lanken Avenue.
Paragon: 1919 to 1921, 6545 Carnegie Avenue.

Cleveland (Chandler): 1919 to 1926, 17325 Euclid Avenue.
LaMarne: 1919 to 1920, 7800 Finney Avenue.
Kurtz Automatic: 1920 to 1925, 3748 W 143rd Street.
Marsh: 1920 to 1924, 4900 W 73rd Street.
Globe Four: 1920 to 1922, 12217 Euclid Avenue.
Merit: 1920 to 1922, 6505 Cedar.
Rollin: 1923 to 1925, E 193rd Street and Euclid Avenue.
Leon Rubay: 1920 to 1923, 1318 W 78th Street.
Pomeroy: 1919 to 1922, 2210 Harvard Avenue.
Cameron: 1922, 10271 Berea Road.
Hupmobile: 1929 to 1931, 300 E 131st Street; 17325 Euclid Avenue.
Canzol: 1931, address unknown.

Appendix 3: Ohio Automobile Manufacturers by City

Cleveland excluded

Akron

Akron Machine Company
Akron Motor Carriage Company
Chandler, P.J.
Ideal Commercial Car Company
International Harvester Company
Motz, Charles A.
Philion, Achille
Smelser, Luther W.
Summit Automobile Company
Tanner-Hower Manufacturing Company
Williams Foundry & Machine Company
Woodruff Automobile Company
York Machinery Company

Alliance

Alliance Motor Car Company

Attica

Rees Motor Company

Barberton

Horseless Carriage Company
Huhene, E.A.

Bellaire

Bellaire Automobile Company

Bellefontaine

Bellefontaine Automobile Company
Bowman, John and Paul
Zent Automobile Manufacturing Company

Belleville

Lepp Brothers

Bowling Green

Bowling Green Motor Car Company
Coats Steam Car Company
Stewart Motor Car Company

Bucyrus

Frey-Schecker Company
Shunk Plow Company
Sommer Motor Company

Cadiz

Scott, R.P.

Canal Dover

S. Toomey Company
Standard Motive Power Company

Canton

American Motor Car Company
Aultman, Henry
Aultman Company
Berger, J. A.
Berger Manufacturing Company
Blackiston, G.P.
Canton Buggy Company
Holmes Automobile Company
Hydro Motor Car Company
Keller Electric Shops

Carthage

Carthage Motor Car Company
Crescent Motor Company
Jewel Carriage Company
Jewell Carriage Company
Ohio Motor Car Company

Chagrin Falls

Falls Garage Company

Chillicothe

ArBenz Car Company
Houser, Orville E.
Logan Construction Company
Motor Storage and Manufacturing Company
Yaple, Luther P.

Cincinnati

Acorn Automobile Company
Ahrens-Fox Fire Engine Company
Alliance Carriage Company
Altenberg, George P.
Anchor Motor Car Company
Automobile Equipment Company
Blair Motor Company
Brown Carriage Company
Buggy Car Company
Bullock Electric Manufacturing Company
Carrico Motor Company
Charles Behlen Sons Company
Charles Eckert Manufacturing Company
Charles Hanauer Cycle Company
Church, F.S.
Cincinnati Automobile Company
Cincinnati Automotive Trades Association
Cincinnati Motor Car Company
Cincinnati Motors Company
Commercial Motor Car Company
Crane & Breed Manufacturing Company
Crosley Corporation
D.T. Williams Valve Company
Eckert, Charles
Emerson, Victor L.
Enger Motor Car Company
Evans-Eich Manufacturing Company
Foley & Williams Manufacturing Company
George C. Miller Sons' Carriage Company
Grane Brothers
H.W. Fenker Company
Haberer & Company
Haydock Motor Car Company
Heilman, John C.
Herman Motor Company
Hermes Motor Car Company
Hydro Engineering Company
J.H. Louis Automobile Company
John Schilito Company
Lunken, Edmond
Lunkenheimer Motor Vehicle Company
Marathon Automobile Company
Norwood Automobile Company
Powercar Automobile Company
Sayers & Scoville Company
Schacht Manufacturing Company
Schacht Motor Car Company
Specialty Carriage Company
Star Motor Car Company
Stover Motor Car Company
Sumner, Harry
Wagenhal, W.G.
Welbon Motor Car Company
Winder, Jon E.

Circleville

Circleville Automobile Company
Colonial Carriage Company

Clyde

Clyde Cars Company
Elmore Manufacturing Company

Columbus

Allen, E. W., and W. O.
Barcus, Nemo
Bellefontaine Carriage Body Company
Columbus Automobile Company
Columbus Brass Company
Columbus Buggy Company
Columbus Carriage & Harness Company
Columbus Motor Vehicle Company
Consolidated Motor Car Company
Cron & Sons Company
Cummins-Monitor Company
Curtin & Schille
Early Motor Car Company
Eastern Automobile Company
Eclipse Manufacturing Company

Farmobile Manufacturing Company
Gaither Auto Company
Groff-Runkle Motor Vehicle Company
Harmer, Frederick
Harmer Automobile Company
Ideal Light Car Company
Jewett Motor Carriage Company
Keystone Vehicle Company
Kinnear Manufacturing Company
Midgley Manufacturing Company
Monitor Motor Car Company
Neil, Ed
New Columbus Buggy Company
Okey, Perry
Okey Motor Car Company
Oscar Lear Automobile Company
Park Motors Company
Poste Brothers Buggy Company
Reive-Thompson Motor Company
Roberts, O.G.
Rodgers & Company
Seagrave Company
Shrum, J.
Standard Automobile Company
Twyman Motor Car Company
Union Sales Company
United States Carriage Company
Wells-Meeker Motor Vehicle Company

Columbus Grove

Jones, C.H.

Conneaut

Goddard, Wilford and Winfred
Vickers Auto Car Company
Webb, W.H.

Coshocton

Coshocton Motor Car Company

Cuyahoga Falls

Crock Motor Company

Dayton

Apple Motor Car Company
Arnstein, Harry
Baker, J.L.
Bolender, F.P.
Buckeye Wagon & Motor Car Company
Conklin, Oliver F.
Courier Car Company
Custer Specialty Company
Darling Motor Company
Dayton Automobile Company (1906)
Dayton Automobile Company (1911)
Dayton Electric Car Company
Dayton Motor Car Company
Dayton Motor Vehicle Company
De Cross Cy-Car Company
Elliott & Lang
Garrison Machine Works
Geyer Sales Company
Green Engineering Company
Heatherman-Solliday Motor Company
Kepler-Berry Motor Car Company
Kero-Car Motor Company
M.C. Witmore Company
Mead Engine Company
Meeker Manufacturing Company
Research Engineering Company
Ruse, Cordy
Speedwell Motor Car Company
Stoddard Manufacturing Company
Stutz, Harry C.
Stutz Manufacturing Company
Thresher Electric Company

Defiance

Highway Motors Company
Krotz-Defiance Auto Buggy Company
Miller Machine Company
Wright, Fred and Ralph

Delaware

Cook, C.E.

East Liverpool

Chester Rubber Tire & Tool Company

Eaton

Cyriacks Motor Company
Union Motor Company
Washington Motor Company

Elyria

Elyria Auto Sales Company
Falcon Motors Corporation
Garford Company
Troxel Manufacturing Company

Weller Engineering Company
Worthington Manufacturing Company

Findlay

Adams Brothers
Bennett, Harry
Differential Steel Car Company
Findlay Carriage Company
Findlay Motor Car Company
Gilford, George
Grant Motor Company

Fostoria

Allen, W. O., and F. W.
Fostoria Foundry and Machine Company
Fostoria Light Car Company
Fostoria Motor Car Company
Seneca Motor Company

Fremont

Fremont Motors Corporation
Lehr Agricultural Company

Galion

A. Howard Company
Ditwiler Manufacturing Company
Fetzger Automobile Manufacturing Company

Garfield

Alliance
MacDonald Steam Automobile Company

Geneva

Cleveland Auto Cab Company
Ewing Automobile Company
Geneva Automobile & Manufacturing Company

Granville

Witter, E.E.

Greenfield

C.R. Patterson & Sons

Greenville

Dunkle, Ralph W.

Hamilton

Advance Manufacturing Company
Columbia Carriage Company
Columbia Vehicle Company
Hamilton Vehicle Company
Republic Motor Car Company
Ritchie, William
West Side Motor Company

Hammersville

Gatts, Alfred Palmer

Kent

Kitto, A. W.

Kenton

Miller, George J.

Lancaster

Dum, Ed and Harley

Laurelville

Armstrong, Wayne

Leavittsburg

Western Reserve Motor Car Company

Lima

American Motor Car Company
Coe, Adelbert Brown
Independence Motor Car Company
Leach Automobile Company
Lima Light Car Company
Relay Motors Corporation

Lisbon

Kitto, A. W.

Logan

Lutz, Henry

Lorain

Carroll Automobile Company
Lorain Motor Carriage Company

Mansfield

Beardsley & Hubbs Manufacturing Company
Eagle & Vincent Automobile Company
Forth, Charles R.
Forth Motor Car Company
Mansfield Motor Vehicle Company
Richland Buggy Company

Marietta
Kent, A. W.
Pioneer Motor Car Company

Marion
Marion Automobile Company
Stringer Automobile Company
Sweney, Busby P.

Marysville
Marysville Motor Car Company
Tarkington, H.
Turner, Robert S.

Mason
John Kohl Carriage & Automobile Company

Massillon
Croxton-Keeton Motor Car Company
Forest City Motor Car Company
Jewel Motor Car Company
Kessell, Frank E.
Long-Crawford Automobile Company
Massillon Developing Company
Russell & Company
Schworm, Melville F.
Smith Bicycle, Automobile & Light Machinery Company
W.S. Reed Company

Miamisburg
Advance Motor Vehicle Company
Catrow, Herbert
Hatfield Motor Vehicle Company
Kauffman Motor Car Company

Middletown
McAdams, John
Merkel, Joseph F.
Miami Cycle and Manufacturing Company
Middletown Buggy Company
Middletown Machine Company
Moyea Automobile Company
Washington Motor Car Company

Millersburg
Spahr, Otto

Millersville
Millersville Machine Company

Mount Gilead
Cook, James M.

Mount Healthy
Markert, F.G.R.

Napoleon
Napoleon Motor Car Company
Ragan, Brown & Lange Company
Reya Motor Company

New Athens
Burdette, Oliver

New Bremen
Case Motor Car Company

New Carlisle
Credlebaugh, H.S.

New Concord
New Concord Automobile Company

New London
Healy, Caleb E.
Post, Charles Bushnell

Newark
Blair Manufacturing Company
Halladay Motor Car Company
Halladay Motors Corporation

Niles
Harris Automatic Press Company
Niles Auto & Machine Company
Taylor, Will

Norwalk
Auto-Bug Company
Norwalk Motor Car Company
Sly, Ethan E.

Ottawa
Krebs, Mr.

Painesville
Anderson, Leonard
Erie Motor Car Company
Vulcan Manufacturing Company

Piqua
Meteor Motor Car Company
Piqua Motor Company

Plymouth
Plymouth Motor Truck Company

Portsmouth
Ideal Manufacturing Company
Portsmouth Automobile & Machine Company
W.B. Rober & Company

Prospect
Wottring & Sons Automobile Works
Wottring Brothers

Ravenna
Riddle Manufacturing Company

Saint Paris
Brockshire & Robinson Company

Salem
Buckeye Engine Company
Davis, D.L.

Sandusky
Barnes Manufacturing Company
Caswell, Myron, and Harold
Courier Motors
Eagle-Macomber Motor Car Company
Maibohm Motors Company
Ogontz Motor Car Company
Roberts Motors Manufacturing Company
Sandusky Auto Parts & Motor Truck Company
Sandusky Automobile Company
Sandusky Automobile Manufacturing Company
Underwood Motor Company

Sebring
Sebring Motor Car Company

Shelby
Shelby Motor Car Company
Shelby Stove & Manufacturing Company

Sidney
Bimel Buggy Company
Bremac Motor Car Company

Spencer
Spencer Manufacturing Company

Springfield
Brenning Brothers
Foos Gas Engine Company
Koeb-Thompson
Koeb-Thompson Motor Company
Krotz, Alvero S.
Krotz Manufacturing Company
Kuqua & Son
McNutt, John
O.S. Kelly Corporation
Oscar Lear Automobile Company
Owens, H.E.
Russell, Dr. C.W.
Springfield Automobile & Industrial Company
Springfield Automobile Company
Springfield Machine & Tool Company
Thomas Manufacturing Company
Westcott Motor Car Company

Tiffin
Economy Motor Car Company
Hollis Tractor Company
Vogue Motor Car Company

Toledo
American Metal Wheel and Auto Company
Automobile Corporation
Belmont Motor Company
Bissell Electric Company
Burwell, George
Carl Electric Company
Consolidated Manufacturing Company
Cooney & Company
Craig-Toledo Motor Company
Cyclomobile Manufacturing Company
De Luxe Motor Car Company
Dennis Motor Company
Dusseau Fore and Rear Drive Automobile Company
Erie Supply Company
Greyhound Cyclecar Company
Hamel, Charles D.
Harruff, J.W.
International Motor Car Company
Interstate Supply Company

Kaiser-Willys Company
Kirk-Hall Company
Kirk Manufacturing Company
Landmann-Griffith
Lawrence Stamping Company
Lecklider, A.E.
Macinnis Brothers
Milburn Wagon Company
National Juvenile Auto Company
Ohio Electric Car Company
Pilliod Motor Company
Pope Motor Car Company
Rossell Motor Car Company
Sypher Manufacturing Company
Tillotson, Harry
Todd Manufacturing Company
Toledo Auto and Garage Company
Toledo Auto-Cycle Car Company
Toledo Electric Vehicle Company
Toledo Motor Car Company
Toledo Steam and Air Motor Company
Willys-Overland Company

TRAIL

Miller, J.W.

TROTWOOD

Niswender, Roman

TROY

Troy Auto & Buggy Company

UPPER SANDUSKY

Indian Motor Car Company
U.S. Motor Car Company

WAKEMAN

Brenenstul & Carpenter

WARREN

Colonial Motors Company
Hitchcock Motor Car Company

Ohio Automobile Company
Ohio Universal Truck Company
Packard & Weiss
Packard Motor Car Company
Trumbull Manufacturing Company
Valley Automobile Company

WARRENSVILLE

Brice Motor Car Company
Prince Motor Car Company

WASHINGTON COURT HOUSE

Swope Garage and Machine Company

WESTERVILLE

Paine, H. S.
Scharf Gearless Motor Car Company

WILLOUGHBY

Ben Hur Motor Company

WINCHESTER

American Hydromobile Company

XENIA

Baldner, Jacob and Fred
Baldner Motor Vehicle Company
Hawkins Cyclecar Company
Jones, Isaac B.

YOUNGSTOWN

Booth, Dr. Carlos C.
Drury-Wells Motor Company
Flynn, Walter F.
Fredonia Manufacturing Company
Glenwood Motor Car Company
H.B. Wick & Company
Mahoning Motor Car Company
Wick, Henry

Appendix 4: Unusual Vehicle Names

When each inventor finished his automotive creation and was ready, after countless hours of effort, to present it to the public, he anointed it with a name, the final stroke of his genius. Most names were straightforward and conventional, but there were many that provoked astonishment and perhaps a chuckle or two. Here are some of the more unexpected of those appellations.

1896: Self Contained
1898: Krajewski Pesant
1900: Quick
1902: Jaszkowiak
1903: Ripper, Wogglebug
1905: Sadd
1906: Wego, Merciless
1907: Yocum
1908: Skimabout
1909: Skidoodler
1911: Riddle
1913: Zip
1914: Motor Bob
1917: Chummy
1922: Flapper
1925: Mystery Car
1929: Little Mystery
1930: Cootie
1939: Tingle

Bibliography

Periodicals, Newspapers and Trade Journals

American Automobile Digest
Auto Era
Automobile
Automobile and Automotive Industries
Automobile and Motor Review
Automobile Quarterly
Automobile Topics
Automobile Trade Journal
Automotive Industries
Cleveland Leader
Cleveland Motorist
Cleveland Plain Dealer
Cleveland Press
Commercial and Financial World
Cycle and Automobile Trade Journal
Cyclecar Age
Electric World
Electric World and Engineering
Evening Herald (Norwalk, OH)
Horseless Age
Horseless Vehicles, Automobiles, Motor Cycles
Journal of the Cleveland Automobile Club
Life
Motor
Motor Age
Motor Vehicle Review
Motor World
New York Times
SAH Journal
Saturday Evening Post
Scientific American
Steam Motor Journal
Templar News
Templar Topics
Veteran and Vintage Magazine
Wall Street Journal

Books, Monographs, Correspondence and Reports

Alexander, Orion. Testimonial letter regarding Diamond tires. Published as an advertisement by Diamond Rubber Company, 1910.

Baker, Barbara P. *Steamy Dreamer*. Grand Junction, CO: Centennial, 1995.

Case, George. Letter to Lamson & Sessions Co., regarding Kirk-Latty Manufacturing Company construction of experimental vehicles, 1944.

Cleveland Automobile Club. *Automobile Route Book*. Cleveland, OH, 1924.

Cleveland Automobile Club. *Cleveland Automobile Show Program*. 1910.

Cleveland Automobile Club. *Road Map of North Eastern Ohio*, 1924. Cleveland, OH: Cleveland Automobile Club, 1924.

Cleveland Automobile Club, Emergency Service of the Cleveland Automobile Club. *Service Guide*, 1924.

Cleveland Directory Company. *Cleveland City Directory*. 1890; 1898 to 1902; 1904 to 1906.

Cram's Automotive Reports. *Hupp Motor Car Corporation*, 1929.

Cram's Automotive Reports. *Jordan Motor Car Company, Inc.*, 1929.

Historic American Engineering Record. HAER Reports 11-E, 11-G, 11-H. Washington, D.C.: U.S. Department of the Interior, Office of Archaeology and Historic Preservation Heritage Conservation and Recreation Service, 1978.

Jordan, Edward S. *The Inside Story of Adam and Eve*. New York: Howard Coggeshall, 1945.

Kimes, Beverly Rae, and Henry Austin Clark, Jr. *Standard Catalog of American Cars, 1805–1942*, 3d ed. Iola, WI: Krause, 1996.

Kimes, Beverly Rae, and James H. Cox. *Walter L. Marr: Buick's Amazing Engineer*. Boston: Racemaker, 2007.

Kirk-Latty Manufacturing Co. Internal memo regarding specifications for Automobile No. 3. November 28, 1903.

Lackey, James H. *The Jordan Automobile: A History*. Jefferson, NC: McFarland, 2005.

Lamoreaux, Naomi R., et al. *Financing Invention During the Second Industrial Revolution: Cleveland, Ohio, 1870–1920*. Cambridge, MA: National Bureau of Economic Research, 2004.

Manual of Cleveland and Northern Ohio Securities. Cleveland, OH: Borton, Bates, 1936.

McCarthy, J.J. *A History of the Knight Engine in America*. Hershey, PA: AACA Library and Research Center, 1921.

Moulton, E.H. [Testimonial]. Letter to the Cleveland Automobile Company. June 2, 1903.

Rauch & Lang. *The First Hundred Years of Rauch & Lang*. Cleveland, OH, 1953.

Rickenbacker, Edward V. *Rickenbacker*. Englewood Cliffs, NJ: Prentice-Hall, 1967.

Rose, William Ganson. *Cleveland: The Making of a City*. Kent, OH: Kent State University Press, 1990.

Saal, Thomas F., and Bernard J. Golias. *Famous but Forgotten*. Twinsburg, OH: Golias, 1997.

Spitzer, Doreen Canaday. *By One and One*. Canaan, NH: Phoenix, 1984.

Templar Motors Corporation. *To the Stockholders of the Templar Company*. 1920.

U.S. Census Bureau. *U.S. Census of Population, 1910*. Table 59: [Population of Places Having in 1910, 2,500 Inhabitants or More: 1910, 1900, 1890.]

Van Tassel, David D., and John J. Grabowski. *The Encyclopedia of Cleveland History*. Bloomington: Indiana University Press, 1987.

Wager, Richard. *Golden Wheels*. Cleveland, OH: John T. Zubal, 1986.

Worthington Manufacturing Company. History from Wikipedia citing *Horseless Age Magazine*, 1904, and *The Sun* (New York), August 1904.

Index

A. Howard Company 186
Abbott Corporation 10, 30, 31, 71
Abbott Motor Car Company 30
Acorn Automobile Company 145
Adams-Bagnall Electric Company 19
Adams Brothers 145
Advance Manufacturing Company 145, 213
Advance Motor Vehicle Company 145, 184
Aero (automobile) 233
Aerocar Company 31
Aetna Company 20
Ahrens-Fox Fire Engine Company 145
Akron, Ohio 144
Akron Bicycle Company 234
Akron Machine Company 145
Akron Motor Carriage Company 145
Albaugh, Gilbert 120
Alexander, Rob Roy 65
Allen, E. W. 145–146
Allen, W. O. 145–146
Alliance 146
Alliance (automobile) 146
Alliance Carriage Company 146
Alliance Motor Car Company 146
Allison, Robert 7
Allyn, E.E. 27, 31, 112
Allyn, Newton 225
Altenberg, George P. 146
Altman, Henry J. 31
Aluminum Manufacturers, Inc. 31–33
American (automobile) 233
American Automobile Company 33, 34
American Ball Bearing Company 9, 26, 34–36, 38, 119
American Bantam Car Company 233
American Bicycle Company 44, 66, 69, 119, 152, 188, 217
American Broc (automobile) 42

American Electric Car Company 42
American Foundry Company 191
American Gas (automobile) 33, 54
American Hydromobile Company 146
American Metal Wheel and Auto Company 146
American Motor Car Company 146
American Motor Carriage Company 33–34
American Motor Company 146, 170
American Steel and Wire Company 9
Amstutz-Osborn Company 34
Anchor Motor Car Company 146
Anderson, Leonard 146
Ann, C.O. 51
Apple (automobile) 146
Apple Motor Car Company 146
ArBenz (automobile) 147
ArBenz Car Company 147
Armstrong, Wayne 147
Arnstein, Harry 147
Arrow (automobile) 193
Arter, James G. 34
Arter Auto Carriage Company 20, 34
Auburn-Moore Special (automobile) 90
Aultman, Henry 147
Aultman Company 147
Auto-Bug (automobile) 147
Auto-Bug Company 147, 201
Auto Buggy (automobile) 187
Auto Lamp & Radiator Company 20
Auto Plating & Mfg. Company 19
Automobile & Cycle Parts 47
Automobile Carriage Supply Company 34
Automobile Club of America 21
Automobile Club of America Automobile Show, New York 208

Automobile Equipment Company 147
Automobile No. 3 (automobile) 83
Automotive Accessory and Radio Exposition 154
Automotive Corporation 147
Avery, Sewell 26

B & H (automobile) 42
Baker, "Cannonball" 128, 162
Baker, Hartley O. 38
Baker, John L. 147, 164
Baker, Newton D. 23
Baker, Walter C. 7, 9, 22, 26, 34–38, 93
Baker, William E. 38
Baker Electric (automobile) 12, 26, 34–38
Baker Motor Vehicle Company 12, 26, 28, 29, 34–38, 51, 105
Baker Motors, Inc. 38
Baker R&L Company 10, 17, 18, 38–39, 93, 105, 116
Baker Raulang (automobile) 38
Baker Runabout (automobile) 36
Baker Steam Car and Manufacturing Company 38
Baldner, Fred 147–148
Baldner, Jacob 147–148
Baldner Motor Vehicle Company 147–148
Barcus, Nemo 148
Barnes (automobile) 148
Barnes Manufacturing Company 148
Barringer, Irene 221
Battalion Roadster (automobile) 145
Beardsley & Hubbs Manufacturing Company 148
Becker, E.M. 118
Becker, H.V. 167
Behle, John 154
Bellaire Automobile Company 148
Bellefontaine (automobile) 148, 149

Bellefontaine Automobile Company 148, 167, 235
Bellefontaine Carriage Body Company 149
Belmont Motor Company 149
Belmont Six (automobile) 149
Belnap & Schwartz Company 185
Ben Hur Motor Company 149
Bender Body Company 17
Bennett, Harry 149
Benson, A.M. 58
Benson (automobile) 40
Benson Automobile Company 39–40, 58
Benz Spirit (automobile) 156
Berg (automobile) 40, 140
Berg, Hart O. 40
Berg Automobile Company 40, 140
Berger, Henry J. 88
Berger, J.A 149
Berger Manufacturing Company 149
Big Four Flyer (automobile) 147
Billings (automobile) 188
Bimel (automobile) 150
Bimel Buggy Company 150
Bing, J.M. 65
Bingham, Herbert 41
Bingham Manufacturing Company 41
Bingham Motor Car Company 41
Bissell Electric (automobile) 150
Bissell Electric Company 150
Blackiston (automobile) 150
Blackiston, G.P. 150
Blackwell, R.E. 119
Blair, Frank 159
Blair Manufacturing Company 150
Blair Motor Company 150
Blakeslee, C.J. 53
Blakeslee Electric (automobile) 53, 134
Blakeslee Electric Vehicle Company 41, 53
Blue Goose (automobile) 228
Blue Streak (automobile) 193
Bob-Cat (automobile) 193
Boden Brothers 20
Bolender, F.P. 150
Booth, Dr. Carlos C. 150
Borton, Eleanor 12
Bosley, R.H. 71
Boss (automobile) 193
Bowling Green Motor Car Company 150
Bowman, John 150
Bowman, Paul 150
Brackenridge, A.B. 69
Bradbury, George E. 51
Bradley, Alva 124
Bramley, F.M. 127
Bramwell (automobile) 158, 219
Bramwell, C.C. 219
Bramwell, W.C. 219

Bramwell-Robinson (automobile) 219
Breeze (automobile) 188
Bremac Motor Car Company 150, 151
Brenenstul, Mr. 151
Brenenstul & Carpenter 151
Brenning Brothers 151
Brew, Francis O. 41
Brew & Hatcher 41
Brew-Hatcher (automobile) 42
Brew-Hatcher Company 41, 42, 73
Brice Motor Car Company 151
Briggs Company 17
Briggs Manufacturing Company 18, 45
Broc Carriage and Wagon Company 17, 42, 89
Broc Electric (automobile) 42
Broc Electric Vehicle Company 42
Brockshire & Robinson Company 151
Brooks, James C. 31
Brotherhood of Locomotive Engineers 82
Brown Carriage Company 151
Browning, King & Company 20
Bruggemeter, C.F. 118
Brush (automobile) 42
Brush, Charles Francis 7, 8, 42
Brush Electric Company 42, 134
Buckboard (automobile) 90
Buckeye (automobile) 103, 104, 193, 201
Buckeye Engine Company 151
Buckeye Wagon & Motor Car Company 151
Buda engine 149
Buggy Car Company 151
Buggyabout (automobile) 184
Bullock Electric Manufacturing Company 151, 152
Bun, Hutchinson & Company 20
Burdett, Oliver 143, 152
Burnes, W.E. 50
Burwell George 152
Byrider (automobile) 54
Byrider, George 54
Byrider, John 54
Byrider, William 54
Byrider Electric Automobile Company 42, 53–54

C. Schmidt & Sons 27
Cabriolet (automobile) 116
Calhoun, T.J. 78
Cameron (automobile) 43
Cameron, Forrest F. 31, 42–43
Canaday, Ward 233
Canton Buggy Company 152
Canzol (automobile) 43
Car De Luxe (automobile) 166
Carl Electric Vehicle Company 152
Carling Brewing Company 27
Carpenter, Mr 151
Carrico, Mr. 152

Carrico Motor Company 152
Carroll Automobile Company 152, 153
Carroll Six (automobile) 152
Carthage (automobile) 153
Carthage Motor Car Company 153
Case Motor Car Company 153
Caswell, Harold 153
Caswell, Myron 153
Catrow, Herbert 153
Central Automobile Company 43
Cerma, William J. 139
Champion (automobile) 43
Champion Motor Car Company 43, 44
Chandler (automobile) 44, 45
Chandler, Frederick C. 44, 45, 71
Chandler, P.J. 153
Chandler-Cleveland Motors Corporation 18, 44, 46, 49, 77
Chandler Motor Car Company 11, 17, 18, 24, 44–50, 71
Chapman, C.A. 34
Chapman, William H. 71
Charles Behlen Sons Company 153
Charles Eckert Manufacturing Company 153
Charles Hanauer Cycle Company 153
Chester Rubber Tire & Tool Company 153
Chevrolet 233
Chicago Automobile Show 41, 43, 45, 47, 56, 65, 71, 182, 226, 228
Chicago Burlington & Quincy Railroad 26
Chicago Times-Herald Endurance Race 148, 158, 192
Chicago World's Fair (Columbian Exposition) 121, 208
Chrysler, Walter P. 231
Chrysler Corporation 27, 234
Chummy (automobile) 44, 167
Church, F.S. 153
Cincinnati Automobile Company 154
Cincinnati Automotive Trades Association 154
Cincinnati Motor Car Company 154
Cincinnati Motors Company 154
Cino (automobile) 182
Circleville Automobile Company 154
Clark, Albert F. 224
Clark, Robert 50
Clark & Company 46
Clark Electric (automobile) 224
Clark-Norwalk 46
Clark-Norwalk (automobile) 46
Cleveland (automobile) 45–50, 65, 71, 140
Cleveland, Beck, and Lyman Motor Corporation 49
Cleveland Auto Cab Company 154, 170, 179

Index

Cleveland Auto Sales & Manufacturing Company 46
Cleveland Automobile Club (CAC) 21, 22, 126
Cleveland Automobile Company 18, 45, 46–49, 50, 77
Cleveland Automobile Show 41, 42, 46, 65, 88, 90, 95, 96, 98, 118, 126, 147, 182, 226, 228
Cleveland Cap Screw Company 16, 117
Cleveland Chamber of Commerce 24
Cleveland-Columbus-Toledo Reliability Run 74
Cleveland Cycle Car Company 49, 50
Cleveland Electric (automobile) 52
Cleveland Electric Company 50
Cleveland Electric Vehicle Company 50, 52
Cleveland Machine Screw Company 16, 18, 19, 34, 40, 46–47, 51, 67, 119
Cleveland Motor Car Company 40, 50, 51, 140
Cleveland Motor Carriage Company 51
Cleveland Motor Company 103
Cleveland Motor Plow Company 112
Cleveland National Air Races 43
Cleveland Roadster (automobile) 47
Cleveland Six (automobile) 47–48
Cleveland Speed Indicator Company 20
Cleveland Tractor Company 27, 112, 133, 140, 141
Cleveland Trinidad Paving Company 127
Clyde Cars Company 154
Coats (automobile) 154
Coats, George A. 221
Coats Steam Car Company 154, 155
Cobra engine 162
USS Cod (submarine) 26
Coe, Adelbert Brown 143, 155
Collins, Richard H. 26, 102
Colonial (automobile) 156
Colonial Carriage Company 155, 156
Colonial Motors 156
Colt, William 140
Columbia Carriage Company 156
Columbia Motor Buggy (automobile) 156
Columbia Vehicle Company 156
Columbus (automobile) 213
Columbus Automobile Company 156
Columbus Automobile Show 216
Columbus Brass Company 156
Columbus Buggy Company 156, 158, 219

Columbus Carriage and Harness Company 158
Columbus Electric (automobile) 156, 158
Columbus Motor Vehicle Company 181
Commercial Motor Car Company 158
Conklin, Oliver F. 158
Consolidated Car Corporation 30
Consolidated Manufacturing Company 158, 191
Consolidated Motor Car Company 24, 51, 114, 158
Continental engine 9, 81, 87, 88, 102, 152, 226, 227
Cook, C.E. 158
Cook, James M. 158
Cooney & Company 159
Cooney Electric (automobile) 159
Cootie (automobile) 164
Corrigan McKinney Steel Company 9
Coshocton Motor Car Company 159
Courier (automobile) 159, 214
Courier Car Company 159, 222
Courier Motors 159, 195
Covered Wagon (automobile) 162
C.R. Patterson & Sons 152
Craig-Toledo (automobile) 160
Craig-Toledo Motor Company 159, 160
Crane & Breed Manufacturing Company 160, 162
Crawford, John 193
Crawford-Hough Garage Company 51
Credlebaugh, H.S. 162
Crescent (automobile) 188
Crescent Motor Company 188
C.R.G. Special (automobile) 180
Criterion Motor Company 191
Crock Motor Company 162
Cron & Sons Company 162
Crosley (automobile) 162
Crosley, Powel, Jr. 144, 162, 166, 184, 195
Crosley Corporation 162–164
Croxton (automobile) 51
Croxton, Herbert A. 51, 64
Croxton-Keeton Motor Car Company 51, 52, 164
Croxton Motor Company 51, 114, 164
Crum, Fred 90
Cummins-Monitor Company 164
Curtin & Schille 164
Curtis Aircraft Company 231
Custer Specialty Company 164
Cuyahoga Electric (automobile) 52
Cuyahoga Motor Car Company 52
cyclecars 29, 49, 57, 59, 60, 66, 76, 83, 118, 147, 148, 151, 154, 162, 166, 179, 181, 184, 193, 196, 197, 201, 208, 223, 226
Cyclomobile (automobile) 183
Cyclomobile Manufacturing Company 183
Cyriacks Motor Company 164

Darling (automobile) 148, 164
Darling, R.R. 148
Darling Motor Company 164
Davies, Charles H. 66
Davis, A.V. 31
Davis, D.L. 164
Davis Motor Car Company 52
Dayton Automobile Company (1906) 164
Dayton Automobile Company (1911) 164
Dayton Automobile Show 146
Dayton Electric (automobile) 166
Dayton Electric Car Company 164, 166
Dayton Motor Car Company 221
Dayton Motor Vehicle Company 166
Dean, Arthur M. 116
DeCharmes, Alice 147
DeCross (automobile) 196
De Cross Cy-Car (automobile) 162, 166, 196
De Dion (automobile) 98
De Dion-Bouton (automobile) 206
Defiance Carriage Company 200
Defiance 40 (automobile) 200
De Gallier, E.P. 52
De Luxe Motor Car Company (1906) 53, 166
De Luxe Motor Car Company (1910) 52
De Luxe Two-Wheeler (automobile) 52
DeMars, William O. 53
DeMars Electric (automobile) 53
DeMars Electric Vehicle Company 53, 54
De Mooy Brothers 54
Denneen Motor Company 10, 68
Dennis Motor Company 166
Derain (automobile) 54, 55
Derain Motor Company 54, 118
DeTamble (automobile) 188
Detroit Automobile Show 90, 166
Dickey, C.B. 41
Differential Steel Car Company 166
Disbrow (automobile) 55
Disbrow, Louis A. 54, 56
Disbrow Motors Corporation 10, 54–57
Disbrow Quad (armored car) 57
Ditwiler Manufacturing Company 166
Dolan, C.M. 69
Dolnar, Hugh 73
Dorman, Frank D. 33, 51

Doty, Raymond C. 52
Downing (automobile) 57
Downing Motor Car Company 57
Drabek, Charles 51
Drown, W.D. 89
Drury-Wells Motor Company 166
D.T. Williams Valve Company 164
Duck (amphibious vehicle) 187
Dum, Ed 166
Dum, Harley 166
Dumont (automobile) 182
Dunham, George W. 51
Dunk, A.O. 219
Dunkle, Ralph W. 166
Durabile (automobile) 34
Durant, William C. 167, 170–171
Duryea, Charles 147, 148
Dusseau (automobile) 166
Dusseau Fore and Rear Drive Automobile Company 166

E.A. Hammer Company 58
Eagle & Vincent Automobile Company 167
Eagle-Macomber Motor Car Company 167
Early Motor Car Company 167
Eastern Automobile Company 167
Eastman, Henry F. 39, 58
Eastman Automobile Company 17, 58, 59
Eastman Electro-Cycle (automobile) 58
Eastman Metallic Body Company 8, 17, 58
Eaton Corporation 16
Eckenroth, Harry S. 59
Eckenroth, Peter L. 59
Eckenroth, Rudolph H. 59
Eckenroth Automobile Livery Company 59
Eckert, Charles 167
Eclipse Machine Company 103
Eclipse Manufacturing Company 167
Economy (automobile) 167
Economy Motor Car Company 148, 167
Economy-Vogue (automobile) 167
Edison, Thomas 36
Edw. G. Budd Mfg. Co. 81
Edwards, H.J. 222
Edwards Motor Car Company 231
Elco (automobile) 150
electric cars 7, 28, 33, 34–39, 41, 42, 50, 52, 53, 54, 58, 59, 77, 98, 103, 105, 118, 119, 126, 134, 155, 156, 159, 164, 185, 189, 192, 193, 196, 198, 200, 202, 208, 213, 214, 218, 222–224, 227
Elliott, H.E. 167
Elliott & Lang 167
Elmer, Harry 67
Elmore (automobile) 167
Elmore Manufacturing Company 167

Elwell-Parker Electric Company 59, 98
Elwood, Harry H. 198
Elyria Auto Sales Company 170
Emerson, Victor L. 170
Enger, Frank J. 170
Enger Motor Car Company 170
Entz transmission 93
Erie (automobile) 170
Erie Motor Car Company 170, 226
Erie Supply Company 170
Euclid (automobile) 40, 41, 59
Euclid Avenue Automobile Company 59
Euclid Motor Car Company 59
Evans, Oliver 5
Evans-Eich Manufacturing Company 170
Ewing (automobile) 154
Ewing, Levi Edward 154, 170
Ewing Automobile Company 170–171, 179

Falcon (automobile) 59, 60, 173, 182
Falcon Cycle Car Company 59–60
Falcon-Knight (automobile) 173, 233
Falcon Motors Corporation 171–173, 233
Falls Garage Company 173
F.A.M. (automobile) 63
Farmobile (automobile) 173
Farmobile Manufacturing Company 173
F.B. Stearns & Company 121–124
F.B. Stearns Company 26, 28, 121–124
F.C. Pinyoun & Son 20
Fedelia Cycle Car 60
Federal Manufacturing Company 18, 19, 40, 51, 140
Ferris (automobile) 91, 92
Ferris, William E. 92, 93
Ferro engine 167
Ferro Machine & Foundry Company 17
Fetzger Automobile Manufacturing Company 173
F.H. Bultman Company 43
F.I. Burke 20
Findlay (automobile) 173
Findlay Carriage Company 173
Findlay Motor Car Company 173, 179
Firestone-Columbus (automobile) 158, 219
Fisher Body Division, General Motors Corporation 16, 45, 144
Fisher Brothers 18
Flynn, Walter F. 173
Fogarty, F.M. 69
Foley & Williams Manufacturing Company 173
Foos Gas Engine Company 173–174

Ford, Henry 61, 148, 159
Ford Model A 62
Ford Model B 62
Ford Model T 61, 62, 87
Ford Motor Company 11, 16, 18, 60–62, 77, 233
Fordyce, J.O. 69
Forest City (automobile) 62
Forest City Motor Car Company 62, 174
Forth, Clarence 174
Forth Motor Car Company 174
Fostoria (automobile) 174, 216
Fostoria Foundry and Machine Company 174
Fostoria Light Car Company 174, 216
Fostoria Motor Car Company 174
Frayer, Lee A. 204
Frayer-Miller automobile 183, 204
Frazer (automobile) 233
Frazer, Joseph 233
Fredonia Carriage and Manufacturing Company 150
Fredonia Manufacturing Company 175–176
Freeman Motor Car Company 62
Fremont (automobile) 176
Fremont Motors Corporation 176
French-American Motor Company 62
Frey-Shecker Company 176

Gabriel (automobile) 63
Gabriel Auto Company 19, 63, 64
Gabriel Company 9, 16
Gaeth (automobile) 64, 65, 67, 125
Gaeth, Paul 7, 64, 103
Gaeth Automobile Company 64, 65, 125
Gail, Henry R. 51
Gaither Auto Company 176
Gallagher, G.R. 51
Garford (automobile) 176
Garford, Arthur L. 19
Garford Company 18, 19, 51, 176–179, 231
Garrison Machine Works 179
Gas Engine and Appurtenance Company 65
Gates Mills (Ohio) Hill Climb 89
Gatts (automobile) 179
Gatts, Alfred Palmer 179
General (automobile) 65
General Automobile and Manufacturing Company 65, 66, 72
General Automobile Company 65, 66
General Electric Company 9, 31, 93
General Motors Corporation 11, 16, 18, 25, 45, 144
General Motors Electromotive Division 26
General Tire and Rubber Company 164

Index

Geneva (automobile) 179
Geneva Automobile & Manufaturing Company 179
Geo. A. Rutherford Company 20
George C. Miller Sons' Carriage Company 179
Geyer Sales Company 179
Gilford, George 179
Gillie, William H. 41
Githens (automobile) 66
Githens, Herbert A. 66
Githens Brothers, Inc. 66
Glenwood Motor Car Company 179
Glidden Tour 64, 132
Globe Four (automobile) 66
Globe Machine & Stamping Company 19
Globe Motor Company 66
Goby (automobile) 66
Goby, G.S. 66, 67
Goby engine 66
Goddard, Wilford 179
Goddard, Winfred 179
Godfrey, W.R. 86
Goldenbogen, A.F. 118
Gongwer, W.D. 124
Goodrich (automobile) 173
Goodrich, C.C. 218
Gormully, Philip 217
Gotham (automobile) 215
Grace, F. 52
Gramm, Benjamin A. 193
Gramm-Logan Motor Car Company 193
Grane Brothers 179
Grant (automobile) 173
Grant, John J. 5, 7, 8, 27, 67, 143
Grant-Lees Machine Company 67, 125
Grant Motor Car Company 10, 67–69
Grant Motor Company 173, 179, 180
Grant Six (automobile) 67, 68
Great Eagle (automobile) 225
Green Dragon race car 101
Green Engineering Company 180, 181
Greyhound (automobile) 181
Greyhound Cyclecar Company 181
Groff-Runkle Motor Vehicle Company 181, 182
Guide Motor Lamp Manufacturing Company 19
Gulliford, George 182
Gunderman, George V. 52
Guthrie, Bernard 89
Guthrie, Irwin 89
Guthrie, James 164

H.A. Lozier Company 10, 44, 69–71
Haberer & Company 182
Habig, Harry 71
Hackenthal, Paul F. 96
Hahn, J.C. 140
Hal Motor Car Company 31, 69–71
H.A.L. TWELVE (automobile) 70, 71
Halladay Motor Car Company 182
Hallady Motors Corporation 182–183
Hallock, T.P. 71
Hallock Engineering Company 71
Hamel, Charles D. 183
Hamilton, Harry H. 86
Hamilton Vehicle Company 183
H&H Auto Company 69
Hanford, George 7, 109
Hansen (automobile) 72
Hansen, Rasmus 71
Hansen Automobile Company 65, 71, 72
Hanson Car Company 17
Harding, Frank J. 72
Harding Motor Car Company 72, 73
Harmer, Frederick S. 183
Harmer Automobile Company 183
Harris Automatic Press Company 183
Harruff, J.W. 183
Hatcher, Bert 208
Hatcher, William A. 41
Hatfield Motor Vehicle Company 145, 184
Hawkins Cyclecar Company 148, 184
Haydock Motor Car Company 184
Hayes, H. Jay 58
H.B. Wick & Company 182
Healy, Caleb E. 143, 184
Heatherman-Soliday Motor Company 184
Heilman, John C. 184
Henry Ford Museum 32, 179
Henry J (automobile) 234
Herman Motor Company 184
Hermes (automobile) 162, 184
Hermes Motor Car Company 184
Herschel-Spillman engine 85
Highway Motors Company 184
highwheel cars 145, 147, 156, 179, 184, 187, 188, 211, 215, 217, 218, 219
Hinde, J.J. 159
Hines (automobile) 73
Hines, William R. 73, 74
Hines Car Company 73, 74
Hitchcock Motor Car Company 185
Hitchcroft, D.G. 77
H.J. Walker Company 17
H.J. Walker Manufacturing Company 68
Hodgkins, R.T. 140
Hoffman (automobile) 75
Hoffman, Jacob 77
Hoffman, Louis 74, 75
Hoffman, William G. 75, 76

Hoffman Automobile and Manufacturing Company 74, 75, 113
Hoggett, T.H. 119
Hollis Electric (automobile) 185
Hollis Tractor Company 185
Holmes (automobile) 185
Holmes, Arthur 185
Holmes Automobile Company 185, 186
Holtom (automobile) 154
Holtom, Hal 154
Hopkins, E.V.K. 59
Horseless Carriage Company 186
Horstman Auto Top Company 20
Houser, Orville E. 186
Howard (automobile) 186
Howard, Adam 186
Howard Motor Car Company 186
Howe, F.C. 31
Hoyes, W.H. 50
Hoyt, Francis R. 76
Huehne, E.A. 186
Huntington, Harry 12
Hupmobile (automobile) 46, 76, 77
Hupp, Robert C. 76
Hupp Motor Car Corporation 11, 18, 25, 46, 76–77
Hutchcroft & Sons Company 77
H.W. Fenker Company 182
Hydraulic Pressed Steel Company 16, 56
Hydro Engineering Company 186
Hydro Motor Car Company 186
Ideal Commercial Car Company 186
Ideal Light Car Company 186
Ideal Manufacturing Company 187

I.H.C.(automobile) 188
Imperial (automobile) 213
Independence Motor Car Company 187
Indian Motor Car Company 187
Indianapolis 500 Automobile Race 56, 222
International Harvester Company 187, 188
International Motor Car Company 188
Inter-Ocean Automobile Show 126
Interstate Supply Company 188

J. Keller Electric Works 77, 189
Jacob Hoffman Wagon Company 77, 78, 134
Jeep (automobile) 144, 233
Jeffery, Thomas B. 148, 217
Jewel (automobile) 51, 174
Jewel Carriage Company 188
Jewel Motor Car Company 51, 174
Jewell (automobile) 62, 174
Jewell Carriage Company 188
Jewett Motor Carriage Company 188

J.H. Louis Automobile Company 188
John Kohl Carriage & Automobile Company 188
John Schilito Company 188
Johnson-Jennings Company 78
Jones, C.H. 188
Jones, Isaac B. 189
Jordan, Edward "Ned" S. 4, 9, 11, 12, 78–82
Jordan Motor Car Company, Inc. 78, 80, 83
Jordan Motor Car Company 10, 11, 24, 29, 78–80, 83
Jordan Motors, Inc. 78, 82, 83
Joy, Henry B. 208

Kahn, Albert 18, 61, 124
Kaiser (automobile) 233
Kaiser, Henry J. 233, 234
Kaiser Jeep Company 234
Kaiser Motors 233
Kaiser-Willys Company 233
Kauffman (automobile) 184
Kauffman Buggy Company 145, 184
Kauffman Motor Car Company 145
Keeton, Forest M. 51, 164
Keller Electrical Shops 77, 189
Kelly, George H. 119
Kent, A.W. 189
Kepler-Beery Motor Car Company 189, 191
Kero-Car (automobile) 191
Kero-Car Motor Company 191
Kessell, Frank E. 191
Kettering, Charles 185
Keystone (automobile) 226
Keystone Vehicle Company 191
Kimmel, R.E. 71
Kimple, George W. 83
King Cyclecar Company 83
Kinnear Manufacturing Company 191
Kirk-Hall Company 191
Kirk-Latty Manufacturing Company 83
Kirk Manufacturing Company 191
Kirkpatrick, J.K. 52
kit cars 103, 223
Kitto, A.W. 191
Kleybolts, Albert 184
Knight sleeve-valve engine 123, 124, 172, 177, 220, 222, 223, 228–231
Kocian, Joseph 139
Koeb, Emil 191
Koeb-Thompson 191
Koeb-Thompson Motor Company 191
Kohl, Edward 83
Kohl & Gates Motor Company 83
Konigslow, Otto 73, 74, 92, 93
Krastin (automobile) 84
Krastin, August 84

Krastin Automobile Manufacturing Company 83, 84
Krebs, Mr. 191
Krotz, Alvaro S. 191
Krotz-Defiance Auto Buggy Company 192
Krotz Electric Buggy (automobile) 192
Krotz Manufacturing Company 191–192
Kuntz Company 17
Kuqua & Son 192
Kurtz, Cyrus B. 84–85
Kurtz, Theodore 47
Kurtz Automatic (automobile) 85
Kurtz automatic transmission 85
Kurtz Motor Car Company 17, 84, 85
Kurtzner Radiator Company 20

Lakewood (automobile) 215
Lakewood Chemical Company 20
LaMarne Motor Company 85, 86, 109
Lambert, John William 192
Lamson & Sessions Company 16
Landefeld, Bert F. 88
Landmann-Griffith 192
Lang, Charles W. 17, 105, 167
Lang, E.J. 17
Lang Body Company 17
Lautermilch, Florence A. 65
Lawrence Stamping Company 192
L.B. Smyser & Company 182
Le Roi engine 151, 174
Leach Automobile Company 192
League of American Wheelmen 21
Lear, Oscar 204
Lecklider, A.E. 192
Lee, Richard H. 51
Lehr Agricultural Company 192
Lemmon, C.A. 52
Lemmon, C.M. 34
Leon Rubay (automobile) 116
Leon Rubay Company 114
Lepp Brothers 192
Levy, S.M. 86
Lewis, I.H. 126
Liberty Bell Company 19
Lima Light Car Company 193
Lima Roadster (automobile) 146
Lincoln Electric Company 69, 86
Little Custom (automobile) 81, 82
Little Custom Tomboy (automobile) 13
Loeb, H. 88
Logan (automobile) 193, 201
Logan Construction Company 193
Lohse, R. 86
Lohse Automobile Improvement Company 86
Long, J.E. 193
Long-Crawford Automobile Company 193
Lorain Motor Carriage Company 193

Louisiana Purchase Exposition 105
Lozier (automobile) 152
Lozier, Henry A. 69
Lozier, Henry A., Jr. (Harry) 69
Lozier Bicycle Company 152
Lozier Brothers Company 70
Lozier Motor Company 69
Lunken, Edmund 193
Lunkenheimer Motor Vehicle Company 193
Lutz (automobile) 193
Lutz, Henry 193
Lycoming engine 85

MacAdams Company 20
MacDonald, Duncan 193
MacDonald Steam Automobile Company 193
MacInnis Brothers 193
Maclaren, Don P. 86
Maclaren Company 86
Mahoning (automobile) 195
Mahoning Motor Car Company 195
Maibohm (automobile) 159, 195
Maibohm, Peter C. 195
Maibohm Motors Company 159, 195
Mansfield Motor Vehicle Company 148
Marathon (automobile) 162
Marathon Automobile Company 195, 196
Marathon Six (automobile) 195–196
Marion Automobile Company 196
Markert, F.G.R. 196
Marr, Walter L. 7, 33, 34, 89
Marsh (automobile) 43, 226
Marsh, Alonzo 86, 225
Marsh, William 86, 146
Marsh Motors Company 86, 87
Martin, Clyde 59
Marysville Motor Car Company 196
Massillon Developing Company 196
Massillon Six (automobile) 226
Master Motor Car Company 87
May, A.F. 54, 118
M.C. Witmore Company 193
McAdams, John 196
McAleenan, M.G. 119
McCauley Storage Battery Company 19
McIlrath, Benson 59
McIlrath, Wade 59
McIlrath, Webster 59
McIntosh Brothers 87
McLouth, L.P. 39
McNutt, John 197
Meacham, S.H. 77
Mead Engine Company 197
Meader, J.C. 91
Meeker Manufacturing Company 197

Index

Mel Special (automobile) 125
M.E.L. Stringer (automobile) 125
Mercer (automobile) 96
Mercury Motor Car Company 87, 88
Merit (automobile) 88
Merit Motor Company 88
Merkel, Joseph 197
Mertz, William 77
Meteor (automobile) 50, 140, 197
Meteor Motor Car Company 197, 198
Metropol (automobile) 86, 107
Metropol Motors Corporation 107
Metropolitan Garage Company 88
Miami Cycle and Manufacturing Company 198
Miami engine 198
Middletown Buggy Company 198
Middletown Machine Company 198
Midgley Manufacturing Company 198
Milburn (automobile) 198–200
Milburn Wagon Company 198
Mileage Motor Six (automobile) 49
Military (automobile) 170
Miller, George J. 200
Miller, J.W. 200
Miller, William J. 204
Miller Machine Company 200
Millersville (automobile) 200
Millersville Machine Company 200
Minch, Captain Philip J. 88, 89
Moehlhauser Machine Company 73
Monarch Motor Car Company 42, 89, 90
Monitor (automobile) 164, 201
Monitor Motor Car Company 164, 200, 201
Monnot, George 186
Montgomery Ward & Company 26
Moore, A.L. 46
Moore, Frank J. 139
Moore, Harry S. 90, 120
Morgan, Garrett 9
Morris, John T. 51
Morrison, Fred 90, 91
Motor Cycle Company 103
Motor Storage and Manufacturing Company 201
Motorette (automobile) 98
Motz, Charles A. 201
Moulton, E.H., Jr. 47
Moyea (automobile) 201
Moyea Automobile Company 201
Much, C.P. 226
Mulvahy, C. 88
Murray Corporation 151
Murray Ohio Manufacturing Company 81
Myers. Fred C. 225

Napoleon Motor Car Company 201, 212
National Carbon Company 9
National Cash Register Company 78, 164
National Juvenile Auto Company 201
National Screw & Tack Company 73
National United Service Company 147
Neil, Ed 201
New Columbus Buggy Company 156
New Concord Automobile Company 201
New York and Pittsburgh Reliability Run 176
New York Automobile Show 65, 70, 81, 88, 93, 113, 138, 146, 148, 149, 151, 154, 179, 182, 186, 226, 228
New York City Grand Palace 182
New York-Cleveland-Pittsburgh Endurance Run 211
New York-to-Boston Reliability Run 176
Nichols, Andrew B. 65
Niles Auto & Machine Company 201
Niswender, Roman 201
Noble Automobile Manufacturing Company 91
Northup, Amos 151
Northway, Ralph 188
Norwalk (automobile) 46, 147
Norwalk Motor Car Company 46, 147, 201, 202
Norwood Automobile Company 202
Nungesser Carbon & Battery Company 19

O'Brian, J.W. 225
Odelot (automobile) 192
Ogontz Motor Car Company 202
Ohio (automobile) 208
OhiO (automobile) 188
Ohio Automobile Company 205
Ohio Electric (automobile) 202, 204
Ohio Electric Car Company 202
Ohio Motor Car Company 188
Ohio Motor Vehicle Company 91, 92
Ohio Universal Truck Company 204
O.K. Gas Engine Company 146
Okey, Perry 204
Okey Motor Car Company 204
Okey Runabout (automobile) 204
Oldfield, Barney 85
Olds Motor Vehicle Company 95
Only (automobile) 86, 107
Orndorf, Harry W. 59
O.S. Kelly Corporation 202

Osborn-Morgan Company 34
Oscar Lear Automobile Company 173, 183, 204, 205
Otis, Mrs. Kenneth 123
Otis Steel Company 9
Otto Konigslow Manufacturing Company 92, 93
Ottokar (automobile) 92
Overland (automobile) 231, 233
Overland Auto Company 144, 211, 228
Owen (automobile) 95
Owen, Ralph R. 93, 94, 123
Owen, Raymond M. 7, 38, 93, 94, 123
Owen Magnetic (automobile) 10, 26, 38, 93
Owen Magnetic Company 38, 93, 94
Owen Motor Carriage Company 93, 95
Owens, H.E. 205, 223
Oxford (automobile) 174

Packard (automobile) 144, 208, 224
Packard, James Ward 144, 205, 206, 208
Packard, William 206, 208
Packard & Weiss 41, 205–208
Packard Electric Company 206, 208
Packard Motor Car Company 205–208
Paine, H.S. 208, 216
Palmer, Herbert R. 59, 95, 96
Palmer Automobile Manufacturing Company 95, 96
Paragon (automobile) 96
Paragon Motor Car Company 96, 97
Paris Exposition Universelle 105, 119
Park Drop Forge 17
Park Motors Company 208
Parsons, John G. 98
Parsons Electric Motor Carriage Company 97, 98
Patterson, Frederick Douglas 6, 144, 152
Patterson Body Company 140
Patterson-Greenfield (automobile) 144, 152
Peerless Manufacturing Company 7, 98–99, 103
Peerless Motor Car Company 11, 24, 26–28, 72, 73, 98–103
Peerless Truck & Motor Company 102
Pendleton (automobile) 224
Pendleton, William C. 224
Pennington, Edward Joel 103
Penton, E.W. 103
Penton Motor Company 103
People's Automobile Company 103, 104

Perfection Spring Company 16
Philion, Achille 208, 209
Phoenix (automobile) 95
Picard, T.W. 213
Pierce-Arrow Motor Car Company 32
Pierce Supply Company 104
Pilliod, Charles J. 209
Pilliod Motor Company 209
Pilliod sleeve-valve engine 209
Pioneer Motor Car Company 209
Piqua Motor Company 209
Playboy (automobile) 12–13, 80
Plymouth (automobile) 209
Plymouth Motor Truck Company 209, 210
Pomeroy (automobile) 32, 43
Pomeroy, Lawrence H. 31, 43
Pope, Albert A. 44, 69, 119
Pope Motor Car Company 188, 210, 211, 231
Pope-Toledo (automobile) 188, 210, 211
Portage Hotel 21
Portsmouth Automobile & Machine Company 211
Post, Charles Bushnell 211
Poste Brothers Buggy Company 211
Potts, J.F. 103
Powercar Automobile Company 211
Presidential yacht 26
Presidents, U.S. 26, 132, 200, 213
Prince Motor Car Company 211
Prospect (automobile) 234

Quigley, W.I. 88

Radford, William H. 174
Ragan, Brown & Lange Company 211
Ralph Temple & Austin Company 43
Ramapaugh (automobile) 198
Rambler (automobile) 148
Rauch, Jacob 105
Rauch & Lang Carriage Company 17, 26, 28, 38, 105
Rauch & Lang Electric (automobile) 38–39, 105
Rauch & Lang, Inc. 39
Rauder, W.G. 86
Raulang Electric (automobile) 38
Raymond, C.M. 66
R.C.H. (automobile) 76
Rees, John Howard 211
Rees Motor Company 211
Reidel, H.M. 69
Reitz, M. 86
Reive-Thompson Motor Company 211
Relay Motors Corporation 212
Republic (automobile) 212
Republic Motor Car Company 212
Republic Steel 149

Research Engineering Company 212
Reya (automobile) 213
Reya Motor Company 212, 213
Rhoades, W.C. 41
Richard, Francois 85, 105, 107, 109
Richard (automobile) 106, 107
RiChard (automobile) 86, 107, 109
Richard Auto Manufacturing Company 86, 105–109
RiChard Magnetic (automobile) 107
Richie, William 145
Richland Buggy Company 213
Rickenbacker, Eddie 56, 158, 205
Riddle (automobile) 213
Riddle Manufacturing Company 213
Ringle, Charles M. 118
Ritchie, William 213
R.M. Owen Company 26, 95
Robe (automobile) 226
Roberts, O.G. 213
Roberts engine 213
Roberts Motor Manufacturing Company 213
Rochester-Duesenberg engine 87
Rockefeller, John D. 9, 20, 208
Rockefeller, William 208
Rodgers & Company 213
Rogers, Frank W. 7, 109
Rogers, George D. 109
Rogers, Lewis 126
Rogers & Hanford Company 109
Rogers & Thatcher (automobile) 109
Rogers & Thatcher Automobile Company 109
Rolfe, Charles A. 52
Rollin (automobile) 110–112, 141
Rollin Motors Company 27, 109–112
Rolls Royce engines 124
Rossel Motor Car Company 213
rotary engine 92, 109
Royal (automobile) 188
Royal Motor Car & Manufacturing Company 112–114
Royal Motor Car Company 51, 75, 112–114
Royal Tourist (automobile) 75, 113
Royal Tourist Car Company 112–114, 123
R.R. Owen Machine Shop 95
Rubay, Leon 114
Rubay Company 17, 18, 29, 114–117, 125
Rudolph, W.J. 31
Ruhl, James B. 34
Ruse, Cordy 213
Russell (automobile) 117
Russell, C.W. 151, 213
Russell, E.L. 117
Russell & Company 213
Russell Motor Vehicle Company 117

Russell-Springfield (automobile) 151, 213
Ryder, B. 86

S. Toomey Company 214
Saf-T-Cab Corporation 117
Sakhnoffsky, Alexis 102
Salem (automobile) 151
Sanborn, R.W. 86
S&S (automobile) 215
Sandusky (automobile) 214
Sandusky Auto Parts & Motor Truck Company 214
Sandusky Automobile Company 214, 215
Sandusky Automobile Manufacturing Company 214
Santos-Dumont (automobile) 181
Saur, Frank 118
Sayers (automobile) 215
Sayers & Scoville Company 215
Schacht (automobile) 215
Schacht Manufacturing Company 215, 216
Schacht Motor Car Company 215
Scharf Gearless Motor Car Company 216
Schied, C.F. 41
Schlaudecker & Company 20
Schmidt, J.A. 118
Schultz, Olga 71
Schurmer, Edward D. 113
Schwab, M. 88
Schworm, Melville F. 143, 216
Scientific Heater Company 20
Scioto Car Company 146
Scott, R.P. 216
Seagrave Company 216
Sebring (automobile) 216
Sebring Motor Car Company 216
Selden patent 65
Seneca (automobile) 216
Seneca Motor Company 174, 216, 217
Servitor (automobile) 148
Shelby (automobile) 148
Shelby Motor Car Company 148
Shelby Stove & Manufacturing Company 217
Sherbondy, Earl H. 54, 118
Sherbondy, William E. 54, 118
Sherbourne, Edward H. 65
Sherman, H.S. 103
Sherwin-Williams Paint Company 9
Shipley, Otto M. 226
Shrum, J. 217
Shunk Plow Company 217
Silent Knight engine *see* Knight sleeve-valve engine
Simplex Manufacturing Company 54, 118
Simplex Zip (automobile) 56
Sipe & Sigler Company 118, 134
Sixth City Machine Company 118
Sizelan, John H. 60

Index

Skadden, Arthur E. 147, 202
Skeel, Ray C. 118
Skidoodler (automobile) 217
Sly, Ethan E. 218
Smelser, Luther W. 218
Smith, George H. 119
Smith, Joe 146
Smith Bicycle, Automobile & Light Machinery Company 218
Smith-Eggers Company 218
Smith Motor Wheel 183
Snyder (automobile) 118
Snyder, Alonzo 124
Snyder, G.J. 119
Snyder Motor & Manufacturing Company 118, 119
Sommer Motor Company 218
Spahr, Otto 218
Special (automobile) 119
Special Motor Vehicle Company 119
Specialty Carriage Company 218
Speedwell (automobile) 218
Speedwell Motor Car Company 218, 219
Spencer (automobile) 212
Spencer Manufacturing Company 219
Sperry, Elmer A. 7, 25, 119
Sperry Electric (automobile) 119
Sperry Electric Company 25
Sperry Engineering Company 119
Sperry gyroscope 119
Sperry Rand Company 119
Springfield (automobile) 219
Springfield Automobile & Industrial Company 219
Springfield Automobile Company 158, 219
Springfield Machine & Tool Company 219
Squires Company 86
Standard Automobile Company 119, 120, 219
Standard Motive Power Company 219
Standard Motor Parts 31
Standard Oil Company 9, 10, 20
Standard Parts Company 26
Standard Top & Equipment Company 20
Stanley (automobile) 224
Stanley, James 224
Star (automobile) 90
Star Automobile Company 90, 120
Star Motor Car Company 219
steam cars 5, 7, 28, 29, 38, 51, 58, 66, 67, 109, 130, 140, 143, 147, 152, 153, 154, 166, 179, 184, 186, 188, 189, 193, 195, 196, 198, 202, 205, 208, 216, 218, 221, 224, 226, 234
Stearns, Frank B. 4, 7, 22, 24, 26, 49, 69, 71, 85, 121–124
Stearns-Knight (automobile) 26, 123, 124

Sterling, J.G. 124
Sterling engine 174
Sterling-Knight (automobile) 125, 220
Sterling-Knight Company 220, 221
Sterling Motor Company 124, 125
Stewart Motor Car Company 154, 155, 221
Stiverson, Frank E. 125
Stiverson Motor Car Company 125
Stock Exchanges 11
Stoddard, Charles G. 222
Stoddard, John W. 222
Stoddard-Dayton (automobile) 159, 222
Stoddard Manufacturing Company 221, 222
Stover Motor Car Company 222
Stringer, John W. 222
Stringer, Mel 125
Stringer Automobile Company 222
Strong, Edwin L. 126
Strong & Rogers (automobile) 126
Studebaker Brothers Manufacturing Company 65, 176
Studebaker-Stutz, Harry C. 3, 6, 222
Stutz Manufacturing Company 222
Stuyvesant (automobile) 125
Stuyvesant, Frank E. 125
Stuyvesant Four (automobile) 67
Stuyvesant Motor Car Company 65, 67, 125
Stuyvesant Six (automobile) 67
Suburban (automobile) 51
Summit Automobile Company 222
Sumner, Harry 222
Sun (automobile) 147
Superior Automobile Company 126
Supreme Motors Corporation 66, 125, 127
Sweney, Busby P. 222, 223
Swope Garage and Machine Company 223
Sypher Manufacturing Company 223

Tanner-Hower Manufacturing Company 223
Tarkington, H. 196, 223
Taylor, Will 223
Templar (automobile) 96, 128, 129
Templar Motor Car Company 129
Templar Motors Corporation 10, 127–129
Thatcher, A.Q. 109
Thomas, J.V. 124
Thomas B. Jeffery Company 78
Thomas Manufacturing Company 205, 223
Thompson, C.E. 117
Thompson, Ralph P. 191

Thornton, William W. 77
Thre-Dor (automobile) 167
Thresher Electric Company 223
Tillotson, Harry 223
tire companies 144
Todd Manufacturing Company 223
Toledo (automobile) 188
Toledo Auto and Garage Company 223
Toledo Auto-Cycle Car Company 223
Toledo Electric Vehicle Company 224
Toledo Motor Car Company 224
Toledo Steam and Air Motor Company 224
Torbenson Axle Company 16
Torpedo (race car) 36
Torpedo Kid (race car) 36
Traveler (automobile) 148, 235
Troxel Manufacturing Company 224
Troy Auto & Buggy Company 224
Trumbull Manufacturing Company 224
TRW 16, 117
Turner, Robert S. 224
Twyman Motor Car Company 224, 225

Underwood Motor Company 225
Union (automobile) 225
Union Motor Company 225, 226
Union Sales Company 225
Unique (automobile) 184
United Factories Company 129
United States Carriage Company 225
United States Motor Company 159, 222
Unito (automobile) 129
U.S. Motor Car Company 225
U.S. Runabout (automobile) 225

V-12 engines 70, 72, 101, 170, 197
Valley Automobile Company 225
Vanderbilt, Alfred G. 105
Van Etten (automobile) 208
Van Etten, Scott 208
Vickers Auto Car Company 225
Victoria (automobile) 39, 54
Vogue (automobile) 167
Vogue Motor Car Company 167
Vulcan (automobile) 170, 225
Vulcan Manufacturing Company 170, 225, 226

Wagenhal, W.G. 226
Washburn, George A. 7, 8, 129
Washington (automobile) 225, 226
Washington Automobile Company 129, 130
Washington Motor Company 225, 226
Waukesha engine 162

W.B. Robe & Company 226
Webb, W.H. 226
Wehrmeyer, K.C. 86
Weiss, George 206, 208
Welbon Motor Car Company 226, 227
Welch, A. 31
Weller Engineering Company 227
Wells, Frank E. 227
Wells, W.E. 227
Wells-Meeker Motor Vehicle Company 227
West Side Motor Company 227
Westchester (automobile) 188
Westcott (automobile) 227
Westcott, Burton J. 227
Westcott Carriage Company 227
Westcott House Foundation 227
Westcott Motor Car Company 227
Western Reserve Motor Car Company 227, 228
W.H. Gabriel Wagon & Carriage Company 63
Whippet (automobile) 231
"Whistling Billy" (automobile) 132
White (automobile) 130–134
White, Fred R. 22, 34
White, Rollin C. 34
White, Rollin Henry 7, 27, 31, 109, 130, 133, 140
White, Thomas H. 27, 130, 133
White, Walter 133
White, Windsor 22, 27, 133
White Company 9, 16, 17, 24, 27, 28, 130-133
White Motor Company 27, 130-134
White Sewing Machine Company 34, 130-134
Wick (automobile) 182, 228
Wick, Henry B. 182, 228
Willard, Theodore A. 77, 78, 118, 134
Willard Company 126
Willard Storage Battery Company 10, 17, 74-78, 98, 134
Williams, F.B. 119
Williams, H.A. 54, 134
Williams, W.A. 187

Williams Electric (automobile) 53–54, 134
Williams Electric Vehicle Company 54, 134
Williams Foundry & Machine Company 234
Williams Motor Carriage Company 53, 54, 134
Willys, John North 26, 144, 177, 228, 231, 233
Willys Company 172
Willys-Garford Sales Company 177
Willys Jeep (automobile) 233, 234
Willys Jeepster (automobile) 233
Willys-Knight (automobile) 228–231, 233
Willys-Overland Company 124, 146, 177, 228-234
Willys 77 (automobile) 233
Willys Wagon (automobile) 233
Wilson, David 233
Wilson, E.B. 140
Wilson & Hayes Manufacturing Company 17
Winder, John E. 234
Winton, Alexander 4, 57–9, 13, 22, 24, 25, 41, 49, 72, 74, 123, 134–139, 144, 205, 206, 208
Winton Bicycle Company 134, 137
Winton Bullet (automobile) 138
Winton Bullet No. 2 (automobile) 85
Winton Engine Company 25
Winton Gas Engine and Manufacturing Company 139
Winton Motor Car Company 25, 134–139
Winton Motor Carriage Company 8, 12, 28, 134, 137
Wisconsin engine 56, 209
Wissman, Joseph H. 139
Wissman Auto Repair Company 139
Witter, E.E. 234
W.J. Walker engine company 45
Wolfe, Maurice 197
Wolverine (automobile) 202
Woodland (automobile) 140

Woodland Motor Car & Repair Company 140
Woodland Motor Car Company 139, 140
Woodpecker engine 198
Woodruff (automobile) 234
Woodruff, Albert 234
Woodruff, George 234
Woodruff Automobile Company 234
Worldmobile (automobile) 212
Worthington (automobile) 140
Worthington, Charles Campbell 140
Worthington, Henry R. 140
Worthington Automobile Company 40, 50, 140
Worthington Manufacturing Company 234
Worthington Pump and Machinery Company 140
Wottring & Son Automobile Works 234
Wottring Brothers 234
Wright, Frank Lloyd 227
Wright, Fred 234
Wright, Orville 213
Wright, Ralph 234
Wright, Wilbur 213
W.S. Reed Company 226
W.W. Sly Mfg. Company 20
W.W. Taylor Machine Company 16
Wyeth, Nathan 72, 73

Xenia (automobile) 184

Yale (automobile) 191
Yaple, Luther P. 234
Y.F. Stewart Manufacturing Company 154
York Machinery Company 145

Zeder, Fred M. 27, 112, 141
Zeder Motor Company 140, 141
Zent Automobile Manufacturing Company 234, 235
Zephyr (Chicago Burlington & Quincy Railroad) 26
Ziegfeld, Florenz 12

www.ingramcontent.com/pod-product-compliance
Lightning Source LLC
Chambersburg PA
CBHW081547300426
44116CB00015B/2783